UPLIFT CINEMA

UPLIFT CINEMA

The Emergence of African American Film and
the Possibility of Black Modernity

ALLYSON NADIA FIELD

Duke University Press · Durham and London · 2015

Typeset in Minion Pro by Tseng Information Systems, Inc.
Interior design by Courtney Leigh Baker.

Library of Congress Cataloging-in-Publication Data
Field, Allyson Nadia, 1976–
Uplift cinema : the emergence of African American film and the possibility of black
modernity / Allyson Nadia Field.
pages cm
Includes bibliographical references and index.
ISBN 978-0-8223-5907-4 (hardcover : alk. paper)
ISBN 978-0-8223-5881-7 (pbk. : alk. paper)
ISBN 978-0-8223-7555-5 (e-book)
1. African Americans in the motion picture industry—History—20th century.
2. African Americans in motion pictures—History—20th century. I. Title.
PN1995.9.N4F54 2015
791.43'652996073—dc23   2014046259

Cover art: Film still courtesy A/V Geeks.

Duke University Press gratefully acknowledges Harvard Studies in Comparative
Literature, which provided funds toward the publication of this book.

for Werner

CONTENTS

PREFACE

A decade after Booker T. Washington's death and the public outcry against
D. W. Griffith's *Birth of a Nation*, Oscar Micheaux released his thirteenth film,
Body and Soul (1925). A major example of 1920s race film, *Body and Soul* became famous for the screen debut of Paul Robeson and infamous for the controversy over its representation of Black criminality. Typical for Micheaux's
work, the plot is far from straightforward, and its convoluted structure involves an array of figures that represent a range of character types—the full
spectrum of Black humanity. Robeson plays twins who have opposite characteristics: a charlatan masquerading as a preacher named Reverend Jenkins and
his brother Sylvester, an upstanding aspiring inventor. The film centers on the
lives of Martha Jane (Mercedes Gilbert), a laundress, and her daughter Isabelle
(Julia Theresa Russell). Isabelle is in love with Sylvester but Martha Jane pushes
her toward Reverend Jenkins, not realizing that he is in fact a con man. Jenkins
takes advantage of Martha Jane's faith and assaults Isabelle. Because Martha
Jane is blind to the truth of her "pastor," he is able to extort her hard-earned
savings from her daughter. Knowing that her mother would never believe her
word over that of Jenkins, Isabelle flees to Atlanta and dies of starvation, but
not before Martha Jane has found her and learned the truth. No longer deceived by Jenkins, she confronts him in the middle of a Sunday sermon and
turns his betrayed congregation against him. Escaping, Jenkins seeks forgive-
ness from Martha Jane who relents, pardoning the con man. Showing no genuine remorse, he goes on to kill a young male parishioner in a gruesome attack
in the middle of the woods. At this point, to add to the confusion, Martha Jane
wakes up and reveals that it was all a nightmare. Having learned a lesson from
the dream, however, she blesses the marriage of her daughter to Sylvester, the
proper "uplift" man.

On its release, the film was sharply criticized in the African American press for its portrayal of a corrupt minister and inclusion of offensive scenes. In a letter to the editor of the *Chicago Defender*, William Henry wrote: "I would beg space to ask the many readers of our greatest Negro paper their opinion as to which screen production does our people the most harm, The Klansman, Birth of a Nation or Mischoux's [sic] Body and Soul . . . ?" Comparing Micheaux to Griffith, Henry exclaimed: "What excuse can a man of our Race make when he paints us as rapists of our own women? Must we sit and look at a production that refers to us as niggers?"[1] Henry's angry attack implies that it is unsurprising that Griffith would portray African Americans in a negative light, but that Micheaux, as "the czar of Race filmdom," ought to produce positive counterimages to combat filmic racism.[2] Micheaux, in effect, has an obligation to use the medium of film to promote the public image of Black respectability—the assertion of Black citizens' fitness for civic engagement and conformity to middle-class ideals—and, perhaps most significantly, to present these traits to whites so as to be what was often called "a credit to the race."

In response to such criticism, Micheaux defended himself vigorously. He did so, however, not by avoiding the charge of negative representation but by placing it in the context of a readily recognizable figure: "I am too much imbued with the spirit of Booker T. Washington to engraft false virtues upon ourselves, to make ourselves that which we are not. Nothing could be a greater blow to our own progress. The recognition of our true situation will react in itself as a stimulus for self-advancement."[3] Micheaux's vehemence concerning realistic representation was matched by the ardor with which he insisted on the significance of his filmmaking for African American progress as "the greatest achievement ever made by the Race."[4] The debate about representation and progress turned on the meaning and viability of a concept central to the thinking of Washington, Micheaux, and Henry alike: uplift.

Put simply, uplift was an idea, a project, and a rhetorical strategy promoted by Washington and his allies, in which individual self-help was the key to collective progress of African Americans. Uplift philosophy began to emerge during Reconstruction, and by the turn of the century it was the main political, social, and economic program for African American advancement. For its proponents, uplift meant that material improvements (and the ensuing elevated social status) would be attained through individual striving and the self-sufficiency of the race—rather than political or social equality with whites created through legal means. Thus, uplift involved a complex negotiation of ambition and obsequiousness, and of assertion and retreat, along with virtuosic rhetorical gymnastics required to speak concurrently to two divergent audiences.

FIG. P.1 Booker T. Washington, from Charles Victor Roman, *American Civilization and the Negro: The Afro-American in Relation to National Progress* (Philadelphia, PA: F. A. Davis, 1916).

In Black communities the uplift project foregrounded a bootstrap mentality that put the burden of advancing the race on the achievements of the individual. While ignoring some forms of collective action, it posited each individual as potentially significant to the race at large. In so doing, uplift inverted the white paternalistic view of Black dependency by insisting on the possibility of individual, and thereby collective, transformation. Micheaux's life—especially his work as a writer, filmmaker, and distributor—exemplified the uplift ideal, as he worked toward economic independence in an industry that was more hostile than hospitable to African Americans. All the same, as Henry noted, Micheaux did not portray a straightforward notion of Black respectability in his films, nor did he singularly celebrate the advancement and achievements of heroic individuals. For Henry this was in conflict with Washington's vision, but Micheaux argued—accurately—that the uplift project had always been ambivalent about notions of respectability and Black society.

Although projecting respectability was a key component of uplift rhetoric, Micheaux's response to critics of *Body and Soul* points to a different aspect of the uplift project: the explicit acknowledgment of negative features prevalent in the popular imagination of white Americans, particularly Black criminality

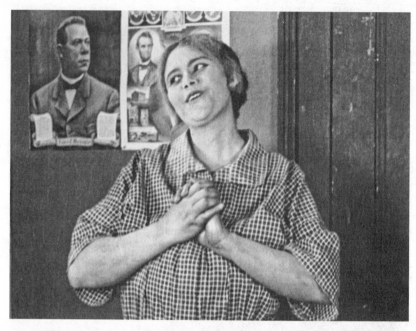

FIG. P.2–P.5 (*above and at right*) *Body and Soul* (Oscar Micheaux, 1925).

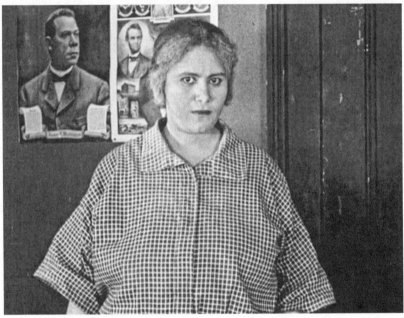

and lack of industriousness. This aspect suggested that the worst features of Black life had to be acknowledged so that progress could be shown. Micheaux was able to defend himself by emphasizing Washington's refusal to champion "false virtues," arguing (however implicitly) that realist representation not only had veracity, but it was also a strategic principle designed to reflect the stereotypes held by many whites. As a result, he implies, his film will be able to overcome, rather than merely contradict, those negative images.

Micheaux's engagement with Washington resonates further in the form of a portrait prominently figured in the interior of Martha Jane's home. In this portrait, an image found in many African American homes of the day, Washington serves not only as a symbol of industriousness and striving but also as an observer of the domestic drama (figure P.1). Although the portrait is certainly a "visual tag to identify laudable character traits," as Pearl Bowser and Louise Spence claim, it has a more complex role, serving as an aloof witness to intraracial crimes of rape and extortion.[5] Micheaux, then, can also be read as using the portrait of Washington to make a pointed critique of the ambivalences of the uplift project and its filmic components. In *Body and Soul*, as in the political enactment of uplift, all manner of sins are overlooked or disregarded in a strategically calculated compromise in service of the promotion of the race (figures P.2–P5). It is, perhaps, a criticism of uplift smuggled into the rhetoric of realism it employed.

To better understand how this complex and nuanced iconographic valence could make sense in *Body and Soul* and other films of the time, we need to account for the larger media presence of the uplift project. In particular, we need to look at how moving pictures took up its visual aspects, using them to give those working for the advancement of the race an image of self-fashioning. Likewise, we need to examine the tensions that film, as a more generally useful medium, generated for uplift as a whole. In other words, if we are to address the complex genealogy (representational, stylistic, and political) of Black filmmaking in the first part of the twentieth century, we must reconstruct the history of uplift cinema. That is the purpose of this book.

The prominence of the portrait of Washington in Micheaux's mise-en-scène provides an occasion to rethink the aesthetic and political strategies of early Black filmmaking. The portrait resonates beyond the visual rhetoric of the image, evoking an entire cinematic practice that preceded it. Despite the fact that no examples of uplift cinema are known to be extant, the forms and strategies of uplift cinema left an enduring and visible legacy in Black filmmaking—carrying with it all the tensions and ambivalences that composed the uplift project as a whole. Uplift cinema, however hidden, has had deep and lasting significance for the development, dissemination, and public engagement of motion pictures with the advancement of African Americans, a legacy that extends to the broader efforts of Black intellectuals, educators, and entrepreneurs to advance claims to racial, political, and economic progress in the twentieth century and beyond.

ACKNOWLEDGMENTS

This book is the product of years of thinking about the role of cinema in shaping African American modernity. It took many institutions, archives, and individuals to develop this project, not only to excavate this history but to understand its significance and give it meaning. At a fundamental level, research support was provided by the University of California, Los Angeles (UCLA), through its Department of Film, Television, and Digital Media; Office of Diversity and Faculty Development; Council on Research; and the Hellman Fellows Program. This book was also subsidized in part by Harvard Studies in Comparative Literature, and I am grateful to the faculty of Harvard University's Department of Comparative Literature for their continued support of my work.

The Dr. Penny Kanner Next Generation Fellowship at UCLA's Center for the Study of Women provided the funding for a manuscript workshop at a crucial time in the genesis of this project. For their detailed feedback, thanks to Kathleen McHugh, the staff of the center, and the workshop participants: especially, Anna Everett, Jacqueline Stewart, and Gregory Waller, as well as John Caldwell, Sarah Haley, Darnell Hunt, Arne Lunde, Samantha Sheppard, and Richard Yarborough. Their generous engagement with my work helped me hone my ideas and shape them into this book. Kathleen in particular helped me find ways to better articulate my arguments, and I am deeply grateful for having such a generous colleague and friend.

This project has its roots in my doctoral work at Harvard. It was in the stacks of Widener Library that I first came across a reference to the Hampton pictures in the Booker T. Washington Papers. From there, a number of individuals and organizations at Harvard—the W. E. B. Du Bois Research Institute at the Hutchins Center, the Radcliffe Institute for Advanced Study, and the Graduate School of Arts and Sciences—generously supported my research to follow the threads to the corpus of works discussed in these pages. Thanks to Harvard's Graduate Student Council, Department of Comparative Literature, Department of Visual and Environmental Studies, and Department of African and African American Studies for the resources they made available to me as I worked on this project. Thanks especially to Cynthia Verba and the Fellowships Office for their generous support of my work.

At Harvard, Werner Sollors, David Rodowick, and Giuliana Bruno were incredible advisors who oversaw the early version of this project as a portion of my dissertation. I want to thank the members of the following workshops and colloquia: American Literature in Comparative and Ethnic Perspectives, American Literature Colloquium, Film Studies Graduate Student Workshop (especially Eric Rentschler), Comparative Literature Dissertation Seminar, and Word and Image Graduate Student Workshop. I am also grateful for the feedback of Henry Louis Gates Jr., Jonathan Crary, Lee Grieveson, Dominique Bluher, Despina Kakoudaki, Laura Murphy, Jessica Callaway Smolin, Julia Lee, Erin Royston Battat, Namwali Serpell, Roxana Popescu, Phoebe Putnam, and Michael Vazquez. Christina Svendsen, comparatist extraordinaire, has been there from the beginning as a writing buddy and critical thinker on modernity.

My research was made possible by staff members at a number of archives, especially Hampton University (thanks to Donzella Maupin and her staff) and Tuskegee University (thanks to Dana Chandler). Thanks also to Rob Hudson at the Carnegie Hall Archives. The George P. Johnson Negro Film Collection at UCLA has been an invaluable resource. As I was completing this book, the Media History Digital Library came online and provided essential access to many crucial early trade publications (thanks to David Pierce and Eric Hoyt for spearheading this valuable resource). Images were generously supplied by the Indiana State Library, the Boston Public Library, the Library of Congress, the U.S. National Archives and Records Administration, Hampton University, Harvard College Library, and the University of California Southern Regional Library Facility (thanks to Diane McMorris and Peter Lacson for the microfilm scans). Mark Quigley provided guidance on frame grabs.

As I was completing this book, I was fortunate to share my research with a number of audiences whose responses and feedback shaped my thinking: at the Chicago Film Seminar thanks in particular to Cynthia Blair who was a thoughtful and helpful respondent; the Visual and Media Cultures Colloquium at the University of California, Santa Cruz; the UCLA Cinema and Media Studies Colloquium; the Black Film Center/Archive at Indiana University, and its conference on Regeneration in Digital Contexts: Early Black Film. Several additional invitations came at key times in the development of this project: from the conference and symposium on Oscar Micheaux: African American Enigma sponsored by Columbia University and the Lincoln Center for the Performing Arts; the Columbia Film Seminar; the Institute for African American Studies at the University of Connecticut; the Department of Visual and Environmental Studies at Harvard; and the W. E. B. Du Bois Institute for African and African American Research. I am also grateful for the feedback I received at the Society for Cinema and Media Studies annual conference, the Berkeley Conference on Silent Cinema, Visible Evidence, and Domitor.

As this project developed over a number of years, I have been fortunate to work with incredibly dedicated research assistants: Brian Brown, Heather Collette-VanDeraa, Jess DePrest, Jessica Fowler, Lindsay Giggey, Artel Great, Andrew Hall, Brandon Harrison, Jane'a Johnson, Daniel Langford, Marissa Leotaud, Ernie Mitchell, Matthew Perkins, Katy Ralko, and Saundarya Thapa. In particular, Daniel Langford oversaw the final details of the manuscript preparation, and I am grateful for his organization, thoroughness, and attention to detail. In deep and profound ways, my teaching and scholarship have been enriched by the presence of Samantha Sheppard.

This book was written while I was teaching in the Cinema and Media Studies Program at UCLA, and I am grateful to my colleagues for their enthusiastic engagement with my work and their support of my research—not least in providing me the necessary time to complete the manuscript. I list them here: Deans Teri Schwartz and Bob Rosen; Chairs Bill McDonald and Barbara Boyle; and Janet Bergstrom, John Caldwell, Chris Horak, Steve Mamber, Denise Mann, Kathleen McHugh, Chon Noriega, Jasmine Trice, and the late Teshome Gabriel. Vivian Sobchack has been a spirited interlocutor and friend. I am also grateful to the students and faculty and staff members of the Moving Image Archive Studies program, the African American Studies Department, and the Ralph J. Bunche Center for African American Studies for creating a dynamic environment of intellectual inquiry at UCLA. I am especially grateful for the collegiality and friendship of Richard Yarborough, who has been a patient and engaged sounding board through my time at UCLA, and the best comrade and moviegoing companion I could wish for. Diana King, Peggy Alexander, and Mark Quigley have been tremendous resources for research at UCLA, and I am deeply grateful for the work they do.

Writing may be a solitary endeavor, but it's far from lonely. I have been fortunate to have a number of colleagues and friends who read drafts, discussed issues, and helped me shape my thoughts about the ideas in this book. Chon Noriega, Cara Caddoo, Joseph Nagy, Jennifer Zwarich, Richard Yarborough, and Jaimie Baron all generously read portions of the manuscript and offered their expertise and valuable insights. Paul McEwan, my guru on all things Griffith, provided key feedback on chapter 4. Quincy Mills provided detailed and insightful feedback on chapter 5. Conversations with Terri Francis, Michael Gillespie, Matthew Bernstein, and Billy Woodberry have shaped my thinking. And Ray Sapirstein's expertise on Leigh Richmond Miner and Hampton's photography provided a key foundation for my thinking about uplift aesthetics; I'm grateful for his generous encouragement through the early stages of my research.

I'm deeply grateful for the support, encouragement, information, and advice I received from Kaveh Askari, Giorgio Bertellini, Pearl Bowser, Scott Curtis, Zeinabu irene Davis, Leslie Eckel, Ken Eisenstein, Jane Gaines, Marsha Gordon, Tom Gunning, Laura Horak, Jenny Horne, Erkki Huhtamo, Patricia Leavy, Megan Luke, Martin Johnson, Jonathan Kahana, Sarah Keller, Maja Manojlovic, O.Funmilayo Makarah, Paula Massood, Donte McFadden, Sean Metzger, Charlie Musser, Rielle Navitski, Christina Petersen, Jennifer Peterson, Sandy Polu, Jennifer Porst, Charlene Regester, Laura Serna, Aparna Sharma, Shelley Stamp, Dan Streible, Julie Turnock, Brigitta Wagner, Haidee Wasson, Allison Whitney, and Josh Yumibe.

Duke University Press has been a dream to work with. I am deeply grateful to Ken Wissoker both for his enthusiasm for this project when it was just an unformed cluster of ideas and for his patience as I took the time to develop it into this book. Thanks also to Elizabeth Ault and Danielle Szulczewski, who so masterfully guided the book through the production process. I am very appreciative of the two anonymous readers who provided thorough and astute feedback on the manuscript and made it a much better book. Thank you!

Jacqueline Stewart was one of the first scholars to take seriously my interest in African American film, and at every step of the way she has guided and shaped my work. In sharing her intellectual and scholarly life with me, she has made me a better film historian, archival researcher, and advocate for Black cinema. This book would not be possible without her example, encouragement, and friendship. I have always been grateful to my family—Nazli Choucri Field, John Osgood Field, and Wasfeya Choucri—for their enthusiasm for my work and their patience through the writing process. Having professors for parents means never having to explain why you're always working; they also set an example of how a scholarly life can be a balanced and rich one. Most of all, this book would not be nearly what it is without Dan Morgan. He read every sentence (several times), helped me find my words, and most importantly has made me a better thinker. His presence pervades this book and my life and has made them both immeasurably better. Finally, I have Werner Sollors to thank for inspiring me to become an Americanist. The entire course of my career changed the moment I entered his seminar on Issues in the Study of American Literature over a decade ago. He has been my benchmark for what a scholar, teacher, and mentor should be. With great appreciation and affection, I dedicate this book to him.

INTRODUCTION

Nothing has done so much to awaken the race consciousness of the colored
man in the United States as the motion picture. It has made him hungry to see
himself as he has come to be. —WILLIAM FOSTER, "News of the Moving Picture"

Writing in the Indianapolis *Freeman* in 1913, the filmmaker William Foster ex-
presses a kind of critique common in African American newspapers throughout the 1910s. He assesses the contemporary status of African American representation in moving pictures and the "resentment" that Black moviegoers
feel against their egregious misrepresentation "presented everywhere." Foster attributes the "hunger" of Black moviegoers for self-recognition to a direct response to the prevalence of grotesque caricatures of African Americans on American screens. Drawing on the uplift philosophy's emphasis on
self-reliance, Foster then shifts from a critique of misrepresentation to a call
for self-representation. Although he celebrates Black movie patrons' protests
against such images, he argues for film production "for ourselves in our own
best way and for our own best good." For Foster, as for many others, the goal
was not to rely on white filmmakers to change their characterization of Black
people but to provide a model for Black filmmakers—and an emerging Black
filmmaking practice—that would avoid the representational problems evident
in mainstream films. In his article, Foster captures the power of moving images
and their potential for resistance and affirmation.[1]

In the early decades of the twentieth century, moving pictures served as
both a mechanism for the misrepresentation of Black humanity and a tool
for asserting it. The former use has persisted, and its history is well documented. However, too little is known about early endeavors toward Black self-
representation in moving pictures, or the ways in which this dynamic medium
served the interests of African American advancement. To fill this gap, this

book is about early African American film practices, focusing in particular on films made in the 1910s. It is also about the role of cinema in the larger social, political, educational, and economic project of African American uplift. Lastly, it is about film history and its methodologies, reconstructing a history of uplift cinema entirely out of surviving archival ephemera. As a whole, this book contributes to a historical understanding of the multimedia operations of the uplift project and brings to the fore alternative uses of the medium of film at a time when its forms and functions were being widely explored by amateurs and professionals alike.

In the 1910s the relatively new medium of motion pictures played a key role in promoting and chronicling the African American experience, especially the broad idea of uplift—the movement of racial advancement based on self-help, service, and the promotion of middle-class ideals that began in the late nineteenth century and continued into the twentieth. Beyond recording instances of African American achievement, moving pictures participated in the self-definition of Black people at a time of vast change and challenge. The uplift project informed early Black filmmaking and provided the impetus for its engagements with the medium. In this way, uplift filmmakers embraced cinema as a useful medium for promoting the interests of African Americans and conveying the possibilities of Black citizenship for both Black and white spectators. *Uplift Cinema* recovers this significant legacy of Black cinema and situates African American uplift filmmaking in the context of African American history, American film history, and the role of visual culture in social and political struggles.

This introduction has three main tasks: first, to provide an overview of the uplift project as a foundation for understanding how Black cinema functioned at the beginning of the twentieth century; second, to put forth critical frameworks for thinking about uplift cinema as an explicitly useful form of cinema; and third, to articulate a methodological imperative that takes up the stakes and challenges of writing film history about only nonextant films. To this end, I conclude the introduction with a call to look beyond decayed and combusted nitrate stock as victims of time and neglect, arguing that we have as much to discover and learn from absences as we do from surviving artifacts. The film itself is but one component of an expansive network of cultural traces that lead to its myriad functions. Uplift cinema is not only best explained in this way, it also provides a test case for a broader methodology of film history.

Uplift films reflected, informed, and participated in the larger movement of African American uplift that was, at the time, the predominant social and political ideology concerning African American progress. The program of racial uplift emphasized individual initiative, mutual assistance, social respectability, interracial cooperation, and economic independence as components of a general strategy for promoting the advancement of African Americans. The uplift project saw individual behavior as the key to communal success, emphasizing personal conduct over systemic critique. This was a view that was cultivated in the acknowledgment of white racist misperception and misrepresentation of African Americans, essentializing and dehumanizing perspectives that needed to be countered by a strict code of conduct. Uplift, Jane Gaines writes, was "a conflation of social and moral elevation [that] sent the message that moral advance meant social advance, as though the one were the effect of the other."[2] As W. Fitzhugh Brundage notes, "by adhering to a code of temperance, thrift, polite manners, sexual purity, cleanliness, and rectitude, blacks contradicted racist stereotypes about their alleged inferiority."[3] In post-Reconstruction Jim Crow America, uplift was not just a strategy for advancement; in the minds of the project's leaders, it was an imperative for survival.

Early twentieth-century Black uplift is inseparable from the figure of Booker T. Washington and the institutions with which he was associated: Hampton Institute (where he was educated), Tuskegee Institute (where he was principal), and the National Negro Business League (NNBL, which he served as president). Though the nerve center of the uplift project was in the South, at Tuskegee, uplift reached into the consciousness of upwardly mobile and would-be upwardly mobile Black northerners as well. Middle-class African American homes across the country commonly featured a portrait of Washington, and his ideals of individual initiative, service, and moral respectability gave a generation of African Americans a model of conduct for them to emulate. Washington popularized uplift, served as its ambassador among whites, and functioned as an image of the uplifted.[4]

Washington's politics of uplift was complex and by no means universally embraced. He agreed to a postponement of social equality in favor of more immediately possible economic remedies, "casting down the bucket" in industries directly connected to an individual's environment. As Washington stated in his 1895 address at the Cotton States and International Exposition in Atlanta, "when it comes to business, pure and simple, it is in the South that the Negro is given a man's chance in the commercial world."[5] (The speech was famously labeled the "Atlanta Compromise" by W. E. B. Du Bois, due to Washington's postponement of demands for political rights and claims for social equality in favor of support for vocational education and economic security.[6]) Washington saw the locus of "chance" for the unskilled and disenfranchised former slaves and their offspring in the mastery of a trade so that they would become indispensable to the larger community and thereby justify their right to rights. His emphasis on chance was further underscored in the address when he asserted that African Americans must begin at the bottom and not permit "our grievances to overshadow our opportunities."[7]

Washington's diplomatic disposition emphasized the usefulness of the Black freedman to the defeated white southerner in improving southern industry and creating an economic situation beneficial to both races, one that would also allow the white population to maintain its desired distance from its previously (and, in fact, currently) subjugated neighbors. Appealing to the broad audience at the Atlanta Exposition, Washington stated that like the "loyal" slaves, Negroes would be a "patient, faithful, law-abiding, and unresentful people" who would give their lives to protect their white neighbors. In this vision, social segregation would not preclude Black labor and enterprise from benefiting northern and southern whites, just as Black uplift would not presume social integration. The goal of the uplift project was to "make the interest of the races one" and thereby bring about gradual improvement to the status of the Black citizenry. But the white man need not fear that Washington was suggesting integration: "in all things that are purely social we can be as separate as the fingers, yet one as the hand in all things essential to mutual progress."[8] The tempered possibility and potential of Black uplift that underlie Washington's measured rhetoric were presented in the service of the "mutual progress" of white and Black Americans. Yet in practice the result was a kind of Faustian pact in which progress was rarely "mutual."

Education was a major component of these efforts, and the "pedagogy of uplift" was a central—and polarizing—component of Black social and political thought at this time.[9] The Hampton-Tuskegee idea of education emphasized normal school education (that is, pertaining to the establishment of standards or norms in education) and training in practical trades. Hampton, Tuskegee, and other normal and agricultural institutes trained teachers and offered students agricultural and industrial training to prepare them to be productive and self-sufficient laborers. Though many groups and individuals, both Black and white, celebrated this model of education for African Americans, others found it controversial. Criticism came both from more progressive Black groups and from socially conservative white southerners. Kevin Gaines argues that the Hampton-Tuskegee philosophy "clashed with the freedpeople's emancipatory vision of education" as well as the views of white southerners who were wary of the potential for Negro education to foster a sense of social equality.[10] To alleviate such concerns, the southern institutional models of uplift emphasized education as a tool for making "useful citizens" rather than social equals or political adversaries.[11] As a result, this educational program, combined with a missionary commitment to service, obfuscated "the brutal realities of conquest and political subordination."[12] This is what made Washington's model of education untenable for Du Bois.

This opposing perspective on the function of education is where Du Bois and Washington diverged most sharply.[13] For Du Bois, education for African Americans should focus on "developing the Best of this race that they may guide the Mass away from the contamination and death of the Worst, in their own and other races."[14] To this end, he advocated higher education for a "talented tenth" of Black elites. Education practically and symbolically highlighted the differences between the two leaders as it played a large part in any vision of the future for African Americans. Quite directly, the form of education (agricultural and industrial or higher education in the liberal arts) anticipated the future role of the Black citizenry.

Faith in education as the gateway to advancement and upward mobility is the cornerstone of the uplift project, and it functioned as a kind of "liberation theology."[15] As Kevin Gaines argues, "describing a group struggle for freedom and social advancement, uplift also suggests that African Americans have, with an almost religious fervor, regarded education as the key to liberation."[16] Although the type and purpose of education was contested, the fact of education as fundamental to uplift was promoted across ideological lines. Gaines shows that "uplift encompassed the tension between competing philosophies of black education orchestrated by the vision of economic development and racial accommodation advanced by white industrialists, reformers and philanthropists."[17] These competing philosophies of education diverged with regard to social class and reflected a fundamental tension in uplift philosophy between the shared effort toward collective advancement and the entrenchment of a "racialized elite identity," through which uplift depended on class stratification as the mechanism for advancement.[18] Fred Moten sees in this tension an uneasy concern with Black criminality, a critique that acknowledges that "the assimilationist cultural politics of normative uplift can never be fully separated from the white supremacism it is supposed to combat."[19] Anxieties about racial advancement were intertwined with challenges to the social order. Education, in whatever form, constituted a threat to Black dependency and therefore had to be advocated with care.

The uplift philosophy focused its strategies for advancement on the notion of the autonomous individual, positing individual self-help as key to communal improvement, which was largely understood as economic independence. To this end, Washington argued that education should facilitate economic self-sufficiency. If agricultural and industrial educational institutes were designed for the educational advancement of African Americans, ultimately this was in the service of economic advancement. The NNBL, founded by Washington in 1900, was the professional nexus of this aspect of the uplift project. Along with "useful" education—or, as the founder of Hampton, General Samuel Chapman Armstrong, termed it, "education for life" (epitomized by Hampton and Tuskegee)—the NNBL represented the significance of economic independence at the heart of the uplift project.[20] The educational institutes, Washington, and the NNBL each promoted the advancements of African Americans in various professions and chronicled examples of demonstrated progress through publications targeted primarily at philanthropists and other members of the nation's economic and political elite. For example, the 1904 pamphlet published at Hampton titled *What Hampton Graduates Are Doing in Land-Buying, in Home-Making, in Business, in Teaching, in Agriculture, in Establishing Schools, in the Trades, in Church and Missionary Work, in the Professions, 1868–1904* exemplifies the uplift philosophy's emphasis on education as the way to affect communities through different forms of labor and public service.[21] The emphasis on economic independence also fostered an encouragement of entrepreneurialism. Black businessmen emerged in all types of enterprises, and higher education was seen as a training ground for businessmen as well as for farmers.

Although the work of the educational institutions and that of the NNBL were central to the uplift project, of equal significance was its public façade. Just as the individual was seen as the key to communal success economically, each person also carried the burden of representing the race through his or her actions and conduct. In an environment saturated with grotesque racist caricatures and representations predicated on racialized ridicule, reclaiming the image of African Americans was an important aspect of the uplift project; the perception of upward social mobility and respectability matched economic advancement in importance. Uplift leaders crafted a rhetoric of uplift to appeal and appease: a rhetoric that thereby reflected the project it represented. To this end, the uplift project communicated its ideals through carefully designed and persuasive uplift narratives.

The idea of the uplift narrative plays a central role in this book. At its most basic level, an uplift narrative is one that presents African Americans as achieving a status as modern, independent, and self-sufficient. It strategically presents a trajectory of progress through a logic of before-and-after examples. Washington's second and most famous autobiography, *Up from Slavery*, is an example of an extremely popular uplift narrative.[22] Chronicling Washington's rise from a slave to the most powerful African American of his time, *Up from Slavery* is an autobiographical narrative that William Andrews has called "one of the most compelling personal myths in the history of American literature."[23] As a postbellum slave narrative at the beginning of the twentieth century, it presents a revisionist account of the so-called peculiar institution that represented "slavery and its significance to the advancement of black people in an increasingly pragmatic perspective."[24] Andrews explains the rhetorical logic in these terms:

> What slavery was in the past is not so important as what slavery means, or (more importantly) can be construed to mean, in the present. A factual view of slavery, for Washington, is concerned less with a static concept of historical truth, frozen in the past, than with the need for rhetorical power in the ever-evolving present. To the postbellum slave narrator, particularly Washington, slavery needed to be reviewed and reempowered as a concept capable of effecting change, of making a difference ultimately in what white people thought of black people as freedmen, not slaves. The facts of slavery in the postbellum narrative, therefore, are not so much what happened *then*—bad though it was—as what *makes* things, good things, happen now.[25]

This harnessing of the narrative of the past to serve particular goals of the present not only necessitated a revision of the slave narrative; it also required a circumscribed presentation of goals. A major component of Washington's accommodationist strategy was, in effect, to reposition the relation of African Americans to whites. Instead of a rhetoric of blame, rights, justice, and restitution, uplift rhetoric emphasized independence and self-help for the "mutual progress" of both races.[26] Throughout Washington's chronicle of his development, he reiterates the principle of service: "The great and prevailing idea that seemed to take possession of every one [at Hampton] was to prepare himself to lift up the people at his home."[27] As an uplift narrative, *Up from Slavery* models a trajectory of progress while carefully negotiating the presentation of its aims and expertly navigating the potential concerns, prejudices, and sensibilities of its intended audience.

Of course, uplift narratives were not simply literary. One of the central points of this book is that uplift was a prescriptive program that was articulated through—and constituted by—a range of media. Uplift discourses traveled across forms, emerging in speeches, literature, pamphlets, pageants, photographs, music, and moving images. In doing so, the broader uplift project encountered new problems at the same time that the multimedia strategy allowed for new possibilities. Uplift cinema in particular conveyed an argument for— and functioned as proof of—African American progress through the most modern form of mass communication, targeting both white and Black (and sometimes mixed) audiences. It aligned African Americans with technological progress while offering a broad-reaching platform from which to vividly project the race's potential for advancement.

Uplift Cinema and Race Film

The dominant way in which historians have studied early African American engagements with moving pictures as producers, subjects, and spectators has been through the discourse on race film. Although race film has received critical scholarly attention since the 1970s, it is a concept contemporaneous to the films' emergence in the 1910s, designated as a term for filmmaking practices by, for, or about African Americans. There were filmmaking concerns owned and operated by whites that sought to appeal to Black audiences with Black cast productions, but African American filmmakers saw themselves as participating in the uplift of the race through motion picture production. Black filmmaking entrepreneurs understood themselves as race men, and the term *race picture* or *race movie* functioned as shorthand for the press, exhibitors, and audiences to understand films made about and for African Americans. In 1920 in the *New York Age*, the arts critic Lester Walton championed "colored motion pictures" as a "new and fertile field offering wonderful opportunities."[28] And, as Jane Gaines has shown, Geraldyn Dismond, an African American writing in *Close-Up* in 1929, defined "Negro films" as films—made by Black-owned or white-controlled companies—with a common "motive": to both present a humanizing portrayal of African American subjects, "showing them not as fools and servants, but as human beings with the same emotions, desires and weaknesses as other people," and to "share in the profits of this great industry."[29] The term *race film* reflected the notion of a separate cinema for a largely segregated audience, but it did not indicate a shared style, genre, or singular point of view.

Since the late 1970s, film historians have endeavored to chronicle and critically assess race films, focusing primarily on narrative fiction films exhibited in theaters to Black audiences. Thomas Cripps defined *race movies* as "films made for exclusively black audiences between 1916 and 1956," following the historical usage of the term.[30] Henry Sampson identified over five hundred films featuring African American casts shown in theaters that catered to an African American audience.[31] Subsequent scholars have built on Cripps's and Sampson's foundational research. Although the focus of scholarly attention has largely been on the Lincoln Motion Picture Company and Oscar Micheaux, other researchers have added to our understanding of lesser known ventures and figures. For example, Christina Petersen has researched and produced a filmography of Reol Productions; Barbara Lupack and Matthew Bernstein and Dana White have traced the history of the Norman Film Manufacturing Company; Pearl Bowser and Charles Musser have researched the Maurice Film Company; and Jacqueline Stewart is producing a comprehensive account of Spencer Williams, including a full survey of his career as an actor, director, and producer.[32] Furthermore, Charlene Regester and Anna Everett have shown that film criticism in the Black press was a constitutive part of race filmmaking at the same time that it critiqued perceived misrepresentations in the films themselves.[33]

The most prolific and successful race filmmaker, Oscar Micheaux, produced nearly forty feature films from 1919 to 1948. His silent era films, only three of which survive from the more than twenty he made, were explicitly oriented by uplift ideals. For example, in *Within Our Gates* (1920), the protagonist Sylvia Landry teaches at a school for Black children in the rural south and is forced to go north to appeal for funds from wealthy white philanthropists to keep the school in operation. *The Symbol of the Unconquered* (1920) centers on a Black frontiersman, and the hero of *Body and Soul* (1925) is an aspiring inventor. At the same time, these films also exhibit inherent ambivalences about the uplift project.

Though Micheaux saw himself as a Bookerite, he did not hesitate to turn his lens on less respectable aspects of Black social life, choosing themes that, as Pearl Bowser and Louise Spence note, were "explosive in their time."[34] His representations of corrupt ministers, rapists, gamblers, and hypocrites drew vociferous criticism, and his portrayals of miscegenation and lynching were nothing short of shocking. Furthermore, as Bowser and Spence note, "Micheaux's notions of racial uplift and individual responsibility challenged white definitions of race without actually changing the terms."[35] Even here, Micheaux's filmmaking project aligns with Washington's philosophy of racial uplift, which was similarly critiqued for setting aside systemic change in favor of modest, incremental challenges to the status quo.

Race film, as it has been historically understood, is nonetheless a category that is too limited for the films under discussion here. Uplift cinema productively expands the epistemological coordinates of race film. This book contributes to the study of race film by introducing uplift cinema as an important component of early Black filmmaking, and then by using that move to reconsider the defining aspects of that filmmaking. The makers of uplift films employed motion pictures as a medium of persuasion and representation in the service of African American advancement and self-definition. Uplift cinema and race film overlap in terms of strategies and practices that extended into the 1920s and beyond. However, unlike race film, uplift cinema was primarily imagined as a form of useful cinema, discussed below. Uplift cinema adds to the historiography on race film by expanding its locations, genres, periods, production and exhibition contexts, and motivations.

Although uplift films have been critically overlooked, uplift itself is not a new concept in the study of race film. Scholars of early Black cinema have described how filmmakers mobilized aspects of uplift to assert the modernity of Black subjects, particularly in northern urban locations.[36] Speaking of race films in their "heyday," Jane Gaines asserts, "in every way imaginable they espoused uplift."[37] She writes: "Like much of the black literary production of the day . . . race movies were thoroughly imbued with the spirit and the letter of uplift, the mode in which race consciousness was publically articulated in the early part of the twentieth century."[38] Uplift cinema may be a distinct practice, but it has implications for how we understand race films, shedding light on the complexities of Black filmmaking in the early decades of the twentieth century.

One consequence of the predominance of the race film model has been an almost exclusive focus on the films made in the north. In this book I show that the emergence of a cinema practice related specifically to African American concerns is rooted in southern rural areas as well as northern urban centers, and that the south played a significant role in engagements with modernization and media culture.[39] African American filmmaking emerged in the south at the same time as it did in the north, in the early years of the second decade of the twentieth century, but it developed in significantly different ways in the two regions. Both northern and southern filmmakers combined popular entertainment with the positive representation of African American life at a time when its prevailing screen image was the visual manifestation of distorted white perception. In the north, Black filmmaking entrepreneurs sought to monetize Black audiences and provide appealing moving pictures for Black theaters. In the south, filmmaking projects aiming to support African American interests emerged from educational institutions rather than commercial ventures. The faculties and trustees, both Black and white, of southern African American agricultural and institutional colleges saw themselves at the forefront of modernity with their proposed solution to the so-called Negro Problem of economic and racial subjugation. To this end, they enlisted moving picture technology by using film as a mechanism for fund-raising, addressing northern white philanthropists who supported the endeavors of Washington and his conservative circle as well as southern Black communities (I examine this practice in chapters 2 and 3).

Attention to race films has focused on narrative fiction, including such genres as comedies, westerns, mysteries, dramas, and musicals. The genre that has received the most attention in race film historiography is melodrama, largely because these films directly engaged with African American social and political issues. In her discussion of the uplift narratives of the Lincoln Motion Picture Company and of Oscar Micheaux, for example, Gaines focuses on melodrama as a form for "the race movie betterment narrative."[40] Other aspects of film culture that have only received brief mention (such as actuality footage, nontheatrical exhibitions at venues such as churches and meeting halls, and versions of the local film) deserve more focused research and sustained discussion because they expand our focus to include a fuller range of the production and reception practices of this period.[41] It is in these broad areas that uplift cinema took shape. Beyond narrative fiction, uplift films extend the uses of moving pictures into other cinematic modes and genres, most notably nontheatrical practices, hybrid forms, and nonfiction filmmaking, such as actualities and local films (discussed below). Films made of Black colleges combined narrative and actuality forms aligned with the rhetorical strategies of fund-raising materials. Even northern Black filmmaking entrepreneurs who made fiction films prior to 1915 were as invested in other forms (such as actualities) that documented aspects of Black civic life, demonstrating the achievement of uplift ideals.

A more overt focus on uplift cinema likewise expands the historiography on race film to include its pre-1915 instantiations. Although scholars do acknowledge that some Black filmmakers were producing films before the 1915 release of *The Birth of a Nation*, Gaines is typical of a broader trend when she argues that "early black filmmaking is inextricably tied to the release of this film, and Griffith's offensive epic was the irritant around which a pearl formed."[42] Yet, as Gaines herself notes, scholarship has repeatedly challenged the notion that Black filmmaking was born as a response to *The Birth of a Nation*.[43] Even if

Griffith's film has a hold in the popular imagination as a flashpoint for Black film history, by the late 1970s historians—most prominently Henry Sampson, Thomas Cripps, and Phyllis Klotman—had traced the filmmaking practices of figures who had worked earlier, such as William Foster, widely considered (until now) the first Black film producer.[44] Still, since not even any fragments of race films made prior to 1915 survive, it became a convenient narrative to posit that Black film endeavors followed from Griffith's film. Such a narrative is supported by the widely publicized efforts to counter *The Birth of a Nation* with films such as *The Birth of a Race* (1918) and, relatedly, by what Cripps calls the notable "failures" of the Lincoln Motion Picture Company and the *Birth of a Race* company.[45] What I show throughout this book is that the landscape of early Black filmmaking practice was far richer than has been understood and offered powerful models of success for filmmakers in the 1920s.

This expansion of the period matters not just because it makes the historiography more accurate but also because it broadens our understanding of the motivation of race film practitioners. Accounts of race film have posited it primarily as a response to representational racism and as the manifestation of a desire to capitalize on a perceived untapped market, African American spectators. The notion of a separate cinema necessitated by a segregated culture is a logical inference. Yet it is only part of the story. The impetus for early Black filmmaking is more nuanced and complex than the familiar narrative of race film suggests: it comes from a wider—and more explicitly multimedia—context.

Along these lines, it is important to recognize that early Black film culture was not an entirely segregated experience. Rather, it was deeply imbricated with the influences and participation of white sponsors. This goes beyond the inclusion of white capital for race film production, or the race film production of white-owned companies.[46] When Gaines discusses the interracial nature of American silent film culture and the "uncanny parallels and volatile intersections of black and white American cultures," she notes that "the race pioneers carved something significant out of nothing—race movies were an audacious invention that helped to make an audience that most white entrepreneurs did not see, that helped to imagine a separate community into existence."[47] Gaines is referring here to the theatrically exhibited films targeting an African American audience produced by figures such as Oscar Micheaux. But such "race pioneers" also included institutions and filmmakers (both whites and African Americans) who thought more expansively about the use of the medium of moving pictures as an agent of uplift. Rather than appearing out of nowhere, these films were the logical extension of already existing multimedia campaign materials promoting African American advancement. As such, their production and exhibition were inherently—though not unproblematically—interracial, as well as intermedial.

Although *The Birth of a Nation* brought the issue of the filmic representation of African Americans to national attention, the leaders of the uplift project had already been using motion pictures to disseminate the message of agricultural and industrial training for several years. As early as 1910, moving pictures were integral parts of the uplift campaigns of the Hampton and Tuskegee Institutes. Speaking generally, African American uplift cinema in the south subordinated entertainment to message, loosely constructing narrative (both fiction and nonfiction) as a means of showcasing Hampton's and Tuskegee's endeavors. The product was Negro education, and the films were vehicles for its sale. In contrast, northern African American cinema was a business venture aimed at visual entertainment for Black audiences. African American entrepreneurs produced and exhibited motion pictures for Black audiences in cities such as Chicago, New York, and Boston. In the north, Black urbanites were "migrating to the movies," as Stewart has argued, to see a reflection of their lives that was positive, realistic, and engaged with contemporary debates concerning Black urban life.[48] The filmmaking projects of uplift filmmakers encompassed various modes of production and different regional requirements, through which they explored alternative possibilities for cinema in the service of African American social and political advancement in the early 1910s.

Myriad in form and content, uplift films shared a cultural context but not necessarily generic characteristics or types of exhibition venues. Uplift cinema included films that spanned several modes of production, were articulated through various genres, and were shown in different exhibition contexts. Although most were ideologically aligned with the Bookerite uplift project, some posited a challenge to uplift philosophy and its practical components (such as uplift comedies that were offensive to some while being highly entertaining to others). Despite their heterogeneity, these films informed, contributed to, responded to, and were otherwise critically engaged with uplift. In all of its forms, uplift cinema functioned as an agent of Black self-fashioning in the early twentieth century.

Frameworks for Conceptualizing Uplift Cinema
USEFUL CINEMA

Uplift cinema is one example of the Progressive Era's response to motion pictures. The National Board of Censorship spoke of using cinema to enact uplift in all audiences, film advocates proclaimed the possibility of using motion pictures as an educational resource, social problem films of the 1910s addressed domestic issues, and the film industry advocated the use of cinema as a tool for the promotion of international understanding—and trade—in the era of the League of Nations.[49]

Along with discourses surrounding theatrical entertainment cinema of the 1910s, recent research on nontheatrical cinema provides a helpful framework for approaching uplift cinema across modes of production and in relation to myriad exhibition practices. As Rick Prelinger has shown, from cinema's emergence moving pictures have been used "to record, orient, train, sell, and persuade."[50] The multiple functions of moving pictures beyond theatrical entertainment are broadly gathered under the category of *useful cinema*. In their discussion of the "multidimensional and flexible concept" of useful cinema, Charles Acland and Haidee Wasson write: "The concept of useful cinema does not so much name a mode of production, a genre, or an exhibition venue as it identifies a disposition, an outlook, and an approach toward a medium on the part of institutions and institutional agents."[51] Acland and Wasson take the term "useful" from Tony Bennett's concept of "useful culture," in which culture is formulated through institutions as a mechanism of power. They extend Bennett's concept to "a body of films and technologies that perform tasks and serve as instruments in an ongoing struggle for aesthetic, social, and political capital."[52] Useful cinema is an effective rubric for considering a broad range of films and film practices that have been receiving greater scholarly attention in recent years.

Useful cinema is not a retronym, however, but rather the restoration of a way of characterizing films that served a purpose beyond entertainment. The notion of utility was a part of the discourse about moving pictures in the early twentieth century. For example, trade publications such as the *Moving Picture World* advertised films like *Adrift* (Lucius Henderson, Thanhouser, 1911) with the slogan: "A picture with a lesson!" The advertisement even spoke to the utility of the film not just for the audience but for the exhibitors themselves: "ADRIFT is a useful film with a big, simple moral that would do much to reconcile the Church to the Motion Picture—if the former knew that this sort of film was so much in evidence."[53] Films were also sometimes explicitly characterized as not useful, as in this review of *The Refugee* (Lux, 1910): "A war story which does not convey any information; nor does it amuse. Its usefulness as a motion picture may, therefore be questioned." The reviewer concluded that *The Refugee* "serves no useful purpose."[54] Utility was also designated for half-reel films that could round out a program, as in the Lubin Manufacturing Company's advertisement of "Those Useful Half-Reel Comedies."[55] Discussions concerning the utility of moving pictures for educational purposes were prolific in the pages of the trade press. For example, in an issue of the *Moving Picture World* from 1911, several articles and notices proclaim the educational value of moving pictures: "The Picture as a Teacher," "Teachers View Historical Films," and "Simplifying the Teaching of History."[56] Similarly, moving pictures such as *The Awakening of John Bond* (Oscar Apfel and Charles Brabin, Edison, 1911) were championed as answers to the current wave of criticism of films. The *Moving Picture World* noted: "These pictures were the entering wedge that pierced the hard shell of conservatism and in less than a year have pried it wide open and forced the recognition of the motion picture by the press, university, state, church and laity as the greatest educational agency since the discovery of the art of printing."[57] The burgeoning film industry thus championed moving pictures as powerful agents of education as well as reform, an argument made most effectively by useful films that explicitly served the greater public welfare.

Sponsored by corporations, governmental agencies, social welfare organizations, and private groups and institutions, useful films were "made to persuade"—functioning as educational films while also striving to entertain.[58] They display industrial processes, technological advances, and lessons in personal and social conduct. Industrial films of this period show industriousness of various sorts: raw materials being turned into products, such as *From the Field to the Cradle* (Lubin, 1911) on milk production and *The Making of a Shoe: From Cowhide Pelt to Goodyear Welt* (Edison, sponsored by United Shoe Machinery, 1915); buildings and infrastructure being built, such as *The Greatest Engineering Feat* (Kalem, 1911) and *Building the Great Los Angeles Aqueduct* (American Film Manufacturing, 1913); the benefits of technology, such as *The Stenographer's Friend: Or, What Was Accomplished by an Edison Business Phonograph* (Edison, 1910); models for conduct, such as *The Little Mothers' League* (Kalem, sponsored by the New York Health Department, 1911) and *The Cost of Carelessness* (Universal Animated Weekly, sponsored by Brooklyn Rapid Transit, 1915); or lessons in hygiene, such as *Boil Your Water* (Pathé Frères, sponsored by the New York City Department of Health, 1911).[59]

Useful cinema is an important lens through which to consider uplift cinema not only because of the historiographical foundation established by Acland

and Wasson (and the contributors to their volume), but also because utility is basic to uplift cinema in two unique and fundamental ways. First, the films were produced and exhibited with a specific purpose in mind—namely, the social and political advancement of African Americans in the first decades of the twentieth century. Second, the films were made with the goal of promoting the idea of African Americans as useful citizens. Thus, in uplift cinema utility is doubly inscribed.

As a form of useful cinema, uplift cinema employed the medium of motion pictures to assert the humanity, respectability, modernity, and utility of African Americans for white and Black audiences at a time when such propositions were, more often than not, challenged by cultural and political norms. In this sense, uplift cinema at once was a public relations project targeting whites and functioned as an agent of positive self-definition for African American participants and spectators. Considered as a kind of useful cinema, uplift cinema can be understood in relation to its social purpose and varying degrees of pragmatism. The uplift project forms a constellation of discursive practices, the filmic components of which are theatrical and nontheatrical, industrial and entrepreneurial, and overlapping iterations of these modes. Uplift cinema is part of this practice of using film as a useful medium, but it extends the stakes of that usefulness to its subject: African Americans as useful citizens. Through various forms, uplift cinema argues that African Americans are modern and industrious citizens, and in this sense, uplift cinema operates at the intersection of making films useful (not just an entertaining frivolity or novelty) and making Black people useful (as workers and citizens). The raw material for many of these films is the Black population.

This fact is explicit in the case of the films made at Hampton and Tuskegee. One such film, *Making Negro Lives Count* (Hampton Institute, 1915), clearly plays on this dual meaning in its title and in a narrative structure that showcases Hampton's ability to transform individuals and, as a result, communities. *Making Negro Lives Count* chronicles the conditions in poor rural communities, the training provided by Hampton to meet the challenges of those conditions, and the results of improvements made in the communities by Hampton graduates. More broadly, the institutes' films were part of the rhetorical arsenal of their multimedia publicity campaigns. With other publicity materials, these films constructed an uplift narrative that was central to the mission of Hampton and Tuskegee: they followed a narrative trajectory of personal and communal transformation in a purported documentary discourse to demonstrate the power of the institutes to bring about concrete change. Following a before-and-after logic—which I will discuss more extensively in chapter 1—

the publicity visualized the transformation that a student would presumably undergo during his or her tenure: what the student was when he or she arrived, and what he or she would be on leaving the school. The publicity materials often featured students (both real and fictitious) living in rural squalor prior to entering the institute, learning how to overcome the disadvantages of their birth through agricultural and industrial training, and then—in the "after" section—returning home to uplift their communities.

The narrative logic of before and after, however, is not exclusive to uplift films but is a mainstay of the rhetoric of useful cinema and, in addition, the rhetoric of advertisements more broadly. It is found in contemporary social welfare and sponsored films such as *The Man Who Learned* (Ashley Miller, Edison, 1910) on the dangers of unsanitary milk production told through the transformation of a stubborn farmer set on the old—and dangerous—ways, and *An American in the Making* (Carl Gregory, Thanhouser, 1913) on the assimilation of an immigrant into a steelworker (featuring lessons on safety procedures).[60] The *Moving Picture World*, for example, championed *The Man Who Learned* as "a very practical as well as useful film" for conveying its lesson concerning sanitary milk production practices by showing "the dangers inseparable from the old order" followed by the details of the "improved methods." Sponsored by the New York Milk Committee, the film also "partially explains the recent advance in price," presumably by telling consumers about the necessity and value of milk safety procedures.[61] In *The Man Who Learned* the modernizing of the production of milk is the subject, while *An American in the Making* combines an assimilation narrative with the showcasing of safety devices and was produced under the auspices of the United States Steel Corporation and distributed by the National Association of Manufacturers (and later by the U.S. Bureau of Mines).[62] The didacticism of these subjects is conveyed through a narrative structure that aims to elicit empathy from the spectator while alerting the audience to the consequences of inaction.

The before-and-after rhetoric, in uplift cinema and in useful cinema more broadly, carried as its subtext an insidious threat: the possibility of failure. In the case of uplift films, the photographic documentary evidence of the before-and-after periods becomes a rhetorical tool for both the promotion of advancement and the cautionary threat of impending downturn. From 1900 to 1917 (when its rhetoric shifted to emphasize Hampton's war efforts), the "what if" scenario featured prominently in Hampton publicity, always calling attention to the other possible paths that might befall a student who did not manage to receive industrial training. This may seem a strange focus on failure in Hampton's publicity, but it is in fact a carefully constructed rhetorical strategy that insists on the need for the institute, a message that would be aimed at both northern philanthropists and southern Black communities.

The double address of the materials meant that the threat of failure was doubled as well. For white audiences, the threat was of the criminal licentiousness of the uneducated Black male who would be governed by "an unbridled body, an ignorant mind, and an undeveloped soul," in the words of one northern white sympathizer.[63] For Black audiences, the threat was the status quo of poverty, dependency, and racial subjugation, highlighting the possibility of failure; for uplift to be a viable goal, there must always be the threat of the impending downturn of a precariously positioned people. The double address thus required a form with which to articulate the social mission of the institutes that would appeal to otherwise conflicting constituents. To this end, the publicity projects used a rhetoric in which formal representational strategies were foregrounded in the service of a political project. In the Hampton and Tuskegee publicity, the iconography of uplift is underscored by ambivalence; failure is always inherent in the promotion of progress.

The rhetoric of before and after that constituted the dominant strategy of the publicity materials of these southern institutes intensified in 1915, after the incendiary release of *The Birth of a Nation* and the ensuing response by mobilized African American groups. In April 1915 Hampton administrators allowed *The New Era*, a film compiled from reedited footage of one of the institute's publicity films, to be appended as an epilogue to *The Birth of a Nation*. *The New Era* was added to the feature to placate the censors and critics of the epic's misrepresentation of American history and African American humanity, and constituted, as I will argue in chapter 4, an "after" to the "before" that was *The Birth of a Nation*. The resulting outcry in the African American press and among the institute's supporters and detractors caused heated arguments over the role of film in Black social struggles. The criticisms were twofold. First, Hampton was faulted for being involved in this project at all, and thereby giving legitimacy to *The Birth of a Nation*. Second, the material Hampton had contributed was described as being not strong enough and not used effectively enough to actually counteract Griffith's film. These two criticisms are related, but they addressed different concerns for the use of motion pictures as an agent of uplift— exhibition context, reception, and efficacy of the material. Indeed, this incident demonstrated the possibility that Hampton's industrial filmmaking could go awry when recontextualized and placed adjacent to such a reviled work.

Yet uplift cinema encompasses filmmaking practices that extend beyond the itinerant screenings in the interest of Hampton and Tuskegee to the more systematic engagement with moving pictures as a business venture by Black entrepreneurs in the north. Apart from the films made at Hampton and Tuskegee, the films discussed in this book were made by entrepreneurs who produced them with the primary goal of financial success. (For example, the *Chicago Defender* referred to the exhibition of William Foster's first film, *The Railroad Porter*, as having been "placed on the market" by Foster.[64]) To call the individual producer-director production mode of uplift cinema *entrepreneurial* is to encompass the three meanings of *entrepreneur*: the director or manager of a public musical institution, the nineteenth-century sense of "one who 'gets up' entertainments," to quote the second edition of the *Oxford English Dictionary*, and the sense of owning and managing a business and assuming the risk of profit or loss. In this sense, the business and entertainment definitions of *entrepreneur* bring uplift into alignment with itinerant exhibitors like Lyman Howe.

Black film entrepreneurs worked with relative autonomy, unhindered by regulation or patent restrictions. There is no evidence to suggest that the Motion Picture Patents Company, which controlled licenses for exhibitors, took any notice of Black film enterprises because they operated outside of the exchange system monopolized by the Patents Company.[65] The term *entrepreneurial* also allows for an understanding of filmmaking that includes narrative and nonnarrative, fiction and nonfiction, theatrical and nontheatrical modes of film production. Although the southern institutes that engaged with motion picture technology did so for a variety of reasons, entertainment was not the primary objective; for independent Black film entrepreneurs, in contrast, the goal was to cultivate and sustain a paying audience through entertaining motion pictures and actualities pertaining to African American life.

Even in entrepreneurial films primarily designated for commercial exhibition, there is still a strong element of useful cinema (which I discuss in chapter 5). In their engagement with nonfiction and actuality forms, in addition to their fiction filmmaking, entrepreneurs explicitly employed moving pictures as agents of race pride and community self-recognition. By filming uplift, and creating uplift through film, they provided an image of Black people that countered the distorted projection of racist paranoia prevalent on American screens and asserted African Americans' humanity and civic belonging through moving pictures.

LOCAL FILM

Among the early moving pictures produced and exhibited by African Americans were iterations of a practice of filmmaking and exhibition known as the local film. The local film—also known as local topicals, local actualities, and local views—was a type of film produced and exhibited for spectators drawn to the theater (or other exhibition site) by the possibility of seeing themselves, their acquaintances, and their communities on screen. Local films appealed to spectators' vanity as well as to their curiosity about how their image would appear when publicly projected. With their targeted address to specific audiences, local films proved to be very popular in the early cinema and beyond; the addition of local views was a common means of increasing audience interest in a moving picture show.[66] In the United States, Edison, Biograph, William Paley, and traveling exhibitors such as Lyman Howe were among early local film producers. And in 2012 Melton Barker's local talent film *The Kidnapper's Foil* (1930s–1950s) was named to the National Film Registry, garnering more attention for the local film.

One of the important features of the local film is that it is often a political gesture of self-recognition as well as a description of a popular practice of early filmmaking. In 1904 American Vitagraph advertised a traveling moving picture show by quoting the Scottish poet Robert Burns, "O would some Power the small gift give us / To see ourselves as others see us!"[67] There is a curious irony in this choice of verse to advertise local films. The Burns poem from which it is taken is titled "To a Louse, on Seeing One on a Lady's Bonnet at Church," and it tells of an upper-class lady in church who does not notice a louse in her bonnet. If we saw ourselves as others see us, the verse continues, "What airs in dress and gait would leave us." To see oneself through the eyes of others, in the poet's imagination, frees the subject from vanity and pretentions. Lice are not discriminating in their prey, whether "beggar," "cattle," or "such fine a lady"; as the poem humorously laments the "impudence" of the louse, it celebrates the creature's democratic reach by gently mocking the lady's assumption that her beauty, rather than the nesting louse, is what has attracted others' eyes. For Burns, to see yourself as others see you is a humbling experience, made all the more so by the divine "Power" that affords this impossible perspective. When applied to moving pictures, however, this "small gift" takes on a broader significance: it allows us to see some of the issues involved in local film practices.

In Burns's poem, class is a central element of the need for self-recognition: the upper-class woman is not able to see herself as others see her (as a host for a louse). Although local film retains an interest in class, it moves in an opposite direction, affording working- and middle-class spectators the opportunity to see an image of themselves projected on a screen in a collective viewing experience—to see themselves as participatory members of a community and as subjects of a film. Thus, in their work on the Mitchell and Kenyon collection in Britain (films largely involving working-class people), Vanessa Toulmin and Martin Loiperdinger point to this act of self-recognition as the central feature of the local film, a phenomenon that Tom Gunning has described (also in reference to the Mitchell and Kenyon films) as "the cry of recognition which baptizes this cinema of locality, as the amazement of a direct connection marks the viewing process."[68] In Martin Johnson's work on American local film in the transitional era and classical Hollywood era (such as home talent films and civic films with largely middle-class participants), he extends the attraction of seeing oneself on screen to consider place recognition as a constitutive aspect of the local film.[69] Where Robert Burns describes a mechanism of humility, the local film offered a means of publicly affirming the individual as an enfranchised member of a particular community.

African American uplift cinema is part of the tradition of local filmmaking, but it is more than that, using more than novelty as the primary draw for its audience. Put simply: African American local film demonstrates a more explicit awareness of existing in response to other images. African American filmmakers were presenting aspects of Black life to audiences (Black, white, and mixed) at a time of prevalent caricatures and degrading misrepresentation of African American images in popular culture. The act of seeing oneself on-screen as a dignified member of a community, then, functioned as a way to counteract the prevailing representational tendencies that existed in the broader culture of circulating images.

When the first film made at Hampton Institute, *John Henry at Hampton: A Kind of Student Who Makes Good* (1913), was shown to students and workers at the school in January 1914, the institute's monthly publication reported: "Nothing is more vitally interesting than 'to see ourselves as others see us' and laughter and applause testified to the intimate appreciation of scenes showing the trials and triumphs of a Hampton student."[70] I discuss this film in more detail in chapter 3. Here, I am interested in how the brief account of the screening refers not only to Burns's poem but also to the definitional discourse of the African American condition theorized by Du Bois as "double-consciousness," the idea of always looking at oneself through the eyes of others, an "other" that is necessarily racially posited. Du Boisian double consciousness is an apt metaphor for the cinematic experience. Referring to Du Bois's famous passage in *The Souls of Black Folk*, Gaines writes: "Suddenly one of the foundational statements in race theory appears as film theory, addressing the question of the execution of power through the trajectory of the eye."[71] Du Bois's passage reads as follows:

After the Egyptian and Indian, the Greek and Roman, the Teuton and Mongolian, the Negro is a sort of seventh son, born with a veil, and gifted with second-sight in this American world,—a world which yields him no true self-consciousness, but only lets him see himself through the revelation of the other world. It is a peculiar sensation, this double-consciousness, this sense of always looking at one's self through the eyes of others, of measuring one's soul by the tape of a world that looks on in amused contempt and pity. One ever feels his two-ness,—an American, a Negro; two souls, two thoughts, two unreconciled strivings; two war-ring ideals in one dark body, whose dogged strength alone keeps it from being torn asunder.[72]

Gaines posits race films—films with Black casts produced for Black audiences—as a kind of antidote to Du Bois's diagnosis: "For blacks there is the hegemonic absurdity of looking at themselves through the same distorted lens that eyes them so contemptuously. For blacks within white society who have historically been looking through the wrong lens, race movies offered a corrected view of things, not a radically new view but certainly an improved one."[73]

There is historical evidence to bear this out. Almost a century after Du Bois's famous formulation, Ossie Davis evocatively described the experience of watching race films in Black theaters, emphasizing the impact of this separate cinema in a space designated for Black spectators:

There were black people behind the scenes, telling our black story to us as we sat in black theaters. We listened blackly, and a beautiful thing happened to us as we saw ourselves up on the screen. We knew that sometimes it was awkward, that sometimes the films behaved differently than the ones we saw in the white theater. It didn't matter. It was ours, and even the mistakes were ours, and the fools were ours, and the villains were ours, and the people who won were ours, and the losers were ours. We were comforted by that knowledge as we sat in the dark, knowing that there was something about us up there on that screen, controlled by us, created by us—our own image, as we saw ourselves.[74]

As Gaines suggests and Davis describes, race film "corrects" the skewed perspective of "the social dimension of looking relations" that is definitional to American hegemonic order.[75]

Uplift cinema, in its interracial foundation, complicates this model. The local films, actualities, and industrial films present images that are at once aspiring and inspiring, but the meanings of the films shift depending on their exhibition context and audience. The practices of entrepreneurial uplift cinema may have more in common with those that race films were known to use, yet the interracial collaboration that defined many of the entrepreneurial ventures also troubles the straightforwardness of Davis's evocative recounting. Double consciousness was not just a mode of spectatorship; for certain uplift films, it was a narrative assumption as well. Beyond this, the terms applied to African American psychology at the beginning of the twentieth century, and to the film experience more broadly, reflect the specific representational or spectatorial structures of the local film. The ideal of the local film is central to uplift because it is the literalization of the principle of seeing yourself as others see you.[76] The imperative of respectability and public presentability that marks the uplift project is mobilized in the reflecting capacities of the local film.

The Archive of Absence: A Manifesto for Looking at Lost Film

Film history is a history of survivors, and scholarly writing is consequently disproportionally weighted toward extant films. However, with more than 80 percent of films made in the silent era considered lost, it is irrational to perpetuate extant-centric film history.[77] Statistical rates of survival and loss are lamented but not presented as a rationale for broadening the scope of analysis. To invoke an Akan proverb, we should not leave the history of hunting to be written by hunters rather than the hunted. I propose that we apply the same scholarly curiosity and inquiry to so-called lost films that we do with extant film artifacts: we must go beyond accumulating filmographic data to ask the same questions of nonextant films, with adapted methodologies, as we would ask of film history's survivors. *Uplift Cinema* is meant to be a model of such a project. To my knowledge, it is the only book-length monograph devoted to nonextant films.[78]

At the same time, as Stewart warns in her work on the Tyler, Texas Black Film Collection, we should get away from celebrating finds at the expense of critical engagement with the way in which the archive produces meaning.[79] This is not to downplay the incredibly important efforts of archivists and scholars who have doggedly labored to find, collect, repatriate, and preserve extant exemplars of early Black cinema or pieces of film history as a whole. Nor is it a call to deprivilege the film print per se, as others—such as Jon Lewis and Eric Smoodin in *Looking Past the Screen* and Jennifer Bean and Diane Negra in *A Feminist Reader in Early Cinema*—have explicitly and implicitly done. Rather, it is a call to not further bury the so-called losers of history by scholarly indifference, a call for work that complements efforts to find, preserve, and restore prints by paying increased attention to films that are, for whatever reason, considered lost. This work should also remind us of the possibilities afforded by extrafilmic research on surviving films. As the increasing scholarly attention to nontheatrical film demonstrates, there is much that we still do not know about surviving films and their history, the cultures in which they circulated, and the audiences for whom they were screened. As I hope to show in this book, we have much to learn from such "losers" if we look beyond what is no longer there.

What does it mean to talk about lost film? This requires a necessarily relational stance. To whom is a film lost? Films and film artifacts that are considered lost to us did, of course, once enjoy projection (beyond the fantasy that our desires might conjure up). Though obvious, it bears reminding that just because we can't see a film does not mean that someone else hasn't, or didn't, see it. But before we start talking about those producers and spectators—the subject of this book—we should think a bit more about our own vantage point. How has the field of film studies dealt with the problem of lost, fragmentary, unreliable, and disappearing print sources?

Language surrounding nonextant film largely falls into three categories of terms, often invoked in combination: the historical artifact, the perishable organic, and the spiritual. In the first category we find analogies and metaphors such as *ruins*, *buried*, *archaeology*, *excavation*, *vacuum*, *holes*, *voids*, *gaps*, and *lacunae*. In the second category are *evolutionary*, *condemned*, *perished*, and *morgue*. The last category answers the perceived lack evoked by the first two, and thereby establishes film restoration and preservation as a near-messianic solution, invoked with terms such as *saving* and *resurrection*. Spatial concepts meet organic metaphors to invoke a divine (or mad-scientist) promise of bringing what was once dead back to life. Once found (and hopefully preserved), a film is then engaged with as a social and material entity. "Excavation," Gaines asserts, "is only the first stage of reclamation."[80]

In *Streetwalking on a Ruined Map*, Giuliana Bruno writes that in an environment where "absence is dominant," one must reflect "on loss and destruction."[81] Discussions of loss in cinema often use terms like *archaeology* that conjure up images of digging through layers of sediment left by time; excavating among ruins; reconstructing fragments; and imagining the past through its artifacts, detritus, and ephemera. This is not wrong. But emphasizing the loss of the object reifies its status as artifact. To effectively address what has been lost to us, we should think of absence a little differently. Instead of defining something by what it is not, this project—and, indeed, the vagaries of film history more broadly—require us to look for the presence in the absence.[82] For those of us who study nonextant films, absence is the archive. Instead of perpetuating a binary of lost and found, we must take as the objects of our inquiry the imprint left by the films' existence and the traces left from conception to production and circulation. Instead of praying for resurrection, we should spend more time with absence. Absence is defined by the object it regrets; it is marked by the location, position, positing, and emplacement (both in time and space) of the missing piece. It is just as temporally and spatially situated as is presence. In a very real way, absence has presence. I propose we look at the presence of absence.

The 1978 International Federation of Film Archives conference in Brighton has become a milestone moment for film historians, what Thomas Elsaesser has called "the beginning of a new era of research."[83] Nearly six hundred films—all produced prior to 1907—were screened at this landmark gathering of archivists, scholars, and enthusiasts, challenging many perceptions about early cinema.[84] As Musser recalls, Brighton "signaled a new integration of academic and archive-based history and fostered tendencies that contributed to the formulation of a new historiography."[85] The historical turn that came out of the Brighton conference shifted the emphasis of early film historians toward empirical research. Going beyond the analysis of a film's aesthetic values, scholars interrogated aspects of production, distribution, exhibition, and reception. It has been increasingly recognized that the film itself is only one element of a broader media universe. As Janet Staiger aptly notes, "being sheltered by studying only film is to work with blinders on."[86] The consideration of films has been bolstered by attention to extrafilmic materials and contextualizing research; historical work is now unthinkable without this broadened perspective.

Even here, however, in the context of the "demotion of intrinsic filmic evidence," film remains the reified object.[87] Although scholars have increasingly engaged with nonextant materials as contextual sources for the study of film, my contention is that even in the best examples of this work, they nonetheless deal with films that serve as models for what such a film ought to look like. That which is extant grounds, orients, and models our understanding of the nonextant. This has varying implications. Almost as a rule, the further from mainstream theatrically screened productions we get, the scanter the surviving evidence becomes, and the more the few extant films gain authority. In terms of African American film history, how we understand race film has been informed by its surviving exemplars. For example, only three of the more than twenty films made by Oscar Micheaux in the silent era are extant, yet they receive almost all of the scholarly attention. This emphasis on surviving material is understandable, yet just as important are the films that are not available to us except as references in contemporary extrafilmic discourse.

Without extant film elements or even surviving photographic evidence, what claims can we make about a particular film? Lost to us today, nonextant films nonetheless existed at a given time and place and functioned in particular contexts, had actual effects on specific audiences, and consisted of certain formal properties. To ignore the formal aspects of these films is to reduce them to their status as facts of history, separate from the effect that they had on real spectators. Just because we cannot see them does not mean we cannot talk about them or about how they affected those who did have the privilege of seeing them. This book argues that nonextant film should be an object of study in its own right, not just a reference point for surviving fragments or items to round out a filmography. Here, too, I believe we can be bolder and assert that nonextant films can be studied, to varying degrees, for their formal aspects. I don't mean to say that these formal elements have been simply denied, but that scholars have been cautious about making claims about them. Although such study does involve speculation, there are solid grounds on which we can base our speculation. Part of the work of archival contextualization is precisely to refine our judgments about what these nonextant films would have looked like and how they could have appealed to spectators. This is the challenge that this project on uplift cinema aims to address. I treat the nonextant body of films that I term *uplift cinema* not merely as products that participated in historical events as facts of the past (events of history), but also as formal works that mobilized various aspects of moving picture technology and cinema's exhibition regimes to create an effect of uplift on producers and spectators.[88]

The context of films' production and exhibition and accounts of their reception provide clues to indicate how they were formally constituted. These formal properties of all lost films fall on a spectrum of known to unknown.[89] Data on such properties as length, format, and narrative elements are often more available, whereas aspects of composition, framing, editing, and mise-en-scène are more difficult to discern—depending on surviving evidence, inferences must be made with caution. We can account for the broader cultural context in which these films were made and functioned (visual culture, discursive engagements, aesthetic properties, and so on). But this means that we have to look adjacently—that is, beyond cinema—to the broader culture of the time. Lewis and Smoodin talk about "looking past the screen," but in the absence of projected images to fill that screen, a composite picture must be proffered from its surviving social, cultural, and economic attendants. More broadly, looking and thinking adjacently mean immersing ourselves in the cultural context of such screenings. Instead of being defeated by the seemingly overwhelming lack of information concerning nonextant film, I propose that we not let this deter us from sustained scholarly inquiry.

Although uplift films may be lost, there is an abundance of archival ephemera that constitute, in the aggregate, a composite portrait of rich filmmaking practices. Three kinds of primary sources make up the raw material for the new model of historiographic study that I am proposing. The first two concern institutional internal discourse. First, at Tuskegee's and Hampton's archives, institutional records and surviving ephemera provided indispensable context for approaching the motion pictures produced at and by these institutes. The materials include the letters and papers of the secretaries of the Boards of Trustees and those of the principals of the institutes from this period; materials related to the institutes' involvement with domestic and international expositions; materials related to the choirs and tours of the singers who accompanied the films; principals' reports; materials related to the Hampton Camera Club, run by the school photographer-turned-filmmaker; records of the photographer/filmmaker; records of special meetings of the Boards of Trustees; and the two most valuable items at Hampton, minutes of faculty meetings and a file on *The Birth of a Nation*. The D. W. Griffith Papers and the NAACP Records have been valuable sources for behind-the-scenes discussions concerning the Hampton epilogue. By connecting the dots across disparate sources, I have been able to piece together the origins of Hampton's filmmaking project, its evolution, and its vexed intersection with the most famous film of its time. The second kind of primary materials concerning Hampton and Tuskegee are the publicity materials, brochures, publications, pamphlets, photographs, and annual reports of the institutes, all of which provide valuable context for their filmmaking projects. These materials demonstrate the rhetorical structures of uplift narratives and provide insights into the way the films would have been designed to work in the fund-raising campaigns of the institutes.

The third group of materials encompasses the public discourse produced by institutions as well as the African American, mainstream, and trade press. This includes published print material such as issues of the *Southern Workman*, the Hampton publication that reported fairly extensively on Hampton's motion picture production and exhibition process, and the Tuskegee student newspaper. African American newspapers have been central in reconstructing the production and exhibition histories of entrepreneurial uplift films. Mining the mainstream press, including trade publications like the *Moving Picture World* and *Motography* as well as regional and national newspapers, provides crucial information, however disparate, on how these films were considered by mainstream—white—writers and exhibitors, how they circulated, and how they were exhibited. The George P. Johnson Negro Film Collection at the University of California, Los Angeles, contains important materials that have fortunately been archived, such as the incorporation papers of Black film companies.

The fact that there are no known extant examples of Black cinema prior to 1920 does not diminish its significance to Black film culture, social life, economic strivings, and issues of self-representation and self-fashioning.[90] It is our responsibility, as scholars of Black film, silent era cinema, and American film and culture, to treat nonextant films as having the same concerns and import as their extant counterparts. If we do not look adjacently at these elements of film history that have fallen into the interstices of dominant narratives, we risk rehearsing the same myths about our cinematic—and, indeed, our cultural—past. Worse, we risk missing the rich, albeit ephemeral, archive of the majority of films produced in this period. Part of the project of media archaeology, as I understand it, is to excavate these forgotten aspects of cinema's trajectory as a means of reassessing the ways in which it took shape, worked in relation to broader concerns, and persisted or disappeared. Uplift cinema is rife with instances of possibilities for the medium of motion pictures as an agent for the social, economic, educational, and political advancement of African Americans. And it includes striking examples of innovative engagements with film form that are part of the era's experiments with the formal possibilities of moving pictures. The fact that some of these possibilities persisted into the race film era and beyond, while others did not, merits further understanding. My hope is that this book will encourage others to look past extant films to the traces that are abundant even in the absence of survivors. Only when we do this will we begin to correct the imbalance of scholarly emphasis and give the so-called losers of history their due and restore their presence.

Uplift Cinema

This book contains five chapters. The first explores the visual culture of uplift in which the motion pictures functioned. This involves, centrally, the campaigns of Hampton and Tuskegee Institutes, both print and live (such as fundraising meetings, concerts, and special events), in the late nineteenth and early twentieth centuries. These campaign materials are important precursors to the uplift films as they established the institutes' multimedia rhetorical strategies that conveyed their political and social program. I examine the role of pamphlets, publications, photography, stereopticon displays, pageants, and singing designed for the promotion of the institutes in their fund-raising campaigns. These campaigns were designed to demonstrate that African Americans were modern, economically self-sufficient people and constituents of what Washington called a southern "new era of industrial progress."[91] Although these materials were primarily targeted toward white philanthropists in the north, they also were circulated among African American communities in the south as models of uplift. The presence of such a double audience and the double address it necessitated was quite prevalent but also complicated. To understand it, I trace the ways in which uplift cinema is rhetorically related to its multimedia precursors by establishing the existing rhetorical strategies that informed the emergence of uplift cinema and that constituted its exhibition context.

In the second chapter, I look at the two films made by northern entrepreneurs at Tuskegee Institute, *A Trip to Tuskegee* (1909) and *A Day at Tuskegee* (1913). The first film was produced by the George W. Broome Exhibition Company of Boston, owned by a filmmaking entrepreneur who made actualities for Black audiences, including scenes of local churchgoers and a film on the Buffalo Soldiers at Fort Ethan Allen, in Vermont. I show that Broome's filming of Tuskegee in 1909 began as a collaboration with the institute, but his entrepreneurial exhibition projects (which were beyond the control of the Tuskegee authorities) led Tuskegee to distance itself from the filmmaker. Thus, for the second film, Tuskegee collaborated with a different company, the Chicago-based Anderson-Watkins Film Company, which screened its film of Tuskegee for northern philanthropists as well as southern Black audiences. In tracing these two histories, I argue that the institute sought to exert greater control over the filming and circulation of these moving pictures. Yet, despite these efforts, the uplift model came into conflict with the ways in which spectators consumed — and wanted to consume — these images.

In the third chapter, I focus on the industrial film production of Hampton Institute, which made three films between 1913 and 1915. Two of the films were fictionalized narratives of a student's progress through the institute; the third was a nonfiction exhibition of the work done at the school. Reading them together with the sponsored filmmaking at Tuskegee, I propose that the motion picture productions made at Tuskegee and Hampton are important components of the history of sponsored and industrial filmmaking. These historical excavations lead to a new account of how cinema functioned in the broader uplift project, serving as a complexly functioning component of uplift education that appealed, successfully and unsuccessfully, to a variety of audiences.

In chapter 4, I discuss the Hampton short *The New Era* and its use as an epilogue for certain screenings of *The Birth of a Nation* in 1915. Here, the industrial filmmaking of Hampton met mainstream commercial filmmaking, which led to a barrage of criticism of the institute for its association with Griffith's racist epic. I show how this controversy brought to the fore the underlying tensions in the representational aspect of the uplift project and underscored the immediacy of the problem of cinematic complicity in the perpetuation of social inequity. I argue that the controversy over the epilogue belied Hampton's naïve faith in the power of a positive image (*The New Era*) to challenge a negative one (*The Birth of a Nation*), producing a sustained crisis in the cinematic promotion of African American modernization. In looking at the controversy the chapter also provides a fuller picture of how Griffith's film was received and responded to by contemporary Black audiences and communities.

In the fifth chapter, I shift my focus to look at early motion picture entrepreneurs working in northern cities. Along with George W. Broome and Louis B. Anderson, filmmakers such as Hunter C. Haynes in New York and Peter P. Jones, Alfred Anderson, and William Foster in Chicago embarked on moving picture ventures. Broome and Louis Anderson made nonfiction films, but Foster, Haynes, Jones, and Alfred Anderson made both nonfiction and fiction films. I discuss how these entrepreneurs engaged with the uplift project through their filmmaking and how their work operated discursively to promote Black modernity through cinema. In this chapter, I trace the rhetorical and social effects that these entrepreneurial films attempted and, to varying degrees, achieved. I consider the connections forged by Black filmmaking entrepreneurs with the broader film industry and the possibilities—both attempted and realized—for African American professional advancement behind the moving picture camera.

I conclude with an epilogue that considers the afterlife of the issues raised in the book, especially those concerning race film and later useful films made in the service of African American causes. Through the example of Oscar Micheaux's *Body and Soul*, I point to a legacy that uplift cinema left for, and that was used by, later filmmakers. Uplift cinema thus becomes a model for alternative uses of motion picture technology that opened up other possibilities for African American engagements with cinema.

My discussion of uplift cinema seeks to demonstrate the importance and vibrancy of Black film culture, however tentative and circumscribed, in the period prior to *The Birth of a Nation* and the proliferation of race filmmaking that began in the late 1910s. With this study, I aim to do two things: first, to complement the rich body of scholarship on African American theatrical fiction film with a thorough consideration of both nontheatrical and nonfiction forms of filmmaking that emerged in this period; and second, to emphasize the major role that cinema played in the self-fashioning of Black civic life in the 1910s, in both northern cities and the rural south. This work entails reconstructing the cultural artifacts that have been lost to history and using them to broaden our understanding of American film history; early Black film culture; and the myriad functions of moving pictures in the promotion of, struggle for, and enactment of African American advancement in the first decades of the twentieth century.

Along with this film historical project, I aim to contribute to critical engagements with the status of modernity, especially in relation to the role of moving pictures and discourses on race. In the context of Black film history, modernity has been understood as concurrently constituted by cinema culture and the color line. This has led to a recognition of different values of modernity. In the early twentieth century, the south was the site of "antimodernity,"[92] issues of race marked a distinctly modern phenomenon,[93] and film was the medium of modernity par excellence.[94] Yet these factors are rarely brought together in critical discourses surrounding Black modernity.[95] As I show, uplift cinema represents an aspect of Black modernity that complicates these divisions and that can be usefully added to genealogies of American cinema and African American engagements with film. Southern institutions for African Americans fiercely fought the ideology of antimodernity, promoting their fight with the most modern means of mass communication. Through this and other case studies—not least, the role of northern Black entrepreneurs—this book places uplift cinema at the center of the debates over Black visual culture, self-determination, the role of moving pictures as a means of social and political protest, and the negotiation of ideologies of racial representation.

1

THE AESTHETICS OF UPLIFT
The Hampton-Tuskegee Idea and the Possibility of Failure

Whatever you become, and even if you fail, you are my fate.
—MR. NORTON in Ralph Ellison, *Invisible Man*

We take these white folks where we want them to go, we show them what we
want them to see.—DR. BLEDSOE in Ralph Ellison, *Invisible Man*

In 1868, after the end of the Civil War and the resulting emancipation of four
million slaves "cast adrift," General Samuel Chapman Armstrong founded
Hampton Institute in Hampton, Virginia, with the assistance of the American Missionary Association (figure 1.1). The institute's goal was the training of
free Black people, former slaves, their children, and, after 1878, Native Americans in useful skills as well as giving students a strong foundation in Christian
morality.[1] With a military structure based on the strict discipline derived from
Armstrong's background in the Union Army, where he led the Eighth U.S.
Colored Troops, Hampton combined practical education and religious-based
character training. Hampton was more than a school; it was a concept. Its educational model was intended to correct the former use of Black slaves as human
capital.[2] The Hampton Idea, as it was known, began as a form of compensatory

4,000,000 former slaves cast adrift at end of civil war

Human Contraband
at Hampton in 1865

THE American Negro, at the close of the Civil War, was ignorant, penniless, propertyless, without leaders, the prey of "carpet-baggers" and his own worst passions. He found himself suddenly thrust into a new world, amid conditions that he was without training or background to meet. Never in modern times had any nation or race faced so crucial a problem!

education for African Americans. Hampton's emphasis on labor and industry was intended to result in replicating skills by training teachers: the institute's graduates were expected to spread the Hampton model of education throughout the south. As William Watkins has noted, a shift from "charity-oriented liberalism to hard-edged, corporate-driven philanthropy" meant that Hampton became "the testing ground and prototype for accommodationist education."[3] The model of corporate philanthropy was inherently political and ideological. Watkins argues that in the case of the education of African American citizens, such philanthropic endeavors were generally motivated by a desire to "guarantee an orderly South and a compliant Black population."[4] Thus, uplift education at its start emphasized the benefit of skilled Black labor as an accommodation to southern white social, legal, political, and economic authority. By 1900 there were over a hundred southern Black agricultural and industrial institutes operating to improve the condition of African Americans by promoting the economic value of a trained Black labor force to the nation.

Founded in 1881 by the Hampton graduate Booker T. Washington, the Tuskegee Normal School for Colored Teachers was both a product of the Hampton Idea—which became known as the Hampton-Tuskegee Idea, as the younger school and its principal gained notoriety—and a generator of Black educators. At its core, the Hampton-Tuskegee Idea emphasized self-help and promoted a model of African American uplift that positioned the individual as the catalyst for the broader advancement of a people. This model was specifically aimed at uplifting the race from the social death of slavery and the postemancipation bonds of neoslavery.[5] The post-Reconstruction period saw the decline of the social and political position of African Americans as the United States became the leading industrialized nation in the world. In fact, the industrial progress of the United States was arguably predicated on the wealth accumulated during slavery and increased after the Civil War through the neoslavery of African Americans, enforced through practices such as convict-lease labor and the systemic economic, political, and social disenfranchisement of Black citizens.

It is in this context that the uplift philosophy became the prevailing political position concerning the so-called Negro Problem in the United States. Despite strong criticism from more radical Black thinkers, the Bookerite principles of humility, work, thrift, and usefulness were widely accepted as the means of African American survival and social viability in the new century. As discussed in the introduction, Washington called on African Americans and white southerners to "cast down your bucket where you are" and develop mutually beneficial economic cooperation.[6] This 1895 speech became known as the "Atlanta Compromise" because of Washington's postponing measures for social and political equality in favor of economic advancement. The imperative for Washington and his ideological allies was to demonstrate that African Americans were modern, economically self-sufficient, and integral to the "new era of industrial progress" in the south.[7] To this end, both Hampton and Tuskegee designed publicity campaigns with the goal of influencing public opinion nationally and raising necessary capital support for southern educational institutes. Targeting white benefactors as well as Black communities, the publicity campaigns of Hampton and Tuskegee used pamphlets, photographs, stereopticon displays, pageants, singers, public appearances, and, after 1910, motion picture technology for the strategic promotion of African American advancement within an accommodationist frame.

The media productions of Hampton and Tuskegee were intended to simultaneously exemplify and present an argument for African American uplift, producing an explicit visual and intellectual effect on their targeted audience. Working across multiple media platforms, the publicity projects of these institutions mobilized a consistent set of narrational, formal, and stylistic aspects in a manner that I am arguing here can be seen as indicative of an aesthetics of uplift. Moving pictures were incorporated into the established culture of uplift aesthetics and served a strategic function as part of a larger project of public persuasion. Uplift cinema emerged from the ambitions of Hampton and Tuskegee to use various media to promote an accommodationist vision of African American advancement and a longer history of experimentation, success, and failure on which these ambitions drew. Thus, uplift cinema—as I will discuss in the following chapters—revealed the same ambivalences that were inherent in the aesthetics of uplift even as it offered new tools and resources in the service of the uplift project.

This chapter explores this broader culture of uplift to give a better sense of why the films developed as they did, and how they functioned and were rhetorically related to their precursors across media. As the locus of uplift was in the south, the southern educational institutions were the main disseminators of uplift rhetoric, yet their message reached the north through the targeting of northern sympathizers and potential donors. Creating the message of Black self-sufficiency and the need for uplift institutions (as well as the needs of such institutions) entailed a delicate negotiation of conflicting concerns. As a result, the culture of uplift consisted of a carefully constructed arsenal of arguments for Black enfranchisement. In print and live appeals, a deliberately organized rhetorical strategy conveyed the uplift message. Yet as a reflection of the uplift agenda, these multimedia publicity campaigns were deeply ambivalent. In the sections that follow, I trace the representational regimes that made up uplift strategy and the necessarily ambivalent functioning of uplift aesthetics. In doing so, I show that the concept of uplift was tied to a rhetoric in which the possibility of failure was centrally employed as a strategic argument for the Hampton-Tuskegee Idea. A greater understanding of the aesthetics of uplift allows for more nuanced insights into the ways in which race-based inequities were perpetrated and challenged through media in a period of great social, political, and economic transformation. An analysis of the aesthetic practices that uplift cinema inherits informs how we understand the development of African American engagements with motion pictures and Black cinema aesthetics in the ensuing decades.

Hampton and Tuskegee disseminated their message of African American uplift through far-reaching campaigns aimed at raising funds and gaining supporters as well as providing a model for Black communities. Uplift discourse was designed to be persuasive, strategic, and didactic. The publication offices of the institutes created brochures to appeal to northern white philanthropists, to provide an example for African Americans, and to present an argument for financial support through demonstrations of the institutes' work. As with any appeal for funds, the tone of the brochures strategically balanced informative content with the carefully constructed rhetoric of success and need. The brochures followed the Hampton-Tuskegee Idea, positing industrial and agricultural education for African Americans as the means by which to foster self-sufficiency and, ultimately, an accommodationist vision of racial harmony.

With his military record and reputation as a missionary and educator, General Armstrong was featured in fund-raising materials long after his death. His image signified an ideal of Christian charity and white philanthropy, as in his statement of the purpose of agricultural and industrial education: "Hampton's aim is to train selected youth who shall go out and teach and lead their people, first by example by getting land and homes; to give them not a dollar they can earn for themselves; to teach respect for labor; to replace stupid drudgery with skilled hands; and to these ends to build up an industrial system for the sake, not only of self-support and intelligent labor, but also for the sake of character."[8] Armstrong appealed to white benefactors by presenting a mission of Black self-sufficiency, bolstered by white philanthropic support, and by underscoring the point that Hampton was a site not of charity but of the creation of transferable skills. Washington's celebrated rhetorical mastery was due in large part to his inheritance of Armstrong's ability to appeal to otherwise conflicting constituencies. As Houston Baker Jr. has argued, Washington's "mastery of form" is a linguistic performance in which he appropriates the "minstrel mask" as a necessary means of communicating with (and in) white America.[9] Baker describes this mask as a "mnemonic ritual object that constituted the *form* that any Afro-American who desired to be articulate—to speak at all—had to master during the age of Booker T. Washington."[10] Tuskegee inherited rhetorical strategies from Hampton and adapted them to the particulars of the younger institute and, especially, to Washington's cult of personality. However, the strategic rhetoric of the promotional materials transcended each campus to constitute a broader aesthetics of uplift, one that had national reach.

The constituent parts of Washington's rhetorical strategy are three main themes that are mobilized in persuasive appeals for support (both sympathetic and monetary) and expressed through different media. Taking form in word, image, and live performance, these themes are syntactically arranged to garner support and have the strongest impact through their careful arrangement and contextual explanation. First is the theme of raw material, in which students are shaped and molded to become effective agents of uplift just as the materials with which they work are transformed by their labor. Second, the theme of success figured as the enactment of labor and education was often represented as a kind of whitening. Third, the theme of failure—or tempered progress, the verso of possibility—was frequently presented as the inverse of success.

Each of these three themes takes shape through a rhetorical structure of before-and-after sequencing. Even when these themes are not literally positioned in that order, they nonetheless operate with that meaning attached to them. The prevalence of before-and-after pairings in the publicity arsenal suggests that readers and spectators would see these elements in this syntactical arrangement as well: raw material is the raw material for something; success as the enactment of labor suggests something else—that is, failure. In this way, the before-and-after structure governs uplift media just as the concept of uplift is itself temporally and spatially situated. Uplift as an aspirational concept presumes a time and space from which to move. Temporally the move is from slavery to freedom and from neoslavery to a viable present. (This advancement in time is inherent in the concept of progress.) Spatially it is a progressive movement consisting of a vertical trajectory from point A to point B: in practical terms, from poverty to livable wage, or from the cabin to the house. However, the spatial aspect of uplift is necessarily limited to the south; uplift rhetoric, as Washington and his allies delivered it, is adamantly antimigration. The emphasis on before in uplift rhetoric results in the past's haunting the insecure present, so that depictions of success are tempered by the possibility of failure. Uplift aesthetics push this further. Hampton's promotional materials even focused on the institute's dropouts, using these examples of failure to show that, even in these cases, some success had been achieved. This apparent paradox—success in failure—underscores the dual nature of the concept of possibility as practiced in uplift aesthetics. Possibility conveys hopeful aspiration as well as limited achievement. Thus, the ambivalence of possibility pervades the culture of uplift.

Industrial training at Hampton and Tuskegee focused on transforming raw materials into goods or infrastructures, primarily in the service of Black communities and only secondarily for the general citizenry. Aiming to materially improve the lives of Black citizens through a kind of trickle-down training, the uplift project was concerned with the transferability of tangible skills and the very real circumstances in which they could be put to use. However, vocational training had a more insidious side: many white supporters advocated it as a means of creating both a useful working class of Black labor and a fixed limit on Black uplift. Men could become skilled laborers in agriculture or industry and productive heads of households; women could become domestic servants, wives, and mothers. Black agricultural and industrial training was, in the minds of white southern sympathizers, a continuation of the "civilizing school" of slavery, with ongoing emphases on religion and hard work.[11] As noted above, the raw materials for the educational industry were the students themselves, often explicitly identified as such. For example, describing the cycle of education in *Working with the Hands*, Washington explains: "At Tuskegee, for example, when a student is trained to the point of efficiency where he can construct a first-class wagon, we do not keep him there to build more vehicles, but send him out into the world to exert his trained influence and capabilities in lifting others to his level, and we begin our work with the raw material all over again."[12] Raw material is posited as the ur-before to uplift's mission. Students are trained to reproduce their education in other communities, extending the after throughout rural areas as they enact the regeneration of uplift. In the most utopian of imaginings, the whole south was figured as a before to the possibility of a viable national after for African Americans. This envisioning reflected the image of the south as the supplier of raw material (cotton) for the industrial north and the rest of the world.

Uplift's mobilization of the raw material concept mirrors the rhetoric of industry itself. Industrial logic depends on the transformation of raw material into replicable assets, goods, and commodities. When applied to human capital, the transformative capacity of raw material implicitly challenges contemporaneous perceptions of the innate mental inferiority of nonwhite peoples. In contrast to eugenics discourses, it implies a Lockean blank-slate concept of education and knowledge acquisition.

In an undated Hampton brochure from around 1910, there is a photograph depicting a young boy in ragged clothes, holding an apple at chest height (figure 1.2). He looks straight at the camera with a hint of a grin; his hat is cocked back,

FIG. 1.2 "The Hampton Normal and Agricultural Institute" (Hampton, VA: Hampton Institute Press, c. 1910). Courtesy Harvard College Library.

"RAW MATERIAL" AT HOME

sitting askew on his head. The caption to the photograph reads: "'raw material' at home." In uplift photographs, captions are key components in conveying meaning. As we see in this photo, the words are, in Roland Barthes's phrase, "parasitic on the image": the image is not so much a mere illustration of the text as it is the text's primary connotative element.[13] Yet the text does important work in constituting meaning, with the quotation marks in the caption signaling the double meaning of "raw material" as both products and human labor. The caption thus conveys the doubled purpose of the photograph: it identifies the figure of the boy as "raw material," something to be molded and shaped, and it creates a spatial context for the figure as located "at home," in contrast to a presumed "other" space — the site of molding and shaping. The location of the boy is ambivalent; he stands against a blank background and could have been photographed either inside or outside, and no specific "home" is evident apart from the caption. It is a careful aesthetic choice; the neutral background allows the image's meaning to become universalized. As an argument for Hampton, the image asks its viewer to recognize the potential of this child clothed in the rags of rural poverty and to support the institute's efforts to remove such potential from its source and provide him with the training necessary for an improved future. The frontal pose and staged setting evoke formal portraiture. Lit from a high angle on the left side of the figure, the loosely draped cloth at his feet (a traveling sack or grain sack) echo the chiaroscuro effect of his tattered jacket. The boy looks right into the camera and, though his eyes are shadowed, he evokes an unshaken faith in progress as if he is captured at the threshold of his education, in limbo between a before that is trapped in destitution and an after that has overcome the economic and social obstacles to advancement. With his face half cast in the shadow of ignorance, the boy is eager for an education, ready for schooling, and poised with an apple for the teacher.

Philanthropists familiar with social welfare photography of the time, like that of Lewis Hine, might recognize the latent talent suggested by the representation of this figure.[14] The nameless subject, identified only as "raw material," is a symbol of Black boyhood, dependent on white benefactors for the possibility of transcending the "home" that has relegated him to the rags that costume him for this photo. The clothes, slanted hat, and frontal posture of this child cast him as a performer of a condition. The child as "raw material" is an apt metaphor here, for he may have been presented as the future beneficiary of Hampton Institute's training but he is also the more "raw" expression of the ambivalent functioning of its rhetoric.

It is even possible to see the "raw material" child as a doubled Washington, reflecting the young Booker who famously swept his way into Hampton (tested with a broom-sweeping "examination") and wondered at "eating on a tablecloth, using a napkin, the use of the bathtub and of the tooth-brush, as well as the use of sheets upon the bed."[15] Casting himself as a primitive child who was civilized by Hampton, Washington writes an uplift narrative in which he presents himself as the successful product of Black agricultural and industrial education. Like the "raw material" child, he enters Hampton to be molded into a citizen and imbued with the values of self-sufficiency that define the uplift mission.

The "raw material" child is also the proto-adult Washington who would evoke such memories in his appropriation of the "minstrel mask," as Baker has argued, to craft his autobiography in the service of his social program. Understanding the efficacy of these vignettes, Washington writes himself into the teleology of progress characterized by Hampton's before-and-after publicity rhetoric. The strategy behind his self-effacement is one in which, as Baker writes, "he struts his minstrel stuff so grandly that there is no choice but to lay twenty thousand on him."[16] The child as "raw material" is doubly inscribed by the caption, cast as material of both education and public promotion. If the child's future at Hampton is implied in the photo and through its caption, the unspoken possible outcome for the child is less positive. The threat of failure is posited as more dangerous—the inverse of raw material could be unbridled raw passions—so that actual failure is the unwillingness to get on the path to uplift. To this end, even the absence of ostensible success could be a positive outcome, as a failing student still represents the successful avoidance of the criminal failure of the nonuplifted. Just as Hampton evoked the possibilities inherent in such "raw material," it also voiced the potential of unachieved education in fictional figures such as Cunningham, a Hampton "failure" who nonetheless serves his community despite his inability to complete the course of study at Hampton.

The Success of Failure

In Isabella Andrews's story "The Failure of Cunningham," first published in 1892 in the children's magazine *The Youth's Companion*, the fictional title character arrives at Hampton posing as a Native American because he heard that the government would subsidize Indians' education. Through the narration of a white Hampton teacher, the fictional Miss Burt, Andrews—a white author—attempts to write humor into her characterization of Cunningham and her awkward attempt to capture his presumed dialect. Cunningham's "coal-black face" and "unmistakably African personality" and "unmistakably African speech" mark him as humorous to the narrator, who informs the reader that the teachers "thought Cunningham very funny indeed."[17] Eventually, Cunningham gives up "his longings for luxurious ease" and instead works hard to become a blacksmith.[18] He works for two years in the night school but, to his dismay, is unable to move through the course of study to instruct others; as he tells the narrator, "I feel the spirit ob desire posessin' me toe go out an' uplif' my own people."[19] The narrator lauds his ambition to "elevate" others but laments his limited aptitude: "Could we send out the blind to lead the blind? We were beginning to consider him one of the hopeless cases." Cunningham is unable to advance beyond basic academic principles, though he proves "faithful, patient and eager to learn."[20] Although he had come to Hampton looking for a handout, "the development of a worthy purpose had greatly changed him. . . . There was no shirk in Cunningham now."[21] After failing to be promoted to a higher grade, he must leave Hampton to care for his "destitute" family following his father's death. He is forced to go home to "Baptist Hill," North Carolina, a place described like the presumed "home" of the "raw material" child: "It was just a cluster of tumble down Negro cabins a few miles back from the railroad. The men were too lazy to work the little farms that would have amply repaid the scantiest care; the women too shiftless to do anything but smoke and gossip; the children too numerous to count, growing up in absolute ignorance and squalor. Poor Cunningham!"[22] The story rehearses racialized discourses of abject poverty and describes the white paternalist imagining in that none of the members of this fictional community are able to actualize their own advancement, sharing the same stereotypical characteristics of laziness and shiftlessness. The story does not challenge the stereotype but imagines a figure like Cunningham who can exist within the stereotype and work toward improving conditions without challenging the worldview that defines him and his community as inferior. He writes to Miss Burt requesting spare books, as he "foun I could do something atter all" by teaching people in his community in between working paying jobs in his trade.[23]

Six months later, by accident of geography the narrator finds herself near "Baptist Hill" and visits Cunningham. She discovers that he is a schoolteacher in the manner in which he had been taught at Hampton, spreading both education and the values of uplift to the most lowly. The steer-cart driver who brings Miss Burt to "Baptist Hill" remarks, "Dat young Cunningham, he made right smart of a change roun' heah, miss," as he drops her off in the center of the community. She narrates, "We had driven into a bit of settlement that looked as little as possible like my notion of what Baptist Hill was. The road appeared to have been raked with a garden rake, so clean it was. Every poor little hut, hanging like a bird's nest to its big outside chimney, was gleaming with whitewash and surrounded by a rude whitewashed fence."[24] There are a few "loungers," but others are seen at work. Though the women smoke, they also are seen washing and hanging laundry. Again, stereotypes are not contradicted, but the story challenges their absolute applicability. When Miss Burt finds the rudimentary schoolhouse, "the pathetic little room went to my heart," and through the window she observes nearly twenty children paying rapt attention to their teacher, Cunningham.[25] When students get an arithmetic answer correct, Cunningham responds, "toe be sho," and aids the students in counting out pine needles to assist in performing calculations.[26]

The example of Cunningham is meant to show that even Hampton's weakest students can make a positive impact on the lives of others. In fact, the story argues that such "failures" are needed in order to "form little centres of light and influence in some of the darkest corners—corners into which less rude and ignorant and simple workers could hardly penetrate."[27] Such examples of rudimentary educational methods are presented as a stepping-stone toward the more advanced techniques of Hampton, with the institute promoting a kind of trickle-down educational model. Cunningham becomes a community leader, exemplifying cleanliness and religiosity, and a teacher who uses surplus Hampton texts in his classroom. In contrast to the "coal-black face" that had come to Hampton, his educational enlightening influence in his community is described as a racial lightening as well, conveyed by the praise given him: "'He jus' done mek us white,' said one old turbaned mammy."[28] Just as the cabins are whitewashed, so are the people. Here, educational and religious metaphors converge as the blank slates of the students' minds are equated with religious associations of being cleansed by the blood of Jesus. Yet the presumed humor conveyed through the ironic juxtaposition of the rude dialect and the assertion of racial transformation underscores the contained progress celebrated in the story. As an example of uplift, it is a safe one: ambitions are small, and impacts are circumscribed.

The story is built around several assumptions and exceptions. Cunningham is industrious but not gifted. He comes from a place where men are "lazy" and women "shiftless." He arrives at Hampton looking for a handout but soon adopts the goal of bettering his race by becoming a teacher. Narrativizing the before-and-after trajectory, the story is a tempered representation of progress: Cunningham does not achieve the middle-class ideal, but rather returns to where he came from with crude arithmetic and religious zeal. The progress represented by the after Cunningham is not revolutionary; he brings only basic improvements to his community, and its isolation is underscored by the narrator's account of her long journey to "Baptist Hill," in which she emphasizes its distance from even a "desolate junction."[29] The isolation of the locale accentuates the imperative for the community to be self-sufficient. The modesty of this uplift story is part of its persuasive rhetoric, as it seems to appease potential critics: fear not, donors—uplift is not analogous with uppity, and a little education is not a dangerous thing.[30] In fact, an incomplete education can be beneficial to the larger community. Hampton helps communities become more self-sufficient but does not promote systemic change or integration. The celebration of tempered progress is underscored by Andrews's emphasis on presumably intended humor and her use of dialect.

Yet despite the levity of the modest story, there is a very real undercurrent of terror that pervades *The Failure of Cunningham*. When Miss Burt enters the schoolroom, she shocks her former student, who "looked as if he saw a ghost," and causes the students to cry in fear.[31] This extreme reaction is of course a reflection of the stereotypes of Black cowardice and superstition, but it also evokes the very real fear that the presence of a white woman in a Black community could elicit. Though she is well meaning, her presence is an embodied danger that threatens the peaceful existence of the rural community in a time and place in which schools were shut and lynchings occurred for far smaller presumed offenses.[32] Furthermore, Cunningham borrows a horse and cart from his neighbors and accompanies Miss Burt back to her modest hotel, driving "in the fast falling twilight." He sleeps at the hotel as well, "in order to say goodbye in the morning," but leaves in the night when he is summoned to attend to "a sick man back in the woods," and the morning farewell is left "unsaid." The story concludes: "And this was our failure—our hopeless case! It was all poor and plain and mean and sordid, but I went back to Hampton and told my story in humbleness of heart. I did not need to point the moral there. Perhaps I need not here."[33] To the northern reader, the moral might rest on the surface of the story, yet the southern reader would note the cues in the text to serious breaches of interracial conduct; the twilight carriage ride and the shared lodgings would certainly raise eyebrows. The emphasis on silence—the unsaid farewell and the unspoken moral—echo the unacknowledged reality of the open secret of the prevalent practice of lynching. Andrews, a Texan, would not have been unaware of these associations. Cunningham's sudden disappearance "back in the woods" haunts the text with the specter of the wrongly condemned Black man. If the Hampton-Tuskegee Idea elided issues of justice and emphasized material improvements over philosophical questions of humanity and equality, the reality of the persistent threat of violence toward Black men and women nonetheless haunted the uplift project.

Written in 1892, *The Failure of Cunningham* was reprinted with permission by the Hampton Press in 1898 and used in fund-raising tours for at least the next two decades. The reprint included several drawings by the famed American illustrator Henry Alexander Ogden, known for his historical and military paintings.[34] The sketches that illustrate the story represent the before-and-after transition. Ogden's illustrations echo *Harper's Weekly*'s "Blackville" cartoons, drawn by Sol Eytinge Jr. in the 1870s and 1880s, and Edward Winsor Kemble's "Coontown" caricatures of African Americans from the late nineteenth and early twentieth centuries—although Ogden's sketches were relatively sympathetic rather than hostile. The first sketch depicts Cunningham in tattered clothes, holding a stick and a straw hat (figure 1.3), but in the second sketch

FIG. 1.3–1.4 (*Right and facing page*) Illustration by Henry Alexander Ogden in Isabella Andrews, *The Failure of Cunningham* (Hampton, VA: Hampton Institute Press, 1898). Courtesy Harvard College Library.

he is finely dressed and neatly coiffed, and a book and pen have replaced the ragged straw hat and stick (figure 1.4). The second sketch shows Cunningham standing in the front of the classroom at a makeshift chalkboard, teaching basic arithmetic to a roomful of stereotyped "pickaninnies" perched on log benches and complete with spiky braids and minstrel-like exaggerated features. (When it came to African American subjects, Ogden was no naturalist.) A white woman, the story's narrator, is peering in the schoolhouse from outside the window, an "unseen listener" and outsider in this segregated scene, barely perceptible yet positioned opposite from the implicit viewer.[35] Curiously, it is not her perspective that the viewer occupies; rather, the viewer is a witness to the triangulation of these figures and the different attentions that are fixed on Cunningham. Indeed, in the story, the narrator goes out of her way to present

herself as an outsider in "Baptist Hill" and as someone visiting across a line that is permeable in just one direction.

In a 1904 speech in New York City, Hampton principal Hollis B. Frissell used, without irony, the fictitious Cunningham as a "concrete example" of Hampton's work. He stated: "I have asked to have placed in your seats a short story called 'The Failure of Cunningham.' It is an account of a dull colored boy who was unable to make his way through the school, and was obliged to return to his home in the back country. It tells how one of his former teachers found him in a poor log schoolhouse and of the tremendous influence for good he exerted in his community. Will you take it home and read it? It will give you an idea of what hundreds of the dullest of Hampton's returned students have done."[36] Although Frissell's rhetoric is a strangely tempered means of demonstrating Hampton's work—how often does a principal promote his school with examples of the worst-case scenario?—the goal is to thwart fearful critiques of Black education by saying, in effect, that there is little danger of a Black insurgency coming out of Hampton. With the commitment to service and the high failure rate, the worst that could happen is that a quasi-literate teenager would teach illiterate children how to become quasi-literate as well.

Frissell importantly contrasts a successful failure in the figure of Cunningham with a real failure, which would be not even moving on the path to uplift. Cunningham's return home is an amelioration of the threat of criminal failure even without the ostensible success of achieving the uplift ideal. By celebrating the failure of Cunningham, Frissell demonstrates the significance of the uplift project to mitigate white fears. "To attract white largesse," Kevern Verney points out in his study of Washington, "it was desirable to portray blacks as victims, unable to save themselves without outside help. Examples of blacks effecting their own uplift therefore needed to be carefully rationed less they prove counterproductive in fundraising terms."[37] This was difficult to do when the message was one of self-sufficiency inherent in the notion of uplift. With Cunningham, it is the white narrator who effects uplift, through the "dull" tool of her former pupil. The claim that Cunningham "done mek us white" functions to underscore the modesty of Cunningham's contribution while naming the actual fear that African American educational advancements would, in effect, efface difference. The fictional "mammy" identifies the underlying conflation of disparity based on education and that based on racial difference.

Cunningham's return home is a successful failure, since he goes back to his community to pass on his modest knowledge instead of migrating north. Uplift rhetoric posits northern migration as another kind of failure. Contemporaneous with the ambivalent publicity represented by *The Failure of Cunningham*, in 1910 Edward Smyth Jones, a son of former slaves from Natchez, Mississippi, made his way to Cambridge, Massachusetts, from Indianapolis without any money, "to seek the lore deep laid" and "to learn in Harvard Square"—only to land in a Cambridge jail when he was arrested for vagrancy, having failed to find shelter for the night.[38] With the support of Judge Arthur P. Stone, the Black attorney Clement Morgan, and William H. Holtzclaw, principal of the Utica Normal and Industrial Institute in Mississippi, Jones was released and given work on Harvard's janitorial staff. Jones studied at Boston Latin School but, because of lack of funds, was unable to finish his secondary education and never entered Harvard.[39] Jones moved to New York City, got a job as a waiter at the Columbia University Faculty Club, and was featured in an article in the *New York Times* in 1913, which gave his ordeal wider publicity.[40] Given the institutional ties between Hampton and Harvard at this time (Harvard President Charles Eliot and Harvard Professor Frances Greenwood Peabody were trustees of Hampton), the publicity materials and their rhetoric of failure would have evoked Jones's ordeal and, likely, elicited more sympathy. Despite the support of powerful figures, Jones failed to realize his educational ambitions. Hampton would have been seen as a more suitable goal for him, and, through the support of the institute, other ambitious African American students could be kept in the south—thereby curtailing the flood of northern migration.[41] The antimigration message of Hampton was the subtext, and often the overtly expressed goal, of agricultural and industrial training for African Americans. The fictional Cunningham and the real Jones are both examples of ambitious students who fail yet are celebrated for their efforts and their modest successes. Indeed, the theme of the possibility of failure pervades uplift culture and is a central component of Hampton's and Tuskegee's self-representation.

In *Working with the Hands*, written as a sequel to *Up from Slavery*, Washington outlines the work done by graduates at other schools that had been developed with the same educational model as Tuskegee: "I do not wish my readers to get the impression that all of Tuskegee's men and women have succeeded, because they have not. A few have failed miserably, much to our regret, but the percentage of failures is so small that they are more than overshadowed by those who have been, in the fullest sense of the word, successful."[42] Again, success is presented not as graduation, but as self-sufficiency and respectable productivity. This assertion is followed by the final chapter, titled "Negro Education Not a Failure," in which Washington analogizes the Hampton-Tuskegee Idea to Christianity. He writes: "Years ago some one asked an eminent clergyman in Boston if Christianity is a failure. The Reverend doctor replied that it had never been tried. When people are bold enough to suggest that the education of the Negro is a failure, I reply that it has never been tried." Washington cites the fact that 44.5 percent of African Americans are illiterate (in 1904) and points to the disparity in educational expenditures per capita in the south for white and Black children.[43] His plea is for opportunity, but an opportunity based on "self-help" in building schools in conjunction with the public school system.[44] Graduates from Tuskegee, he argues, can extend the support of state-funded education and encourage "patience and self-control" to thereby avoid "a war of races." He concludes: "Every Negro going out from our institutions properly educated becomes a link in the chain that shall forever bind the two races together in all the essentials of life." Emphasizing that "an inch of progress is worth a yard of complaint," Washington addresses *Working with the Hands* to white allies and potential supporters.[45] Thus, it presents a measured and tempered view of African American advancement that, as with all Bookerite rhetoric, emphasizes the value to whites of Negro education in the Hampton-Tuskegee model. To this end, the resulting ability of graduates to generate self-help rather than strain civic resources is a recurring theme of uplift media.

Publications of Hampton and Tuskegee trumpeted success stories of former students as evidence of the impact of the institutes' educational models. A 1904 brochure titled *What Hampton Graduates Are Doing in Land-Buying, in Home-Making, in Business, in Teaching, in Agriculture, in Establishing Schools, in the Trades, in Church and Missionary Work, in the Professions, 1868–1904* features case studies of Hampton success stories. Before-and-after photographs of decrepit cabin birthplaces and new homes built by graduates for themselves and their families illustrate prose accounts of the graduates in a section titled "out of the one-room cabin." The photos, recycled from the series shot by Frances Benjamin Johnston in 1899, function as proof of the accounts of Hampton's successes. Reiterating the antimigration message that constitutes a central component of uplift rhetoric, one story tells of a graduate, Boyd Rhetta, who returns home after graduating from Hampton in 1901 to fill the void caused by his father's vices. He is lauded as one of the first graduates to build a better home for his mother with the skills learned at Hampton and at the Calhoun Colored School in Alabama, which was founded on the Hampton-Tuskegee model of education. The brochure proclaims: "On his return home he found his mother and brothers and sisters in a very uncomfortable one-room cabin, and heard the story of his father's thriftlessness, debt, and misused opportunities. Inspired by the Hampton and Calhoun ideas of self-help and self-support, he determined to join the land company, get a good farm for himself, and make a new home for his mother." This anecdote contrasts the father's "misused opportunities" with the son's industriousness. The brochure points out that Rhetta "is determined to show that the people of Lowndes County can, if they will, make a good living from their farms."[46] This anecdote presents a before-and-after success story shadowed by the alternative unsuccessful ending represented by the express reference to the father's inability to make constructive use of the opportunities supposedly given him. Rhetta replaces his father as provider for his family and, in so doing, represents a generational replacement marked by Hampton's training for uplift. Notably, the story is illustrated with two contrasting photographs (figure 1.5). The first shows a dilapidated cabin in a desolate environment identified in the caption as the "birthplace of Boyd Rhetta." The second depicts an orderly, well-constructed new home surrounded by tall trees and a manicured lawn with the caption "house built

BIRTHPLACE OF BOYD RHETTA

HOUSE BUILT BY BOYD RHETTA FOR HIS MOTHER

FIG. 1.5 Hampton Institute, *What Hampton Graduates Are Doing* (Hampton, VA: Hampton Institute Press, 1904). Courtesy Harvard College Library.

by Boyd Rhetta for his mother."[47] The images provide the visual evidence for Rhetta's transformational impact on his family's material condition, illustrating the metamorphosis from blight to ideal (before and after).

Another success story in this collection features Thomas C. Walker, a lawyer who helped Black residents of Gloucester County, Virginia, to build homes and buy land, leading to the improvement of churches and schools. As a result, "the migration to Northern cities was stopped, and for a space of five years no Negro was sent from that county to the penitentiary."[48] To appease white fears of Black dependency, Principal H. B. Frissell emphasized, in a speech in New York City in 1904, that "no graduate of Hampton becomes a drag on the community to which he goes."[49] A key element of the before-and-after rhetoric is the insistence that Hampton graduates become self-sufficient, implying that a Hampton education corrects African Americans' woeful reliance on government handouts, white neighbors, or northern migration. This emphasis on self-sufficiency promotes the sense that to "cast down the bucket where you are" would be a viable option; graduates would thereby have the internal resources to make life in the often oppressive south possible.[50]

"Learning by Doing": Displaying Labor

Along with "raw material" and the attention to failure, the uplift project emphasized labor, specifically laboring students in its promotion of agricultural and industrial education. The discourse of self-fashioning promoted the transformation of the raw material of oneself. Printed on the page facing the one showing the "raw material" child is another photograph, this one of students installing a window in a newly constructed building with the caption: "Learning by doing at Hampton" (figure 1.6). The students perform their work for the camera and illustrate both "skilled hands" and the literal building of their own environment.[51] In one sense, the changed environment is the product of the education, but the students themselves are depicted as products whose progress is recorded throughout their tenure at Hampton and after graduation, "so that the full results of scholarship gifts may be followed by the donors."[52] Put more crudely, donors would thus be able to chart their investments. Furthermore, donors played more than a supporting role, as they were able to indicate if their contributions would go toward academic or industrial scholarships or both.

The performance of labor for donors was also enacted through live demonstrations and pageants (theatrical displays and processions). Each spring, Hampton's annual anniversary exercises enacted the narrative teleology of

FIG. 1.6 "The Hampton Normal and Agricultural Institute" (Hampton, VA: Hampton Institute Press, c. 1910). Courtesy Harvard College Library.

LEARNING BY DOING AT HAMPTON

progress that represented the institute's purpose. The "Story of Hampton," a pageant designed by Cora Folsom, was presented over two days to benefactors visiting the school. There were three "chapters": a student's life prior to entering Hampton, a thorough demonstration of the work and "spirit" of the institute, and an account of the success stories of graduates several years after graduation. Performances of the "ever-welcome plantation songs" were interspersed in the various demonstrations of practical coursework.[53] The visitors, members of northern Hampton clubs and associations, concluded their visit with the annual meeting of the National Hampton Association. The enactment of uplift, the pageant was also a ritual whose formula mirrored the message embodied in Hampton's publicity materials that demonstrated progress through a before-and-after narrative trajectory in print and photographic media.

Hampton initiated its arsenal of before-and-after photographs in 1899 when Principal Frissell commissioned Frances Benjamin Johnston, a celebrated white photographer, to create a series of photographs at Hampton for the American Pavilion at the Paris Universal Exposition of 1900 and for publicity materials.[54] The resulting series of 140 photographs included a segment of photographs through which Johnston presented the change in African American rural life brought about by Hampton.[55] The January 1900 issue of Hampton's the *Southern Workman* reported that Johnston's photographs "constitute a pretty complete pictorial representation of the various activities of the school, and the making of them was the chief event in the early part of December."[56] In the thirty-second annual report of the principal, Frissell noted the "remarkably fine series" and how the photos "further illustrate our plans and methods."[57] The *Southern Workman* reported that the central theme of the photographic series was to depict "the relation of the various subjects in the school's curriculum to the central one of agriculture" and how "every part of the school life bears upon the home and the farm."[58] While at Hampton, Johnston also exhibited her own work and that of other photographers, including Gertrude Kasebier, F. Holland Day, Rudolph Eickemeyer, Alfred Stieglitz, Alfred Clements, and Henry Troth. Hampton's Camera Club, made up of faculty members and administrators, "was present in full force."[59]

The before-and-after series presents a teleology of progress through the juxtaposition of images. The January 1900 issue of the *Southern Workman* reported: "It is part of the plan of the exhibit to contrast the new life among the Negroes and Indians with the old, and then show how Hampton has helped produce the change." Through Johnston's contrast of the old and the new, Hampton aimed to present its methods to the world at the Paris exposition and to northern benefactors through stereopticon lectures, and to "[make] clear to the school itself what it is doing."[60] The photo series was a success in Paris, and Johnston received a Grand Prix as well as medals and acclaim. Frissell used the photos in subsequent publicity brochures, and for at least fifteen years the *Southern Workman* drew from Johnston's photographs to illustrate various articles.

In her discussion of the Hampton series, Laura Wexler notes how the politically decontexualized photographs are deliberately uncontroversial and "sublimate all marks of domestic racial struggle into the appearance of social harmony" as they represent the "socially passive black identity" that Hampton was attempting to incorporate in its students.[61] Johnston's output was in keeping with Frissell's mission, and her "averted gaze" was in line with Hampton's own promotion of the illusion of uncomplicated uplift.[62] Wexler notes the narrative dimension of the grouping of photographs collected in Johnston's *Hampton*

Album: "As a shooting script, such categories project a particular kind of spatial and temporal plot upon the material. They show the where, what, and when of a very concrete, very substantial Hampton. A second characteristic of the shooting script is its explicit hermeneutic of black history as progress initiated by the action of the Hampton Institute and illustrated by the 'before' and 'after' Hampton shots. As *tableaux vivants* choreographed by the photographer and enacted by a willing body of students and faculty, the images and titles represent material accomplishment and the solidity and measurability of development."[63]

However inadvertently, Johnston's images portray the ever-lurking possibility of failure, emphasizing the tangible presence of destitution as "before." This attention to failure underscores the precariousness of uplift. These images are mapped onto time, but it is a temporality excised of historical and social context. More than a focus on the triumphant overcoming of difficulties, uplift aesthetics figure failure as an ever-present threat to potential achievement. It is an attention to failure in which the present is elided and folded into a vague after. Unlike the anniversary exercises, where the emphasis is on the current work of Hampton, in Johnston's photos the future is cast as a perpetual present of uplift. Uplift then becomes not a means to an end, but the end in itself. The "shooting script" that Wexler sees in Johnston's photos speaks only of a hermetically encapsulated world of enacted progress, not a progress that leads to actual improvements beyond Hampton's borders. The medium of photography assists with this process through the frozen image. Moving images, then, present the opportunity for other possibilities for their subjects.

Wexler's assessment of Johnston's images as a "shooting script" echoes Ralph Ellison's Invisible Man's description of the Negro college he attends, and from which he is subsequently expelled for showing a trustee the nonuplifted outskirts of the campus:

As I drove, faded and yellowed pictures of the school's early days displayed in the library lashed across the screen of my mind, coming fitfully and fragmentarily to life—photographs of men and women in wagons drawn by mule teams and oxen, dressed in black, dusty clothing, people who seemed almost without individuality, a black mob that seemed to be waiting, looking with blank faces, and among them the inevitable collection of white men and women in smiles, clear of features, striking, elegant and confident. Until now, and although I could recognize the Founder and Dr. Bledsoe among them, the figures in the photographs had never seemed actually to have been alive, but were more like signs or symbols one found on the last pages of the dictionary.[64]

Ellison describes the photographs of the early years of Black colleges as empty symbols of uplift depicted through the photographic representation of an un-individuated and passionless "black mob" corralled by self-satisfied whites. The experience of the Invisible Man at his college is one in which the façade is more important than the substance. The uplift image becomes the tool of uplift and, ultimately, uplift itself. This passage also marks his realization that the before could not be erased by the after. He narrativizes this by going from the college to the nonuplifted outskirts on the misguided tour, giving this concept a narrative twist and belying its broader transformational promise. As he moves away from the campus, the uplifting potential of the college is revealed to be a myth.

Given that Hampton's emphasis on service always concluded with a litany of proof of its impact on actual communities, it is strange that Johnston's photographs are so inward looking, emphasizing (in Wexler's terms) "station, stillness, and solidity."[65] In the effort to seal out the contemporary critiques of radical Black thinkers and the hostility of some whites, strange bedfellows that threatened the singular message of the institute, progress could only be of the most conservative kind, exemplified by the idyllic yet somber bourgeois family scene of "A Hampton Graduate at Home" (figure 1.7). Here the image is the uplift. Indeed, that is the point: figures and statistics may present abstract evidence of the progress of the southern Black populace, but the image of a refined, middle-class, respectable (and relatable), and nonconfrontational (only the children meet the camera's gaze) family is the performance of uplift staged for the white philanthropist's eye.

In the Johnston series, the staging of the photographs and their doubling in the before-and-after sequence create an environment of uplift without a space for resistance. Johnston's photographs present staged scenes of uplift, organized for the camera, whose stasis represents a controlling immobility that suggests the greater political and social obstacles that conspire to circumvent racial advancement. As Wexler has shown, Johnston's photographs are consistent with Hampton's "dominant narrative": "In an ominous, familiar, over-determined, and claustrophobic formula, the concept of *race* in the Hampton of Johnston's camera is homologous with a principle of *place*."[66] The notion of progress in an accommodationist context depended on the delay in seeking certain rights (such as voting) and the deferral of claims (of equality) in favor of a slower, cyclical process of self-sufficiency and contained uplift. This is expressed through the visual display of labor.

The rhetorical strategy of displaying labor as an element of uplift aesthetics was common; indeed, Washington's *Working with the Hands* included a series of photographs of Tuskegee by Johnston taken in 1902 (three years after she

FIG. 1.7 "A Hampton Graduate at Home," Frances Benjamin Johnston, 1899. Courtesy Frances Benjamin Johnston Collection, Prints and Photographs Division, Library of Congress, LC-USZ62-38150.

photographed Hampton). In the book, Washington describes how he became disabused of the "warped" notion that "freedom from slavery brought with it freedom from hard work" and that "education of the head would bring even more sweeping emancipation from work with the hands." With work, Washington describes a newfound "self-respect, an encouragement, and a satisfaction that I had never before enjoyed or thought possible." Washington's belief in example is expressed in *Working with the Hands*: "Quietly, patiently, doggedly, through summer and winter, sunshine and shadow, by self-sacrifice, by foresight, by honesty and industry, we must re-enforce arguments with results. One farm bought, one house built, one home neatly kept, one man the largest tax-payer and depositor in the local bank, one school or church maintained, one factory running successfully, one truck-garden profitably cultivated, one patient cured by a Negro doctor, one sermon well preached, one office well filled, one life cleanly lived—these will tell more in our favour than all the abstract eloquence that can be summoned to plead our cause." He concludes by imagining people as buildings, asserting that "we cannot begin at the top to build a race, any more than we can begin at the top to build a house." Here, the notion of people as materials is reinforced through his evocation of a mix of animate and inanimate examples: "An industrial school is continually at work on raw material." Evoking the "raw material" trope, Washington posits individual successes, however modest, as having more impact than "abstract eloquence," certainly a critique of Black intellectuals who argued for broader concerns of justice and equality.[67] Washington's trajectory of advancement is not from idea to change but from labor to change.

Though taken only a few years later, Johnston's photographs for *Working with the Hands* are far more dynamic than those she shot at Hampton for the 1900 Paris Exhibition. Students are shown at work, casually captured rather than carefully posed. The exceptions to this are the photographs of the women's departments. For example, the women workers depicted in photos such as "Learning Dressmaking," "Mattress-Making," "Basket-Making," and "Barrel Furniture" (figure 1.8) for the Tuskegee series are shot as if in staged tableaux, consistent with Johnston's earlier compositional tendencies. But the exterior shots of men in the cane fields (figure 1.9), sawmill, foundry, and machine shop are more chaotic and frenetic, less crisp in line and orderly. Even the illustration for "Mechanical Drawing Class at Tuskegee Institute" (figure 1.10), which most closely approximates the orderly repetition of the Hampton series, has a more dynamic energy as the legs of the white tables cut through the center of the image like the legs of dancers in a chorus line on a stage. The tension between the stillness of the human subjects and the compositional busyness of the environment shown here betray a more profound tension in Johnston's view than is evident in the tidy world she created for the Paris exposition. In "Roof Construction by Students at Tuskegee Institute" (figure 1.11), the compositional chaos is most sharply divergent from the orderly world composed of Hampton. And the human figures in "Wood-Turning Machinery" (figure 1.12) are difficult to discern in their frenzied environment. The visual confusion captured by Johnston's lens reflects a larger sense of agitation that challenges the orderly containment of the figures in the frame.

In this series, Johnston's framing seems to anticipate the incident that shortly followed her visit to Tuskegee, when she attempted to visit the Ramer Colored Industrial School in rural Alabama and was caught in town at night in the company of several Black men who were escorting her.[68] White defenders of racial propriety threatened the interracial party with gunshots, and Johnston narrowly escaped. As a result of Johnston's breach of southern codes of interracial conduct, the Ramer school was closed for a number of years. Wexler has demonstrated that the irrational threat of violence marked a "livid" Johnston, yet the photographer ultimately complied with Washington's request not to pursue the matter further.[69] Wexler notes that Johnston's photographs of other rural Alabama sites reflect "the placid, beautiful scenes" of her 1899 Hampton series, and "their pastoral quality gives no hint of the dangers Johnston had just witnessed."[70] Even though the Tuskegee photographs were taken prior to this incident, they display the confusion and incomprehensibility of their Alabama subjects that is unlike the orderly world she had framed in Hampton, Virginia, a few years earlier.

Published a decade after *Working with the Hands*, the 1915 brochure *The Need for Hampton* employs a rhetorical strategy of before-and-after pairings, underscoring the work of the institute for the betterment of Black southern life and, by extension, better "race relations":

Slowly, but surely, the dilapidated cabins are giving place to well-built and sanitary houses; the worn-out fields to flourishing farms; the leaky churches to handsome structures; the tumble-down schoolhouses to modern buildings; the idle street loafers and the shiftless housewives to good citizens and wise and capable mothers and sisters. Well-lighted and sanitary streets are supplanting dirty, unpaved ones in the Negro quarters of cities; race relations are constantly growing more friendly; Southern white men and women are working in church and school and settlement for their backward neighbors; the problem of two races differing in color and advantages living side by side in harmony and mutual respect is on the way to solution.[71]

The presumption that training in citizenship is the basis for improved race relations is also folded into the before-and-after rhetoric. *Hampton's Message*, a brochure of the same year written by Sydney Dodd Frissell, executive secretary of the National Hampton Association and son of Principal Hollis B. Frissell, continues to promote agricultural and industrial education as the antidote to race problems: "Through Hampton outposts and graduates, the method of industrial training has become thoroughly established as the educational solution of a race problem. Hampton today has become the headquarters of an army of uplift."[72] The accompanying photographs of uniformed students demonstrating militaristic discipline underscores the image of an "army of uplift," which Washington also fondly recounted in *Up from Slavery*. This rhetoric alludes to the military organization of Hampton, beginning with General Armstrong's emphasis on military discipline and the regimental organization of the students from untrained "raw material" into men fit for service.

The Need for Hampton is illustrated with a series of photographs depicting

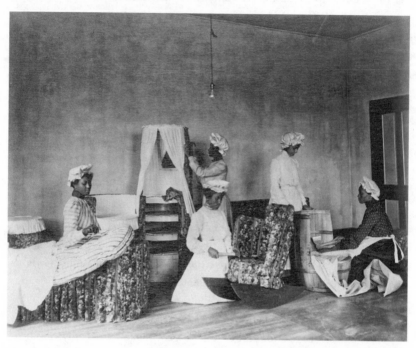

FIG. 1.8 (*facing page, top*) "Students Making and Upholstering Barrel Furniture," Frances Benjamin Johnston, 1902. Courtesy Frances Benjamin Johnston Collection, Prints and Photographs Division, Library of Congress, LC-USZ62-24333.

FIG. 1.9 (*facing page, bottom*) "Cutting Sugar Cane on the Marshall Farm, Tuskegee, Ala." Frances Benjamin Johnston, 1902. Courtesy Frances Benjamin Johnston Collection, Prints and Photographs Division, Library of Congress, LC-J694-185.

FIG. 1.10 "Mechanical Drawing Class at Tuskegee Institute," Frances Benjamin Johnston, 1902. Courtesy Frances Benjamin Johnston Collection, Prints and Photographs Division, Library of Congress, LC-J694-109.

FIG. 1.11 "Roof Construction by Students at Tuskegee Institute," Frances Benjamin Johnston, 1902. Courtesy Frances Benjamin Johnston Collection, Prints and Photographs Division, Library of Congress, LC-J694-107.

FIG. 1.12 "Wood-Turning Machinery." Frances Benjamin Johnston, 1902. Courtesy Frances Benjamin Johnston Collection, Prints and Photographs Division, Library of Congress, LC-J694-112.

the before-and-after transformation. One example is a juxtaposition of images of "the old home and school" and "the new home and school," in which the decrepit interior of the old schoolhouse is contrasted with an exterior shot of the newly constructed school (figure 1.13). These images reflect the brochure's conflation of poverty with idleness and the assumption that the underlying causes of racial conflict would be ameliorated through the training of the Black citizenry. The frontispiece to the brochure is one of the most striking examples of this rhetorical strategy, as it contrasts two images on facing pages. On the left is the photograph of a Black teenager "before he came to Hampton" and on the right is the same figure "ready to leave Hampton" (figure 1.14). The photographs are shot from a similar angle. In each photograph, the figure is represented against a different background, a cabin on the one hand and a neoclassical building on the other hand, a visual contrast consistent with the before-and-after images of architectural structures that were a common feature of the Hampton brochures. Moreover, the shabby clothes of before are contrasted with the pressed uniform of the cadet, while the slouch (coding him before as lazy and shiftless) is juxtaposed against his perfect posture after.

More insidiously, the first image keeps its subject's face in partial shadow and his hands hidden in his pockets. The interior of the cabin against which he leans is completely obscured, its door covered with illegible graffiti. The space is presented as threatening and contains an implicit cautionary warning to the philanthropic recipient of the brochure. In this setting, the man is not merely lazy or passive, but evokes a latent criminal threat that such a lack of industriousness breeds (suggested by his slouching posture and hidden hands). He represents the real failure—that of failing to aspire to uplift—in contrast to the successful failure of Cunningham. To the target white audience, the implication of this iconography would be clear: the threat embodied in the Black male can be harnessed into usefulness if molded by proper education. In the final chapter of *Working with the Hands*, Washington takes special care to point out that "not a single graduate of the Hampton Institute or of the Tuskegee Institute can be found to-day in any jail or State penitentiary." He continues: "If the Negro at the North is more criminal than his brother at the South, it is because of the employment which the South gives him and the North denies him."[73] In this respect, Washington concurs with Du Bois's assessment in *Some Notes on Negro Crime*—published the same year as *Working with the Hands*—of "Negro criminality" as socially caused rather than racially determined.[74]

In contrast to the claustrophobic framing of the first image, the second rebalances the figure so that he is not centered in the frame but positioned in the lower left corner, allowing the building to occupy the center and the sky

THE OLD HOME AND SCHOOL

THE NEW HOME AND SCHOOL

FIG. 1.13–1.14 (*above and at right*) Hampton Institute, *The Need for Hampton* (Hampton, VA: Hampton Institute Press, 1915). Courtesy Harvard College Library.

in the upper right corner to balance the figure. The only sky available in the first image is through the cabin door out of the background window of the obscured interior. The only shadow in the second image is cast by the cadet who is clearly out in the open: erect, free standing, and isolated. Paired in this way, these images articulate the relation between environment and individual, and in so doing present an argument for Hampton as a civilizing force. Thus, the pairing enacts what Baker characterizes as the "marshaling of the black body to attention, discipline, regimentation, rudimentary craft, and agricultural skills" that indicates the uplift project's white missionary roots.[75] In Baker's assessment, agricultural and industrial education for African Americans functions as a kind of "sanitizing" of the Black southern masses ("to *clean them up*").[76] Such an effort to bring "the body under control" is literalized through this pair of photographs.[77] Although not explicitly extending Baker's argument, Fred Moten argues that what is in particular need of control, according to whites as well as Black uplift leaders, is Black criminality. He astutely notes that the "discord and disorder" that signifies Black criminality is held up as evidence of the need for socialization, yet in all kinds of ways "blackness" and "black social life"

BEFORE HE CAME TO HAMPTON   READY TO LEAVE HAMPTON

are coded as criminal: "To be black, to engage in the ensemblic—necessarily social—performance of blackness, is to be criminal."[78] This paradox is visualized in the before-and-after syntax of uplift photography. Here, Hampton draws on a longer tradition of juxtaposing images to present a vivid argument for the possibility of transformation.

In his discussion of similar before-and-after photographs taken in 1864 of Hubbard Pryor (figures 1.15 and 1.16), an escaped slave and enlistee in the Forty-fourth U.S. Colored Troops Regiment, Maurice Wallace demonstrates how the juxtaposition of these images is a visual corollary to the rhetorical tool of the chiasmus, most famously employed by Frederick Douglass and theorized by Henry Louis Gates Jr.[79] Extending Wallace's observations, I would argue that the chiastic structure of before-and-after photography is central to the visual rhetoric of uplift in the late nineteenth and early twentieth centuries. Such a structure suggests a more complex temporality than the before-and-after structure, as the images inform the legibility of one another. As with the juxtaposition of the "visual propaganda" of the Pryor images, the before-and-after pairings of uplift's persuasive rhetoric derive meaning from a Barthesian

FIG. 1.15 Before photograph of Private Hubbard Pryor, 44th Regiment, USCT; Enclosures M750-CT-1864; Colored Troops Division—Letters Received; Records of the Adjutant General's Office, Record Group 94; National Archives and Records Administration, Washington, DC. Courtesy U.S. National Archives and Records Administration.

"third effect," in which their adjacent sequencing proffers "an ideological argument in its appositional excess."[80] In the case of the frontispiece to *The Need for Hampton*, the threat of implied criminality is neutralized by the military discipline of the opposite image, a juxtaposition that serves as an argument for environmental rather than innate causes of "Negro criminality," a question that was debated in the popular discourses of eugenics and phrenology. By placing the figure so specifically in contrasting settings, the institution argues that the "need for Hampton" is to directly mitigate Black criminality. The captions even elide the actual education the student would have received at Hampton. Like Hubbard Pryor's after image, the recently graduated Hampton stu-

FIG. 1.16 After photograph of Private Hubbard Pryor, 44th Regiment, USCT; Enclosures M750-CT-1864; Colored Troops Division — Letters Received; Records of the Adjutant General's Office, Record Group 94; National Archives and Records Administration, Washington, DC. Courtesy U.S. National Archives and Records Administration.

dent is a spectacle of redemption. Thus, the image is more significant than its implication: that is, neither Pryor nor the Hampton graduate are shown doing anything—their significance is derived from the spectacle of their being. Of course, the fact of their existence, a fact evidenced by photography, is a form of action; the uplifted image is an argument for the agents of uplift. The interstices of the before-and-after apposition constitute the realm of uplifting—before demonstrates the need for uplift, and after exhibits its possibility.

A Tuskegee pamphlet from around 1912, *Making Useful Citizens*, performs a similar function. It identifies a dilapidated cabin as a "type of one-room cabin from which many students come" and juxtaposes it with a hillside two-story home with a wraparound porch and white picket fence, "the new type of home" that belongs to A. R. Stewart, a graduate of Tuskegee (figure 1.17). This precedes a two-page illustration that juxtaposes a photograph of a Tuskegee student "just as he arrived" with two photographs of a man and a woman as "the finished product" (figure 1.18). Like his Hampton counterparts in *Everyday Life at Hampton Institute* (discussed below) and *The Need for Hampton*, the Tuskegee arrival slouches, whereas the graduate stands erect, his sword echoing his perfect posture.[81] This is an odd juxtaposition, however, since the man in the arrival photograph is clearly not the same as the graduate on the facing page. Most strikingly, he is much darker skinned than the male and female graduates, an aesthetic decision that imbues the comparison with the weight of the social politics of skin color. Like Cunningham's enlightening-as-whitening message, the implication here is that to be a "useful citizen," the Tuskegee student must become white or, rather, closer to white: less Black. In this vein, the *New York Age* once misquoted Washington in a way that inadvertently commented on Tuskegee's civilizing mission: "Fifty-seven per cent of our race can read and white [*sic*]."[82] As with the photographs in *Making Useful Citizens* and the repeated instances of whitewashing in *The Failure of Cunningham*, Washington's before-and-after rhetoric contains a presumption of whitening as the necessary corollary to full citizenship. Although uplift leaders were ostensibly critical of eugenics, uplift narratives often contained prejudice related to physiognomy. For example, Hampton Principal Frissell described Thomas Walker, the lawyer celebrated in *What Hampton Graduates Are Doing*, as he first appeared as a new student: "a small, thick-lipped negro boy from a back country."[83] The before-and-after rhetoric writes physiognomy as a marker of ignorance. The conflation of racialized description and the emphasis on the manipulation of white charity characterize the before figures in the anecdotes that are used to prove the need for Hampton's existence.

Leigh Richmond Miner

Everyday Life at Hampton Institute, a 1907 brochure, contains some of the most striking photographs of all of the publicity materials. These were taken by Leigh Richmond Miner, Hampton's director of applied art and resident photographer. In addition to the frontispiece, the brochure contained twenty-eight photographs, each with a short paragraph as a caption. The captions describe the photo and then connect it to the aspect of the school that they are meant to illustrate. As its title suggests, the brochure offers a virtual tour of the work of

Type of One-Room Cabin from Which
Many Students Come

Home of A. R. Stewart, a Tuskegee Graduate
—the New Type of Home

Just as He Arrived

The Finished Product

FIG. 1.17–1.18 Tuskegee Normal and Industrial Institute, *Making Useful Citizens* (Tuskegee, AL: Normal and Industrial Institute, c. 1912). Courtesy Harvard College Library.

the institute, highlighting the training it provides, and is structured as a kind of walk-through from a student's matriculation to his or her achievements after graduation. In terms of structure, it follows the pageants and other publicity materials.

In contrast to Johnston's long shots and group compositions, Miner's images are framed more tightly and are more interesting in terms of their formal range and compositional layout. With attention to depth of frame, these photographs add dimension to the scenes depicted and appear more like film stills than choreographed static moments. Though they show posed students, they evince a fluidity that suggests an action in time rather than the frozen suspension of time, in contrast to Johnston's Hampton series. The brochure itself is organized narratively, starting with a photograph of Memorial Church and its reflection in the water as the frontispiece (figure 1.19). This initial image announces the aesthetic vision of Hampton as a nineteenth-century idyll; the reflection of the church tower in the water is impressionistic, and the horizontal symmetry creates a doubling effect that is temporally concurrent (as opposed to the before-and-after pairings that comprise much of the photographic arsenal). The photo also posits the concrete Hampton as if rising from a primordial or spectral inversion; the image suggests the very real way in which the institution exists because of and in response to the spectral hauntings of American history. The image, in my reading, is thus a nostalgic vision consistent with American Romanticism's sublime concurrence of utopian vision and ghostly illusion. As the first image, it also establishes the theme of reflection that will carry through the brochure: image and its reflective text, concrete evidence and its subtext. Positioned opposite the title, *Everyday Life at Hampton Institute*, the photo suggests that everyday life consists of these opposing dualities, the image of the institute and how that image is reflected. Situated this way, the photograph reflects the efforts to control the meanings of disseminated images of the institution, its work, and the very representation of uplift.

The opening pages narrate two new arrivals, an African American and a Native American "fresh from the plains."[84] Although this practice is not consistent throughout the brochure, most of the right-side images depict Native American students even though they made up only around 10 percent of Hampton students at the time.[85] The African American "new arrival" sits on his trunk, perched among the luggage of other recent arrivals waiting to be enrolled in the school (figure 1.20). It is a composition that foregrounds the baggage and captures the figure in a full shot, looking out of the frame. Unlike the before images or the "raw material" child, the new arrival is well dressed, wearing a coat, tie, and hat, and has three trunks and a bag's worth of possessions.

FIG. 1.19 Leigh Richmond Miner photograph in Hampton Institute, *Everyday Life at Hampton Institute* (Hampton, VA: Hampton Institute Press, 1907). Courtesy Harvard College Library.

MEMORIAL CHURCH

In fact, he looks like every other teenage student arriving at boarding school. The very fact of his normalcy, like Johnston's portrait of "A Hampton Graduate at Home," makes him relatable to the white philanthropists for whom this would be a familiar scene. The opposite photograph depicts a Native American arriving at the Wigwam, the dorm for male Native American students (figure 1.21). He, too, wears a hat, but he carries only a small bag. He is greeted on the steps of the dorm by a uniformed student who reaches out as if to help with his bag or to shake his hand—a gesture not reciprocated in the photograph by the not-yet-civilized arrival. Yet unlike the African American arrival, the Native American arrival is shown in medias res, on the threshold of the dorm and of his transformation through education.

FIG. 1.20-1.21 (*right and facing page*) Leigh Richmond Miner photograph in Hampton Institute, *Everyday Life at Hampton Institute* (Hampton, VA: Hampton Institute Press, 1907). Courtesy Harvard College Library.

A NEW ARRIVAL AT HAMPTON, SEATED ON HIS TRUNK WHILE WAITING HIS TURN TO BE ENROLLED BY THE COMMANDANT OF CADETS.

HAMPTON INSTITUTE HAS (1907) 1295 STUDENTS, INCLUDING 487 CHILDREN IN THE WHITTIER TRAINING SCHOOL. OF THE 808 BOARDERS, 315 ARE GIRLS.

As Ray Sapirstein has shown in relation to the photographic illustrations of Paul Laurence Dunbar's poems made by members of the Hampton Institute Camera Club (of which Miner was a leading participant), the visual trope of the threshold was a recurring theme in such materials. In this way, the cadet in the before-and-after pairing in *The Need for Hampton* is figured on the threshold of the cabin and of the neoclassical building, his position there reiterated by the captions. On the Dunbar illustrations, Sapirstein notes: "The threshold potentially represents a thwarted escape, from incarceration and slavery into freedom and citizenship, from ignorance and superstition to civilization, from the shadows into the open, from the past to the future."[86] Coupled with the

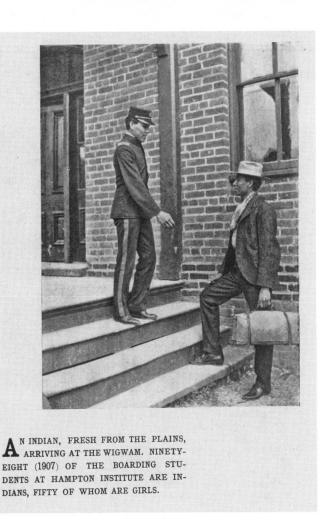

A N INDIAN, FRESH FROM THE PLAINS,
ARRIVING AT THE WIGWAM. NINETY-
EIGHT (1907) OF THE BOARDING STU-
DENTS AT HAMPTON INSTITUTE ARE IN-
DIANS, FIFTY OF WHOM ARE GIRLS.

recurrence of the domestic cabin motif, the Hampton Camera Club photos convey the precariousness of freedom and the liminality of African Americans in the post-Reconstruction era. In the case of *Everyday Life at Hampton Institute*, the threshold is explicitly temporal: the two new arrivals move from an old way of life to a new one through the modernizing institution. What follows, then, are intimate views, albeit staged for Miner's camera, of individual students engaged in various activities. Yet instead of focusing on the education and training, the brochure is overwhelmingly dedicated to demonstrating the self-sufficiency of students who are shown cooking (figure 1.22), cleaning, doing laundry (figure 1.23), and gardening.

A FIRST-YEAR BOY AT WORK IN THE STUDENTS' KITCHEN. THE NEW NEGRO BOYS WORK AT VARIOUS KINDS OF UNSKILLED LABOR FOR ONE YEAR, GOING TO SCHOOL TWO HOURS IN THE EVENING. BY SUCH WORK THEY ACCUMULATE A CREDIT BALANCE WHICH HELPS THEM TO MEET THEIR EXPENSES.

These photographs are formally distinct from the series taken by Johnston or the other images commonly used in printed pamphlets or published in the *Southern Workman*. Different from other campaign photos, the images in this brochure share compositional similarities that have no immediate explanation. Nearly all of the figures are depicted leaning over some task and are shown in profile or three-quarter angle facing toward or away from the camera. They are shot with bright natural light coming through the windows that dramatically illuminates the figures from the side. Certainly, the bending posture reflects the nature of the work being depicted. Yet when the brochure is seen in its entirety, its recurrence has a rhetorical function that is not found in any single

FIG. 1.22–1.23 (*facing page and left*) Leigh Richmond Miner photograph in Hampton Institute, *Everyday Life at Hampton Institute* (Hampton, VA: Hampton Institute Press, 1907). Courtesy Harvard College Library.

A TYPE OF THE NEGRO GIRLS WHO DO THE LAUNDRY WORK FOR NEARLY 1000 PERSONS, AS WELL AS FOR THE BOARDING DEPARTMENTS OF THE SCHOOL. OVER 25,000 PIECES ARE WASHED EVERY WEEK. EACH GIRL IS TAUGHT HOW TO DO ALL PARTS OF THE WORK AND IS, BESIDES GIVEN LABORATORY INSTRUCTION IN LAUNDRY CHEMISTRY.

image alone.[87] According to the second edition of the *Oxford English Dictionary*, the verb *bend* is derived from the term for bondage, to fetter, confine, or put into bonds; the word came to its modern meaning through the image of a bow whose string and arch hold an arrow in tension. Bending could be read as stooping in subservience or reverence, recognizing the authority of both the photographer and the implied white viewer. But it could also convey prayerfulness, reflecting the religious and moral training instilled in students at Hampton. Furthermore, the angle from which the subjects are captured heightens the naturalism of the scenes and creates a dynamism that is absent in Johnston's Hampton series. The angle and posture of the subjects suggest movement and put the figures in further relief, so that they sculpturally inhabit their space. Given Miner's extensive background in the fine arts, the sculptural evocation of his framing was certainly deliberate.[88] This movement serves to undermine the suggested subservience of the posture. It offers a point of tension in which the angle of the figures counters the deferential postures. It also creates a space in which the viewer of the image is figured in the space but not entirely privileged in the way that Johnston's photographic tableaux lay out scenes for the viewer or that the pageants unfold before their spectators. Miner's images are quieter, more intimate portraits of individuals performing tasks; in the context of an institution that trained students to gain skills that would make them useful, the task was understood as constitutive of the individuals. Yet Miner lovingly frames his subjects so that, even when partially obscured, they are individuated. The brochure has a clear addressee, the white philanthropist. The captions address potential donors, ensuring that the images function similarly; the brochure also concludes with a direct appeal for funds. But the images perform more than simple supplication. Their subjects' averted gaze may be deferential, but it is also indifferent. And in the context of the publicity brochure, such indifference is a small form of resistance, one that carries with it an assertion of humanity—or at least a certain definition of it. In the Hampton-Tuskegee ethical worldview, humility is a key virtue that leads to full humanity. As the caption to an image of a woman helping teach another woman to sew states, "the idea of service is inculcated in every possible way."[89] The brochure seems to assert that humanity is more valued than citizenship. Being a "possible man" is more crucial than being an enfranchised citizen.[90]

There is another aspect to this posture, one that mirrors the white paternalism that is foundational to the Hampton-Tuskegee educational model. The "white patriarchal stance," as Wexler notes, that celebrated interracial cooperation was one in which "the whites had to stoop and the blacks and Native Americans had to stretch."[91] Removing the white figures from the scene, the brochure nonetheless leaves their trace, as students are shown helping and teaching one another.

The repeated bent posture also recalls Miner's collaborative photographic illustration of a young woman bent over a bowl kneading for Paul Laurence Dunbar's poem, "Dinah Kneading Dough," published in *Candle-Lightin'
Time*.[92] *Candle-Lightin' Time* has three photos depicting Dinah (figures 1.24–1.26). Although the middle one largely echoes Miner's images in *Everyday Life at Hampton Institute*, the other two do something different. The first image presents "Dinah" standing upright in front of a large brick fireplace where a fire has been lit, her hand on her waist and the other resting on the mantle,

just beneath a framed photograph of a woman (presumably herself) and her sweetheart or husband. She is smiling confidently and looks out toward and beyond the position of the camera. She is posed and posing, but she has a natural look and an expression that is intimately beguiling. Yet there is also a hint of defiance in her posture and sideways gaze: she is confident and has an air of ownership in the home. This sense of belonging and the intimacy of the scene are intensified in the last image. Here, she is shown standing above the dough that she is kneading, resting from the work and looking out (toward a space out of the frame, perhaps at a door) with a wider smile. Although she is positioned at the far end of the table with her back to the hearth, the photo is taken from across the room so that the fireplace is seen in relation to the table where she kneads, uniting the spaces depicted in the previous photographs.

Considered as a sequence, the series of three photographs depicts the work of bread creation from the intention expressed in the first photo (the lit fire, a hand gesturing toward her sweetheart—the implicit kneading lover who narrates the poem) to the mixing of ingredients in the bowl and then to Dinah standing over the kneaded dough smiling, presumably, at her sweetheart who cherishes this image. The photographs show the process of bread making, in keeping with the raw material-to-product trajectory of the before-and-after images as well as contemporary industrial films. What we are shown, as well, is a few moments of extreme intimacy between two people. There is room for expression and individuality. As with Johnston's images that "construct a black identity from an external vantage point," Miner and his camera are interlopers in these intimate scenes.[93] Since the subject is not looking at the camera, the viewer is not put in the position of the poem's narrator but is rather an invisible witness to this domestic scene. Of course, the photo is posed and framed for the presumed viewer, but the action unfolds without deference to the spectator. This tension between deliberateness and indifference characterizes the bowed stance of Dinah and the related images in *Everyday Life at Hampton Institute* as well as the photographic aesthetic of Miner overall. Wexler describes the Dunbar illustrations, including those for "Dinah Kneading Dough," as nostalgic images.[94] Nostalgia is an operative mode, but we should not dismiss the photographs as merely nostalgic. The "nostalgic" images have a dynamism that is absent in (or erased from) Johnston's Hampton series. It is resistant to the "socially passive black identity" of the Johnston series that so well captured the purpose of the institute.[95] Miner's subjects are deferential but not passive. Although subject to external vicissitudes, they are active, working subjects. Furthermore, the hint of defiance in the first image of Dinah and the warm smile in the last image suggest a depth of interiority absent from the Johnston

FIG. 1.24–1.26 (*facing page, left and below*) Leigh Richmond Miner photograph for "Dinah Kneading Dough," Paul Laurence Dunbar, *Candle Lightin' Time* (New York: Dodd, Mead, 1901).

oeuvre. The accommodationist position could be seen as submission to white hegemony, but the bowed posture—like the political position it reflects—is a deliberate and strategic one. This posture is consistent with Washington's efforts to appeal to northern capitalist interests in the economic usefulness of the southern Black populace.[96]

"Dinah Kneading Dough" is the only poem in *Candle-Lightin' Time* that is in standard English, and Dunbar was aware that his dialect poems were far more popular with both Black and white readers.[97] Although we can read a subversive intent in his dialect poems, it is the act of writing in standard English that was a gesture of formal resistance. In the context of *Candle-Lightin' Time*, "Dinah Kneading Dough" is a marker of uplift. Despite Dunbar's masterful and arguably subversive use of dialect, Gates notes that dialect connotes "black innate mental inferiority" and is the linguistic marker of the "continued failure" of uplift.[98] If the poetic use of dialect signified blackness as difference and functioned as an index of the minstrel and plantation traditions, the poems in standard English subvert those associations and assert a stronger claim to humanity by means of assimilation achieved through education.[99] Dinah, a name frequently used for female characters in minstrelsy, is reclaimed from the minstrel tradition and recast in respectable domesticity and praised in standard English.[100]

These illustrations demonstrate that Miner's photographic aesthetic, representational emphases, and compositional tendencies are a distinct iteration of uplift aesthetics. In contrast to Johnston's photographs, Miner's images depend on a humanizing portrayal of individuals at work, enacting progress. And unlike Johnston's series, Miner's photographs individuate Hampton students and represent them with a past, present, and future. But although Miner and Johnston represent two trends in uplift aesthetics, in both the orderly collective world composed by Johnston's lens at Hampton and the individuated world depicted by Miner, the claim of Black humanity ambivalently coexisted with the presumption of Black inferiority.

Uplift publicity did not presume to the scientific level of discourse in Du Bois's *Types of American Negroes, Georgia, U.S.A.*, which operates, as Shawn Michelle Smith has argued, as a "counterarchive" to contest and resist racialized scientific and popular discourses from eugenics to caricature.[101] Though Washington disapproved of the prevalent belief in scientifically determined racial inequity, his rhetoric skirts the issue of eugenics but does not directly challenge it—and Du Bois directly criticized Washington for accepting "the alleged inferiority of the Negro races."[102] The visual culture of uplift is not the "antiracist propaganda" of the *Crisis* either, the official magazine of the NAACP, edited by

Du Bois, in which photography was mobilized in the struggle for social justice.[103] To trace the visual culture of uplift is to trace accommodation to racist paternalism as much as resistance to supposed scientifically determined Black inferiority. By working against a certain notion of a racial hierarchy (or the violent enactment of it), the uplift project reinscribed—and reentrenched—racial hierarchies. By not challenging Black subordination, it aimed to assert Black humanity. As Washington argued in his 1895 speech in Atlanta, "it is from the bottom of life we must begin," and the claim for Black humanity functioned as the first rung on the uplift ladder.[104] This worked through a multipronged rhetorical strategy that functioned in multiple media. The publicity images and uplift narratives produced by Hampton and Tuskegee reflected the complex negotiation involved in demonstrating African American self-sufficiency as key to the progress of the race while simultaneously arguing for financial and political support for the educational work of the institutes. Their rhetorical strategy hinged on this balance, one that attempted to be "void of offence" to its mainly white audience: Kelly Miller criticized Washington for allowing southern whites "to believe that he accepts their estimate of the Negro's inferior place in the social scheme."[105] Thus, it is not surprising that a century later we would read these images as laden with misguided and racist paternalism, just as we have come to question the pedagogical methodologies of the institutions that employed them. Yet they are also part of a visual and textual rhetorical strategy that served a specific goal: to raise support for Black agricultural and industrial education while also publicizing to Black communities the progress achieved by these institutes. These images, then, are part of a longer lineage of strategies of representing African American progress that has relied on a precarious balance between lauding social and political advances and perpetuating the underlying inequities that blocked further improvements.

In this context, it is logical that cinema was a natural successor to uplift photography and its narratives. As many people were recognizing in the early twentieth century, cinema permitted a narrative unfolding in time and thus allowed the before-and-after syntax to be fleshed out to include the during—that is, the process of uplift itself. Uplift cinema emerged in the broader culture of uplift and operated adjacent to other promotional materials. At Hampton, Folsom's pageants provided the framework for conveying the institute's narrative through film, and Miner translated his dynamic aesthetics of uplift to the moving pictures that he produced for the institute. In the north, Black filmmaking entrepreneurs saw the possibility that cinema could permit a new level of self-representation unmitigated by the ambivalent rhetoric of uplift's southern roots. In this entrepreneurial strand, uplift cinema took part in the assertion of a project of Black self-representation that was wholly separate from the influence of the Hampton-Tuskegee model of advancement. Thus, although uplift cinema developed most prominently in conjunction with the promotion of so-called Negro education as practiced at the southern institutions, it also broadened the representation of Black civic culture, shifting the epicenter of uplift away from the rural south and toward the northern destinations of increasing numbers of African American migrants.

2

"TO SHOW THE INDUSTRIAL PROGRESS OF THE NEGRO ALONG INDUSTRIAL LINES"

Uplift Cinema Entrepreneurs at Tuskegee Institute, 1909–1913

The country has gone crazy over moving pictures.
— "MOVIES," *Chicago Defender*, March 8, 1913

Marvel, indeed, is the progress.
— CARY B. LEWIS, "Film Co. Incorporated," *Freeman*, March 8, 1913

At the beginning of the twentieth century, for African Americans and for the nation at large, Tuskegee was a metonym for uplift. This was true largely because its principal, Booker T. Washington, was the foremost representative of the possibilities of African American advancement. But the promotion of uplift was not just confined to Washington's persona alone. Washington was quite conscious of the impact of the institute's print campaigns, realizing the importance of using photographs of the school and its students in raising capital and other support as well as spreading the message of the uplift project. As I argued in the previous chapter, the media produced by the institute emphasized both its achievements and what Washington termed the "ideals, the possibilities of the Tuskegee trained man and woman."[1] More broadly, the political, social, and cultural possibilities represented by Tuskegee made it an attractive location for Black filmmakers, who capitalized on its popularity in their quest to appeal to

African American audiences. As the epicenter of the uplift project and the object of powerful brand recognition in the north, Tuskegee was a logical subject for Black filmmaking entrepreneurs. Between 1909 and 1913, two northern filmmaking enterprises, the George W. Broome Exhibition Company and the Anderson-Watkins Film Company, visited Tuskegee and produced moving pictures of the institute, intending to document and publicize its methods and impact. Such collaborations seemed to be mutually beneficial for Tuskegee and the Black-owned film companies. However, in practice, the confusion of the multiple purposes of moving pictures—for education, fund-raising, and entertainment—generated conflicts between the institute and the film companies. The Tuskegee films demonstrate the divergent views on how moving pictures should reflect, promote, and shape African American uplift.

The Broome Exhibition Company of Boston

In 1909 the Boston-based African American entrepreneur George W. Broome asked to produce moving images of Tuskegee's campus.[2] Broome was an old acquaintance of Washington, having been introduced to him by the composer Harry T. Burleigh in 1897, when Burleigh was soliciting Washington's help in organizing a benefit concert at Carnegie Hall in 1897 for the Pickford Sanitarium for Consumptive Negroes in Southern Pines, North Carolina.[3] Broome aligned his mission with that of Tuskegee, saying (as reported by the *New York Age*) that his motion picture company aimed "to show the industrial progress of the Negro along industrial lines by means of moving pictures."[4] Broome argued that motion pictures, by showcasing the achievements of the institute, could be an effective agent in building support among benefactors. He convinced Washington that motion pictures would surpass print campaigns and work in conjunction with live appearances to raise awareness about the work of Tuskegee. Appealing to Washington's desire to promote Tuskegee as a cutting-edge and modernizing institution, Broome wrote: "I feel that you are interested in this work because of the great possibilities and advantages the moving pictures have over the old style of pictures."[5] Given Washington's emphasis on public promotion and image management, it is not surprising that he took Broome's advice and turned to the new medium of motion pictures as a tool of African American uplift through broadly disseminated, but tightly controlled, representation. During their association, however, he was surprised by how difficult it was to manage Broome, by Broome's own exhibition of the motion pictures for the purpose of entertainment, and by Tuskegee's unwitting association with seemingly less uplifting aspects of Broome's filmic enterprise.

Though the details of their arrangement are not completely clear from the surviving records, it appears as though Broome filmed with the full cooperation of Tuskegee and without any financial or legal obligations. After filming concluded, Broome maintained ownership of the motion pictures and distributed the prints himself. He also received a fee of $100 plus expenses for exhibiting the motion pictures on behalf of Tuskegee at fund-raising events.[6] According to Broome, *A Trip to Tuskegee* (1909) cost over $2,320 to produce.[7]

In late November 1909, Broome began shooting with the assistance of "one of the most expert photographers in Boston at a great expense."[8] Prior to filming, Broome requested access to "every possible subject in and around the Institute," including Washington himself—whose presence was considered crucial enough by both Broome and school officials that shooting was delayed until the principal's return to Tuskegee.[9] Few records survive concerning the actual filming or the details of Broome's visit to Alabama, but he shot enough footage to compile a thirty-five-minute film titled *A Trip to Tuskegee*. The film consisted of exterior scenes of the institute (including shots of Washington), views of the buildings erected by students, and images of students constructing roads and working in the institute's fields and dairy. Though Broome shot interior footage, none of it was included in the final cut due to exposure problems. Because of these technical issues, footage depicting the girls' industries and the mechanical industries were excluded from the film.

The film's structure followed the format of the pageants and live demonstrations of the trades that students performed for benefactors. For the institute, one of the main advantages of motion pictures was to streamline the presentation of the work of the school and bypass the live demonstrations on which it had relied to that point. Prior to the use of motion pictures, the institute had students perform tableaux of trade learning for northern philanthropists. One press account described the staged work presented at an annual meeting at Carnegie Hall in vivid terms: "When the curtain rose after one of the addresses, students in overalls were seen busily engaged in the actual work of carpenters, blacksmiths, wheelwrights, and other tradesmen, thus giving an ocular demonstration to the great audience of the industries which the school offers."[10] This "ocular demonstration" required the cumbersome apparatus of props, materials, and students who would otherwise be in class. In front of potential donors, students were presented as actors in the enactment of their schooling, creating the visual impression of Black bodies at work, performing labor. In this context, the use of motion pictures was a cost-effective alternative that conveyed the uplift message without requiring the physical presence of labor-enacting students.

Broome's production of a moving picture seemed to address Tuskegee's concerns and support its fund-raising goals. However, his association with the institute soon revealed their competing visions of filming uplift. Initially, Broome worked in concert with Tuskegee's interests, yet their relationship soured in the months following the film's New York and Boston showings. Despite Broome's amicable visit to Alabama, his independent exhibition of *A Trip to Tuskegee* to predominantly Black audiences in Boston elicited sharp concern on the part of the institute over the film's images and their circulation. Although touting the impact his pictures would have in Tuskegee fund-raising campaigns, Broome largely focused on generating and then entertaining Black audiences independently of the institute. His mission, as he described it, was "to produce some pictures that would show colored people what colored people are doing."[11] Black filmmaking entrepreneurs saw Tuskegee as a potential draw for Black spectators, but the institute expressed no interest in reaching a general and indiscriminate Black audience. Tuskegee was primarily concerned with its philanthropic audience, and the institute tightly controlled the promotional materials disseminated to predominantly white benefactors. Its concern with Broome centered on the perception of motion pictures as merely a form of entertainment and also as a primarily working-class diversion frequently associated with moral corruption and vices, which were anathema to the uplift ideal. By keeping the exhibition of its motion picture in the context of fund-raising efforts, Tuskegee could avoid such problematic anti-uplift associations.

Under the auspices of promoting the institute, Broome revealed a more commercial motivation for taking motion pictures of the school than its representatives were comfortable with. Tuskegee had planned to premiere the motion pictures at a major fund-raising event at Carnegie Hall on January 24, 1910, organized by the institute's benefactors. Yet earlier in the month Broome held his own screenings in Boston that were loosely modeled after Tuskegee's fund-raising programs but apparently had considerably less polish and that included elements deemed objectionable by Tuskegee supporters for their association with common amusements and popular entertainment. The Boston program offers a glimpse into what the screenings of the uplift films for Black theatrical audiences entailed—that is, screenings separate from the nontheatrical screenings sponsored by Hampton and Tuskegee. Although the films were shown to Black communities around the country and were screened primarily in churches and meeting halls, few accounts of these screenings survive. Thus, the reports of Broome's Boston screenings are especially valuable in under-standing how the exhibition contexts differed when films were screened for Black audiences rather than for white benefactors.

On January 4, 1910, Broome held a public screening of *A Trip to Tuskegee* at Tremont Temple in Boston, a Baptist church with a long history of social justice advocacy. Not to be confused with Tremont Theatre, where *The Birth of a Nation* was screened in 1915, Tremont Temple was often rented out as a venue for lectures, events, and concerts. The advertisements for the exhibi-tion implied that the screening was sponsored by and for the benefit of Tuske-gee, yet the screening was not an official institute event. In fact, Broome was capitalizing on the fame and popularity of the institute to appeal to potential ticket buyers. The program was arranged in the manner of an illustrated lec-ture: Broome featured the Tuskegee motion pictures accompanied by a quar-tet imitating the popular Tuskegee Singers. He also screened his other films, including a series on the cotton industry and the Tenth Cavalry, known as the "Buffalo Soldiers," which had arrived at Fort Ethan Allen in Vermont in July 1909. No accounts of these films survive, but presumably they featured African American laborers working in the production of cotton and footage of Black soldiers in the Tenth Cavalry. Finally, Broome included a novelty section of local actuality pictures, which was the segment of the entertainment that drew the greatest delight from the audience and the sharpest criticism from Tuske-gee officials.

The rhetoric of publicity did not go unnoticed by the members of the pub-lic in attendance. A former Tuskegee teacher and Hampton alumnus, Samuel Courtney, was a Boston physician who worked as a northern agent for Tuske-gee. He attended Broome's exhibition at Tremont Temple, assuming that the institute, which regularly held fund-raising events in northern cities, was spon-soring the event. Courtney wrote to Emmett J. Scott, Washington's chief aide and personal secretary, recounting that the crowd was small due to the tem-perature—it was reportedly the coldest night to date in Boston's history—but that Broome's pictures were "*fine*" despite needing some "improvements in his machinery." While praising the use of motion pictures, Courtney noted that during the screening Broome "had a lot of cheap singing" that was a poor imi-tation of the Tuskegee Singers who usually accompanied Washington on his fund-raising tours to entertain the nostalgic white benefactors with plantation melodies. Believing Broome to be working at the behest of Tuskegee, Court-ney recommended cutting out the subpar singing in favor of a talk from Scott or Washington.[12] Hampton's Vice Principal George Phenix attended the same screening and had a more critical reaction to the event. Expressing his concern to Washington, he wrote: "I do not know whether this meeting was held with your knowledge. If not, you certainly ought to know about it. The posters in front of Tremont Temple were conspicuous for at least a week before the meeting. They had your picture, and the advertising matter was such as to lead people to think that the Tuskegee School was responsible for it. The price of admission was fifty and twenty-five cents. For the first hour of the evening there was no reference to Tuskegee in anything that was represented. Then came the moving pictures which were obviously of Tuskegee, but which did not strike me as very good."[13] Phenix enclosed a copy of a letter, with the sender's name redacted, sent to him by a friend who had heard about the "most disappointing" screening:

> It appears that a colored man by the name of Broome has secured some slides and motion pictures of the school and gives an entertainment with them without having anybody with him who directly represents the institution. From the description of the meeting I should say that it would do the school as much harm as good. Ninety percent of the audience was colored. . . . There were very few people present and the proportion of whites was extremely small, which would seem to indicate that the general public was not mislead [sic] by the poster which certainly gave me the impression that there was to be a meeting in the interest of Tuskegee. If but few people are being deceived by the entertainment I suppose little harm is being done but for the sake of the cause as a whole it seems unfortunate that such a performance is going the rounds.[14]

The friend of Phenix concluded by warning that "if the time ever comes when you have moving pictures made at Hampton take care that they are kept in your own hands."[15] For both Phenix and his friend, the worry was that screening the films to a predominantly Black audience would tarnish Tuskegee's image.

Perhaps it was an expression of snobbery, or an implicit bias, that the only audience that mattered was a white audience. But there was an overriding concern over what is today understood as brand control. The main worry was the inclusion of the Tuskegee pictures in a program that included other, less informational forms of motion picture entertainment, including local filmmaking—the filming of community members who were then invited to see themselves on screen, a common strategy of itinerant exhibitors. The anonymous source complained of such actuality entertainment when writing that "the first section of motion pictures showed the congregation coming out of the churches in Boston which are made up of colored people. While this called forth considerable applause on the part of the locals who saw themselves parading on the screen it was far from edifying for those who had come to be interested in the cause."[16] Washington himself forwarded these accounts to Scott, warning that "we shall have to watch the moving picture exhibit for New York and Philadelphia very closely to keep out nonsense."[17]

The Tuskegeeans' concern about the institute's visual image and the danger in associating that image with less formal types of motion picture entertainment — "nonsense" — is understandable when considered in the context of other images of African Americans in motion pictures, especially the narrative and nonnarrative comedy entertainments of racial ridicule. For Washington, the challenge was to exploit motion picture technology for its advantages in communication and verisimilitude while avoiding the perpetuation of stereotypes antithetical to the uplift project. This was not an easy task considering the forms of representation historically articulated through the medium of moving pictures. And although local films operated differently, their fairground and itinerant associations meant that they were understood as a primarily working-class diversion rather than as a means of reaching wealthy supporters. The "see yourself" films, however popular, were less serious than Tuskegee wanted, and they did not have the purpose of garnering support for the institute. Anything not directly contributing to Tuskegee's campaign was deemed superfluous and, in the Bookerite view, potentially harmful as well.

The issue of audience is the other key aspect of the complaint against Broome's entrepreneurial use of the Tuskegee pictures. At the objectionable January 4 event at Tremont Temple, the audience was overwhelmingly made up of Black Bostonians. The lack of a sizable white audience was a relief to the Tuskegeeans, who were principally concerned with the reputation of the institute in front of its financial benefactors. As a result, Tuskegee distanced itself from Broome and rebuffed the filmmaker's repeated overtures for continued collaboration. However, Broome exhibited his films independently in New York with the same program that he had mounted at Tremont Temple in Boston. For example, under the auspices of a Bible class at Mother Zion A.M.E. Church on the Upper West Side, Broome screened a program of his films on February 14, 1910, charging twenty-five cents admission. He highlighted his footage of Tuskegee, including "realistic pictures of the students at actual work learning trades," actualities of congregations of Black Bostonians "leaving Church on a Sunday morning," shots of "Negro Industrial Progress in the South," and other "interesting pictures."[18] He also showed the films on March 4 in Atlantic City, New Jersey, for the benefit of Emmanuel Presbyterian Church, a notable event in the African American press for being "the first affair by members of our race" held at the white YMCA.[19]

Despite his entrepreneurial efforts to build a Black audience for his moving pictures, Broome's independent exhibitions were not financially successful. By November 1910, a year after he began filming at Tuskegee, Broome was ready to give up the commercial exhibition of A Trip to Tuskegee. He hoped to sell the prints to Tuskegee for the exclusive use of its publicity department, but the institute refused and he was unable to sell the pictures (likely due to their uneven quality). Broome ended up keeping the prints and continued to use the Tuskegee film in his motion picture exhibitions.

The politics of this first Tuskegee film and the pictures' ultimate fate were far from simple. Broome may have made a marginal profit in his show, but it was an unwitting Tuskegee that became the star of the motion pictures and was frequently mistakenly credited as a producer in the "moving picture business."[20] Tuskegee may have been critical of Broome's exhibition, but in terms of publicity it turned out to be a boon. An editorial in the *Chicago Defender* proclaimed "that Booker T. is way ahead of the game" by displaying his model of education through moving pictures. Describing an exhibition put on by Broome at the Tremont Temple in December 1910, the *Defender* wrote of a reporter being lured in from the sidewalk by a large banner stretched across the front of the building announcing Tuskegee moving pictures: "He dropped in and to his surprise saw the workshops, drill of the men and the whole school walking and working. The sight that struck him most was N. Clark Smith leading his band. The *Defender* will do all it can to have Tuskogee [*sic*] brought to Chicago. . . . Then our would-be leaders can see what makes Booker T. so great."[21] This praise is particularly noteworthy given that the *Defender* was the most militant African American newspaper in Chicago and, although generally friendly to Washington and his National Negro Business League, strongly argued for racial equality and against accommodationism. It is not entirely clear who is the target of criticism in this short piece ("our would-be leaders"); the "greatness" of Washington seems to be as much in the entrepreneurialism evidenced by the use of moving pictures (the headline proclaims that Tuskegee is in the "moving picture business") as it has to do with Washington's politics or Tuskegee's educational mission per se. The reporter is simply thrilled by the fact of the moving pictures, which transport him to Tuskegee, and he desires to bring the campus to Chicago through the power of motion picture technology.

Tuskegee's conflict with Broome reveals the disagreements among African Americans about different models of uplift. Washington was concerned with promoting the Hampton-Tuskegee model of education as a means of uplifting the race, but Broome's image-making was itself another form of uplift—that of a Black-owned film company dedicated to capturing subjects of interest to a Black audience that would be entertaining. To the Tuskegeeans, however, Broome was an uncontrollable rogue. Although much of Tuskegee's efforts were motivated by a desire to control the circulation of its image, it is not clear that the institute's leaders had (or believed they had) the opportunity to intervene in Broome's enterprise, to buy his prints or negatives (at this stage), or to challenge his right to exhibit them. For an enterprise that insisted on control (self-control, image control, and even economic and political control), Tuskegee found the element of hazard in Broome's exhibition unnerving. Yet Broome's interest in African American self-representation in motion pictures suggests the possibility of uplifting public perception that the medium of film allowed—an image of uplift that could affect both white and Black audiences.

Broome's model of uplift cinema consisted of a combination of actualities with the local film, a type of filmmaking whereby spectators were drawn to a motion picture exhibition by the possibility of seeing themselves and their communities projected on screen. With their special appeal to specific audiences, local films proved to be very popular in early cinema and beyond; the addition of local views was a common means of increasing audience interest in a moving picture show.[22] As was the case with the local "topicals" of motion picture operators such as Mitchell and Kenyon in Britain and William Paley and Melton Barker in the United States, a large part of the appeal of these films was the audience's thrill at seeing itself projected on screen. Broome's actuality filmmaking was one of the earliest assertions of African American self-representation in cinema. Although no public accounts survive of Broome's audiences or of the reception of his films, his filmmaking practice represents a significant attempt to reclaim the medium from its employment in the ridicule of the race.

In Broome's exhibition, local African American spectators were shown an image of themselves as respectable and communal—a fully constituted social body. The footage is not extant, and therefore we can only speculate on its representational capabilities. But the very fact of the actuality footage—and its enthusiastic reception by a public—is an assertion of resistance to the dominant misrepresentation of Black people in cinema of the era. Likewise, the fact that Broome filmed churchgoers in particular underscores the emphasis on an image of respectability and middle-class values as well as the showman's effort to present a "high class" entertainment.[23] Broome's ambitions are also evident in his letterhead, which announces, beneath his name as general manager: "An exhibition for showing Moving Pictures of the Advancement of the Negro Race in Education, Manufacture, Commerce and Science."[24]

Broome's local films, through their recording of individuals and a specific community and their targeted address to particular audiences, are therefore indicators of significant counterpractices that position Black spectators as constitutive of their own self-image as well as the screen representation of that image. The instances of identification that Broome's audience members would have experienced both seeing themselves coming out of the local churches and recognizing their neighbors and their community function as an assertion of civic belonging and public respectability. Furthermore, in the adjacency of these local views with Broome's other pictures, audiences could see themselves in conjunction with images of industriousness (advances in the cotton industry), civic pride and national valor (the Tenth Cavalry), and racial uplift (Tuskegee Institute). In its totality, Broome's program projected an image of African American uplift that made spectators into participants in the social, political, economic, and educational advances of the race. It might not have corresponded to the model that Tuskegee propounded, but the act of movie-going in this case was a form of self-fashioning that cast Black spectators not as stereotypes or spectacle but as subjects and agents of uplift.

The idea of the Black public as spectacle was taken up in the Black press in the later 1910s. The Chicago-based filmmaking entrepreneur William Foster, writing under the pen name Juli Jones Jr., proclaimed: "There is a future for the race in the Motion Picture world actively and passively. Let every one so live and conduct himself as if he were to be caught on a 'close-up' or a 'long shot' he will be so acting and living that he will help the race he represents."[25] Jacqueline Stewart has discussed how the Black press criticized the lack of public decorum, viewing "Black readers as spectators of their own embarrassing daily performances."[26] Broome's actualities anticipate the self-fashioning of a respectable Black urban populace through cinema. In this sense, it is a cinematic articulation of what Evelyn Higginbotham has termed the "politics of respectability."[27] In Higginbotham's discussion of Black Baptist women in the early decades of the twentieth century, she argues that respectability "assumed a political dimension" by answering racism as well as promoting intraracial class differentiation.[28] To this end, individual conduct was extrapolated to broader social structures of race relations.

Despite their differences, Broome worked with a form of uplift rhetoric's before-and-after model that closely resembled the strategy of Tuskegee. The opportunity for positive self-reflection in his local films counters the negative images perpetuated by filmic stereotypes and functions like a corrective after to the distorted before. More strikingly, it is a model of self-uplift that does not rely on white largesse. As such, Broome's exhibition practice was seen as pointless and even harmful to the Tuskegee authorities, who were primarily concerned with raising funds for the institute.

Moving pictures proved to be more complex agents than other media employed in conveying the uplift project. In the opinion of the uplift leaders of Hampton and Tuskegee, the Tremont Temple event helped crystallize the distinction between moving pictures that seemingly threatened African American uplift and those that furthered it. From that point on, Washington exerted more control over the exhibition context of the Tuskegee pictures. He also publicly commented on the dangers of "objectionable" motion pictures in the months following the Boston screening, calling for "pictures that would have a wholesome and uplifting effect."[29] Washington's image of Black modernity depended on the representational uplift of African Americans and the concurrent crusade against tawdry and demeaning motion pictures (which would, for Washington, culminate in his public denunciation of *The Birth of a Nation* shortly before his death in 1915). But the Tremont Temple event also highlights the different iterations of the uplift project. Although Washington and Black filmmaking entrepreneurs like Broome believed in African American advancement in keeping with the uplift ideal, the tensions over the projection of that ideal underscore the complexity of the seemingly simple objective of positive representation. Uplift aesthetics manifested itself in sometimes contradictory ways.

For the important New York fund-raising event on January 24, 1910, Tuskegee authorities exerted strict control over the program. After the unauthorized exhibition in Boston, Tuskegee campaign directors wanted to preview the film prior to the Carnegie Hall event. Thus, one week before it, Broome held a private screening at the Crescent Theatre in New York for a small audience including Scott and the eminent sociologist Robert E. Park. The *New York Age* reported the private screening the following week, referring to "forty-three subjects" of scenes at Tuskegee.[30] The newspaper told its readers: "It is the intention of the Broome Exhibition Company to show the industrial progress of the Negro along industrial lines by means of moving pictures."[31] There were concerns, however, over Broome's mastery of the medium, not least in his interior filming. Although enthusiastic about the pictures, Scott expressed disappointment that only the exterior footage was viable. After the private screening, Scott reported back to Washington that he thought the pictures were strong enough to cut out the stereopticon photos from the program, so that only the moving pictures would be used to illustrate Tuskegee, a departure from the standard program template. Yet, realizing that the films needed some narrative context, he suggested that a spokesman from Tuskegee introduce the images. He wrote Washington:

> *As a whole*, they are very good & yet only the outside work can be shown—none of the girls [*sic*] industries & none of the mechanical industries except in the case of masons & carpenters on new heating plant. The farm pictures are very good. I think quite frankly that it is needed to have a word said about some features of the moving pictures—the others all agree with me. Just who ought to do this is a problem. The pictures will take 25 minutes only at the outside & with this cost & also the cost of a man from Tuskegee will make it quite considerable. Mr. Broome will give full rehearsal the morning of Jan 24 with anyone we may select.[32]

Scott acknowledges the semantic ambiguity of cinematic images in his argument for a lecturer to explain the scenes, since such oration offered Tuskegee another way to frame and control the message conveyed through the images. No records survive of who provided commentary for the moving pictures, but Tuskegee's leaders worked to control the ways in which the event would be reported in the press and thereby shaped the broader public discourse concerning the institute and its use of moving pictures.

In advance of the event Scott met with the Sunday editor of the *New York Tribune*, a mainstream newspaper, and secured the publication of "a special article bearing upon the Moving Picture & other features" prepared by Park.[33] The article, titled "Bring School Here. That Is, by Means of Moving Pictures," emphasized the economy of moving pictures as a means of showcasing the institute. Prior to the use of moving pictures, highlighting the various departments of the school was difficult to do without an on-site tour. Park's article recounts the story of President Theodore Roosevelt's visit to Tuskegee: it had been too short for a proper tour, so the departments had come to him. Park writes: "They got together several hundred wagons, loaded a large part of the school upon them—enough, at any rate, to show all the thirty-seven different industries, as well as the other departments of the institute's work—and hauled them in procession before a reviewing stand which had been erected for Mr. Roosevelt and his party" (figure 2.1).[34] The article heralded the use of motion pictures to address the challenge of garnering wide public support for the Hampton-Tuskegee Idea, "to find some method of showing people a thousand miles away just what the school is actually doing and what industrial education, as Booker T. Washington conceives it, means." In this announcement of Broome's achievement, Park anticipates that the medium of film would be a means of "solving the problem" of communicating over distances, both geo-

FIG. 2.1 President Theodore Roosevelt and Booker T. Washington reviewing the sixty-one "industry" floats, Tuskegee, 1905. Courtesy Stereograph Cards Collection, Prints and Photographs Division, Library of Congress, LC-DIG-stereo-1s02155.

graphical and cultural. Park continues: "This year a new method of solving this problem has been adopted. At the public meeting to be held January 24 at Carnegie Hall it is planned to bring the work of the school home to a New York audience by showing it in the form of moving pictures. By this means it will be possible to show students at work in the fields, planting, ploughing, milking, working in the dairy and building roads, as well as pictures showing the whole body of sixteen hundred students in motion, marching to chapel, all in life-size moving pictures." Additionally, Park gives credit to Broome for originating the plan "to put Tuskegee into a moving picture show" and announces the new company's goal by echoing Broome's own language of self-promotion: "They conceived the idea that it would be a good thing, as well as a paying investment, to produce some pictures that would show negroes what negroes are doing." The article championed Broome's plan to send the Tuskegee pictures to Black churches around the country in order to display Washington's "large and novel educational experiment" and to dispel the criticism of the institute by its detractors who "believed that a school which taught negroes to work was going to be an obstacle to the higher education of the race." Park notes: "Those who have been most opposed to the work of Tuskegee Institute, however, have often been those who were ignorant of its scope." Broome's pictures, therefore, perform an important public relations function for Tuskegee, Park concludes:

"They have thus performed an important educational work among the masses of the negro people, because the pictures of what the school is actually doing are the best argument that can be made in its favor, and it is important to the success of the work that Dr. Washington is trying to do that all the negroes, as well as all of the white people, should understand and appreciate the large and novel educational experiment he has undertaken for the masses of his race."

Not surprisingly, Park's article considers the "Tuskegee in action" images to be the "most successful" of the Broome Company's works, which included a series on the cotton industry and the Tenth Cavalry at Fort Ethan Allen.[35] Tuskegee must have sent Park's article to several newspapers and journals, as an abbreviated version of it appeared in a May 1910 issue of the trade journal the *Nickelodeon*.[36] Although the acknowledgment of the Tuskegee pictures by a trade publication is significant, the *Nickelodeon* does not mention Broome or the fact that the films were produced by an African American company, instead emphasizing the subject of the pictures and the way in which they solve the problem of conveying the concept of industrial education over distance.

At the Carnegie Hall event, *A Trip to Tuskegee* was the principal feature.[37] In addition to the film screening, the program included speeches and a performance of the Hampton Singers, who toured the country to raise funds for both Hampton and Tuskegee. The addresses given on this occasion provide an important context for understanding the stakes of these moving pictures. In addition to a speech by Washington, there were remarks by former New York mayor Seth Low (a Tuskegee trustee), President John Huston Finley of City College, and Benjamin Franklin Riley of Alabama, the author of a self-published monograph called *The White Man's Burden: A Discussion of the Interracial Question with Special Reference to the Responsibility of the White Race to the Negro Problem*.[38] Low praised the late General Armstrong for pioneering industrial education with the founding of Hampton. Finley told the audience: "I've never been [to Tuskegee], but I am glad to honor it because of the glorious work it is doing to reach our humblest citizens. The Negro in the past has had an unbridled body, an ignorant mind, and an undeveloped soul. We don't want him in our houses as our social equal, but this is not because he is colored; it is because, up to the present, he has lacked intellectual and moral education."[39] Apart from the racist rhetoric articulated by a supposed friend of Tuskegee, the before-and-after structure is again evoked here in the allusion to a past that threatens present race relations. The civilizing mission of Tuskegee is also presented as a type of domestication to make the "humblest citizens" fit social company for white Americans. Finley's phrasing follows the logic of uplift rhetoric, however perversely, and reveals the ways in which Broome's rogue use of *A Trip to*

Tuskegee might have freed the film from this compromised discourse. Broome projected the Tuskegee moving pictures to Black audiences outside of the fundraising context, thereby removing the contingency of enlisting the images in the service of the paternalistic worldview framed by the white speakers and unchallenged by the uplift leaders.

Like Finley, Riley, a white southerner speaking to northerners, reminded the audience of the perceived postemancipation Negro problem: "In the initial stages of the Negro's freedom predictions were prolific that when left to himself he would lapse into paganism. But theories have vanished on the arrival of the facts." More daringly, Riley also reminded the audience of the uncomfortable fact that the north had benefited from southern slave labor and that the entire country owed a debt to the Negro, who "is steadily vindicating his merits by his deeds."[40]

The speeches presented arguments promoting Negro education, but the proof of uplift was carried by the moving pictures, bolstering the arguments of the speakers and providing an idyllic scene of the south in order to appeal to northern philanthropists. Riley underscored the need for positive images in his assessment of the public relations problem of African Americans: "One of the chief things from which the Negro suffers in the South is that the crimes of the few are exploited in the public prints to the neglect of his worthy deeds. A crime is flared in the public press, but nothing is said of his steady progress and of his achievements."[41] In the context of the program and the moving pictures, Riley's comments place a burden of representation on the film: to counter the popular impression of criminality (propagated in the white media and in popular eugenics discourses), the film must argue the case of progress more strongly.

Washington concluded the event with a characteristically hyperbolic concession that "no one objects to the educated Negro nowadays, because the Negro race is over the silly period which it went through thirty years ago. The type of 'educated' Negro with high hat, cane, patent leather shoes, eyeglasses and overlarge cigar has disappeared. Social service—service of head, service of hand, service of heart is now his motto. He doesn't think that labor, that work, is degrading any more."[42] With his caricature of the "'educated' Negro," reminiscent of his anecdotes about emancipated slaves' "entitles" recounted in *Up from Slavery*, Washington presents a before-and-after scenario in which Tuskegee's project corrects the posturing, labor-averse Reconstruction Negro with a modern, service-oriented New Negro. He thereby takes a common trope of reform rhetoric and adapts it for his purpose, conjuring up stereotypes familiar to his audience and replacing them with an image of the uplifted Black man.

Washington concluded the event with an appeal for funds for student scholarships.

Later that week, the *New York Age* ran a front-page article with the headline "Moving Pictures of Tuskegee." In the reportedly sizable audience at Carnegie Hall, "there were present many who have contributed largely to the work of the Institute, but whose information about the school had been only gained by hearsay." Through motion pictures, the paper reported, the audience saw buildings erected by students, and the labor of those students in the fields, roads, and dairy. The paper observed that "if applause is to be taken as a criterion, the 2,000 spectators were very favorably impressed with the moving picture exhibition, which proved to be quite an education."[43] The motion pictures gave the audience a fuller sense of "just what Tuskegee Institute is actually doing and what industrial education means." In this sense, the film was celebrated for documenting the work of the school and serving as an argument for its fund-raising efforts.[44]

Following the *Age*'s announcement of the motion pictures of Tuskegee, the institute received a number of inquiries from Black schools, churches, and theaters interested in exhibiting them. On behalf of Washington, Scott referred the inquiries to Broome with polite detachment. To Robert Motts, director of the Pekin Theatre in Chicago, Scott wrote, "I am sure such pictures as these will go a long way toward helping the work of the institution."[45] J. O. Spencer, the president of Morgan College in Baltimore, wrote to Scott after having read "in a New York paper" about the moving pictures that showed "various forms of work among the colored people."[46] Broome took the motion pictures to Philadelphia and held a screening at the Cherry Memorial Baptist Church on February 11, the evening following Washington's appearance at the Philadelphia Academy of Music. Cherry's pastor, William Creditt, wrote to Washington requesting his presence at the exhibition, noting that it would not be necessary to make an address, merely to attend the event as a "drawing card."[47] Washington frequently received requests to speak and attend events, yet this is the first request for his presence as complementary to the motion pictures, rather than as the central feature of an event. In February 1910, Washington met with Broome in Boston and requested an estimate for the reproduction of the motion pictures. But when Broome estimated that a reprint would cost $250 for 1,000 feet of film, Washington chose not to respond.[48] Broome told Washington, referring to Charles Winter Wood, head of Tuskegee's English and Drama Departments and director of campaign publicity, that "where we have been exhibiting the pictures, I find every one seems to be greatly interested, and I think they could be used to a great advantage by Mr. Wood in his exhibitions and lectures." Broome also requested photographs of Tuskegee to publish in a book to sell at the motion picture exhibitions.[49] At Broome's exhibits, he projected slides of Washington, and at one point he requested a photo of Washington "in a standing position as if delivering an address for a moving picture film" to use in conjunction with his other films.[50] Scott responded that no such photograph was available, though he indicated a willingness to provide one to Broome if such a photo were to be taken in the future.[51]

Broome continued to travel with the Tuskegee pictures, giving itinerant screenings in Black churches. Although few records survive of his tour, one announcement of a screening at Mount Zion A.M.E. Church in Trenton, New Jersey, suggests that Broome might have passed himself off as a representative of Tuskegee rather than as an independent entrepreneur, or at the very least allowed his affiliation with the institute to remain vague.[52] By June 1910 Broome was running out of money and unable to continue exhibiting *A Trip to Tuskegee*. He wrote to Washington, asking for $500 "to carry the work on," in exchange for the free use of the motion pictures "whenever you would care to use them." Broome implored Washington: "I am very sure that the continued use of such pictures showing the industrial progress of the Negro will have a great influence on the philanthropic people, if they can be placed where they can see them."[53] Washington replied that he was unable to suggest any way of circulating the pictures more widely, but that they would be used "very extensively" in the fall and winter campaigns. He did not acknowledge Broome's request for $500.[54] A month later, Broome inquired whether Washington cared to use the motion pictures during the National Negro Business League convention in New York, suggesting they could make an "interesting part of the program" or be screened at the banquet.[55] Washington curtly replied that "there seems to be no place on the program where they might be introduced."[56]

Despite the institute's unwillingness to finance him (and his subpar moving pictures), Broome continued to use the Tuskegee film in his motion picture exhibitions in Boston, though it is not clear how long such exhibitions continued. By November 1910, a year after he initially filmed at Tuskegee, Broome was ready to give up the commercial exhibition of *A Trip to Tuskegee* and have the prints be exclusively used by Tuskegee's publicity department. At the encouragement of Tuskegee trustees William Jay Schieffelin and William G. Willcox, Broome wrote to Washington, "I feel that the pictures can be put to better use by the Institute than by me."[57] Broome prioritized filming for Black audiences over being useful to Tuskegee's institutional self-promotion and fund-raising efforts. The image he projected of African Americans exhibited the pride and autonomy of its subject in a manner that might be jarring to white philanthropists. Instead of an image of dependency, Broome's exhibition projected a self-sufficient, albeit segregated, community. In this respect his filmmaking practice was echoed by subsequent Black entrepreneurs working in the north, such as Hunter C. Haynes in New York and Peter P. Jones and William Foster in Chicago (I discuss them further in chapter 5).

Although he had difficulty raising funds to continue his moving picture ventures, Broome continued producing cultural artifacts of African American subjects throughout the next decade, including a series of phonograph records in 1919 featuring baritone and composer Harry T. Burleigh and soprano Florence Cole-Talbert.[58] Not only was Broome probably the first Black filmmaking entrepreneur, but in 1919 he founded the first record label owned and operated by an African American, the Broome Special Phonograph Records Company.[59] In 1920 Broome released a recording of Washington delivering his famous Atlanta Exposition address of 1895. The recording had been made at the Columbia studios in 1908, but Broome applied his label over that of Columbia and sold the recording through his company.[60] Though his relationship with the Tuskegeeans may have soured, Broome—ever the entrepreneur—recognized the commercial potential in a posthumously released recording of Washington's most famous speech.

Broome's investment in Black audiences as subjects marks an engagement with cinematic modernity that is at the forefront of the possibilities of the medium at this historical moment. Stewart has argued that "Black viewing practices can be read as a reconstructive process, whereby Black viewers could reconstitute themselves as viewing subjects in the face of a racially exclusionary cinematic institution and social order."[61] Stewart develops a concept of reconstructive spectatorship, extending Hazel V. Carby's and Henry Louis Gates Jr.'s interest in "the Race's image of itself" from the literary realm to the public sphere, where Black spectators function as consumers of mass culture.[62] Broome's actualities literalized this construction of a cinematic self-image.[63] Broome's aesthetics of uplift focused on promoting a Black self-image on screen to Black audiences rather than formulating one for white philanthropists or mixed audiences, as Tuskegee had intended. Broome's local films did not invite white sympathy or financial support. Instead, they projected an image of pride and autonomy that left no room for white philanthropic intervention. Broome's independence, and the context in which he projected his Tuskegee pictures, caused conflict between him and the institute—yet it also constituted a significant instance of resistance to representational racism through the medium of cinema.

The Anderson-Watkins Film Company of Chicago

Tuskegee administrators hoped that the motion pictures of the institute would be evidence of the impact of its model of agricultural and industrial education and of the uplift project more broadly. Yet with *A Trip to Tuskegee*, they were confronted with challenges to their idea of uplift—a necessarily conservative, even rigid one—as they discovered that the motion pictures did not carry the uplift message in a vacuum but functioned in and were often defined by broader exhibition contexts. They might have been able to control the campaign programs and the press coverage of the motion pictures, but they could not control Broome's exhibition practices. After their experience with Broome, the Tuskegee authorities were more circumspect in allowing moving pictures to be taken of the institute. When they permitted Tuskegee to be filmed for a second time, they chose Louis B. Anderson, someone from the inner circle of Chicago's Black elite and a close ally of their uplift interests (figure 2.2). Anderson had graduated from the Virginia Normal and Collegiate Institute, a historically Black land-grant university (now Virginia State University), and had gone to Chicago in 1890. There he worked as a writer for the *Daily Columbian*, the official publication of the World's Columbian Exposition in 1893. He then went to Kent Law School and became an assistant county attorney and a community leader in Chicago.[64] Anderson was a representative uplift man, and his photograph was featured in Washington's *A New Negro for a New Century*.[65] Anderson gained some notoriety in 1905 when, as an assistant county attorney, he was mugged and shot his attackers with a gun in his pocket; the papers celebrated the "nervy man" who fatally wounded one of his assailants.[66] Anderson served as a lieutenant in the Eighth Illinois Regiment under Colonel John R. Marshall, a graduate of Hampton and the first African American colonel (figure 2.3).[67] He became an alderman of Chicago's second ward.

In October 1912 B. F. Moseley, chairman of the Appomattox Club, asked Anderson to be a part of a committee of "representative Chicago Colored citizens" that would prepare a written statement for the press to address the Johnson-Cameron episode.[68] A month after the wife of Jack Johnson, the famed boxer, committed suicide, he was charged under the Mann Act with abducting a white woman, Lucille Cameron (he married Cameron a few months later). Johnson was the uplift proponent's nightmare, but this scandal offered respectable Black leaders the opportunity to critique the media hysteria over Johnson's alleged transgressions. Anderson's participation on this committee and his cosigning of the statement indicate his prominence among race men in Chicago. The Appomattox statement criticized the public discourse for "im-

FIG. 2.2 (*right*) Louis B. Anderson portrait from Booker T. Washington, *A New Negro for a New Century* (Chicago: American, 1900).

FIG. 2.3 (*below*) Colonel John R. Marshall portrait from Booker T. Washington, *A New Negro for a New Century* (Chicago: American, 1900).

LOUIS B. ANDERSON,
Assistant County Attorney Cook County, Illinois.

COL. JOHN R. MARSHALL,
Colonel of the Eighth Illinois Infantry in the Spanish-American War.

pliedly condemning the entire Negro race for the alleged misconduct of one of its members" and affirmed allegiance with "the law abiding White citizens of Chicago to promote the highest civic betterment along all lines for the moral uplift of all classes."[69] Johnson was present at the Appomattox Club to answer the allegations that he had claimed to be able to "get any white woman in Chicago with his money," a comment that had served as fodder for salacious journalism.

Johnson's presence did somewhat appease the critical audience of prominent African American men. However, without editorial comment, the *Broad Ax* (famously critical of Washington and Tuskegee) reported that Johnson slandered Washington by bringing up an incident that had caused great embarrassment to the Tuskegeeans. In what was known as the Ulrich Affair, Washington had been beaten by a white assailant on March 19, 1911, near New York City's seedy Tenderloin district. Washington was exonerated of any wrongdoing, but questions lingered in the last years of his life as to what business he had had in the neighborhood.[70] The *Broad Ax* reported that "Booker T. Washington was sent to the mat by Champion Jack, who declared that the great wizard of Tuskegee was beaten up in New York City in 1911, for peeping into the wrong keyhole and for attempting to enter the wrong flat occupied by a White lady, and he intimated that Brother Washington must have been looking for some light chicken at the time he received his beating, and attempted to beat it or run away in an effort to save his life and reputation."[71] In his rehashing of the Ulrich Affair, Johnson was likely retaliating for Washington's statement a few days earlier to the United Press Association, which had solicited a response to the "Nationwide agitation" caused by Johnson "to restore sane public thought."[72] Washington pithily asserted, likely to the fury of Johnson, that "no one can do so much injury to the Negro race as the Negro himself." Washington continued, "What makes the situation seem a little worse in this case, is the fact that it was the white man, not the black man who has given Jack Johnson the kind of prominence he has enjoyed up to now and put him, in other words, in a position where he has been able to bring humiliation upon the whole race of which he is a member."[73] Johnson's dig at Washington was as much a critique of the notion of representativeness as it was a response to the evident embarrassment with which race leaders handled the question of Johnson's actions. The specter of interracial sex complicated uplift ideology; Johnson's public flaunting of his sexuality and the rumors surrounding Washington's proclivities put into relief and made more urgent the issues of representativeness, respectability, and performance that were at the fore in these debates.

Anderson's endorsement of the "official" line indicated why he was the ideal figure to produce the second film made at the institute, *A Day at Tuskegee* (1913). It is not clear what led Anderson to enter the business of motion picture production, and he did so with discretion rather than self-promotion.[74] Anderson partnered with William F. Watkins, a dentist in Montgomery, Alabama, to create the Anderson-Watkins Film Company with the intention of filming African American institutions around the country.[75] Watkins was also a public figure: he had been president of the Montgomery Negro Business League and had served in the Philippines with Colonel Robert Lee Bullard and Captain W. P. Screws.[76] His leadership in the league and his prominence in Montgomery society made him an attractive associate to the Chicago-based Anderson. Anderson and Watkins then asked Colonel Marshall to work with the company. Marshall's alliance with Tuskegee was cooperative and mutually beneficial, and the significance of the Eighth Regiment as a point of pride and symbol of possibility for Black citizens cannot be overstated. Marshall himself declared that "the Colored people in the State of Illinois have no better asset in the matter of their advancement and recognition than this organization [the Eighth Regiment]."[77] A celebrity, Marshall was a popular figure and represented the possibilities for full citizenship that involvement in the military was seen to promise.

At the behest of Anderson-Watkins, Marshall visited Tuskegee in January 1913, where he oversaw the filming of the motion pictures and directed the accompanying cameramen from the National Moving Picture Company of Chicago.[78] Little information survives concerning this company outside of its involvement with Anderson-Watkins, but it appears to have been a local film company that hired out equipment and camera operators to independent producers. While at Tuskegee, Marshall was the guest of honor at a "stag party" during which he talked about the Eighth Regiment and its campaign in Cuba in 1896. He also gave a talk to students in the institute's chapel, where he spoke "most encouragingly to the students of the Institute and was warmly and cordially welcomed by them," according to the *Tuskegee Student*.[79]

As uplift insiders, Anderson and Watkins received "exclusive rights" to filming and exhibiting motion pictures of Tuskegee.[80] Tuskegee, however, remembered the earlier difficulties caused by Broome's independent entrepreneurial endeavors and so kept tighter reins on the exhibition and public discourse surrounding the films. During Marshall's trip to Tuskegee, for example, Scott sent a prewritten news item to Anderson with instructions for him to arrange with the prominent African American newspaperman Cary B. Lewis, the Chicago correspondent for the Indianapolis *Freeman*, to run it in both the Chicago papers and the *Freeman*.[81] The article announced Marshall's visit and his accompaniment by moving picture producers, the talks he gave, and the warm reception he was given by the students and faculty and staff members of the institute.[82] Although Tuskegee was interested primarily in the fund-raising potential of the moving pictures, which meant white viewers, Anderson and Watkins wanted their work to reach African Americans, and their press efforts indicate that they emphatically solicited a Black audience.

A Day at Tuskegee consisted of 3,300 feet of film and showed the development of the institute from 1881 to 1912.[83] Although frame rates were variable, at sixteen frames per second, 3,300 feet of film would run for approximately fifty minutes. Like Broome's A Trip to Tuskegee, A Day at Tuskegee was designed to showcase the institute's work; however, it placed more emphasis on Washington's cult of personality than the previous film had done. A Day at Tuskegee opened with a contemporary shot of Washington dismounting from his horse in front of the executive building, then it cut to an image of the shack that was the first school building in 1881. This was followed by scenes of a hundred vocational tradesmen and the institute's regiment and band.[84] Anderson described the film in a letter to Scott: "It is a truely [sic] wonderful story shown with its varied activities and scenes numbering nearly one hundred in active physical life, the operation needing only the living voice to perfect them. You can get an idea of what an impressive, educational lesson this exhibit makes."[85] The Broad Ax echoed this sentiment, stating that "the voice of Dr. Washington will make the scenes all the more perfect."[86]

In March Anderson placed an ad in the Moving Picture World indicating that state rights were available for purchase (figure 2.4).[87] This indicated a change in distribution strategy for Tuskegee. "State rights" involved selling the rights to a film for a particular state or region, after which the owner of the rights could then exploit the film as he or she saw fit. Thus, once sold, there would be no way to control the context in which A Day at Tuskegee was exhibited. This would open up the possibility of misuse of the print in a way that had already happened with Broome. It may be that Tuskegee's leaders did not consider that possibility, or they weighed it against the potential impact of broader publicity reach enabled by the moving pictures. Or perhaps they were not worried because the film had been produced by Tuskegee insiders and presumably would have resisted the effects of recontextualization. In any case, potential worries were rendered moot; there is no evidence to suggest that Anderson-Watkins was able to sell any state's rights.

Anderson sent invitations to the Chicago press and the city's "prominent people" for a private advance screening at the Washington Moving Picture Theater on State Street on March 6, 1913.[88] The letterhead used for the invitations

A Sure Success

Three-Reel Educational Feature

"A Day at Tuskegee"

Showing nearly one hundred Industrial Activities and scenes of

Booker T. Washington's

Famous Industrial Institute at
Tuskegee, Alabama

*"Booker T. Washington has devised the best system
of vocational education in America."*—Harry Pratt
Judson, Prest. University of Chicago.

**Great Lobby Display, Including Photos and
Life Size Portrait of Mr. Washington**

State Rights Open

Anderson-Watkins Film Company
184 W. Washington St., Chicago, Illinois

identified the company as "sole owners and distributors of 'A Day in Tuskeegee,' [*sic*] a feature film showing in moving pictures the Various Activities of
Booker T. Washington's great Industrial Institute. An educational Exhibit designed for entertainments in Churches, Colleges and Schools."[89] By identifying
its moving pictures as "educational," Anderson-Watkins explicitly presented its
product as a nontheatrical production, in contrast to Broome's theatrical and
commercial project.

In advance of the premiere, Anderson requested from Scott a number of
"life size lithographs" of Washington printed with his name and "Principal,
Tuskegee Institute," as well as a series of photographs from the Tuskegee *Annual Catalogue* from 1911–12 to create lobby displays. Anderson suggested to
Scott that they plan to sell pamphlets with images from the film along with a
cover photo of Washington to raise funds for "scholarships for needy colored
youth," equating the "booming" of the pictures with that of the institute.

Anderson also eagerly anticipated getting back "some of the coin of the realm, which we have so liberally expended in making this very big thing."[90] Scott collaborated with Anderson in the procurement of the photos, arranging for the Tuskegee printer to make prints at cost. As Scott told Anderson, "we appreciate the fact that Tuskegee Institute will largely profit from this advertising, and we are pleased to make the figure as low as possible."[91] Scott complimented Anderson on his endeavor: "You have certainly gone after this moving picture business in great shape and you have our very best wishes for your success."[92]

Following the private screening, Anderson arranged for the public premiere at Orchestra Hall to fit Washington's schedule, telling Scott that Washington's presence at the event "would be of tremendous advantage both to the School and the pictures. The mention that Mr. Washington would be present would absolutely insure a capacity house."[93] The *Chicago Defender* wrote in advance of the event, "No public affair given in Chicago in recent years has created as much interest as the coming of Dr. Washington and the 'movies.'" The *Defender* emphasized that the moving pictures thoroughly captured the work of Tuskegee, "making you feel as though you were on the campus." The paper advised its readers that "Tuskegee Institute and its various vocational activities will be brought within your vision and the voice of Dr. Washington will make the scenes all the more perfect."[94]

Anderson-Watkins hired Lewis to serve as publicity agent for *A Day at Tuskegee* and invited him to introduce Washington after the Orchestra Hall screening of the film (figure 2.5). Anderson-Watkins also hired Clarence Goines of Springfield to work as advance agent and W. H. Smith for his experience in theatrical promotion.[95] Through Lewis, Anderson-Watkins targeted ministers, churches, their congregations, and other Black citizens with invitations to the exhibition.[96] They also wrote to principals of public schools, club presidents, and other prominent citizens.[97] Lewis undertook an enormous publicity effort, sending personal letters to over 750 people and mailing over 5,000 heralds to a mailing list compiled from white and Black clubs; he also posted ads in newspapers and hung posters in each elevated train station in Chicago.[98] Prominent ministers were each given two complimentary tickets and club presidents one.[99]

In advance of their release, Lewis wrote several articles for the *Freeman* extolling the Tuskegee pictures. Given that he was both the Chicago correspondent for the paper and a paid press agent for the film, there was certainly a conflict of interest, but this was a fairly common practice at the time and does not render irrelevant the evidence that he provides for the film's reception. In the first article, Lewis wrote:

FIG. 2.5 Cary B. Lewis portrait from *Freeman*, January 25, 1913.

CARY B. LEWIS,
Chicago Representative of Indianapolis
Freeman.

Your correspondent has had the pleasure to witness a private exhibition of the pictures. They are great. We have not adjectives enough in our vocabulary to praise this wonderful production. It is perfect and needs only the human voice to make it complete, with the exception of a personal visit, and observing with the naked eye the wonders of this great institution. The pictures give a splendid and comprehensive idea of the stupendousness of Tuskeegee [*sic*]. All the various activities are shown with nearly three thousand students and faculty in action. The exhibit starts with the picture of Mr. Washington dismounting his famous charger at the executive building, then the shack in which Mr. Washington started in 1881 is shown. Marvel [*sic*], indeed, is the progress. We are impoverished with English in which to express it. We are gradually carried from the primitive state to its colossal greatness as depicted by the "movies." No longer do you have to go to Tuskeegee [*sic*] to see young men and women actively engaged in all the trades for this wonderful scene is brought to your home to be seen with the naked eye. We raved over the pictures when we saw activities in the tailor shop, mechanical building, dairy, carpentry, tinning, electricity, millinery, laundering, cooking, academic, musical, model house-keeping, and blacksmithing departments. The scenes of the agricultural industries are superb—a continuous interest running throughout. Likewise is [sic] shown scenes with the institute regiment, the band playing martial airs, making you feel as though you were on the campus. Then there is [sic] the faculty and executive officers and the live stock; altogether the films make the most interesting educational exhibit now before the public.[100]

Given that Lewis was the agent for the film, his synopsis is the closest we can get to a description of what the filmmakers and Tuskegee thought they were doing. Through the repeated comments about the inability of language to capture the images, Lewis underscores the significance of moving pictures as an approximation of live presence. In this way, they operated as travel films, a popular genre of actuality filmmaking at the time. Touring the educational departments of Tuskegee, the moving pictures demonstrated the possibility of African American advancement and vividly conveyed that message to the audience, thereby becoming agents of uplift themselves.

The following week, Lewis wrote another front-page article for the *Freeman* lauding the Tuskegee pictures and listing the prominent figures scheduled to speak at the April 1 event.[101] The *Defender* announced the moving pictures with an emphasis on Marshall's role, reporting in advance of the screening that "Colonel John R. Marshall, who is actively identified with movements tending toward uplift of the race, personally visited Tuskegee and directed the photographer, with the result that the exhibit of the various activities of this world-famed institution will be brought to our doors and will do more to convince the doubting white element that the Negro is building a foundation upon which to rear the structure of a permanent and enduring success."[102] The identity of the "photographer" is unknown, but it likely was a white camera operator and, if so, it is significant that the *Defender* describes Marshall as the director of the scenes.

Leading up to the premiere, there was a great deal of discussion about Washington's travel schedule and his ability to appear on April 1. Scott appealed to Washington, who was then on the road, saying, "Tuskegee Institute, it seems, will get a great deal of free advertising out of this moving picture business."[103] Anderson equated the impact of the moving pictures with that of the persona of Washington himself, stating "the Institute will be given a character of publicity and advertisement such as no other agent, except Dr. Washington per-

FIG. 2.6 Advertisement in *Broad Ax*, March 22, 1913.

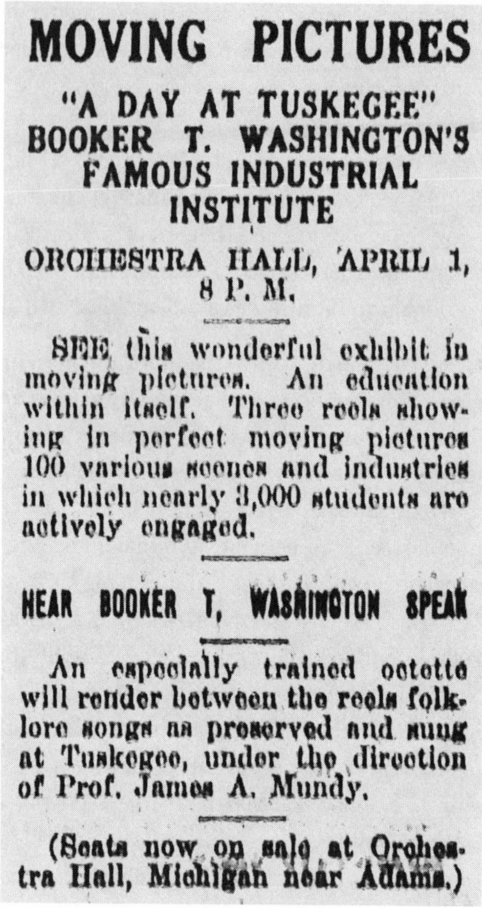

MOVING PICTURES

"A DAY AT TUSKEGEE" BOOKER T. WASHINGTON'S FAMOUS INDUSTRIAL INSTITUTE

ORCHESTRA HALL, APRIL 1, 8 P. M.

SEE this wonderful exhibit in moving pictures. An education within itself. Three reels showing in perfect moving pictures 100 various scenes and industries in which nearly 3,000 students are actively engaged.

HEAR BOOKER T, WASHINGTON SPEAK

An especially trained octette will render between the reels folklore songs as preserved and sung at Tuskegee, under the direction of Prof. James A. Mundy.

(Seats now on sale at Orchestra Hall, Michigan near Adams.)

sonally, could afford."[104] Curiously, although Washington was usually the main attraction for a Tuskegee event, the Orchestra Hall program was advertised in the African American press highlighting the moving pictures above Washington's presence (figure 2.6).[105] Tuskegee also highlighted Marshall's celebrity (as Broome had done with Washington's), yet it was the new medium that took top billing.

In advance of the Orchestra Hall screening, the film was shown in Springfield, Illinois, at the Chatterton Opera House on March 24 and 25. An announcement of the Opera House screening—sent to five hundred people—proclaimed: "These Pictures should be seen by every one, as they are an exact reproduction of the World's greatest Industrial Institute."[106] Although Anderson was targeting prominent residents of Illinois, he was concurrently considering a southern tour for the films. Anderson asked Scott to send him the names of "prominent colored people" in the south from whom he could solicit bookings of the film and, he hoped, broader distribution through the southern states.[107]

On April 1, 1913, *A Day at Tuskegee* premiered at Chicago's Orchestra Hall. Seats ranged from twenty-five cents to seventy-five cents; boxes were a dollar.[108] The musical accompaniment was promoted as representing "folk-lore songs as preserved and sung at Tuskegee."[109] Anderson had requested sheet music for the songs from Tuskegee, but as Tuskegee had not published scores to such songs, Scott referred him to John W. Work of Fisk University, a collector of southern spirituals.[110] The singers—four men and four women under the direction of James A. Mundy, a prominent Chicago choirmaster—sang songs and entertained the audience between reel changes.[111] As the images were likely accompanied by an explanatory lecture, the songs served to create the ambience for the moving pictures. Given the popularity of Black musical traditions, they would have distracted audiences from the necessary pauses between reels.

Anderson produced announcements for the Orchestral Hall occasion. One four-page announcement consisted of photographs reproduced from Tuskegee's media arsenal and textual descriptions of the work of the institute, announcing that the film was "an education in itself" and showing that the film functioned like returned students, spreading the uplift gospel to spectators far and wide. The cover featured a large photograph of Washington captioned by two quotes lauding Tuskegee (figure 2.7). The first quote, taken from Harry Pratt Judson, president of the University of Chicago, asserted that Washington "has devised the best system of vocational education in America." The second quote, taken from the *Chicago Daily Tribune*, pointed to the institute's founding in 1881 and exclaimed that there can be "no doubt" of the need for the school "nor of the value of the work it has done during the last thirty years." As a companion piece to the film, the announcement emphasized change over time and posited the moving pictures as evidence of that change as well as an argument for the continued "imperative need of its service." After a lengthy description of the composition of the school, the announcement concluded with a note on the moving pictures, evidently with convenient amnesia about Broome's earlier venture at Tuskegee: "This is the first time in the history of moving pictures that vocational industries have ever been put together and exhibited. The fame of Booker T. Washington and the phenomenal growth of his world-famed Institute are known throughout the civilized world. Thousands of persons yearly travel thousands of miles, spending thousands of dollars, to see this wonderful Institute, and the thousands of students actively engaged in their vocational studies. It is now brought to your home at a small price. It can

FIG. 2.7 Announcement for the premiere of *A Day at Tuskegee*.

"A DAY AT TUSKEGEE"

contains more than 100 activities and beautiful scenes of this World Famed Industrial Institute

SEE This Wonderful Exhibit in Moving Pictures—An Education in itself. No one Should Miss it.

"A DAY AT TUSKEGEE" is in three reels Showing In Perfect Moving Pictures the Various Industries in which Nearly 3000 Students are Actively Engaged.

BOOKER T. WASHINGTON, Principal Tuskegee Institute

"Booker T. Washington has devised the best system of vocational education in America."
—Harry Pratt Judson, President University of Chicago

"Tuskegee was founded in 1881....There can be no doubt of the imperative need of its service...nor of the value of the work it has done during the last thirty years."
—Chicago Daily Tribune, March 1, 1911

TUSKEGEE INDUSTRIAL INSTITUTE Is Brought to YOUR DOOR

be seen in moving pictures, perfectly depicted, needing only the human voice to make it complete."[112] In addition to these announcements made by Anderson, Tuskegee printed pamphlets to be sold, with the proceeds going to charity. Although the pamphlets were printed by the school printer, the cost was paid for by Anderson: Tuskegee insisted they remain a "private affair" since, as Scott argued, the school "could not go into the business side of furnishing the pamphlets and selling them on consignment, etc."[113] Anderson told Scott, "I have every reason to believe that this is the biggest undertaking ever launched by colored promoters."[114] Scott praised Anderson for producing the print materials, which, in his words, showed "that you have gone after this matter in the most up-to-date manner."[115]

Lewis wrote an article that appeared in the *Tuskegee Student* on April 5, 1913, as a special dispatch from Chicago, noting that the Orchestral Hall event "is expected to be the grandest and most largely attended affair ever given in Chicago." The article is worth quoting at length:

> When Colonel John R. Marshall of the 8th Illinois National Guard made a special visit to Tuskegee Institute, Alabama, only a few of his friends knew his mission. The public afterwards learned that he went to personally direct a photographer with the purpose of having the various activities of this world-famed institution taken for moving pictures.
>
> The subject of the "movies" is, "A Day at Tuskegee." These pictures comprise 4,000 feet in reels of 1,000 feet each, containing a complete story in moving pictures from the shack started in 1881, its varied vocational industries, the colossal buildings, the Institute Regiment and Band.
>
> In order to give the pictures a formal "send off" the management has invited Dr. Booker T. Washington to appear on the night of the exhibition, April 1st, at Orchestra Hall on Michigan Avenue. . . . These pictures will be shown in every city, county and state in this country, and later representatives will show them wherever Tuskegee is known and Dr. Washington's books have been read.[116]

The films were not shown on campus until May, but the student newspaper chronicled Marshall's visit and the production of the moving pictures with great interest. Lewis's article gives a sense of how he marketed *A Day at Tuskegee*. However subtly, he subordinates Washington to the moving pictures, implying that the famous leader is a bolster for the promotion of the film, not the other way around. Although the film highlighted the figure of Washington in its portrayal of Tuskegee, the institute could not control its effective meaning once it was projected. Tuskegee's leaders exerted greater control over the production and exhibition of *A Day at Tuskegee* than they had with Broome's moving pictures, but once again the medium itself was the main attraction, taking prominence over the uplift message it was attempting to disseminate.

Press coverage of *A Day at Tuskegee* extended to the motion picture industry trade magazines, which saw the film largely as an educational novelty. In the same issue that ran an advertisement for the film, the *Moving Picture World* featured *A Day at Tuskegee* in its "Chicago Letter" column, noting: "This fine educational exhibit is especially designed for entertainments in churches, colleges and schools."[117] The announcement reiterated the details of Lewis's press release for the Orchestra Hall screening. Several months later, the trade journal included *A Day at Tuskegee* under the topic of sociology in its listings of new educational films.[118] In June 1913, the *Moving Picture World* lauded "the introduction of pictures in schools and churches" and "special pictures" like *A Day at Tuskegee*, concluding: "Oh, it's great for the moving pictures."[119]

A Day at Tuskegee appeared at an important juncture in the evolution of the possibilities of cinema as a broadly educational medium. The Progressive Era's investments in modernization and education coalesced around the proliferation of educational moving pictures.[120] The *Moving Picture World* championed the "great educational value" of moving pictures as early as 1911, when it launched a column dedicated to educational films.[121] Educational film was a component of the broader campaign for the uplift of cinema. In its inaugural educational film column, the *Moving Picture World* stated: "It has been predicted in these columns repeatedly that the moving picture would outgrow the commonplace and the vulgar" and that the moving picture should rise "to the level of its highest ideals."[122] The uplift of cinema coincided with the educational mission of Tuskegee and the respectable use of motion pictures in schools and churches. The Tuskegee films projected the possibilities of Black uplift while also functioning as educational tools and participating in the broader uplift of cinema.

However, the educational appeal of the films did not guarantee their economic viability. Reporting back to Scott on the Orchestra Hall event, Anderson noted that the screening was "a decided artistic success, but not financially so," selling only 800 out of a possible 3,000 tickets. Despite positive reviews in the Black press and the attention given to the film in the trade papers and other newspapers, *A Day at Tuskegee* could not get public support because of the high ticket prices being charged.[123] The event was advertised as having a range of seat prices, starting at twenty-five cents, the cheapest tickets actually sold were fifty cents, apparently deterring spectators accustomed to paying five or ten cents for a moving picture show. Anderson had expected Washington's presence to justify the higher cost, but that did not happen. Putting a positive spin on the low attendance, Anderson told Scott that the majority of the audience was white "with the 'brother' showing in some strength in the 50¢ tier," and that those present "were the classiest of the classy and the exhibition and Mr. Washington were both enthusiastically applauded." Despite the disappointing numbers, Anderson reported, "I am not, however, deterred, because I know this is a good thing and will in the end show handsome returns."[124]

Given that the publicity surrounding the event subordinated Washington's presence to the exhibition of moving pictures, it is perhaps not surprising that many potential spectators considered the ticket prices too high for such an attraction. There were also criticisms of the presentation, particularly the absence of commentary delivered by a lecturer to explain the images and give "a little more life" to the pictures.[125] Insofar as *A Day at Tuskegee* functioned as a travel film as well as an educational film, the lack of explanatory framing of its scenes rendered the images less legible to an audience with no firsthand knowledge of Tuskegee's operations. The singers performed during the reel changes, and though it is not clear what kind of music accompanied the moving pictures, it is likely that some did, as complete silence would have been uncommon and certainly noteworthy. Regardless, the desire for an explanatory framing of the images suggests a general expectation on the part of the audience for an integration of the moving pictures with the live speeches and performances. It also suggests that the three ways in which Tuskegee was represented at the event—through moving pictures, lectures, and songs—were experienced as an integrated spectacle rather than as two aural forms supporting the images. In the absence of singers or lectures, the moving pictures could not stand autonomously. Anderson-Watkins advertised the three-reel "educational feature" for rent from March to November in the trade press and Black newspapers.[126] Anderson also received requests from white churches for the rental of the films for Sunday afternoon programs.[127] Despite this interest, the film was a financial failure, and *A Day at Tuskegee* would be the only production of the Anderson-Watkins Film Company.[128]

In terms of their rhetorical value, Washington was pleased with the films and saw them as bringing Tuskegee "in closer touch with the masses, as well as the classes," according to a letter from Anderson. Washington suggested that Anderson-Watkins incorporate colored photographic slides that showed buildings not featured in the moving pictures, "thereby giving the audience a larger view of the scope of the institution." Anderson agreed with Washington and noted that "it happens that those of the scenes in the 'movies' which may be classed as 'bad' are buildings and therefore can be easily eliminated" and replaced with colored slides.[129] Anderson made twenty-five slides of buildings and scenes at the institute, rendered in color, and inserted them into the moving picture exhibition. In his view these changes yielded "a comprehensive and thorough exhibition of the Institute, its scenes and life." Anderson wrote to Scott about the positive press reports of the moving pictures, adding that "even the *Broad Ax*, notoriously anti-Tuskegee, graced its columns with a full column laudatory in the highest degree."[130] The *Broad Ax* indeed noted that Anderson-Watkins had "met with unusual success" in its exhibition and had "exerted unusual effort" in the scope of its advertising campaign for the film. Anderson-Watkins had "introduced an innovation entirely new in every detail" and "placed before the people of Illinois the possibilities of seeing Tuskegee at a moderate expense." The article continued:

> The pictures began by showing the photo of Tuskegee's famous educator which was followed by showing the old house in which the school and its beginning in 1881 [sic]. The exhibitor then with great precision and care, led the audience step by step through the increasing growth and development up to the present day of the now famous school. The activities of the institution were vividly portrayed in all of its various phases and departments, showing corps of teachers and pupils at work in the many class-rooms, the demonstrations were indeed wonderful and the exhibition of the growth of the institution justifies that eloquent tribute of Andrew Carnegie to Booker T. Washington, in which he said, at Cooper's Institute in New York City with his hand upon his shoulder, "here stands the greatest climber in all history."[131]

The *Broad Ax* outlined how the pictures served as models for advancement, emphasizing the way in which the motion pictures conveyed possibility to their African American spectators. Pointing to the persuasive power of the motion pictures, the paper proclaimed: "No Negro could look upon that exhibition and [absorb] the importance of what his eyes beheld without being inspired with the realization of the great possibilities which lie in reach of any Negro of character, ability and ambition. The exhibition of these pictures are [sic] within themselves a practical education; no Colored person should permit an opportunity to pass without seeing them, and every white person, especially those who have such little conception of the magnitude of Tuskegee, should avail themselves of the opportunity of seeing these illustrated pictures."[132] In this respect, the Tuskegee pictures aimed to educate audiences as well as portray the educational transformations brought about by the institute. Although the audience for the pictures was likely to be made up mostly of Tuskegee supporters, the *Broad Ax* suggests that the film's persuasive potential could have a strong impact if presented to a wider audience as well.

The media attention given to *A Day at Tuskegee* did not escape the notice of an indignant George Broome. He considered *A Day at Tuskegee* a breach of understanding between his company and Tuskegee over the rights to film the institute. When he read of the upcoming Orchestra Hall event in the *New York Age*, he wrote to Washington, complaining that the pictures taken of the school by Anderson-Watkins "practically makes my pictures valueless and a great loss for me." Yet he was not in a strong position to take legal action and could only assert, "I feel that I am entitled to some consideration in this matter," again offering to sell his films to Tuskegee outright.[133] Scott forwarded the letter to Anderson, who allayed any concerns that the Tuskegee authorities might have had by noting that Broome had been permitted to take his pictures "quite a while ago, which didn't turn out good," and that Broome's "rights were limited to the ownership of the pictures taken by him, and that's all."[134] Tuskegee denied having made any exclusive arrangement with the Bostonian, who was left with his Tuskegee footage and a broken relationship with the institute. Broome also wrote to Anderson, who ignored his complaint; Anderson told Scott that "I have disregarded it and intend to continue to do so."[135]

A Day at Tuskegee in the South

Although the Tuskegee authorities were more concerned with using moving pictures to promote the institute among northern benefactors, the filmmaking entrepreneurs who worked with them were invested in reaching Black audiences. Broome sought an audience among Black Bostonians, and Anderson-Watkins turned to southern Black communities. Watkins even suspended his dentistry practice to promote the moving pictures across the South. Anderson-Watkins hired an expert operator to travel with a projector, slides, and films, and he arrived in Montgomery from Chicago on May 2, 1913.[136] To better promote the film, the Chicago stockholders sent Colonel Marshall to Montgomery to accompany the operator and Watkins on the film's southern tour.[137] Once again, Anderson requested support from Tuskegee in terms of targeted publicity, noting that "official approval" would increase interest and help generate a strong audience turnout in southern cities and towns.[138] The first southern showing was in Montgomery on May 7, after which the men followed a route that had been tentatively planned in Chicago.[139]

Watkins exhibited the moving pictures to Tuskegee students and faculty in the campus chapel on May 8, 1915. If A Day at Tuskegee served as a travelogue in other exhibition contexts, at Tuskegee it functioned as a local film, a "see yourself" actuality. The Tuskegee Student reported that "students and teachers enthusiastically applauded the various persons and scenes recognized in the pictures."[140] Scott, who had not seen the moving pictures prior to their screening at Tuskegee, reported to Anderson that "quite a number of them were dim" and could not be made out, "but, as persons were recognized, they were enthusiastically applauded" by the "very large and very enthusiastic" audience.

Given Tuskegee's dismissal of Broome's local film "nonsense," the celebration of *A Day at Tuskegee* on campus might seem contradictory. However, it was screened for the campus community rather than for the express purposes of fund-raising; different audiences meant different exhibition contexts and expectations for the moving pictures. It also permitted the Tuskegee leaders to get a better sense of how southern Black audiences might receive them. Anticipating some of the difficulties that Watkins would have on the southern tour, Scott told Anderson: "I do not believe you will have a larger audience anywhere than the audience given the pictures here at Tuskegee."[141]

Watkins was permitted to charge students and teachers fifteen cents for admission to the screening at the Tuskegee Chapel. Although Scott did not specify the terms of their arrangement, Watkins was likely permitted to keep all of the proceeds for the Anderson-Watkins Company rather than sharing them with Tuskegee, which was in keeping with their collaboration for the northern exhibitions. These persistent attempts to capitalize on the interest in the moving pictures are likely due to the cost of their production. In retrospect, Scott told Anderson that it would probably have been preferable for the Pathé cameramen to shoot the film rather than the National operators, who charged thirty-five cents per foot, ten cents more than Scott reported that Pathé would have charged, "and the Pathé pictures are much clearer." He was pleased, however, with the inclusion of the slides, which "were in every way much clearer than the others."[142] The technological limitations of the camera used to shoot *A Day at Tuskegee* might have limited the success of the Tuskegee pictures. (Ironically, Washington was ultimately shot by Pathé cameramen, who captured his funeral in November 1915.)[143]

In Montgomery, *A Day at Tuskegee* was shown at the Montgomery Theater for twenty-five cents, with "special arrangement for white people."[144] (It is not clear if the "special arrangement" indicates a screening exclusively for white people—there was a matinee screening as well as an evening screening—or if white people were given a separate section.) After Montgomery and Tuskegee, the film traveled through Georgia and was shown in LaGrange, Atlanta, Savannah, Augusta, Macon, and Columbus.[145] In Savannah, the film was shown both at St. Philip's A.M.E. Church and the Beach Institute, an African American school.[146] The problem that Anderson-Watkins faced in the south was that exhibitions were planned for Black churches and schools that were often not wired for electricity. Watkins bemoaned the lack of an advance agent to mitigate "the many inconveniences we are experiencing." However, he noted that "the people seem to be wild over the pictures everywhere." Ultimately, though, because of the quality of the pictures "due to atmospheric conditions," Watkins

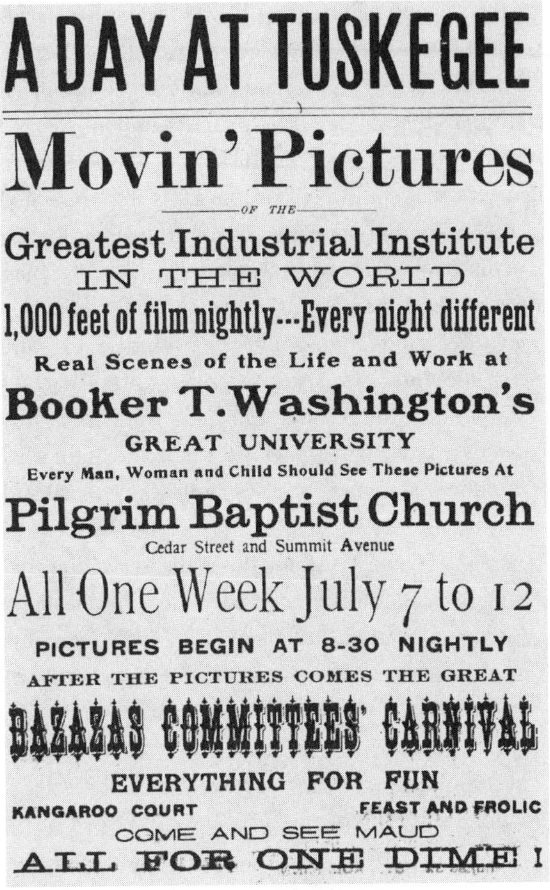

FIG. 2.8 Advertisement in the *St. Paul Appeal* July 5, 1913.

reported a "general dissatisfaction" with the film.[147] Problems such as ticket costs, inclement weather when the films had been taken, and lack of reliable electricity in nontheatrical southern venues combined to prevent the success of the Anderson-Watkins venture.

Despite this, Anderson-Watkins attempted to turn a profit on the Tuskegee pictures, and Tuskegee continued to cooperate with and encourage the endeavor. At the end of May 1913, Washington personally sent a still photograph to Anderson, believing it to be "a very effective one," to incorporate into the moving pictures.[148] In July 1913, Anderson-Watkins screened *A Day at Tuskegee* at the Mid-Summer Carnival at Pilgrim Baptist Church, an African American church in St. Paul, Minnesota (figure 2.8). They charged ten cents admission and in their advertising claimed to show a different reel each night for a week, imploring potential spectators to "see them all and get the whole story."[149]

Tuskegee's calculations that the moving pictures would be successful in terms of advertising (if not financially so for their producers) proved to be correct, as interest in moving pictures of Tuskegee persisted. Lewis suggested in an August 1913 article in the *Freeman* that Anderson was in discussions to send the Tuskegee moving pictures to the Lexington, Kentucky, Fair Association in September.[150] No records survive that could verify if the films were screened on that occasion, although *A Day at Tuskegee* was screened at the First Baptist Church in Lexington in November 1913.[151] Later that month, Hunter C. Haynes, the general manager of the Afro-American Film Company, wrote to Scott at Tuskegee, announcing the intended production of a five-thousand-foot feature titled *Notable Achievements of the American Negro*, intended to travel across the country and through Europe (the film, released in 1914 as *Notable Negroes and Their Achievements*, is discussed in chapter 5). Haynes asked Scott for a list of "the notable and most prominent Negro enterprises, both commercial and agricultural."[152] He also asked if it would be possible to include the pictures taken at Tuskegee. Scott referred Haynes to Anderson-Watkins, stating that it "has the privilege of showing these pictures for considerable time ahead."[153] Scott's reply suggests that Anderson-Watkins had been given exclusive rights to film Tuskegee and exhibit the pictures. Once again, Tuskegee's priority of reaching benefactors took precedence over its address to Black spectators, often against the wishes of the filmmakers.

The question of control over moving picture production and exhibition was central to Tuskegee's negotiation of motion picture use. The institute's leaders exerted greater control over the second Tuskegee film, but they could not predict how the spectacle of the medium could overshadow Washington's own star power. Although symbiotic in many respects, the intersections of entrepreneurs and Tuskegee resulted in a model for industrial filmmaking that Hampton chose to avoid. At Hampton, filming uplift was entirely controlled by the institute. Yet in spite of its leaders' close management of its screen image and the dissemination of that image, they could not control how audiences responded to their films, a fact that became evident in their misguided association with *The Birth of a Nation*.

3

"PICTORIAL SERMONS"

The Campaign Films of Hampton Institute, 1913–1915

_____

At nine o'clock on Saturday morning, January 6, 1912, the senior faculty members of the Hampton Institute met for the first time in the new year. At 10 degrees, it was the coldest day they had experienced so far and unusually chilly for Tidewater Virginia. As was typical for faculty meetings, they heard specific students' cases. One student's father pleaded for his son to be given a second chance before being expelled, and the student was granted a month-long provisional status. Another student who had been sent away for two years returned, hoping to be readmitted, but was deemed by the faculty to be "coarse and unsatisfactory" and was asked to leave "at once." The faculty debated, with no conclusion, the question of which church the twelve Episcopalian Native American students should be allowed to attend. For the final order of business, the faculty selected students to participate in the chorus for the spring fund-raising campaign in the north. It was decided that the selected students would be excused from work at 4:30 PM three times a week for rehearsals. At the end of the meeting, Vice Principal George Phenix presented Cora Mae Folsom's plan for demonstrating the progress of a Hampton student through his education by using motion pictures.[1]

For over a decade, Folsom had been head of Hampton's Photography Department and had written the school's pageants and plays, live costumed displays enacted by students to commemorate national holidays such as Independence Day and to provide illustrations and entertainment for Hampton's campaign events. When she became curator of the Hampton Museum in 1903, she took charge of exhibits and entertainments, becoming responsible for showcasing the institute's work as well as engaging students in performances.[2] In 1911 she turned to full-time development work for the museum and devoted herself to the campaign pageants.[3] In this context, the production of moving pictures in the service of the uplift project was a logical development from Hampton's and Folsom's other representational methods. Hampton had a far more sophisticated media operation on its campus than did Tuskegee, whose public presence centered on the figure of Booker T. Washington as a national celebrity and overshadowed the on-the-ground endeavors of the institute. Hampton's media work reflected this sophistication. As an extension of the institute's leaders' investment in photography and pageantry, Hampton's engagement with moving picture technology demonstrates their recognition of a changing media ecology and the power of visual images to serve persuasive ends. It also reveals their commitment to image control and message dissemination.

The administration of Hampton believed that the institute had a dual purpose: the training of skilled African American and Native American labor in the service of uplift, and the promotion of the positive representation of both groups. Hampton expended considerable resources on its publicity efforts, justified by the goal of challenging negative public opinion of both African American and Native American education. Through the institute's official publication, the *Southern Workman*, the press office of Hampton described its mission in these terms: "It is doubtful if the work done on the Hampton School grounds is more important than [the] education of public sentiment to a belief in our brothers in black and red."[4] It was this faith in the power of positive representation to change misperceptions concerning African Americans that led Hampton to expand its publicity arsenal through an array of mass communication media. Its first two films, *John Henry at Hampton: A Kind of Student who Makes Good* (1913) and *Making Negro Lives Count* (1914), follow the model of uplift aesthetics established by its campaign materials. These films were highly regarded and welcome additions to the campaign programs. But this belief in the persuasive power of moving images would lead to a project that proved deeply controversial, even damaging. In the wake of protests over the release of *The Birth of a Nation* in 1915, Hampton's leaders agreed to allow their films to be used by D. W. Griffith in an attempt to diffuse the anger and appease the censors. Footage of Hampton was thus inserted as a coda to *The Birth of a Nation* under the title *The New Era*, an act that immediately catapulted Hampton into the national debate over racial representation, film censorship, and "history written in lightning."[5] The controversy over the association of the "Hampton pictures" with *The Birth of a Nation* was a defining moment for the institute and its filmmaking project. Although Hampton's leaders had intended to counter negative images with positive ones, the resulting criticism caused them to rethink their narrative strategies and, ultimately, abandon motion picture production until after World War I.[6]

In retrospect, the controversy into which Hampton was catapulted, and which took its leaders by surprise, could have been expected. It was not a change in Hampton's strategy or a crucial mistake in judgment that led to the controversy; rather, it was a logical outgrowth of the basic strategy for using mass media. Hampton's films, operating in the context of the institute's fundraising campaigns, were explicitly constructed in line with the rhetorical strategies of the uplift project. Just as the visual and textual materials that represented uplift reflected the tensions embodied by the project, the films likewise manifested the tenuous status of African American possibility. The next two chapters are linked. Chapter 4 will work through the controversy over Hampton's involvement in *The Birth of a Nation*, and this chapter lays the groundwork for that episode, showing how Hampton's previous films successfully employed the logic, rhetoric, and tradition of uplift to present a distinct and powerful image of a southern, rural Black modernity.

Discussions at Hampton proposing the use of moving picture technology had begun much earlier than the faculty meeting in 1912. On December 15, 1909, the Hampton faculty began to consider the idea of having motion pictures made of Hampton for promotional purposes.[7] At a meeting on January 13, 1910, the faculty referred the issue to a committee. The committee was certainly aware of Tuskegee's investment in motion pictures: the Hampton Singers were to participate in a New York fund-raiser at Carnegie Hall on January 24, 1910, during which Tuskegee was to debut *A Trip to Tuskegee*. The screening was reported with acclaim in the African American press, but three days after the event Hampton faculty members determined that the Tuskegee pictures were "not altogether satisfactory," and their discussions turned to the possibility of producing motion pictures themselves rather than hiring an outside company.[8] The abbreviated faculty meeting minutes do not elaborate on what was unsatisfactory about *A Trip to Tuskegee*, but from the discourse surrounding the Tuskegee motion pictures we can presume that the faculty members were dissatisfied with the quality of the images, the lack of institutional control over their dissemination (reported by Phenix), and the fact that Tuskegee's films did not directly contribute to the education of the institute's students (since they were not made primarily as campaign films). The Hampton faculty members sought to address these concerns in embracing motion picture production as a new element in their multimedia campaign arsenal.

Discussions about the production of moving pictures of Hampton lasted from December 1909 to December 1911, when Principal Hollis B. Frissell told the faculty that he wished "the question of making moving pictures of the school pushed."[9] Again, the minutes of the meeting indicate a strong desire to keep the production in the hands of the faculty and administration: though the faculty discussed the possibility of hiring the Edison Manufacturing Company to produce a series of moving pictures of Hampton, it appears that nothing came of this plan.[10] The faculty members determined to produce films themselves rather than hiring a production company in large part because they were unimpressed by the Tuskegee films.[11] Phenix had attended the screening of *A Trip to Tuskegee* at Tremont Temple in Boston and had witnessed George W. Broome's exploitation of the footage. Phenix had been warned by a friend, as discussed in chapter 2, that "if the time ever comes when you have moving pictures made at Hampton take care that they are kept in your own hands."[12] Hampton heeded that advice and embarked on the new venture by turning to its own resources, purchasing a Snyder camera and charging Cora Folsom and Leigh Richmond Miner, Hampton's director of applied art and school photographer, with the task of producing the moving pictures. Folsom and Miner had experience organizing pageants; anniversary exercises; and photographic exhibitions, magic lantern, and stereoscopic displays of Hampton. They were thus able to draw on their own expertise to create scenarios and undertake the shooting themselves. Though Miner took charge of the production, the concept for the film was Folsom's—a fact that marks Hampton's moving picture enterprise as an early and significant instance of a woman's involvement in filmmaking.

In contrast to the Tuskegee films' emphasis on showcasing the physical plant and the figure of Washington, the Hampton films employed a range of narrative techniques beyond the before-and-after structure, including a focus on specific, albeit fictitious, students and an innovative use of flashbacks. From

1913 to 1916, Hampton produced three films—the two mentioned above plus *Cephas Returns* (1915)—that depicted the work of the institute. All three were each fiction films that included elements of actuality filmmaking demonstrating the various departments of the school and highlighting the educational course through the example of a representative student. By fictionalizing the trajectory of a typical student's course of study at Hampton, the institute could narrativize the actuality footage and mobilize it in the service of a story. All three films followed the logic of the print campaigns, which emphasized the teleology of progress. The narrative form of Hampton's uplift films was motivated by their expected purpose, just as the exhibition context was determined by the larger rhetoric of the campaign program. The films functioned in symbiosis with musical performances: songs accompanied the images, which concurrently illustrated the musical entertainments. Moving pictures were integral parts of campaign meetings, for which they were projected in a carefully choreographed context. Divorced from their prescribed role in the campaign program, however, they could be exhibited with consequences that conflicted with and, arguably, undermined the uplift project's directives.

John Henry at Hampton:
A Kind of Student Who Makes Good (1913)

───────────

Miner supervised film production at the institute. Miner's photographic aesthetic, as discussed in chapter 1, presents a humanizing portrayal of Hampton students and workers while operating within the parameters of the uplift project. Hampton's first film, *John Henry at Hampton: A Kind of Student Who Makes Good*, premiered to students on June 28, 1913.[13] The film, written by Folsom and shot by Miner, follows the template of demonstrated progress as it traces a fictitious student through his time at Hampton.[14] The institute's administrators considered the film and its emphasis on the student experience as a boon to their fund-raising campaign in the north. The *Southern Workman* reported that the students and workers "formed an interested and appreciative audience" for the film and unanimously agreed that it would be an asset to the campaign.[15] *John Henry at Hampton* was screened on campus on several other occasions between 1914 and 1916, along with fiction films that were brought in for entertainment over school holidays.[16]

News about the Hampton moving pictures had reached Chicago alumni by July 1913, when Robert S. Abbott, class of 1896 at Hampton and editor of the *Chicago Defender*, called for the organization of a local Armstrong League, the fund-raising organization that supported Hampton, to make arrangements for the moving pictures and glee club to visit Chicago.[17] The African American newspapers *Broad Ax* and *Cleveland Gazette* both ran articles on Hampton's new use of moving pictures, with the headline: "Moving Picture Story: Achievements of a Hampton Student Portrayed in Didactic Manner." The newspapers published the scenario of the film, most likely furnished by Hampton's press office, which emphasizes John Henry's education in several trades "so as to be truly useful to his people back in the country districts." In addition to emphasizing John Henry's usefulness, the two articles note the "sacrifice" of his parents and emphasize the cyclical nature of Hampton's training: "The country teacher, one of Hampton's graduates, who influenced John Henry to break his home ties and go to Hampton, witnesses the happy scene."[18]

A description of the film in the August 1913 issue of the *Southern Workman* is worth quoting in its entirety, as it is the most detailed extant account of the film's narrative structure:

In the first scene John Henry's school-teacher, a Hampton graduate, visits him and his parents in their little cabin in the country and persuades them to send him to Hampton. John Henry, found plowing, willingly agrees although when the time comes he leaves his mother with evident regret. He is next seen arriving at Hampton Institute in an oxcart and admiring its beautiful buildings. He is taken to his room where his roommate, an "old" boy, gives him a lesson in bed making.

John Henry spends his work year on the farm, caring for the chickens and farm animals, and doing various other chores. He then enters the cabinet-making department and learns that trade thoroughly in three years. Meanwhile he learns something of several other trades, harness making, shoemaking, bricklaying, and upholstery, in order to be useful when he goes back among his people. He is also seen assisting in the cooking and laundry departments, and helping the rug weavers.

In his Senior year John Henry sits at the head of his table and represents his class in athletics, being seen in the track meet and in an exciting football game. His life on Sunday is shown in the Sunday morning room inspection and in the battalion drill before church. He also appears as a teacher at the Whittier School, leading the procession of children to their morning salute of the flag. He takes his part in the Anniversary procession, and in the last picture he is seen, such a change from the awkward country youth of the first picture, receiving his diploma from the hands of Dr. Frissell in the presence of his happy parents and teachers.[19]

Although details on the production of the film do not survive, John Henry and the other characters were likely played by actual students and teachers; both groups were often involved in campaign pageants and demonstrations. Produced as a campaign film, *John Henry at Hampton* also functioned as a local film for the Hampton students and faculty members who shared in the collective projection of moving pictures of their community. As was the case with Broome's Boston actualities and Anderson-Watkins's screening of *A Day at Tuskegee* to Tuskegee students, members of the Hampton community could see themselves projected on screen. As the first audience for the Hampton moving pictures, the students were reportedly amused and intrigued by the reels reflecting back to them their own images and those of their classmates and teachers.[20]

The main use of *John Henry at Hampton*, of course, was as a fictionalized actuality for publicity and fund-raising outside of the campus, as the John Henry figure provided a narrative framing for the scenes of Hampton's campus, vocational department, and principal. John Henry, in effect, is presented as a successful counterpart to the character in Isabella Andrews's *The Failure of Cunningham*—a student who, as described in chapter 1, left Hampton to return to his community and became an inspiring teacher and effective community member. Unlike the failed Cunningham, John Henry is a model of Hampton's possibilities. His skill at various endeavors provides the narrative structure, demonstrating a variety of the trades learned at the institute. The narrative also emphasizes the circularity of uplift: a Hampton graduate encourages John Henry's parents to send him to Hampton, and while at Hampton John Henry participates in the training of the young children at the Whittier School. The model of education presented by the film is one that emphasizes the self-uplift of the race; Frissell gives John Henry a diploma in the end, but John Henry is found by a graduate and guided through Hampton by an "old boy." The synopsis emphasizes that his education is for the purpose of being "useful when he goes back among his people." The mention of his ultimate return home, combined with the scene between John Henry and his mother, underscores the goal of Hampton's course of study—to change individuals for the better so that they may in turn bring advances to their communities. The film presents the mother's sacrifice in sending her son away as rewarded by his eventual return; it is a narrative frame that provided a model for rural Black families and an emotional note to the story, as well as a relatable moment for the philanthropic spectators. Importantly, the circularity of the uplift ideal and its reflection in *John Henry at Hampton* confine the uplift narrative within Black communities. The film is explicit in its message that Hampton is not a training ground

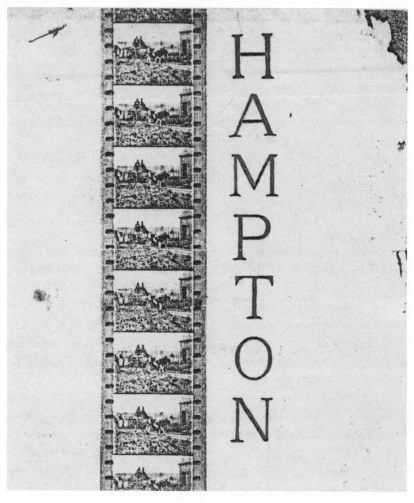

FIG. 3.1 Undated program, c. 1914, Hampton University Archives.
Courtesy Hampton University Archives.

for systemic change or a challenge to the segregationist status quo: John Henry
is not going to compete for a job with southern whites, nor does he aspire to
move north.

The ethos of *John Henry at Hampton* was further reflected by the printed
program that toured with the film in its fund-raising campaign. The cover demonstrates the centrality of the film for the 1914 campaign (figure 3.1). Though
undated, the program was filed with a 1915 invitation in the Hampton University Archives, indicating that *John Henry at Hampton* might have been used

well into that year, when it was replaced by *Making Negro Lives Count*.[21] The cover shows a film strip with seven frames vertically aligned with the seven letters in the word *Hampton*, displayed in block letters, and is the only surviving photographic reproduction of an uplift film that I have found.[22] The strip depicts the journey of John Henry in an oxcart, riding across a rural landscape with a companion (presumably the mentor who inspired him to attend Hampton), framed in a long shot so their features are indiscernible. Inside the program, opposite the order of events, the film is described as follows:

> The story of an average boy coming from the country to Hampton is told in the experience of John Henry. A Hampton graduate has inspired him with the desire to become a competent farmer. The big family trunk is packed (with very little) and the old steer takes him to the landing. He gets his first view of the beautiful school grounds from the deck of the steamer, is met on his arrival by one of the old students, and instructed in many details of his new life. He has to work his own way through the course in agriculture, but finds time for many interesting experiences before the glad day when he receives his diploma in the presence of his proud and happy parents.[23]

This description differs in tone from the account in the *Southern Workman*. It also differs on a key narrative point. Rather than cabinetmaking, the program states that he is focusing on agriculture. This relatively minor change indicates a concern for the different audiences of the film. To the southern Black audience, the skill of cabinetmaking implies upward mobility through the mastery of a trade. For a northern white audience, the focus on agriculture suggests an investment in uplifting the agrarian South, an antimigration appeasement measure (also important to southern audiences of both races).

Hampton's campaign meetings followed a standard format, and this one differed only in the integration of moving pictures into the program. The program begins with plantation songs, followed by an introduction. Labor songs then lead to the film, which is accompanied by the Hampton Singers. The film is followed by an address, and the program concludes with "trade song in costume."[24] Although there are no surviving records of exactly which songs were sung in the 1914 campaign, the 1913 campaign selections give a sense of the kinds of songs performed on these occasions. In 1913 songs were performed along with the staging of "picturesque tableaux" that presented the progress of Native American and African American students, enacted by students traveling along with the singers.[25] A Native American student portrayed "the Indian in history and song," and African American students sang "plantation melodies" and formed illustrative tableaux.[26] The *New York Times* described a performance at Carnegie Hall on March 10, 1913, as follows: "The first scene had to do with historic events at Hampton, and negro and Indian students from the institute were the actors. John Smith's visit to the Indians on the lower Virginia Peninsula was represented, and the first slaves finding a home was another scene. The scene representing negroes in the cotton fields and the announcement of the emancipation of the slaves were the subjects of brilliant tableaux. The scenes traced the history of the negro from the days of slavery to the first Freedmen's School, and the establishment of what is now the Hampton Institute."[27] The singers illustrated each of these scenes with a selection of "plantation melodies" divided into five sections: "The First Slaves Find a Home," "In the Cotton Field," "Emancipation," "Refugees," and "The First Freedmen's School." The program concluded with the song "Fifty Years of Freedom," sung by a Hampton graduate who was supported by the chorus called Men of Hampton. Each section had one or two songs. For example, in the cotton field section, the songs included "Dis Cotton Want Pickin' So Bad" and "I's Gwine Pick Off Massa's Pea[nut]s," and the staged action was described as follows: "Slaves sing as they pick the cotton and carry it to the scales, then break into an informal dance."[28]

Modeled after the successful Fisk Jubilee Singers, who began performing traditional African American spirituals on tours to raise funds for Fisk University in 1871, the Hampton Singers had begun touring in 1873. Starting in 1902, they incorporated secular work songs into their concert repertoire, along with stage settings "representing the actual physical conditions under which the songs were composed and used." The secular songs included work songs, cradle songs, game songs, and dance songs, and they were performed accompanied by "proper dramatic action."[29] As R. Nathaniel Dett, the director of vocal music at Hampton, wrote in 1918, "this was the first time in history that the secular songs of the Negro were given so public and proper a hearing, and by their use a new light was thrown on what slavery really meant to the Negro; and the value of his music as a characteristic means of racial expression was clearly demonstrated."[30] From that point on, secular songs joined spirituals and Native American tribal songs on Hampton's campaigns "for friends and funds."[31] Dett observed that "the effect of the secular songs has often been intensified by the use of appropriate and carefully worked out drama."[32] The songs also functioned to assert pride in Black musical traditions in the context of blackface minstrelsy. Discussing the "emancipation of Negro music," Dett quotes Major Robert R. Moton, then Tuskegee principal and a former Hampton faculty member, describing his embarrassment as a result of blackface minstrelsy: "I felt that these white men were making fun, not only of our color and of our songs, but also of our religion. It took three years' training at Hampton Institute to bring me to the point of being willing to sing Negro songs in the presence of white people. White minstrels with black faces have done more than any other single agency to lower the tone of Negro music and cause the Negro to despise his own songs."[33] It is in this context that Dett emphasizes the "serious utility of Negro music."[34] In this sense, the spirituals and secular songs had a double use: fostering pride in Black music among African Americans and appealing to predominantly white audiences for financial support. Given the popularity of the Hampton Singers, fund-raising campaigns were built around the performances of songs and advertised primarily as concerts in the interest of the institute. With the incorporation of *John Henry at Hampton*, moving pictures replaced the cumbersome pageant, reducing the number of students involved and the costumes, props, and sets required for these elaborate tableaux.

These songs also had a more direct purpose. The back cover of the program used for the 1914 campaign summarizes the operational needs of the institute, which involved "many thousand dollars" each year: "In order to raise this sum a little band of students gladly sacrifice their precious days at Hampton and go forth, with their God-given gift of melody, to do their part toward creating and holding the interest and confidence of their friends in the cause that means so much to them."[35] Moving pictures and the songs of the Hampton Singers were valued for their utility in appealing to potential donors. To this end, the campaign synergistically combined moving pictures and live performances of songs that showcased the "God-given" musical abilities of the singers. Students were engaged in fund-raising efforts and entertained prospective donors with "beloved Negro singing." Francis Peabody, a Hampton trustee and professor of social ethics at Harvard, wrote that the Hampton Singers "set themselves to 'sing up' Virginia Hall," a new building paid for by funds raised by the traveling entertainers.[36] Hampton students actively participated in all aspects of the construction of the school's buildings, which became a key point in publicity material, stressing the guided self-uplift of a race.

The success of the campaign program in attracting attention depended on the interrelation of narrative and spectacle. The performance of the singers supplemented the spectacle of the motion pictures, and the film provided a contemporary note to the typical program: the relatively new medium of film aligned Hampton with the most modern mode of mass communication and reiterated the story conveyed by *John Henry at Hampton* in print, image, music, and the accompanying speeches. Underlying these iterations of Hampton's

John Henry is the legend of the heroic John Henry, the so-called steel-drivin' man who raced the steam hammer, won, and then died of exhaustion.

The rise of southern railroads coincided with the establishment of southern agricultural and industrial schools for African Americans in the years following the Civil War. The John Henry legend proliferated among the southern states, though until recently common consensus was that it had probably originated in 1872 with the completion of West Virginia's Big Bend (or Great Bend) Tunnel on the Chesapeake and Ohio Railway line, the terminus of which was at Tidewater Virginia, just north of Hampton. In 2006, however, the historian Scott Nelson published his discovery that convicts leased from the Virginia Penitentiary worked side by side with a steam hammer in the construction of the nearby Lewis Tunnel. One such convict was the real John Henry, arrested for theft, tried under the "black codes" of Virginia in 1866, and sentenced to ten years in the state penitentiary. Lengthy sentences at hard labor were not uncommon. During the period of Radical Reconstruction, the state's military government turned to the penitentiary as a source of cheap labor for railroad construction. Prisoners began as unskilled laborers and worked in increasingly dangerous conditions, leading to the death of more than a hundred men in the construction of the Chesapeake and Ohio Railway. By 1870 convicts were drilling alongside the steam drills in the Lewis Tunnel, and convict labor completed the tunnel. During the next decade, convict workers died at a rate of 10 percent a year, most—including John Henry—died as a result of acute silicosis, a deadly occupational lung disease. Indeed, in his excavation of the buried history of John Henry, Nelson discovered that the original versions of the song were cautionary tales rather than the boastful legends that they would become.[37]

The convict labor subtext of the legend also serves as a parallel narrative to the Hampton arrival whose fate, following the logic of uplift, depended on his acquiring a proper training, as provided by the institute. Between 1900 and the U.S. entry into World War I, Virginia's economy grew because of the extensive railroad network and the navigable waterways that could be used to transport goods to northern cities.[38] The legendary John Henry, a former slave, represented both the individual contribution and resistance to the collective enterprise of industrialization and American modernization. In 1965 the folklorist Richard Dorson commented on the John Henry legend: "The ballad commemorates an obscure event in which several lines of American history converged—the growth of the railroads, the rise of the Negro, the struggle of labor. Various interpreters have read in the shadowy figure of John Henry symbols of racial, national and sexual strivings."[39]

The concern over Black criminality—perceived or real—was intricately linked to uplift proponents' investment in training workers in the most modern technologies of agriculture and industry, training that would combat idleness and contribute to a workforce indispensable to white interests. In an increasingly industrialized south, the possibility of the individual worker's being replaced by machinery was a looming threat. As Nelson has shown, "among trackliners who lived by their strength, the song of John Henry found its home as a story of heroism, one tinged with anxiety about the future."[40] At an also anxious Hampton, John Henry was a fitting cinematic hero who embodied the conflict between the agrarian past and industrial modernity, with its attending pressures and promises.

The cinematic image of John Henry arriving at Hampton on an oxcart is thus ironic. The "steel-driving man" sits atop a slow-moving, antimodern means of transportation. Hampton neutralizes John Henry's strength by placing him on an oxcart, disassociated from the railroad and from symbols of strength (physical or sexual), and then reconstructs him within the uplift ideal. With this image, Hampton suggests that John Henry can become the legend only through proper training (or taming). But it is a different kind of legend. Racing the steam hammer kills the legendary John Henry, but the Hampton student has no such ambition; he wants "to become a competent farmer." This revision of the John Henry legend and the addition of Hampton is part of the film's negotiation of the institute's geographically disparate constituents and the film's double address to two separate audiences with different interests: the film could inspire African Americans across the country while remaining unthreatening to wealthy white philanthropists. It thereby represents the ambivalences of the uplift project. It is technologically advanced in the training offered to students and representationally positive in the image conveyed to the world, but it contains an underlying conservatism that functions as a tether to the uplift narrative.

Despite its conservatism, the rewriting of the John Henry legend in Hampton's first motion picture is not an entirely antimodern gesture. The film participates in cinematic modernity in a distinctly southern way by emphasizing the up-to-date qualities of Hampton's agricultural training, a rhetoric that speaks not only to the interests of white benefactors and patrons of the institute but to Black audiences as well. By removing any reference to the train in the film, Miner ensures that John Henry is not killed by industrialization, a martyr to its destructive path; instead, John Henry capitalizes on it by "casting his bucket down" and learning the most advanced methods of farming.[41] The experience of modernity is here given a southern, rural framework. In contrast to the industrialized north, this rural modernity centers around the Reconstruction and post-Reconstruction ideal of technological advances in the trades and agricultural skills for which the ostensibly premodern African American workforce could be trained. Hampton's modernity is thus not marked by trains, urban crowds, or temporal confusion; instead, it creates a space for Black spectatorship through a presentation of a southern modernity (challenging the association of the south with backwardness) that in turn figures Black life as translatable, realist, and progressive. Although white audiences could see Hampton as a catalyst for Black modernization, *John Henry* presents Black spectators with a model for their viable participation in modernity—a modernity they might otherwise miss out on.

As Dorson notes, industrialization, labor, and the African American male converged in the story of John Henry. These were also three convergences that marked Hampton's assertion of its own modernity. The institute's use of motion pictures added a fourth: the moving image as modern representational technology. If nineteenth-century train travelers "encountered themselves as moderns," as Alan Trachtenberg has noted, then early twentieth-century African Americans, as spectators to the itinerant projection of uplift, saw themselves in *John Henry at Hampton* as possible moderns, participating in a shift from the agrarian past to an agrarian modernity—and perhaps even to an industrial modernity.[42] White philanthropists, as earnest if self-serving patrons of what was called the Negro cause, saw (or at least were shown) African Americans as modern subjects, but operating in a different field. For example, Hampton's representation of John Henry sharply contrasted with the image of Jack Johnson, the contemporaneous African American boxing champion, whose cinematic image set off a flood of new legal restrictions on moving pictures in response. Although both figures represented Black strength and masculinity, Johnson was seen as the epitome of the nonuplifted and as further evidence of Black criminality and licentiousness, a perception of Blackness against which the uplift ideal ardently fought. For the uplift project, Johnson's notoriety represented the imperative for the public presentation of its own image and exemplified a reputation against which it strove to define itself. The legend of John Henry filled this need.

In advance of the 1914 northern fund-raising campaign, Hampton faculty members were invited to view the moving pictures and campaign program on January 10. At the following faculty meeting, they discussed the strengths and weaknesses of the program, concluding that the story of "John Henry" was not "representative enough" of Hampton and its work and suggesting the inclusion of stereopticon slides of the grounds, buildings, and interiors. They also agreed that the program should consist of "less singing and more explanation of the pictures." After meeting with Folsom, they decided to retain the singing and leave the use of stereopticon slides to the discretion of those in charge of the campaign.[43] The moving pictures were again shown to students and teachers at the chapel services on Sunday, January 17, 1914, and on the following Wednesday for those who missed the Sunday screening. Students and workers were reportedly delighted by the scenes depicting "the trials and triumphs of a Hampton student" and responded to *John Henry at Hampton* with "laughter and applause," demonstrating their "intimate appreciation" of the moving pictures.[44] These campus events served as practice run-throughs of the campaign program while also displaying to the students and faculty members the way in which their work was explained to the outside world. In this sense, the discourse of uplift education was shared with its primary constituents through moving pictures of themselves, an example of the complex logic of the local film.

Hampton's 1914 northern campaign began on January 25 in New York City, with three events: one each at the Ethical Culture Hall, the music hall of the Brooklyn Academy, and Carnegie Hall.[45] At the Brooklyn meeting, Job E. Hedges, Republican candidate for governor of New York, spoke before Moton's appeal for funds, stating, according to the *Afro-American*: "Hampton is a good place for white people because it makes them whiter. There you find a sanctity of emotion that makes you ashamed. At Hampton true religion is to be found. We sometimes go to church because it is decent. They go because they've got to have it." He concluded: "I know of no place where a dollar will breed more dollars of value than at Hampton," emphasizing Hampton's model of return on investment through the self-uplift of the race.[46] The African American newspaper did not comment on Hedges's use of egregious stereotypes about Black religiosity (or Hampton's alleged blanching effect on whites), but his comments reveal the way in which the music reinforced stereotypes just as it fought others (like those perpetuated on the minstrel stage). Following Hedges, Moton turned the terms of the discussion: "The white race taught us that anything black was to be despised. Hampton has taught my race to be proud of itself. God intended that the Negro should be as good as any other race."[47] The *Afro-American* remarked that, in addition to the popularity of the speakers, "the most interesting feature of the meetings was the moving pictures."[48] It is clear that the moving pictures in these events functioned as both medium and message of uplift, as they offered both counterrepresentations and narratives of successful Black modernity.

The northern campaign continued in Boston, where *John Henry at Hamp-*

ton was the featured entertainment along with the Hampton Singers at a fund-raising benefit at Jordan Hall on February 3. The event was organized by the Massachusetts Hampton Association and presided over by Samuel W. McCall, a former congressman, and Moton. Moton said, as he had in New York, that Hampton "teaches the negro to believe in himself, and not to be ashamed of his color." Emphasizing the "dignity of manual labor" through the transformation of John Henry, the film conveyed to Boston philanthropists the "results" of their investment in Hampton's training.[49] The Boston meeting was followed by a series of events in Pennsylvania: at Horticultural Hall in Philadelphia, the Wilkes-Barre High School, and local church services.[50]

The use of motion pictures in the campaign caught the attention of the *Moving Picture World*, which reported on the Hampton pictures on February 21, 1914, in the "Correspondence: New England" section, and on March 7 in the "Moving Picture Educator" column.[51] The mainstream recognition of Hampton's motion pictures is especially important as it publicized the institute's film venture to a world beyond the already sympathetic audiences at campaign events. The trade journal noted the use of moving pictures, for the first time, as "an advertising medium for a great educational institution."[52] It reported on the quality of *John Henry at Hampton*: "The moving picture itself was one that would command a goodly rental fee at any first-class photoplay house, as the pictures of plantation life were synchronized with appropriate negro melodies, sung behind the screen by the noted Hampton Quartet."[53] Whether this was referring to the scenes of John Henry's home, confusing the campus with a plantation, or—more likely—conflating the rural campus with the iconicity of a southern plantation, it championed the scenes represented in the film as an attraction. It is also interesting that the *Moving Picture World* reported that the singers were positioned behind the screen and "synchronized" their songs to the moving picture scenes. Some accounts of campaign events indicate that the singers performed between the reels and that a speaker would explain the moving picture scenes, while other accounts suggest that the singers performed during the screening. This disparity may be explained by variations in the program, speakers, and types of venue. In either case, the moving pictures and the musical performances functioned in a symbiosis that was core to the campaign events.

Although newspaper reports on campaign events emphasized the popularity of the singers, the *Moving Picture World* naturally focused on Hampton's use of cinema. The "Moving Picture Educator" column featured Hampton's motion picture "advertising," noting that "much good is anticipated by the advantage of these kinematograph exhibitions." The review concluded that, through his education, "the boy" — John Henry — "is sent out into the world, in many respects the equal of his more fortunate white brother." The trade journal suggests that the moving pictures powerfully represent the success of uplift education, even surpassing the rhetoric of the Hampton-Tuskegee Idea by raising the issue of equality, a concept carefully rationed in uplift rhetoric.[54]

Though the primary aim of its motion pictures was to raise funds, Hampton promoted the uplift project among Black communities through designated screenings during the campaign tours. Hampton also received requests for the moving pictures apart from the campaign, though the institute's authorities kept close control over the reels, having learned from the experience of Tuskegee and the perceived misuse of its films. African American groups and entrepreneurs in the north and south alike requested the rental of Hampton's films on several occasions. In October 1914, the Cincinnati branch of the African Union Company, a trading firm, requested moving pictures of Hampton.[55] After some debate, the content of which is not recorded, the faculty decided not to send the company any motion pictures.[56] On another occasion, the faculty discussed the possibility of engaging a moving picture agency to present Hampton's films more broadly, though "no action" was taken.[57] The faculty did, however, vote to copyright the film to prevent unauthorized duplication after a mistaken report of "John Henry" pictures circulating in the south was brought to their attention.[58] With the attention given to Hampton's moving picture venture by national and local newspapers and the *Moving Picture World*, there is reason to suspect that the moving pictures could have been viable entertainments both theatrically and nontheatrically. However, Hampton carefully balanced its desire to spread the uplift message and the imperative of protecting the institute's public image and reputation.

Moreover, Hampton's desire to publicize its work and promote Black agricultural and industrial education was in constant conflict with an equally strong drive to protect the institute from criticism. This is probably why, in 1913, the faculty turned down W. E. B. Du Bois's request to use Hampton's motion pictures for the Emancipation Proclamation Commission exercises in New York, though the stated reason was that "the films are incomplete and not ready to send out."[59] Instead, Hampton offered Du Bois stereopticon pictures to use during the ten-day exposition celebrating the fiftieth anniversary of Lincoln's Emancipation Proclamation. Despite this caution, the attention given to the moving pictures by the press and their successful integration into the campaign programs encouraged the institute to continue employing films. Following the success of *John Henry at Hampton* and after Hampton officials' initial trepidation over sharing the films had faded, they sought to realize the potential for wider impact among white and Black audiences through the extended employment of moving pictures.

Making Negro Lives Count (1914)

The Hampton authorities were pleased with the incorporation of moving pictures into their campaign program and continued to develop their motion picture production. Following the portrayal of the fictional student John Henry, Miner made a film in 1914, *Making Negro Lives Count*, for the Panama-Pacific International Exposition in San Francisco and Hampton's 1915 fund-raising campaign. Rather than fictionalize the trajectory of a student's tenure at Hampton, *Making Negro Lives Count* was similar to the Tuskegee films in that it presented Hampton through the discourse of actuality filming. Like *John Henry at Hampton*, *Making Negro Lives Count* showcased the need for, work of, and impact of Hampton through the before-and-after structure of the uplift narrative.

Dissatisfied with the quality of the Snyder camera that he had used to make *John Henry at Hampton*, Miner appealed to the faculty's business committee in October 1914 for a new moving picture camera and lobbied faculty members to approve the purchase. Weighing the relative merits of a new Snyder camera and an expensive Pathé model, Miner also lobbied the faculty to agree to have an expert visit Hampton to take the images or to coach Miner in filming. The faculty assigned Miner the task of traveling north to assess the options and to meet with Frissell (who was in the north at the time), consulting with him "as to the school's future policy about taking moving pictures."[60] A week later, Miner returned to Hampton after testing Pathé, Snyder, and Erneman cameras. He opted for buying the last and hiring a camera operator to visit Hampton for twenty-five dollars per week "until a series of satisfactory moving pictures of the place have been taken." He also suggested that a former student by the name of Warner be instructed by the visiting camera expert "so as to become a trained camera man."[61] This mention of a former student named Warner is a brief yet significant indication that Hampton considered, or was beginning to consider, its motion picture production as an educational site as well. Although the Camera Club was exclusively made up of faculty and staff members, the participation of students and former students in the production of *Making Negro Lives Count* suggests that the faculty saw the possibilities for professional training in moving picture operation. This is not surprising, given that students "sang up" buildings that they themselves built in keeping with the principles of uplift education. Unfortunately, no record survives of Warner or other students who might have participated in film production at Hampton or beyond. Still, the faculty meeting minutes suggest that moving pictures were seen as both a boon to the fund-raising campaign and another trade that could be taught at Hampton. Deferring to Miner's recommendations, the faculty approved his proposal.[62]

In early December 1914, Miner and Leo Bock, the hired moving picture operator, filmed footage in and around Hampton "to show by these pictures the needs of the people, means of meeting them and results through Hampton's work."[63] No details survive about Bock other than that he came from Long Island and spent over a month at Hampton assisting Miner in filmmaking.[64] During his visit, he gave a lecture on color photography, displaying photographs, to the faculty and museum staff.[65] The very title *Making Negro Lives Count* points to the uplift project's mission of transforming Black communities through agricultural and industrial education. The idea of "making lives count" likewise reflects Hampton's economy of harnessing the natural resources of the raw material of Black labor for the material progress of African Americans. The title also implicitly refers to the possibility of failure inherent to the strategic rhetoric of the institute's publicity campaigns, as if to paternalistically suggest that Hampton was necessary for "negro lives" not to be wasted. The more insidious implication is that the before-and-after trajectory inscribes the before's unfulfilled potential not just as a lesser form of life but as a kind of nonlife. According to this logic, only an uplift education could create life and give it meaning. Tied up with its paternalistic assumptions, the title returns to a concern for the assertion of the humanity of African Americans in the vein of antebellum antislavery arguments, rather than the more contemporary issue of addressing a perceived problem. Strategically, this anachronism serves to describe uplift education in nostalgic terms while serving current concerns.

In March 1915, the *Southern Workman* published a detailed synopsis of *Making Negro Lives Count*, indicating that it was a scene-by-scene summary of the film's narrative:

The first pictures show conditions in the rural communities from which most of the students come—dilapidated one and two-room cabins, broken down fences, and untidy yards. An ox-cart meanders slowly along the road. Then come scenes which tell how Hampton trains Negro youth to meet these conditions. Battalion drill and inspection on Sunday morning show the boys erect and soldierly in their dark uniforms. The girls are seen coming from church. The boys are shown at work in the Trade School, making furniture, painting, printing, making uniforms in the tailor shop, shoemaking, and blacksmithing. The girls are seen in their home economics classes—sewing, cooking, weaving, gardening—in the manual-training room, and in the laundry. That it is not "all work and no play" for them is demonstrated by a spirited hockey game. In the agricultural department, students are learning proper methods of farming and caring for farm animals. Scenes from the Farmers' Conference—the horse-judging contest and the plowing match—illustrate Hampton's extension work.

The last pictures show the results of this training—returned students raising the standard in their communities. In Slabtown the Negroes are having a "clean-up day." In marked contrast to the cabins of the first picture are the homes now shown. The houses are simple, but well built and attractive in appearance. In Gloucester County a home is made more attractive by planting trees near the house. A school-teacher encourages her pupils to beautify their school grounds with trees and shrubs. A model schoolhouse and playground appear; a farm-demonstration agent shows an ignorant farmer how to plough deeply. The final scene illustrates happy home life, the farmer returning from the fields, the wife and children running to meet him.[66]

The structure of *Making Negro Lives Count* follows the typical uplift narrative of before-and-after while also highlighting the educational departments of the institute. This is similar to *John Henry at Hampton*, but there is now more emphasis on the girls' program. The gendered structure of the education evidenced by the photographs of Frances Benjamin Johnston and Miner are underscored in the film, as girls are shown coming from church, taking home economics courses, and working in the laundry. Evidently, the institute recognized an advantage in showing a more general perspective on the work of the school rather than focusing on the career of one fictitious student, especially as it allowed for scenes of the girls' departments. Likewise, the film reinforces the ideal of uplift in the ripple effect of individuals and the values of a traditional family supported by the farming father and living off the land.[67]

The *Outlook* reported on Hampton's production of *Making Negro Lives Count* as part of its 1915 educational and financial campaign. Unlike the description in the *Southern Workman*, the summary of the film in the *Outlook* uses evocative language that underscores "the disheartening conditions that still exist among Southern Negroes" and the work being undertaken at Hampton to address those challenges. The summary describes these conditions and the institute's response to them:

Shabby cabins and ramshackle outbuildings, ill-kept fields with pigs, chickens, and ragged children galore, tell the story of neglected rural life among Negroes. The sad old mule and the ill-fed steer, dragging by the doorway where the Negro woman washes early and late for a mere pittance, give a true picture of every-day life in hundreds of communities. Street scenes peopled with many loafing Negroes show the need of getting black folks to work and build up country life.

The scene changes to Hampton Institute, where tradesmen, teachers, and community leaders are being trained. Boys are shown busy at their every-day work in the common trades (carpentry, bricklaying, and blacksmithing) and at farming, just plain farming—plowing, harvesting, and caring for stock. Girls are seen washing, ironing, sewing, cooking, weaving, and making gardens. They are being trained for home-making and school-teaching. Farmers by the hundreds come to Hampton to learn how to do better plowing, to judge cattle, and grow better farm crops.

This film story of Southern black life, careless and backward, also shows what Hampton-trained Negroes do when they return home: clean up houses, back yards, and outbuildings; teach children to plant flowers, shrubs, and trees around newly painted or whitewashed fences and buildings; show the farmers how to make a better living and really love the land; make clean, attractive, Christian homes.

Industrial training and good citizenship go hand in hand. Nearly eight thousand Hampton graduates and former students, for example, have been quietly demonstrating the truth of this proposition for nearly fifty years.[68]

The rhetoric of the *Outlook* echoes other accounts of the film, though with more florid language, and suggests that the Hampton press office sent a press release to various publications (the reference to the "sad old mule," for example, is also in the *Moving Picture World*).[69] This description also recalls the language of *The Failure of Cunningham*, in which the seeming primitiveness of rural conditions is met with the discipline and industriousness of a Hampton graduate.

Making Negro Lives Count was first shown to Hampton students, workers, and faculty members in Cleveland Hall Chapel on January 30, 1915.[70] Given the participation of students in the production of the moving pictures, both in front of and behind the camera, it must have been an exciting experience for them to see moving pictures of themselves and their classmates (as they had

FIG. 3.2 Program for "Hampton Meeting," Carnegie Hall, February 8, 1915. Courtesy Hampton University Archives.

done with *John Henry at Hampton*). The idea that their lives could "count" was literalized through the filmic representation of their labor and progress.

A week after its initial screening at Hampton, *Making Negro Lives Count* was shown at a fund-raising event at Carnegie Hall on February 8, 1915. Unlike the cover of the program for the *John Henry* event at Carnegie Hall the previous year, which featured a facsimile of a filmstrip from *John Henry* (figure 3.1), the program for the 1915 campaign featured a color-pencil drawing by Miner (figure 3.2). The drawing depicts an African American woman in profile, balancing a woven basket on her head, with pine trees and a small one-room cabin in the background. She has a hint of a smile and her eyes, positioned at the center of the drawing, serenely gaze beyond the borders of the image. Unlike the drawings that illustrated *The Failure of Cunningham*, Miner's illustration is relatively naturalistic. The sketch features one of Miner's favorite subjects, a student named Portia Peyton, who Miner featured in several photographic series.[71] This scene is not part of the film's narrative and seems an unlikely choice for the program cover. However, the text inside the program situates the image: it is a representation of Dixie, meant to invoke nostalgia and fondness for "a sunny-natured race." At the same time, however, it invokes Du Bois's analysis of the "sorrow songs":[72]

> Would you know the souls of black folk? Listen, then, to the old plantation songs by Hampton Singers.
> "Nobody knows de trouble I've seen"
> "My Lord, what a morning, when de stars begin to fall"
> "De ole ark a-moverin' along"
> The moan of anguished despair, the high, wild note of jubilant thanksgiving and happy wonder, the irrepressible laughter of a sunny-natured race, are in these three songs and a score of others which the Hampton Quartette is singing this spring from Old Point Comfort to Palm Beach, and from Virginia to the states beyond the Mississippi.
>   You dream of Dixie and the land of cotton when you hear the slave-day melodies. You see Virginia, the cabins and the cornfields, passing in motion before you. You see Hampton Institute training leaders, tradesmen, farmers, and teachers.
>   Back among the Southern pines again, among their own people, you watch a miracle of change, where Hampton graduates are leavening the lump.
>   Whether the scenes move you to laughter or tears you will know that there are faithful black folk at work today whose service for our country spells "peace on earth, good will to men."[73]

In this context, the sketch of Peyton presents symbols of southernness (the basket, cabin, and pines) that surround the central female figure "among [her] own people." The nostalgic imagery is mobilized to appeal to northern philanthropists and to work, quite literally, in concert with the "sorrow songs." The program frames the music with an infantilizing discourse that essentializes Black expression and presents it as the projection of the imagination of the spectator. This mental image called up by the songs ("you dream") is then corroborated by the projected images of Hampton ("you see"). However, the images might work to undermine the authority of the characterization of the emotionally ebullient "sunny-natured race." The systematic visual catalog of Hampton's departments and the before-and-after structure that demonstrates the institute's impact are evidence of material conditions that are at odds with the nostalgic imagery that mediates the moving pictures for the spectator. As a means of translation, the program text provides a point of entry to the images that temper progress through familiar and comforting tropes of "faithful black folk."

The Carnegie Hall event attracted an audience of 5,000 people, the largest crowd to have gathered at a New York benefit for Hampton. Many of the Black attendees were reportedly drawn to the event because of Washington's appearance.[74] In his speech, Washington "set at rest his position relative to the higher education of the race" by addressing the role of Hampton in contrast to that of other Black colleges and universities: "Although we need Hampton, I do not mean to say that such colleges for the higher education of the Negro like Fisk, Atlanta and other universities are not needed. Through such institutes the Negro has been able to live in this country along beside [sic] the white man and survive."[75] Though his statement, as reported by the *Freeman*, is vague, it reflects the increasing tension between proponents of industrial education and supporters of liberal arts education, a tension that Washington sought to diffuse, however evasively.

The program opened with the Hampton Quartet, whose members were Hampton graduates: Charles H. Tynes, class of 1898; James A. Bailey, 1901; Samuel E. Phillips, 1912; and John H. Wainwright, 1890.[76] After Washington's address, Harry T. Burleigh, the celebrated African American baritone and composer, sang a selection of his own compositions.[77] Following that, *Making Negro Lives Count* was screened—"scenes from the hopelessness of the old life through Hampton's industrial training to the joy of service, interpreted by plantation melodies by the Hampton Singers."[78] Burleigh then sang several songs, including "Why Adam Sinned," and concluded by joining the quartet for the final number.[79]

After appearing in key northern cities, *Making Negro Lives Count* was the feature of Hampton's western campaign, the pinnacle of which was the 1915 Panama-Pacific International Exposition where the institute participated in the Bureau of Education, Bureau of Labor, and the state of Virginia exhibits. Accounts of the Carnegie Hall event focus on the famous figures present, such as Washington and Burleigh, but accounts of regional screenings as the campaign moved west provide more details about the way the songs and moving pictures combined to form a spectacle of uplift. In many cities the Hampton representatives appeared before groups composed primarily of white philanthropists and at separate venues for Black audiences. The party was composed of the quartet, Moton, and Sydney Dodd Frissell, son of Principal Hollis B. Frissell and author of the 1914 campaign pamphlet *Hampton's Message*.[80] The Hampton representatives also traveled with an electrician, presumably to set up and operate the moving pictures and thereby avoid the problems that the

Anderson-Watkins Company had while touring Black communities in the south with *A Day at Tuskegee*.[81] The *Chicago Defender* identifies two "moving picture operators" who traveled with the Hampton representatives, Captain Allen Washington and Fred Scart, though there is no further information available about either of these figures (nor is it clear that their names were accurately reported).[82]

Fund-raising events took place across the country and, of necessity, varied depending on location and region, something that permitted Hampton's representatives to craft their appeals to specific audiences. The western campaign began on March 14, 1915, in Hot Springs, Virginia, with a screening of *Making Negro Lives Count* "interpreted by plantation melodies" and accompanied by an explanatory speech and fund-raising appeal.[83] Two days later, the Hampton representatives held a meeting at the Shubert Masonic Theater in Louisville, Kentucky.[84] Sydney Frissell reported that "the far South was entered with trepidation, but from this untried field came whole-souled response" in a packed house in Louisville, where "the sight of a Southern audience rising to its feet to applaud the conclusion of Hampton's plea . . . and the generous aid of the best of Kentuckians are memories which speakers and singers will always treasure."[85] The following week in Indianapolis, the *Freeman* reported that the appearance of the Hampton representatives "was heralded by a large amount of white and colored friends."[86] The program was given first at Roberts Park M. E. Church for a wealthy, predominantly white audience and on the following day at the African American YMCA for schoolchildren and at Tomlinson Hall, a major public meeting site with 3,500 seats, in the evening.[87] The Indianapolis meetings were successful both in terms of turnout and financially, with Madam C. J. Walker pledging enough money for a full scholarship for both academic and industrial education. The famous African American businesswoman and millionaire attended the event at the Park Church, considered "a white church of the aristocracy of the city."[88] Walker also held a lavish dinner in honor of Moton and the other members of the Hampton party at her home between the YMCA and Tomlinson Hall performances.[89] The "Indiana Brief Notes" column in the *Moving Picture World* of April 10, 1915, noted that "motion pictures portraying the life of the negro in the South are making a big hit in Indianapolis, where there is about 20,000 colored population in one neighborhood."[90] The column is almost certainly referring to *Making Negro Lives Count*, given the press attention paid to the Hampton film and the absence of other similar films on exhibition at that time.

Details of these events reported in local newspapers provide insights into how the moving pictures were integrated with musical performances and fund-raising appeals. The songs performed by the Hampton Quartet mirrored the narrative trajectory of *Making Negro Lives Count*. The program for the April 1, 1915, meeting at the First Baptist Church in Lawrence, Kansas, shows that the songs, whether performed during the screening or during reel changes, illustrated the three sections of the film: "scenes from the old life," "scenes at Hampton," and "scenes from the new life." The first song, "There's a Meeting Here Tonight," opened the program, followed by "Nobody Knows the Trouble I've Seen." This either accompanied or preceded the "scenes from the old life." Then the singers performed "Ezekiel Saw De Wheel" and "Swing Low, Sweet Chariot" to accompany "scenes at Hampton," followed by "Lord, I Don't Feel Noways Tired" and "Let de Heaven Light Shine on Me" for the "scenes from the new life." Following Moton's delivery of "Hampton's Message," the quartet concluded with unspecified songs.[91] As the program was published the day before the meeting, Hampton's advance agent, who booked the venue and arranged for press coverage to advertise the event, likely provided it.[92] The following week in Cedar Rapids, the quartet was "encored again and again," until the local leader who was presiding over the evening "was forced to declare that one more selection was all they possibly could give." The songs identified by the local paper include those performed in Lawrence as well as "There's One More River for to Cross," "Suwanee [*sic*] River," and "Old Kentucky Home," demonstrating the combination of spirituals and secular songs in these performances.[93] Although press coverage of the tour frequently highlighted the popular singers, some accounts emphasized the moving pictures. The press coverage of Hampton's meetings in Washington is representative of the enthusiasm garnered by the moving pictures. For example, the Spokane *Spokesman Review* reported:

> The entertainment which the Hampton (Virginia) singers gave last evening at the Metropolitan Theater was deserving of the widest patronage, if only for the reason that it brought back in the most vivid manner, by means of pictorial scenes, the actual presentation of a life which, with its occasional gleam of light, was still a life of the deepest shadow. Scene after scene, portrayed with fidelity and minuteness of detail, made real the drama of the past. A picture of the new life with its lessons of usefulness and hope followed the portrayal of the old life of wretchedness and want. These pictorial sermons were interspersed by songs typical of the Negro temperament.[94]

Referring to the Hampton pictures as "pictorial sermons," the newspaper rhetorically aligned the moving pictures with the spirituals performed and the speeches representing the fund-raising efforts. In addition to the songs mentioned in other accounts, according to the Seattle *Daily Times* and *Post Intelligencer*, the singers also performed "Roll de Ol' Chariot Along," "Dem Golden Slippers," and "Roll, Jordan, Roll," as well as "the ancient Negro 'Juba' patting song and some other like chants of African origin."[95]

Events tended to be arranged by Hampton field agents and organized in conjunction with local groups. For example, in Eau Claire, Wisconsin, the local Women's Club arranged for the Hampton representatives to appear at the First Congregational Church, with all of the offerings going directly to Hampton. The local paper reported that the singers performed between reels and that "the pictures shown gave realism to the work being done."[96] They went on to a three-day series of performances in Minnesota, organized by F. A. Whipple, a Hampton field agent who had visited St. Paul a few weeks earlier to arrange the events.[97] In the Duluth and Minneapolis areas, events were held at the Pilgrim Congregational Church, where the quartet furnished the musical program for the vesper services; the Commercial Club; and the First Methodist Church, whose auditorium was reportedly crowded with interested listeners.[98] The *Chicago Defender* reported on the Minnesota events: "The moving pictures of Hampton's one hundred and seventeen buildings and grounds were shown in various clubs, and other churches in the city, and each audience was eager and responsive in the right way. Financially each showed every evidence of being pleased."[99] In Anaconda, Montana, the quartet performed in the Broadway Theater on June 12, 1915, an event that was announced in the local paper: "In addition to the singing, a series of most interesting moving pictures, showing life in the cotton fields in the South, will be shown, with an interesting description by William S. Dodd, the well-known lecturer, who infuses into his talk many amusing incidents of life and customs beyond the Mason and Dixon line."[100] Although the details of the program and characteristics of the venue varied depending on the location, the meetings all strategically sought to promote the work and idea of Hampton to gain financial backers and supporters of its cause.

From Washington and Oregon, the party headed for San Francisco and the Panama-Pacific International Exposition. Few records survive of the quartet's residency at the exposition, but they won a gold medal for their performances at the Palace of Education, where the Hampton exhibit appeared under the auspices of the U.S. Bureau of Education, the Bureau of Labor, and the state of Virginia. After returning from the exposition, Sydney Frissell described Hampton's exhibit in these terms:

Surrounded by furniture constructed by the tradesmen of Hampton and pictures showing the everyday life of this pioneer school of industry and the work of its graduates, the quartet sang every day for two months the old plantation melodies, which are seldom heard on the Pacific Coast. Scenes depicting the hopelessness of the old life, with ramshackle cabins, ragged children, and rickety steer carts dragging past shanties where Negro women washed, followed by scenes on "the drill ground of a people's leaders," training in shop, classroom, laundry, farm, and on the parade ground, were shown by motion pictures. Then back to the cabins and the pines again [where] Hampton's graduates were seen carrying a message of new life to their people. Interpreted by the singing of plantation songs, these motion pictures of Hampton drew crowds which overflowed the auditorium twice every day. Although no opportunity was given to ask financial aid at the Exposition, the carrying of Hampton's message of hope and good will to men, to many thousands from all parts of America, is a noble accomplishment.[101]

Additionally, Hampton's exhibit with the Bureau of Labor also displayed the institute's motion pictures, showing the work of the departments of the Trade School along with fifty-two slides and charts illustrating carpentry training. Hampton also participated in the Virginia Building, presenting an oak rack made by students to hold sixty large sepia photographs of the institute.[102]

The Panama-Pacific International Exposition was a celebration of modern capital and industry, showing new industrial methods as a reflection of American ideals of modernity and progress. The Hampton exhibit for the Bureau of Education included two reels of moving pictures accompanied by a lecturer and the Hampton Quartet, performing in the Simplex Theater Number 1 in the Palace of Education. Reporting on this exhibit, the *Moving Picture World* noted that Hampton's "excellent pictures" make it "one of the most effective and popular features" of the exposition. The trade journal also noted the novel fact that "Hampton is equipped with a moving picture machine" and that moving pictures are a regular part of Hampton's curriculum.[103]

Following their two-month residency at the exposition, the Hampton group continued the campaign as they returned to Virginia. In Salt Lake City, they gave two performances at the Utah Theater, on September 10 and 11. The *Salt Lake Tribune* announced: "Their programme is composed of what many musicians consider the only real American folk music, the old plantation songs of the south. All the pathos of the negro's long enslavement, all the joyousness of his character and all the romance he has contributed to the south are expressed in this music and, it is claimed, interpreted with rare musicianship by the Hampton singers."[104] Hampton deployed its media as an agent of the uplift cause; the western trip provided extensive publicity for the institute, and, through the entertainment of music and moving pictures, Hampton spread the uplift message across the country.

As with *John Henry at Hampton, Making Negro Lives Count* caught the attention of the motion picture trade press outside of its appearance at the exposition. The *Moving Picture World* reported on the March 16 screening at the Masonic theater in Louisville, noting that the moving pictures illustrated "the hopelessness of old plantation times as well as the new efficiency made possible by the industrial training" of Hampton. The article goes on to describe the screening: "The program will be divided into three parts. The first will include scenes from the old life—ramshackle cabins, ragged children in the sunlight and the sad old mule dragging by the doorway where the negro woman washes. The second group of the pictures will illustrate the work done at Hampton Institute. The last pictures will show how Hampton graduates carry the message to their own people." G. D. Crain Jr., the Louisville correspondent of the *Moving Picture World*, commented on the "plantation songs" that accompanied the film with language that echoed the tone of Hampton's printed program: they "show 'the soul of the black folk' in its varied moods of wonder, weird despair and irresistible laughter." Noting that the pictures were produced at Hampton, "and naturally appeal strongly to Southern people," the trade magazine proclaimed: "The show will undoubtedly be one of the biggest things in the motion picture line ever handled in this city."[105] This attention by the trade press led to inquiries by theater managers hoping to rent the pictures. For example, H. H. Mack of the Effingham Theatre in Portsmouth, Virginia, wrote to Hampton and was told that "no films for general distribution" were available: "It is an experiment and the school is not yet prepared to distribute them."[106] Determining that it was "not advisable" to permit the general exhibition of the moving pictures, the Hampton administration refused the requests, screening the films primarily for campaign purposes and keeping the moving pictures under their control, as they had with *John Henry at Hampton*.[107] Hampton officials' desire to show the films everywhere—in the context of the campaign program—and their simultaneous unwillingness to permit anyone else to screen them indicate their conceptualization of the motion pictures as a useful component of the larger program, one that depended on such a context for its meaning—at least, the meaning preferred by the institute.

The Hampton authorities had learned a lesson from Tuskegee's example, and they were becoming increasingly aware of the problems that could arise from projecting Hampton's moving pictures outside of the controlled context of the campaign program. The main headline of the *Moving Picture World*'s report on the Louisville screening of *Making Negro Lives Count* was "Pictures That Disturb," referring to the censorship of *The Frank Case* (George K. Rolands, 1915), a five-reel film that advocated for the acquittal of Leo M. Frank, who would eventually be lynched in August 1915.[108] The film was banned from Louisville "on the grounds that the film is contrary to good morals." The *Moving Picture World* reported: "This order stirred up a good deal of interest in moving picture circles as it is the first time in months that any movement has been started or any strong feeling of opposition shown to any moving picture scheduled in the city."[109] Following this account of the suppression of *The Frank Case* came the announcement of *Making Negro Lives Count*. The *Moving Picture World* could not have known that the Hampton moving pictures would also become "pictures that disturb" and thereby gain notoriety — not for the novelty of their southern scenes but for their association with *The Birth of a Nation*.

Hampton's use of moving pictures was an economical means of conveying the practicality of the uplift project. It was fundamentally proactive, as the institute's representatives embraced the medium for its utility and efficacy. Initially conceived of as useful cinema, Hampton's campaign films strategically targeted audiences already sympathetic to the cause of African American agricultural and industrial education. Yet no filmmaking enterprise concerned with issues of race could expect to remain wholly separate and controlled, especially when projected on the national stage. If the films were designed to pictorially showcase Hampton to audiences across the country, Hampton was reflected in those projections. In the case of *The New Era*, the Hampton epilogue appended to *The Birth of a Nation*, Hampton's engagement in the world of dominant commercial cinema starkly revealed the limitations of uplift logic and belied the optimism of the images of African American progress.

4

"A VICIOUS AND HURTFUL PLAY"

The Birth of a Nation and *The New Era*, 1915

———————

In his 1901 autobiography, *Up from Slavery*, Booker T. Washington recalls that around 1877, while he was teaching in Malden, West Virginia, the Ku Klux Klan "was in the height of its activity" during a period that was "the darkest part of the Reconstruction days." He concludes this lone mention of vigilante violence against African Americans in the book by contextualizing it in the now-forgotten past: "I have referred to this unpleasant part of the history of the South simply for the purpose of calling attention to the great change that has taken place since the days of the 'Ku Klux.' To-day there are no such organizations in the South, and the fact that such ever existed is almost forgotten by both races. There are few places in the South now where public sentiment would permit such organizations to exist."[1] Fourteen years later, the release of *The Birth of a Nation* would belie Washington's strategic idealism. In fact, one of the last major issues that he dealt with before his death on November 14,

1915, was orchestrating Tuskegee's responses to the film. Though he would not live to see the rebirth of the Klan on Thanksgiving of that year, following the Leo Frank lynching in Atlanta on August 16, Washington was well aware of the divisive potential of the film.[2]

At least a year prior to *The Birth of a Nation*, Washington had been in various stages of negotiation over the possibility of a film adaptation of *Up from Slavery*. Following the release of D. W. Griffith's film, these efforts were renewed with more vigor, as Emmett J. Scott, Washington's chief aide and personal secretary, also began looking for a producer for *Up from Slavery*.[3] In a letter written in October 1915 to Edwin L. Barker, the general manager of the Advance Motion Picture Company in Chicago, Scott wrote: "It has occurred to me that the Barker-Swan Service might be disposed to consider filming the story of 'Up From Slavery.' I am quite sure that an interesting picture can be made which should include not only Dr. Washington's personal strivings, but also the strivings of the race climbing up from the tragic period represented by slavery in America. I write to inquire if the matter in any way interests you."[4] Scott included a copy of the book as well as reviews, telling Barker that he recently had secured the film rights from Doubleday, Page and Company, the publisher of *Up from Slavery*. These efforts were halted with Washington's death on November 14; a film version of the "Representative Man's" widely read autobiography was never produced.[5]

All that proved moot, as Washington's efforts were overshadowed by controversy surrounding Hampton's response to *The Birth of a Nation*, when the institute cooperated with the National Board of Censorship of Motion Pictures, the industry's self-regulatory body, and the Griffith camp in furnishing moving pictures to be appended to *The Birth of a Nation* as an epilogue under the title *The New Era*.

The New Era was Hampton's answer to the nefarious representation of African Americans in *The Birth of a Nation*. Believing in the persuasive evidence inherent in their films of African American uplift, the institute provided footage taken from *Making Negro Lives Count* to append to Griffith's epic. Contemporary and subsequent criticism has generally described this association as a straightforward mistake, yet Hampton was responding to complex sets of problems and demands. To understand this, we need to consider not only the context of Hampton's own filmmaking project—discussed in chapter 3—but also the broader African American response to *The Birth of a Nation* on its release.

For Black leaders across the political spectrum—from Washington to W. E. B. Du Bois to William Monroe Trotter—the popularity of the film demanded a response, which ranged from letters to legislators, newspapers, and Black leaders through rotten eggs thrown at the screen to full-blown riots. The struggle over censorship of *The Birth of a Nation* has been well documented and marks a significant moment in the history of institutions such as the NAACP.[6] As Thomas Cripps has shown, responses to the film by Tuskegee representatives, the NAACP, and the Black press were overwhelming, but they also presented African American leaders with a dilemma. He sums up the possibilities: "They could ignore the film and its hateful portrayal, knowing not what damage it might do. They could urge censorship. Or, and least likely, they could finance and make their own films propagandizing favorably the role of Negroes in American life."[7] In the months following the release of *The Birth of a Nation*, Carl Laemmle and two employees of the Universal Film Manufacturing Company, Rose Janowitz and Elaine Sterne, began working on a response to Griffith's film (eventually titled *Lincoln's Dream*) with the support of the NAACP and, a little later on, the Tuskegeeans.[8] Indeed, Black filmmakers (such as the Johnson brothers and Oscar Micheaux) would work throughout the following years to counter the damage perpetrated by the film with films of their own. However, overshadowed by attention to the censorship battles and by the subsequent work of African American filmmakers was the immediate attempt to improve the film—in effect, to fix it—by incorporating an uplift film into screenings of the controversial epic. *The New Era* was one strategic response to the problem of prolific filmic racism. Along with debates about the need for Black filmmaking, this "least likely" solution was interwoven with the immediate outcry against the filmic version of Thomas Dixon's novel and stage play *The Clansman*.[9] The idea of "answering film with film" to appease censors, calm protestors, and promote positive images of Black progress was an immediate reaction to *The Birth of a Nation*.[10]

The Birth of a Nation in Boston

Hampton's willingness to furnish its own moving pictures as an appendix to Griffith's spectacle requires contextualization in the broader exhibition circumstances of *The Birth of a Nation*, specifically with regard to its controversial appearance in Boston. From the moment of the film's national debut there were protests against it and pressures placed on local censorship boards to suppress it.[11] When the film premiered in Boston at the Tremont Theatre on April 10, 1915, an organized campaign had already been launched against it, leading to a hearing before Boston Mayor James Michael Curley on April 7. After a preview screening on April 9, the mayor indicated that certain scenes should be cut, and the exhibitors complied to maintain political goodwill.[12] However, they capitalized on the controversy in advertising on the eve of the premiere, announcing that "this is the play agitators will tell you is not fit to be seen in Boston" and quoting from supporters whose "praise completely drowns out [the] antiphony of a few opponents."[13]

Following the Boston premiere of *The Birth of a Nation* at the Tremont Theatre, Philip J. Allston, a member of the National Negro Business League, wrote to Washington describing his encounter with Griffith at the screening. Allston reported that he and his colleague William Alexander Cox, a Black dentist and lawyer, had talked with Griffith in the lobby after the film and that the filmmaker suggested that he wanted to "reproduce in pictures" Tuskegee and was "considering the matter very seriously." Allston told Washington: "I feel no one should be allowed to make capital of Tuskegee, without some financial benefit to the Institution in return financially [*sic*]."[14] This letter was followed a week later, on April 19, by an enraged missive from Samuel Courtney advising the ousting of Allston and Cox for misrepresenting the National Negro Business League in response to the film. Courtney was a former student of Washington's from Hampton who had become a physician in Boston and a member of the Boston Board of Education. He wrote Washington that "these two men voluntarily called upon the management of this photo play and endorsed it, and the general impression is that they represented *you* and *your* sentiments." He urged Washington to ask them to resign from the league: "Mr. Washington, I cannot adequately describe to you the intensity of the feeling against these men today. Since Saturday night it has been considered dangerous for them to show themselves on the street. Not only are they condemned by the colored people but by the whites as well."[15] Cox and Allston were denigrated as "traitors" by a large number of attendees at a protest meeting in Faneuil Hall on April 18.[16]

Washington's response from Tuskegee, however, was measured as far as the censuring of Allston and Cox was concerned. He expressed hesitation in taking explicit action against them, stating that "I have found it always safe not to act in the midst of excitement" and that "freedom of opinion and action is rather tenaciously held to in most parts of the country." He expressed concern about the possibility of inadvertent publicity for the film that public outcry might bring about: "I am satisfied that the same crowd of people who are handling this play were the ones who got up 'The Clansman' and in that case I happen to know in New York and other places they actually paid some colored people to oppose the play for the sake of advertising." However, he encouraged a fight against what he considered the Griffith camp's probable legal preparedness against efforts toward censorship, concluding that "our friends should spare no pains to see to it that they get the best lawyers they can get to take the matter into the courts."[17]

Included in this letter to Courtney, however, is also a telegram that represents Washington's official position on *The Birth of a Nation*:

Have just returned from educational campaign through Louisiana. Did not know Birth of Nation being played in Boston until very recently. From all can hear is vicious and hurtful play. If it cannot be stopped it ought to be modified or changed materially. Best thing would be to stop it as it can result in nothing but stirring up race prejudice. Do not believe play will be permitted in its present form in any of our Southern states. Glad to hear people in Boston are against play and hope their efforts to stop it will be successful. Particularly unfortunate to have this play at present time when we were entering upon era of good racial feeling throughout country such as we have not experienced lately.[18]

Subsequent correspondence indicates Washington's general approval of the various steps toward censorship that were undertaken in Boston and Chicago.

Although this effort would eventually coalesce around *The New Era*, curiously it was not the first addition to the film. *The Birth of a Nation* had undergone various—and varied—edits to appease protestors, but there was also a major attempt to improve it with the addition of educational slides. In Boston, where the film premiered on April 10, Mayor Curley held a meeting on April 12 at which Charles Fleischer, a prominent Boston rabbi, suggested to the Tremont Theatre managers that they incorporate in the screening "the vital facts of the negro's real progress since emancipation," believing the suppression of the film to be "undemocratic and un-American." Fleischer stated: "I would like to urge strongly upon the producers that they present a series of pictures, in connection with their play, which shall tell the story of the progress of the negro from the date of the birth of our Nation in 1865 up to date. The play thus enlarged appeals to me as a far-reaching opportunity to serve not only the cause of the negro, but likewise the Nation as a whole." Fleischer positioned *The Birth of a Nation* as an educational opportunity, arguing that it could be used to allow the whole nation to see the advancement of African Americans and their demonstrated progress from slavery to the contemporary moment. Fleischer's optimism hinged on the broad exhibition of *The Birth of a Nation*, far beyond the limited reach of champions of the "Negro cause."[19]

Fleischer's proposal was submitted to Griffith, who was reportedly "so interested" that he began planning for such an addition.[20] From New York, Griffith wired Joseph J. McCarthy, business manager for *The Birth of a Nation*, concerning the additional materials to be added to the film, including images demonstrating the "progress of the negro race since the Civil War" and "astonishing facts and figures" demonstrating "negro advancement."[21] On April 16, "title material" was added to screenings of the film to chronicle "the record of advancement" of African Americans. The material included the names of key figures like Frederick Douglass "in statesmanship," Booker T. Washington "in education," W. E. B. Du Bois "in oratory and philosophy," Henry O. Tanner "in art," and Paul Lawrence Dunbar "in poetry."[22]

It is unclear if this "screen record" was composed of simple text intertitles or if it also included photographs, but it certainly did not include moving pictures.[23] According to the *Boston Globe*, the addition was made "a permanent part of the picture" and "completed the story from the time the negro as shown in the first part of the picture was brought in chains from Africa up to the present, when he has developed extraordinary resource and skill in the arts, professions, crafts and agriculture." The inserts demonstrating "the marvelous record" were reportedly "heartily applauded" by Boston audiences.[24] The newspaper reported that the titles were added at the suggestion of Fleischer and other "friends of the play," who "felt that while the tale of carpetbagger and negro excesses during Reconstruction as pictured by Mr. Griffith was true to history, yet in fairness the wonderful advances made since Reconstruction should also be presented."[25] These "advances" were conveyed through the additional titles that interrupted rather than altered the course of the narrative. They were inserted "naturally" following the reported "series of historical events" in the film's opening scenes on the introduction of slavery to America, extending through the Civil War and "the troubles between the Southern whites and the carpetbaggers and negroes after the war."[26] Thus, the added titles would have followed the "disunion" caused by the introduction of slavery and the agitation of abolitionists "demanding" emancipation but come before the introduction of the principal characters.

These efforts did not satisfy the film's critics. On the one hand, the "screen record" would have lent veracity to the preceding scenes; on the other hand, the length of the ensuing drama would have overwhelmed the brief interlude of facts and figures. Although Mayor Curley had requested the removal of the intertitle "The bringing of the African to America planted the first seed of disunion," that was the only cut made to the opening.[27] This is an important point. There is a significant shot, missing in surviving prints of *The Birth of a Nation*, that was one of the most contested parts of the film in 1915. In the abolitionist meeting in the film's opening sequence, the shot of the abolitionist preacher taking the young Black boy through the congregation is intercut with a shot of "a motherly looking old lady" who, according to a review in the *Moving Picture World*, "stretches out her arms in sympathy toward the child, but immediately repulses him with every manifestation of disgust caused by the odor which we must assume the boy carries around with him."[28] This shot was removed from some screenings, but there is no evidence to suggest that it was cut in Boston when the "screen record" was added.[29] If the abolitionists' empathy for the child is undercut by the gestures of the repulsed woman, the progress stated by the added intertitles could not have addressed the visceral distaste for proximity to African Americans that the woman represents. The "screen record" might deal with the intellectual claims about history, but not with the deep-seated emotional impulses and commitments that allowed these claims to flourish—and that *The Birth of a Nation* advanced. History "written by lightning" is no so easily unwritten or repaired.[30]

With or without this lost shot, the insertion of the "screen record" inter-titles at this particular juncture in *The Birth of a Nation* raises many questions. The opening sequence sets the historical precedent for the unfolding drama to come, yet the inserted titles speak to the contemporary audience of the demonstrated "progress" of the vilified African Americans—a confusing gesture when set between the abolitionist meeting and the Civil War and Reconstruction. The ambiguity—even illegibility—of this sequencing indicates the ineffectiveness of the "screen record." This example also points to the semantic instability of *The Birth of a Nation* itself. In the abolitionist meeting scene, a hollow-eyed preacher leads an African American child through the meeting toward the camera (figure 4.1).[31] However brief, this is a haunting image, in which the man displays the child for the camera while the child confronts the spectator with a direct gaze. If this is the last scene before the insertion of the "screen record," how would it change with that addition? How is the reading of this image of the child affected by the adjacency of statistics on "negro progress"? Is the implication that the child grows up to be a post-Reconstruction hero? Does he go from being an abolitionist poster boy (Frederick Douglass) to the early twentieth-century liberal patron's accommodating ally (Booker T. Washington)? Without the insertion of the possible alternative destinies for the child, is he implicitly cast by Griffith as a proto-Gus? Or a proto-primitive legislator? And what of the abolitionist? Is he presented as being responsible for the crimes that will unfold in the drama? Is he offering up the child to the camera and, by extension, to the spectator? Or is he challenging the spectator to, in effect, deal with this "problem"? Is the film articulating the moment of transition from the assertion of the "Negro as person" to the "Negro as problem"?[32]

FIG. 4.1 *The Birth of a Nation* (D. W. Griffith, 1915).

Of course, how a spectator might understand the opening depends on his or her own subject position. Regardless, the ambiguity created by the insertion of the "screen record" undermines its own claims to historical truth. If the "screen record" purports to demonstrate how the problem has been solved, or at least signals that progress has been made, this is undone by the way the semantic power and instability of Griffith's film renders those claims problematic. As the drama unfolds, the progress rolls back and belies the veracity of the inserts.[33] With three hours of narrative drama to go, the "screen record" would likely be a distant memory—if even that—by the film's conclusion.

Although *The Birth of a Nation* was protested and fought from its initial appearance in Boston, it was not until after the addition of the "screen record" of "negro advancement" that protests reached a critical mass. The *Boston Daily Globe* announced this in a front-page article with the headline "'Birth of Nation' Causes Near-Riot."[34] The managing editor of the African American newspaper the *Boston Guardian*, William Monroe Trotter—a prominent figure connected to the NAACP but considered too radical to be a central member of the organization—led the protest against the film, reprising the campaign he had mounted against Dixon's play in 1905. On the night of April 17, Trotter and a group of followers attempted to purchase tickets at the Tremont Theatre and were refused on the ground that the film was sold out. However, Trotter claimed that white patrons were able to purchase tickets. The theater was in fact acting on rumors that a Black mob intended to seize and destroy the film and had enlisted the protection of plainclothes police officers. Several protestors were able to enter the theater, and during particularly offensive scenes they released stink bombs in the theater and assaulted the screen with rotten eggs. Jane Gaines has extensively discussed the practice of throwing rotten eggs at the screen, focusing on the Boston incident, in which she considers the political strategy and "hermeneutic act" of egg throwing. She writes: "The separation between the world of the audience and the world of the screen is dramatized by the egg that is directed at race hatred in the world but hits the motion picture screen instead."[35] The Boston egg thrower, Charles P. Ray, threw fresh eggs and "odoriferous bombs" at the screen until he was arrested.[36] Although the egging occurred around the Gus chase scene, the eggs could also be understood as directly engaging with the moving picture itself; the visual and olfactory assault on the screen answered the visualized olfactory insult of the abolitionist scene.

There is no direct evidence that the inserts catalyzed the protests, but it is clear that they were not enough to stop them. Trotter reportedly objected to the apparent ignoring of Mayor Curley's negotiated deal with the producers to edit out the most offensive scenes, claiming that the parts "had been enlarged rather than reduced."[37] Although the edits were not made consistently or with precision, the only certain addition to the film at this point was the "screen record," so Trotter's objection might very well have included the material added to show this image of African American progress. It is not clear that anyone thought the "screen record" worked well. An editorial in the *Fitchburg Daily Sentinel* called the added statistics of progress "a miserable apology," stating that "tables of statistics do not appeal to the imaginative like moving pictures."[38] The paper called for "some representation of negro valor, fidelity and patriotism, of which there are ample illustrations."[39]

The protests intensified on April 19, when nearly 2,000 people gathered on the Boston Common in front of the State House as Trotter and his associates met with Governor David I. Walsh (figure 4.2).[40] For several days, Walsh had been negotiating with the moderate politician and lawyer William H. Lewis, who had served as the nation's first African American assistant attorney general and was an ally of Washington, and Butler R. Wilson, a member of the NAACP. Lewis had decided both to pursue legal action against *The Birth of a Nation* and to push for a new state censorship law.[41] Given hopeful signs from the statehouse, further protests were delayed.

THE PROTEST ON BOSTON COMMON
Courtesy of *Boston Post*

FIG. 4.2 *Crisis*, June 1915, 88.

All evidence suggests that the inserted "screen record" was never imagined as anything other than a temporary solution until moving pictures could be furnished to supplement further showings of *The Birth of a Nation* at the Tremont Theatre. In the midst of the protests, the *Boston Globe* announced on April 18 that the theater "expected to add to the play this week the supplemental film being prepared by Mr. Griffith, showing the progress of the negro race since reconstruction and thus rounding out the great cycle of historical events from slavery until now."[42] On April 20, the managers of the Tremont Theatre announced that they were in compliance with the law and that the requested edits had been made. However, throughout the film's run in Boston, there were conflicting accounts regarding the consistency of the changes, with some people claiming that the objectionable scenes had been left in or, as Lewis commented, "The 'Gus' scene is worse now than it was before they changed it" (which may be what Trotter was referring to as well).[43] On April 21, Judge Thomas H. Dowd ruled on the censorship of the film in the Municipal Court, effectively overturning Mayor Curley's requests for numerous edits and requiring only one cut:

There is one scene which is offensive and immoral. This is the scene where the renegade and degenerate negro, "Gus," pursues a child of 12 years, with an expression upon his face which leaves no doubt of his state of mind. There is not any question of his purpose in pursuing the white girl; he is plainly actuated by the lowest passions of mankind. This would be the same were he a white man.

This is the only scene which in my mind is covered by the statutes. There is nothing else in the play covered by the statutes. I have no doubt that parts of it are more or less disgusting to colored people; but there is nothing in the statutes which covers them.[44]

For many people, the titles demonstrating "negro progress" underscored the "negro problem" that Rabbi Fleischer insisted would be the result of "a wonderful achievement—whether measured pictorially, dramatically and historically." Fleischer asserted that *The Birth of a Nation* would "fairly force Americans to face the negro problem and to work toward its wise and just solution."[45] Lewis objected to Fleisher's logic, asking: "Why should I be a problem to any man? I am a problem only to the man who seeks to take away my rights as a human being, and to such a man the negro must be a problem."[46] Members of *The Birth of a Nation* camp did not see the "screen record" as salt poured into the wounds caused by the film's more offensive scenes; rather, they sought to, in effect, double down: to expand on the counterbalancing "progress" material with supplemental motion pictures and hence do away with objections once and for all. To this end, in addition to the "screen record" demonstrating the progress of African American citizens, on April 21 the Tremont Theatre premiered what the *Boston Journal* reported to be "pictorial scenes further illustrating their progress" (figure 4.3).[47] These new images were added as a coda to the film under the title *The New Era*.

The Hampton Epilogue: *The New Era*

Despite widespread reports, the epilogue was not in fact filmed by Griffith but was furnished by Hampton Institute from its publicity arsenal. The sheer fact of Hampton's role in this enterprise is intriguing and curious. Yet however perplexing, the actions of Hampton's representatives were entirely consistent with the logic of uplift media that they employed and embraced. Uplift media presumed the persuasiveness of the image as evidence of the guided progress of the race and the ability for individual and collective transformation. Hampton's media arsenal (containing texts, photographs, moving images, and songs) was designed to counter negative representations and prejudicial impressions of African Americans with demonstrations of the impact of uplift education.

FIG. 4.3 *Boston Journal,*
April 21, 1915. Courtesy
Trustees of the Boston
Public Library.

PRODUCER OF "BIRTH OF A NATION"

DAVID W. GRIFFITH
Who staged the great photo-play which is objected to by Boston
negroes.

The institute provided the "after" to the "before." That logic would prove to
be greatly flawed—indeed, *The New Era* publicly revealed these flaws—and
Hampton officials faced a tremendous backlash to their efforts to improve the
misrepresentation of African Americans in Griffith's epic through an uplift
film appended to it.

Initially, Hampton became involved at the behest of William G. Willcox and
Frank Trumbull, two prominent New Yorkers who were Tuskegee trustees. On
April 10, the same day that *The Birth of a Nation* opened in Boston, Hampton
faculty members discussed a telegram sent by Willcox and Trumbull asking
for moving pictures of Hampton that would show "the progress of the Negro
race and the work being done at Hampton and Tuskegee so as to offset the unfortunate effects so far as the Negro is concerned, of the moving picture play
entitled 'Birth of a Nation.'"[48] No records survive to indicate how the Tuske-

gee trustees became involved in the first place, but they had consulted with William Jay Schieffelin, a Hampton trustee, and come up with the idea of adding the Hampton pictures.[49] The faculty had also received a telegram from William D. McGuire Jr., the executive secretary of the National Board of Censorship of Motion Pictures, indicating the board's interest in appending the Hampton films to *The Birth of a Nation* "throughout the leading theatres of the country."[50] Four days later, the board requested two reels of Hampton pictures.

Why would the censorship board have sought to augment *The Birth of a Nation* with footage from Hampton? What interest would its members have had in changing the structure of a popular film? To understand their motives, it is necessary to briefly discuss the organization and its objectives. The board was formed in 1909 as an industry self-regulatory body aimed at deterring calls for official censorship of films and the impositions of greater state and federal governmental control over motion picture exhibitions.[51] As Lee Grieveson has shown, it was also an effort to stave off the charge by the recently formed Motion Picture Patents Company that any perception of the cinema as immoral or licentious was the fault of exhibitors. Grieveson writes: "A struggle emerged between exhibitors and producers who, although united on some level in the necessity of responding to regulatory discourses and practices, were divided as to the proper course of action—with producers suggesting theater space was the problem and exhibitors suggesting film content was responsible for the troubles besetting the industry."[52] In response to these concerns, exhibitors worked with the People's Institute, a progressive civic organization, in founding the National Board of Censorship of Motion Pictures to serve as a voluntary review mechanism for the industry. The People's Institute was friendly to motion pictures (and hostile to the monopolistic Motion Picture Patents Company), seeing the potential for the medium to aid in social reform endeavors and provide a wholesome alternative to the allures of urban vice. The censorship board quickly became a national organization that reviewed up to 85 percent of the films produced for commercial exhibition. Shelley Stamp argues that, as it was lacking in legal authority, the board exerted what its chairman, Frederic C. Howe, called "moral coercion": instead of suppressing objectionable films, the board sought to intervene in the portrayal of "delicate issues" and thereby improve the overall quality of films.[53] This largely had to do with public morals. To this end, films featuring vice did so within a moralizing frame and could thereby arguably serve an educational purpose; *Traffic in Souls* (George Loane Tucker, Universal Film Manufacturing Company, 1913) and other so-called white slavery films were a case in point. When such films neglected a punishment or redemption in the conclusion or "the heavy-handed sermonizing" that Stamp describes as important to the censors, they left themselves open to broader objections.[54] As Grieveson notes, by associating with the People's Institute, exhibitors "succeeded in aligning an influential reform organization with a commercial strategy of 'uplift.'"[55]

Championing the cinema as an agent of broad social uplift thus was good business for producers and exhibitors. After all, it did not require a change in the content of a film but rather its narrative framing.[56] And it was this logic that brought the censorship board in line with the project of African American uplift rhetoric. As I argued in chapter 1, the rhetoric of uplift employed a model in which the structure and organization of the presented material was designed to shape reception of the educational institutes' message. Indeed, with its use of and emphasis on a before-and-after structure, the rhetorical strategy of uplift became, in effect, the message itself. As the board's members viewed motion pictures as "an agent which can educate," linked to the social improvement of its audience, it makes sense that they would see the Hampton pictures as didactic and edifying.[57] Though coming from widely different realms, the board and the Hampton Institute shared an investment in the educational potential and useful capacity of moving pictures. Both, then, saw the addition of *The New Era* to *The Birth of a Nation* as a logical step. If moving pictures had what Constance D. Leupp, a prominent reformer, termed "the double duty of holding interest and giving instruction," then *The New Era* could be the instructional component of the unequivocally interesting epic (the quality of whose own instructional capacity was virulently debated, if its effectiveness was not).[58]

Plans were quickly put in place. Hollis B. Frissell and Leigh Richmond Miner, both in New York at the time, met with the censorship board. Frissell expressed his "strong disapprobation" of *The Birth of a Nation* but was told, as he later recounted, that "it would be impossible to discontinue it and that no court would take action against it."[59] In his annual principal's report (published in May 1915 and probably written around the time he was deliberating about adding the Hampton pictures), Frissell wrote: "Thousands of people in New York City are now attending a moving-picture show called 'The Birth of a Nation,' which presents an utterly false and abhorrent picture of Negro life. The papers of the country dwell upon the crimes of the Negro race, but not upon its progress. It seems incumbent upon schools like Hampton to help people realize that under proper conditions the Negro can be fitted for Christian citizenship."[60] Frissell consulted with several Hampton trustees and sent Miner to Boston to work with the censorship board on the materials. On behalf of the board, McGuire requested 1,800 feet—two reels—and Miner worked with him to furnish the material.[61] On April 20, the faculty voted to approve the use of

Hampton's motion pictures in conjunction with *The Birth of a Nation*.[62] However, the faculty approval was either a formality or a gesture revealing the misguided presumption of their authority, as it came just one day before the first showing of *The New Era* in Boston on April 21 at the Tremont Theatre (figures 4.4 and 4.5). This timeline indicates that plans were already well under way to include the Hampton footage as a supplement to the "screen record." At best, the Hampton epilogue was a rushed attempt to address the protests, calls for censorship, and legal challenges to *The Birth of a Nation* in Boston, carried out with little deliberation or discussion.

The day that *The New Era* premiered, McGuire wrote to the progressive philanthropist and Hampton trustee George Foster Peabody, stating that "we believe that the Hampton pictures will go a long ways toward correcting unfortunate impressions given by 'The Birth of a Nation.'"[63] He also offered Peabody tickets to the Tremont Theatre, saying that the Hampton pictures had been "substituted" for the scene depicting the deportation of African Americans to Liberia, reportedly with the intertitle "Lincoln's Solution," "giving Hampton Institute large credit for the work being accomplished there and indicating that the industrial education of the Negro is the important solution to the race problem confronting the South."[64] The exclusion of the deportation segment is not certain, but McGuire's letter suggests that the Hampton epilogue was considered, at least by the censorship board, to be a substitute conclusion—and thereby solution—to the racialized problem articulated by *The Birth of a Nation*.

The New Era was pieced together from the last section of *Making Negro Lives Count*, the sequence depicting Hampton's departments and the community improvements made by its graduates. Aside from its length, we do not know how much of the final section of *Making Negro Lives Count* was actually used, but given the speed with which it was brought to Boston and exhibited, it is doubtful that major edits were made. The before, during, and after segments appeared to give *Making Negro Lives Count* a modular structure, allowing for the easy reappropriation of the last section. However, the pieces of the before-and-after structure of *Making Negro Lives Count* were necessarily linear and relied on the other segments and exhibition context for their meaning.[65] Although *Making Negro Lives Count* was made to be used as a campaign film, it was adapted to serve another function when excerpted to append to *The Birth of a Nation*. Along with this recontextualization came new—and higher—stakes. *Making Negro Lives Count* conveyed its message in a controlled and carefully planned context, with clarifying speeches, illustrative songs, and a receptive audience. In contrast, *The New Era* was expected to speak for itself

FIG. 4.4 Cover of the Tremont Theatre program, week of April 26, 1915. Collection of the author.

and to serve as a counterargument for the preceding three-hour motion picture epic. In effect, the epilogue tried to make *The Birth of a Nation* as a whole into an uplift film, subsuming it in the greater logic of uplift: Griffith was to be the before to Hampton's after.

The position of *The New Era* as an after is generated by its image of a farming family, an image that emphasizes the uplift ideal of self-help. Before turning to the impact of *The New Era*, the logic of its proponents and criticism of its detractors, it is worth considering how the epilogue might have formally functioned in the larger context of *The Birth of a Nation*, and how it informed and was informed by its preceding scenes. This is not a simple task, given that—as we have seen—*The Birth of a Nation* itself was an unstable text, subject to the demands of censors, whims of exhibitors, and suggestions of legislators.

How might the end of *The New Era*, with its final scene of "happy home life," have functioned as a coda to *The Birth of a Nation*?[66] Although the "screen record" intertitles from the prologue of the film might be forgotten by the end,

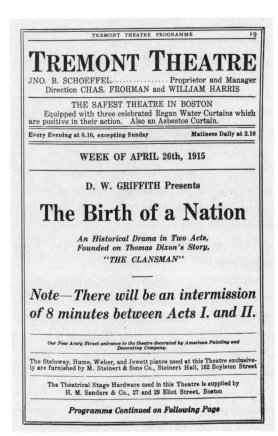

FIG. 4.5 Title page of the
Tremont Theatre program,
week of April 26, 1915.
Collection of the author.

the image of an African American farmer father and his family in *Making
Negro Lives Count* would now serve as the final word to the epic, an emblem of
sorts—or a tableau. If this scene was in fact included in *The New Era*, it would
represent a remarkable parallel with the conclusion of *The Birth of a Nation*. On
the surface the echoed ending seems to propose an African American equiva-
lent to the white domestic ideal that concludes Griffith's film. However, there is
a deep asymmetry: the double honeymoon scene in Griffith's film comes only
after a rapid sequence of events following the climax of the film—the ride of
the Klan—a context that troubles any reading of parallelism. After the parade
of the Klansmen, a title announces "The next election," and a brief scene follows in which African Americans emerge from their homes on voting day,
only to be met by a wall of mounted and armed Klansmen who intimidate
them into retreating back into their homes. The next title, "The Aftermath.
At the sea's edge, the double honeymoon," announces the unions of Margaret
and Phil and Ben and Elsie. This is followed by superimposed shots of "bestial

War" being defeated by "the gentle Prince in the Hall of Brotherly Love in the City of Peace," intercut with Ben and Elsie, before the final intertitle "Liberty and union, one and inseparable, now and forever!" If there was a parallel in the form of the endings of *The New Era* and *The Birth of a Nation*, then, the same was not true of the content provided. The last shots including African Americans in surviving prints of *The Birth of a Nation* appear in the sequence of voter intimidation. Thus, *The New Era* in effect appears not as a mirror of domestic bliss but as an implied consequence of the voter intimidation. It shows African Americans back on the farm and contained in a domestic frame: after three hours of the threat of miscegenation, Hampton's domestic scene suggests not a parallel force but a neutralized Black threat. Instead of contradicting Griffith's presentation of history, *The New Era* legitimizes its thesis—however unwittingly—by positing the uplift project as a logical extension of, rather than a challenge to, the white supremacy advocated by the film.

There is still another aspect to the epilogue at work here. The ambitions of *The New Era* are further complicated by its adjacency to another part of the conclusion of *The Birth of a Nation*, a deportation scene that does not exist in surviving prints. Reportedly, following the intertitle "Lincoln's Solution," there were shots of the mass deportation of African Americans to Liberia.[67] This scene was cut out of the 1921 re-release but apparently left intact in most prints in 1915, and it is unclear if it was shown in Boston.[68] If the deportation scene was there, it poses an interesting possibility for *The New Era*—allowing Hampton to refute (or at the very least replace) *The Birth of a Nation*'s proposed solution of the mass deportation of African Americans. In this case, the Hampton footage would argue not just that African Americans were useful citizens, but—more fundamentally—that they were viable Americans.

The most thorough account of an early screening of *The New Era* comes from a Boston spectator, a veteran of the Union army, who wrote a letter to the *Boston Journal* praising *The Birth of a Nation* as an illustration of events that should serve as a history lesson. The presumably white author, C. F. Lothrop of Everett, Massachusetts, described the end of the film this way: "The last scene shows pictures and statistics to show the great advance made by the negroes in every desirable way since the Civil War. They should be proud of it and glad to see it portrayed in the moving picture medium. But it is necessary to show their early unlovely, brutal but unfortunate conditions as newly freed slaves to teach by contrast what any freed people can do."[69] Lothrop's account of the epilogue suggests that the "screen record" was moved from the opening of the film and placed at the end with the Hampton pictures.[70] It also rehearses the narrative logic of the before-and-after structure that the inclusion of the Hampton footage created. Additionally, Lothrop's account demonstrates the seamless integration of the new footage with Griffith's epic; without an overt indication of difference in authorship, production context, or film stock, the epilogue seemed to be the logical and consistent conclusion to the drama just witnessed.

Members of the Griffith camp duly absorbed *The New Era* into their repertoire of counterarguments against critics. In response to a letter from A. E. Pillsbury of Boston that denounced *The Birth of a Nation* in the *Boston Journal*, Joseph J. McCarthy wrote a detailed rebuttal that was published alongside Pillsbury's complaint. Without indicating its independence from *The Birth of a Nation*, McCarthy points to the Hampton epilogue as evidence of the film's commitment to "national unity":

> The producers of "The Birth of a Nation" are not trying for a repeal of the 14th and 15th Amendments. They are not insidiously attempting to bring back slavery (the very thought provokes a smile), and they are not actuated by political motives. They do not share Mr. Dixon's radical view of a future Liberia for American negroes; over against the imaginative scene of the great Liberia once dreamed of by Lincoln is displayed the happy recount of negro progress and prosperity since the war. And any schoolboy could have told Mr. Pillsbury that the depiction of the antics and excesses of recently freed negroes, as shown in the play during Reconstruction times, does not in any manner indict or malign the negro of today.[71]

This logic was pervasive, and it did not just come from those in the Griffith camp. Unwittingly echoing this line of argument in his call for censoring the film, Washington stated: "The play is fundamentally wrong in that it attempts to deal with the development of America since the abolition of slavery by ignoring the substantial progress of the Negro race and emphasizing the cruel misunderstandings of the readjustment period, in which unfortunate individuals of both races figured."[72] According to this logic, the Hampton epilogue would mitigate the damage perpetrated by the film's account of history because it provided that crucial after demanded by narrative logic: without *The New Era*, offense; with it, uplift. Furthermore, the publicity garnered from the wide distribution of *The Birth of a Nation* and the film's tremendous popularity with audiences catapulted Hampton into a far wider arena than that of its typical audience. Hampton authorities considered both the uplift logic and the widespread publicity to be irrefutable justifications for their involvement with an otherwise deplorable popular spectacle. They welcomed the opportunity to, in effect, correct the preceding misrepresentation even if in so doing they (inadvertently) reinforced rather than refuted it.

With its high profile as both a cinematic achievement and a flashpoint for race debate, *The Birth of a Nation* elicited strong and often emotional responses. Many people turned to Washington, as the nation's preeminent Black leader, for decisive action. On May 3, Jesse Harris, a Hampton alumnus and president of the Hampton Alumni Association, wrote to Washington from Boston concerning the struggle against the film, imagining the mobilized African American response as the catalyzing force against factionalism. Harris was active in the campaign against *The Birth of a Nation* and told Washington: "I saw in my mind a meeting in this city in the Old Liberty Hall—the speakers Washington, Walters, Du Bois—Trotter and others—where all things of the past would be buried. And a race of Ten Millions of Negroes would be united. A Nation would *really* be *Born*."[73] Harris optimistically saw the possibility of a unified fight against *The Birth of a Nation* and was encouraged by a telegram of support from Washington that had reached him during the screening.[74]

June was an intense month for Washington in regard to *The Birth of a Nation*, and it ended with a letter that he sent to Florence E. Sewell Bond, a former cataloger at the Carnegie Library at Tuskegee who had moved to Boston and heard rumors that Washington would allow images of Tuskegee to be screened along with *Birth of a Nation*.[75] Her "friendly warning" implied—incorrectly, as Washington knew—that Lewis approved of Griffith's film. Washington replied that he had "no idea" of permitting any pictures of Tuskegee to be shown in connection with *The Birth of a Nation*. He continued: "We have been appealed to to make such an exhibit but have refused on the grounds that such an exhibit would be an indirect endorsement of The Birth of a Nation. We consider The Birth of a Nation a thoroughly harmful and vicious play, and want to do everything possible to prevent its being exhibited. I feel quite sure that you have been misinformed regarding the attitude of Mr. William H. Lewis. He is thoroughly opposed to the play, as I know."[76] Although Washington presented his position as having refused to allow Tuskegee footage to be appended to *The Birth of a Nation*, he nonetheless encouraged Hampton's involvement.

This is a curious inconsistency in Washington's position that we should not overlook. Why did the Tuskegee board members approach Hampton for the moving pictures? Why did they not try to produce the material themselves? The answer underscores the complexity of the uplift project and the political navigation required to intercede in the *Birth of a Nation* controversy. Washington himself was on an educational campaign in Louisiana and out of reach until the 23rd, at which point he wrote the telegram calling *The Birth of a Nation* a "vicious and hurtful play." Although Washington told Bond that Tuskegee refused to offer moving pictures to be added to *The Birth of a Nation*, he said nothing of the Tuskegee trustees' encouragement of Hampton's involvement. Two things are significant here: first, Tuskegee was not in a position to provide motion pictures, as they did not retain control over the moving pictures shot of the institute; and second, Washington exhibited greater media savvy—owing to his experience on the national political stage—than the Hampton authorities, who operated on the seemingly straightforward logic of uplift. But there is likely a third, even more important, reason Washington turned to Hampton: people there knew uplift cinema in a way that Tuskegee officials did not. As discussed in chapter 2, the two films that were shot at Tuskegee in 1909 and 1913 were not under direct control of the institute but were made through vexed partnerships with northern Black filmmaking entrepreneurs. The Tuskegee films also had significant technical flaws that prevented them from being an economic success and even from reaching a broad audience. Hampton had done much better cinematic work. Washington may have known how the national political discourse worked, but Hampton was a place where they knew how to do cinema—and how to do cinema in the service of African American uplift. It made complete sense that Hampton would have been the go-to place for uplift cinema (the fact that it provided political cover for Washington was of course an additional benefit).

From its first appearance on April 21, *The New Era* was shown with *The Birth of a Nation* throughout its Boston run at the Tremont Theatre. The Hampton epilogue was so integrated into *The Birth of a Nation* that the theater listing for the Tremont Theatre in the *Boston Daily Globe* during June and July 1915 conflated the Hampton footage with the fictional epic. For example, the listing from June 8 described Griffith's film as follows: "The story takes up the theme of National growth from the introduction of slavery 300 years ago to the awful struggle between the North and the South and the troubles of reconstruction, and its final course shows the wonderful advances made by the ex-slaves in their 40 years' progress since reconstruction times."[77] On June 27, an extended plot summary concludes: "it shows how Aryan supremacy was finally won, the North and the South were reconciled, and under the new arrangement the negro, who had been the object of these struggles, made wonderful advances in progress and prosperity."[78] On July 4, of all days, the announcement for the film went so far as to suggest that *The New Era* itself provides the key to the meaning of the title, *The Birth of a Nation*. This plot summary reads: "The story travels with the main currents of American history following the immortal Declaration of July 4, 1776; shows as by succession of lightning flashes, the titanic conflicts that rent North and South in twain; exhibits the comedy, pathos annd [*sic*] romance of the old South reconstruction and, after an eloquent indictment of the horrors of war and a happy picture of the recent progress of the negroes, shows America reborn, a new Nation out of that awful nine years' struggle of 1861–70."[79] In these plot summaries, *The New Era* is simply incorporated into Griffith's epic as its conclusion.

Though the Hampton epilogue was regularly screened in Boston, when it was sent to other cities it was not always shown. Washington himself wrote in private correspondence in May 1915 that the Hampton pictures were not being consistently shown in New York City, commenting: "I was surprised to learn that the moving picture people are not keeping faith with Hampton and do not show the Hampton pictures regularly. It seems they do not show them [*sic*] only when the spirit moves them."[80] Still, *The New Era* was seen as a means of thwarting potential protest and was in circulation through the entire first run of *The Birth of a Nation*; it was even on the print that screened in the 1922 re-release in New York.[81] The film screened in Baltimore in February 1916 with *The New Era*, mentioned in the local press as "an epilogue showing the negro of today as he is being taught at Hampton."[82] When the film was shown in Harrisburg, Pennsylvania, in February 1916, one local paper noted that the police were on hand "to quell any outbreak" and that, along with the police presence, "the promoters have taken the precaution to soothe any wounded feelings by concluding the picture show with views of Hampton Institute and other colored institutions along with proof of the wonderful development made by the colored race since the dark days of reconstruction."[83] When the film played in a regional theater outside Boston in September, the local paper quoted a press agent for *The Birth of a Nation*, who stated that the opposition to the film was "unreasonable" given that the "showing of the carpetbagger and the negro excesses during the reconstruction period is counter balanced by the marvelous depiction of the colored man's progress since reconstruction particularly where the scenes at Hampton Institute are shown."[84] It suited the proponents of *The Birth of a Nation* to absorb *The New Era* completely into the epic, though this was not always the case. The Chicago censorship board challenged the presumption of cohesiveness that was being asserted by the surrounding discourse.

Following its Boston and New York runs, *The Birth of a Nation* opened in Chicago in June 1915, despite efforts to suppress it. *The New Era* was denied an exhibition permit in Chicago on the ground that it was not part of the film initially submitted to the censors for approval. This fact was reported with some amusement by the *Boston Daily Globe*: "'The Birth of a Nation' is now being shown in Chicago, and what do you think the censors have made 'em cut out? Well, the after-part showing the colored race's advancement. A technicality is responsible."[85] The municipal censors rejected the argument that *The New Era* was part of *The Birth of a Nation*, recognizing that it functioned instead as an attempt to circumvent censorship. McCarthy alleged that the municipal authorities were disingenuous in their concern about the representation of African Americans. Objecting to the actions taken by Major Metellus Lucullus Cicero Funkhouser, head of the Chicago censor board, McCarthy argued:

The city authorities say they are concerned for the negro. That is the reason they give for objecting to the photoplay.

But there must be another explanation. Otherwise they would be anxious to have us show "The New Era." We prepared this part of the picture at the request of the trustees of Hampton and Tuskegee institutes. But when we asked permission to exhibit it Maj. Funkhouser said "Nothing doing."

"The New Era" gives a vivid impression of the progress of the race. It shows that in the last fifty years since the passing of the carpet bagger and his trail of evil influences over the colored people their wealth has increased from $17,000,000 to $300,000,000.

It shows how Hampton institute is making valuable citizens. It shows the agricultural advance of the race. It exhibits progressive types of colored men and women. In fact, it is a tribute to the qualities of the race and their capabilities for industrial and social progress. Yet Maj. Funkhouser won't let us show it.[86]

Judge William Fenimore Cooper issued an injunction against the city, effectively overturning its censorship of the film. Although his opinion did not explicitly mention *The New Era*, Cooper noted that "the negro race has advanced almost immeasurably" since the period depicted in Griffith's drama, an assertion conveyed by *The Birth of a Nation* through the inclusion of the Hampton epilogue.[87] The trade journal *Motography* lauded Cooper's decision, noting that the city had argued that the film was libelous of Black citizens but that argument was undermined by the inclusion of *The New Era*:

At the request of two negro institutes a picture entitled "The New Era" was prepared and arranged to run as a postlude to "The Birth of a Nation." This postlude shows the development of the negro race and the important part it is taking in modern civilization. Apparently the censors should have welcomed it—doubly so after they had been enjoined from interfering with the master film. Did they receive it in all sincerity as a solution of their difficulty? They did not. Those powerful and intelligent arbiters of the people's rights refused to allow "The New Era" to be shown, on the ground that it was not a part of "The Birth of a Nation" when a permit was granted for that film. And they refused to issue a separate permit for it. Is that judicial action, or is it small-minded retaliation for defeat? What better evidence can we ask [for] of the quality of our "censors"—those vested with the sacred and responsible duty of protecting the public morals—than that they refuse to do a good act because they resent being caught in a bad one?[88]

It is not clear if *The New Era* was included in Judge Cooper's decision or if it ever was shown in Chicago. However, in at least one case, the Hampton pictures were explicitly treated as part of *The Birth of a Nation* rather than as a separate film. When *The Birth of a Nation* was banned in Ohio in early October 1915, Charles G. Williams, the chairman of the Ohio Board of Censors, listed the board's objections to the film and concluded: "It is also true that there are a few scenes on the end of the last reel of said film that show the colored race in a favorable light. But to my mind, after considering all that has gone before, it is similar to forcing a very nauseating concoction down the throat of a man and then giving him a grain of sugar to take the taste out of his mouth."[89] The socialist leader Eugene V. Debs wrote, referring to the "screen record" that was moved to the end of *The Birth of a Nation* with the addition of *The New Era*: "The chief commercial statistics exhibited at the close of the play to show the progress made by the colored race is but a weak attempt to excuse the wanton insults heaped upon that race. Intelligent colored men will not be deceived. The progress they have made is mainly due to themselves. They owe little to the white race as a whole, save their exploitation and degradation." Debs's image of self-help is not the uplift ideal based on philanthropically guided self-improvement, but an education "to develop their minds and do their own thinking."[90]

No matter how the censors or judicial authorities assessed the film, many spectators—particularly African Americans—felt strongly that the inclusion of seemingly positive imagery was not enough to counter the offense of the film's negative representation of African Americans. Although the epilogue was appended as a corrective coda to *The Birth of a Nation* with the best intentions of the Tuskegee and Hampton trustees who suggested it, Black civic groups quickly protested its association with Griffith's film. One group in Atlantic City challenged the institutes' "miscreant leaders," stating that "the manifest object in showing Hampton Institute in connection with the play is to divert the mind of the colored people from the racial hatred which the play engenders" and that the leaders who "consented and recommended" that pictures of Hampton be shown with *The Birth of a Nation* should be "condemned as traitors of the Negro race."[91] May Childs Nerney, secretary of the NAACP, said quite plainly that it was "really adding insult to injury."[92] To the dismay of the Hampton authorities, the mere inclusion of relatively brief images of uplift could not counteract the epic film's harmful misrepresentation of African Americans. As John P. Turner, a prominent Black Philadelphian, told the African American newspaper the *Philadelphia Tribune* in response to an article in which he was mistakenly represented as approving of *The Birth of a Nation*, "while the last five or six minutes of Hampton School scenes, and statement of the colored man's progress, is inspiring, this to my mind cannot heal the terrible indignities heaped upon us for the two hours preceding. It appeals to the passions of race hatred, and to my mind, can do the colored people of this country none other than harm."[93]

The Black women's club movement, whose members were politically engaged and mobilized, facilitated a large-scale coordinated campaign against *The Birth of a Nation* and Hampton's perceived complicity with its racist vision. The Northeastern Federation of Colored Women's Clubs, whose president at the time was Margaret James Murray (Mrs. Booker T. Washington), organized letter-writing campaigns to protest Hampton's association with *The Birth of a Nation*.[94] Letters were also sent from other clubs and from unaffiliated individuals. One letter from the Frances E. W. Harper Club of Ansonia, Connecticut, is representative: "We do not approve of having pictures of young men and young women who are striving to raise the standard of manhood and womanhood shown at the end of this film to offset nefarious pictures shown in the beginning."[95] The *New York Age* reported that one Jersey City club sent resolutions to Frissell requesting that he "withdraw from that infamous play, 'The Birth of a Nation,' the scenes of Hampton Institute."[96]

These campaigns had an effect. The Pennsylvania Armstrong Association, a branch of an organization of philanthropists dedicated to raising funds for Hampton, fielded questions throughout the fall of 1915 and turned to Frissell for guidance on how to answer such inquiries. Educators at other schools and institutes wrote to people associated with Hampton to express concern. For example, Leslie Pinckney Hill, the principal of the Cheyney Training School for Teachers in Cheyney, Pennsylvania (the oldest institution of higher learning for African Americans, founded in 1837), wrote to the Pennsylvania Armstrong Association asking that organization to intercede with Hampton to have the pictures removed. In her letter, Hill assumed Hampton was motivated by "advertisement" but stated that it is "inconceivable" that they should "tolerate advertisement of this sort." She concluded: "There may be a scintilla of good connected with this show, but nobody thinks of this when one considers the world of evil which it brings upon us all."[97] Letters also came in from Hampton alumni, asking how such an alliance could have occurred. All of the letters Hampton received regarding *The New Era* implored the institute's authorities to withdraw their pictures from screenings of *The Birth of a Nation*.

The Black press, campaigning against *The Birth of a Nation*, closely followed the various efforts to challenge the film and criticized perceived missteps in the struggle. James Weldon Johnson—a prolific writer and critic and a contributing editor to the *New York Age*—denounced the potential association of Hampton with Griffith's film in a column that appeared several weeks after the first screening of *The New Era*. Titled "A Trap," the belated publication of the column suggests that his cautionary tone carried a strong undercurrent of irony. Johnson refers to the Hampton pictures appearing early in *The Birth of a Nation* rather than at its conclusion, possibly conflating the "screen record" intertitles and *The New Era* (though following its appearance at the Tremont Theatre, the positioning of the Hampton scenes would have been at the discretion of exhibitors). Johnson's critique is worth quoting in its entirety:

> Word comes to us indirectly that the producers of "The Birth of a Nation" are showing their kindly feelings toward the Negro by offering to introduce into the first part of the picture some views of Hampton Institute. If this is true, the Dixon-Griffith combination is laying a trap in which, we are quite sure, the Hampton people will be too wise to walk.
>
> If there was ever a case for the application of the old saw, "Beware of the Greeks bearing gifts," this is one. No good will toward the Negro need be expected or hoped for from Tom Dixon and his associates. There is absolutely nothing in their hearts but blind hatred for the race; and any protestation to the contrary is based on some hidden motive.
>
> This "The Birth of a Nation" gang is evidently feeling the attacks made on their hell-inspired production; but it is not for Hampton to save them. If the picture can be killed, let it die, from first scene to last; for there isn't enough good in it to merit saving any part. The whole representation was conceived only in hatred for the North and contempt for the Negro; so let it die! Kill it!
>
> The final effect of introducing views of Hampton Institute into the first part of the "Birth of a Nation" would be to have spectators feel at the end of the play that education for Negroes is a failure. In doing this the producers would obtain the powerful endorsement of Hampton and

thereby disarm criticism and repel attack, and still not change the main lessons taught by the play.

It is inconceivable that the Dixon-Griffith people after spending thousands of dollars to produce a picture whose sole purpose is to convince the North that it made a mistake in fighting to free the slaves, and to convince the nation that it must "keep the nigger down," it is inconceivable, we say, that these people would consider introducing into their picture views from a colored school in such a manner and to such an extent as to change the whole play into a propaganda of glorious uplift for the Negro. No such change of heart can be expected.

The offer to introduce these views, if it has been made, is nothing more than a trap. A trap, as we said, into which Dr. Frissell and the Hampton authorities will be too wise to walk.[98]

Johnson's column highlights several significant aspects of the debate over *The New Era*. First, the suggestion of a potential "hidden motive" in the defense of Dixon and Griffith suggests the possibility of nonaltruistic motivation on the part of Frissell and Hampton, an insinuation that reveals Johnson's mistrust. Johnson's ironic and condescending tone is surprising for the pages of the *New York Age*, a paper financed by Washington and considered a conservative mouthpiece for Tuskegeean ideals. In effect, Johnson says what Tuskegee representatives could not state publicly due to Tuskegee's close association with Hampton. Second, Johnson suggests that the association of Hampton with a film that presents Negro degeneracy as history would result in an unwitting "endorsement" from Hampton of its own denunciation. The Hampton film, then, would not counter the negative portrayal of African Americans in *The Birth of a Nation* but rather would be complicit in its racist agenda. Third, Johnson's warning that the proposal to add the Hampton footage constitutes "a trap," and his recognition of the potential of motion pictures for propagandistic purposes, suggests that an association with another film can alter a film's significance. He speaks to the power of context: by juxtaposing representations, alternative meanings could result.

At the end of May, the *New York Age* reported that the efforts to suppress *The Birth of a Nation* in New York City had failed: "It is claimed that some slight changes have been made in the play but from all we can learn they are so insignificant as to make no material difference. We learn, also, that the Hampton Institute views have been put in; from our point of view this can only injure Hampton and not improve the picture. So it appears that, notwithstanding all efforts, very little has been accomplished."[99]

Clearly, *The New Era* did not have its intended effect. But there are other, broader implications to the issues raised by this episode. Critics saw the adjacency of the Hampton images with the racist portrayal of African Americans in *The Birth of a Nation* as undermining the very logic of uplift media itself. The entire publicity project of Hampton was predicated on a tenuous balance of referential imagery: the line between positive representation and the perpetuation of stereotypical iconography was a nonexistent boundary—or at least a line to be finessed—in Hampton publicity. Like Washington at Tuskegee, Frissell aimed to appeal to white benefactors without making his institute, or agricultural and industrial education for African Americans in general, appear threatening to white power. The tone of condescension in Johnson's critique answers the benevolent condescension of Hampton publicity, in which African American uplift is facilitated by white paternal guidance and reported by authoritative white witnesses.

Although Hampton publicly stood behind *The New Era*, behind closed doors its faculty was divided on the issue. Frissell, who was white, approved of the addition, but on May 19, a month after the faculty vote to approve of use of *The New Era* in conjunction with *The Birth of a Nation*, Moton (who would end the year as Washington's successor as principal of Tuskegee) entered in the record of the Hampton faculty minutes his official protest against the use of the Hampton moving pictures in connection with *The Birth of a Nation*.[100] It is unlikely that Moton was speaking only for himself, nor is it clear if the faculty members were divided along racial lines. On May 1, the faculty was told that Howe, chairman of the National Board of Censorship of Motion Pictures, considered the epilogue "a mistake," but that consent to use it had already been given.[101] Howe, a prominent progressive reformer, had refused to permit his name to be included in the official approval of *The Birth of a Nation* and had subsequently resigned as chair of the censorship board over the issue.[102] Also in early May, Schieffelin and Willcox, who had originated the idea of adding the Hampton pictures along with Frank Trumbull, attended a screening of *The Birth of a Nation* in New York City, and Willcox reported that the effect of *The New Era* "was very good indeed, and went far to counteract the unfortunate impression of the preceeding [sic] films."[103] Hampton's Board of Trustees apparently had had internal disagreements from the beginning, though the board took action only later in the summer by breaking with school authorities and sending its secretary to New York to try to get *The New Era* withdrawn from exhibition.[104] The critique by some faculty members and other African American supporters of the institute—and the failure of its white leaders to understand their concerns—exposed the fissures that were emerging surrounding Hampton's self-representation in the broader public sphere.

Still, despite letter-writing campaigns and a barrage of complaints that flooded Hampton for the better part of the year, on November 3 the faculty voted to encourage the censors to append more Hampton pictures to screenings of *The Birth of a Nation*.[105] Perhaps, wedded to the logic of uplift, the question was seen as one of balance, with more positive images needed to outweigh the negative preceding ones. This vote suggests that the majority of the faculty still believed in *The New Era*, and that those who warned against Hampton being directly associated with the slanderous, albeit tremendously popular, *Birth of a Nation* were in the minority. Internal tensions might have resulted in a necessary dialogue at Hampton about its media project, but a greater crisis occurred at this moment. On November 14, a week after the faculty vote to add more Hampton pictures to *The Birth of a Nation*, Washington died, and faculty attention was fully diverted from the controversy around *The New Era*.

Still, throughout the winter and into the new year, Frissell faced ongoing pressures concerning his approval of the addition of the Hampton epilogue. A pamphlet written by the prominent African American Presbyterian minister Francis J. Grimké excoriating *The Birth of a Nation* and Hampton's involvement with it got Frissell's attention. Grimké wrote:

> I confess I was greatly surprised to find that Dr. Frissell and the authorities at Hampton were willing to lend the weight of their influence in giving countenance to a play that is so manifestly hostile to the Negro. That it is only a disguise, admitted simply for the purpose of getting the endorsement of an institution like Hampton, is evident from the length of the time the statement, "THESE PICTURES ARE PRESENTED BY PERMISSION OF DR. FRISSELL," is kept upon the canvas, and the rapidity with which the pictures themselves are crowded on and off. To be able to say, "These pictures are presented with the permission of Dr. Frissell" means, or at least, that is the impression which it is intended to make— means that Dr. Frissell approves of the play, sees nothing objectionable in it, and, so the weight of his influence, as a known friend of the race, is thrown in its favor, which is unfortunate, to say the least.[106]

Hurt yet resolute, Frissell responded to the prominent minister on November 6, 1915, "I wonder if it occurred to you to give a little more charitable interpretation to my action concerning the Hampton pictures." He went on to explain how the association came about and offered his rationale for it: "I wonder if you have not felt that if you can not alter unfortunate conditions it is wise to attempt to improve them. It seemed to me that here was a chance to show to many thousands of people another side of the colored race than that set forth by this play which is so unfair not only to the Negro but to the white man as well, and I embraced this opportunity with the best of motives. I appreciate how strongly you feel but I want you to see the other side of the affair."[107]

Grimké responded that although he appreciated Frissell's motive, he maintained that it was a "mistake" to provide "this little annex," pictures which were "tagged on in such a way as to make them of no value in counteracting the bad impression already made against the race." Grimké pithily explained to Frissell that Hampton's efforts to improve "unfortunate conditions which cannot be changed" resulted in a dangerous endorsement: "In our attempt to improve such conditions we ought to be very careful that what we do is not construed into an endorsement of the very conditions which we are seeking to improve." Grimké urged Frissell to withdraw *The New Era*, concluding: "Your name, as a known friend of the Negro, and Hampton Institute, ought not to be used to popularize on, to break down the opposition to this deliberate attempt to destroy the good name of a race. And one of the things that surprised me was that you did not see that such would be the effect."[108] Grimké's view was shared by many other prominent Black citizens. Monroe N. Work retrospectively recounted the campaigns, protests, and riots against *The Birth of a Nation*, noting: "To meet the objections of the Negroes, and it was said to show that no ill feeling towards the Negro was intended, an additional reel to show the progress of the Negro was added. The general opinion of the Negroes with reference to this addition was that it was clearly out of place."[109]

Throughout the controversy, Frissell remained silent in public, addressing his response to individuals rather than engaging in open debate about the suitability of Hampton's involvement with *The Birth of a Nation*. In response to one women's club, which had organized a letter-writing campaign protesting *The New Era*, Frissell explained his approval of Hampton's involvement with the film by reiterating the rationale for complying with the National Board of Censorship of Motion Pictures:

> I have protested both in public and private against [*The Birth of a Nation*], but when two of the Tuskegee Institute trustees approached me and asked my help, and then, since we were unable to induce the censors to suppress the film, asked my cooperation in improving it, I said I would be glad to do what I could toward this end.
>
> It seemed to a number of us most unfortunate that the large audi-

ences who witness the performance daily should be left with the impression that the Negro race is incapable of the best things, and in order to show these people something of the tremendous advance that the race has made since the days of slavery, the Hampton moving pictures were added.

I think you will understand that this was done for the sole purpose of informing the public as to the true status of the Negro race in this country.[110]

In Frissell's opinion, *The Birth of a Nation* could be improved through Hampton's skill at transforming the raw materials of southern racist oppression into a modern, useful product. The naïve faith in the power of a positive image to challenge a negative one betrayed the fundamental assumptions of uplift rhetoric. Far from being a corrective to a false history or a happy ending to a racist horror, the Hampton epilogue underscored the potential dangers of its purportedly realist representation in the service of uplift.

Beyond the immediate controversies, this episode helps us understand how uplift cinema functioned as a useful cinema—a form of filmmaking designated to bring about specific ends, something made to be persuasive. This is certainly the way uplift institutions understood media. But seeing oneself as useful meant understanding oneself broadly as part of a larger culture in which other kinds of representations flourished. Even if uplift cinema was not imagined as a direct response to white racism—a kind of countercinema—it could not escape functioning, or being evaluated, in those terms.

Cephas Returns (1915)

After Washington's death and the controversies caused by Hampton's association with *The Birth of a Nation*, the institute's authorities exhibited more caution both in the circulation of the pictures and in the narrative structure of their next moving picture venture. Although maintaining the familiar before-and-after uplift trajectory, Miner began to introduce new narrative sophistication through the use of flashbacks. This new structure can be seen as a strategic response, however unwitting, to the critical misunderstanding of Hampton's supporters of the institute's ill-advised involvement with *The Birth of a Nation*.

In the same meeting in which the faculty voted to request the censors to add more Hampton pictures to exhibitions of *The Birth of a Nation*, Frissell announced that Miner would be making a new set of moving pictures to showcase "the results of Hampton's work."[111] Along with an assistant, Miner was sent "at once" to the Penn School on St. Helena Island, a school founded in South Carolina in 1862 to educate freed slaves as part of the Port Royal Experiment.[112] This program, initiated during the Civil War, encouraged former slaves to work independently on abandoned plantations and was assisted by northern philanthropists and missionaries with the goal of preparing these people for self-sufficiency. In 1900 the Penn School became incorporated as the Penn Normal and Industrial School, with Frissell as chairman of the Board of Trustees, and served as part of Hampton's larger outreach work. Miner's goal in filming the school was to record the results of Hampton's extension work for a new film, *Cephas Returns*. Planned in the immediate aftermath of the contention over *The Birth of a Nation*, *Cephas Returns* was imagined as a response to the problems of *The New Era*. The Hampton authorities believed that the new film would showcase the impact of Hampton's model of education rather than merely depict "its immediate work."[113]

In contrast to Hampton's other films, relatively little information survives about *Cephas Returns*. Like *John Henry at Hampton*, the title character's name is an allusion to a legend. The name Cephas likely refers to the Aramaic word for Peter, the builder of the Christian Church; alternatively, it may refer to the king of Ethiopia in Greek mythology, Cephus or Cepheus. Shot in early November 1915, *Cephas Returns* was a multireel film about a Hampton student from the Sea Islands who takes the skills he learned at Hampton back to his South Carolina home and becomes a farm demonstration agent, "returning to his people and his problem."[114] Screened for the first time for Hampton students and faculty members on December 23, 1915, the film was shown at Symphony Hall in Boston on January 12, 1916, and then used in a fund-raising tour from February through April 1916 in Pennsylvania, Florida, and New York.[115] Sydney Frissell, executive secretary of the National Hampton Association, described the return of Cephas to his island in evocative and visual terms: "The land, weary with its continued burden of cotton, appeals to the Hampton-trained farmer, and the neglected fields with poor shelters for homes cry out to him. Under the moss-draped oaks, to his wondering family and the groups of Islanders in the country of the long-stapled cotton, he tells vividly of work and study at Hampton."[116] Frissell's personification of the land and fields suggests an organic bond between Cephas and both the earth and his community, underscoring the uplift ideal as one in which an African American is improved in his "natural" talents and within his "native" environment. Frissell implies that the emphasis in the film is on the improvement to his people and his work "toward an ideal community" that Cephas is able to bring about due to his Hampton training.

Frissell's description also suggests that the scenes of Hampton appear in flashback, as Cephas "tells vividly of work and study at Hampton" to the curious onlookers. As with the other films screened at meetings, the Hampton Quartet sang plantation songs, "interpreting the scenes." Frissell concluded the description of the film by pointing to a broader purpose: "By these meetings it is hoped that the school will gain many new friends."[117]

The before-and-after rhetoric created by the flashback allows the images of training for progress to appear after the "weary" land and "neglected" fields are highlighted. As Kristin Thompson has demonstrated, after 1912 flashbacks were usually expressed as separate shots rather than superimposed vignettes, their "distinct interruptions of the chronological flow" motivated by a character's memory and formally signaled to minimize narrative disruption. This in turn marked them as characteristic of the newly codifying classical cinema.[118] Expressed through this new narrative sophistication, Cephas's flashback demonstrates the process of training that will appear again in the final scenes of the film, when he applies in his community the skills he learned at Hampton.

The flashback structure of *Cephas Returns* is an innovative departure from the earlier Hampton films, but it is shaped by the problems that beset *The New Era*. The narrative point of view is that of the student who recounts his experience and thereby exhibits a level of agency that is absent in *John Henry at Hampton* and *Making Negro Lives Count*. Strategically, the flashback structure contains the images of Hampton in Cephas's narrative so that the after already informs the viewing of the before. The film's premise is established on the already demonstrated success of Hampton's training. As a contained circular narrative structure, *Cephas Returns* tries to preserve the logic of uplift while guarding against the criticisms made of the employment of Hampton pictures with *The Birth of a Nation*.

The Birth of a Nation may have been "a vicious and hurtful play" to Washington, but to many people the real harm was done in the move by members of the Griffith camp and the National Board of Censorship of Motion Pictures to use Hampton, its reputation, and its moving pictures to keep the racist epic in theaters. The incident revealed the complexities involved in the public circulation of uplift films. Although moving pictures allowed Tuskegee and Hampton to promote themselves more broadly, film also presented a challenge to the institutes' control over the dissemination of their images and the context in which they were received. Just as the message of uplift was determined by the organization of content, so did the exhibition context determine the efficacy of its message; this was one prominent lesson of the Hampton epilogue affair. The various kinds of public exposure — to the targeted audience of philanthropists and the wider public sphere of the popular cinema—created a range of deeply ambivalent responses to moving pictures that caused trouble for uplift leaders.

However, taken outside of the philanthropic sphere and considered more simply as a business venture, moving pictures succeeded in providing a new platform for promoting the advancement of the race. For various Black film-making entrepreneurs, moving pictures provided the opportunity to capitalize on their convictions as race men and promote the interests of their communities through the production of films for urban Black audiences. The distinction between business and uplift was not clear in these ventures, if indeed it ever was. Still, as we shall see in the following chapter, uplift cinema in the north served as a mechanism for the self-fashioning of its audiences, the assertion of Black civic belonging, and the promotion of a modern Black visual culture.

5

TO "ENCOURAGE AND UPLIFT"

Entrepreneurial Uplift Cinema

I fear that the Negro does not fully realize what the moving picture
has meant to them [*sic*], or what it is going to mean in the future.
—HUNTER C. HAYNES, "Amazing Figures on 'Movies'"

Writing in mid-1914, the Black entrepreneur Hunter C. Haynes could not have
foreseen that within a year the nation would be in the throes of a debate about
the capacity for motion pictures to cause injury, incite violence, foster national
unity, and castigate a large segment of the population. Haynes could also not
have known that the representation of African Americans would be central to
the major industrial and narrative advances of the moving picture industry and
its most popular products: multireel melodramas (*Uncle Tom's Cabin*, J. Stuart
Blackton, American Vitagraph Company, 1910), epic narratives (*The Birth of a
Nation*, D.W. Griffith, David W. Griffith Corporation, 1915), the emergence of
sound (*The Jazz Singer*, Alan Crosland, Warner Bros., 1927), Technicolor (*Gone
with the Wind*, Victor Fleming, Selznick International Pictures, 1939), anima-
tion (*Song of the South*, Harve Foster and Wilfred Jackson, RKO Radio Pictures, 1946), and television (*Roots*, ABC, 1977).[1] Or that later in the century

Black cinema would constitute a significant part of the mainstream film industry (Blaxploitation in the 1970s and the Black film boom of the 1990s), even rescuing it from financial collapse (as Blaxploitation cinema arguably did).[2] Throughout American film history, African Americans and various aspects of Black culture and notions of Blackness have been central to the development of the industry and its output and have increasingly constituted a significant box-office force.[3] Haynes could not have anticipated these developments even as he recognized the transformational power of moving images.

What Haynes did know in June 1914 is that moving pictures held significant meaning, industrially and socially, for the race. Although moving pictures were a contested site of racist depictions that perpetuated stereotypes and further maligned a marginalized people, more recently the capability of motion pictures to counteract prejudicial representation had provided hope for the possibilities of the medium. Racist representations were most prevalent in comedy, especially in films that drew on longer traditions of minstrelsy and vaudeville. In contrast to this tradition, African American filmmakers had reclaimed comedic racialized representation and recast these tropes, creating new comedic types as well as more respectable representations. This effort was not without complications, but Haynes was able to optimistically postulate a future for Black filmmakers and, by extension, for the medium that would be responsive to the aspirations of a Black audience increasingly desirous of a screened projection of itself as both modern and respectable.

Haynes was not simply a filmmaker or a businessman but an entrepreneur. The position of the entrepreneur was a significant one for the uplift model, demarcating a role in which a wide range of business ventures were combined with a sense of social responsibility. Filmmaking was one of the enterprises into which such businessmen ventured, as it was appealing for both its commercial possibilities and its potential for social impact; Haynes and his fellow filmmaking entrepreneurs thus engaged with motion picture production both as a business enterprise and as a medium that could serve as a tool for uplift. Indeed, cinema had a special role to play in the entrepreneurial project. As an industry, the motion picture business was more than just another realm in which African Americans could achieve economic autonomy. In the early 1910s, there were an increasing number of theaters owned and patronized by African Americans as well as a growing audience for race pictures.[4] Entrepreneurs saw motion pictures as an industry with special significance to African Americans, since film offered the possibilities of self-representation in a culture hitherto representationally hostile to people of color. Photographic media's pretentions to realism and verisimilitude appealed to these businessmen who, like their associates in the Black professional elite, saw their success and their economic viability as a means of uplifting others. The photographic camera could become a "mighty weapon" in the fight against distorted images of blackness and in the assertion of the dignity and humanity of the Black subject.[5] The reproducibility of photographs and the collective consumption of moving pictures could be central to the formation of model citizens whose images were displayed and disseminated according to uplift principles. With an untapped market of spectators eager to see themselves on screen, Black filmmaking entrepreneurs used film to articulate the ideals of uplift by recording the key markers of social, civic, and economic advancement. These entrepreneurs projected possibility, providing audiences with an image of an emerging Black urban life that both conveyed the uplift concept while at the same time serving as a model of civic engagement for the growing urban populations.

Economic success was central to the politics of uplift, and various leaders emphasized the importance of African American economic autonomy. To this end, the promotion of Black business and industry was a main tenet of the uplift project. The uplift idea presumed that economic strength and independence would make Black people indispensable to white interests and thereby catalyze social improvements. It may have been a form of acquiescence to segregationist policies, but it was one that practiced a quiet resistance on the economic front, believing economic advancement to be the key to eventual social equality.

The uplift model of self-help and mutual progress was the most visible, powerful, and prevailing view—even the gospel—of Black political and social thought. It was in following these principles that Booker T. Washington organized the National Negro Business League (NNBL) in Boston in August 1900, for the purpose of serving to "multiply these examples North and South" so that "our problem would be solved." The NNBL was based on the belief in the economic indispensability of African Americans' contributions, with social and political gains to follow economic advancement. Washington recalls the NNBL's founding: the league's members "recognized that a useless, shiftless, idle class is a menace and a danger to any community, and that when an individual produces what the world wants, whether it is a product of hand, heart or head, the world does not long stop to inquire what is the color of the skin of the producer."[6]

Two things are worth emphasizing in this model. First, the burden of representation fell on the Black businessman and -woman to counteract the image problem of the whole race, since he or she had the means and a unique method to intervene. Second, above anything else, the image of respectability was the key to uplift. These two were inextricably linked. As Washington wrote in *The Negro in Business*:

> The advent of the Negro business man has given great encouragement to those who have confidence in his abilities and future. We have been charged as a race with shiftlessness and extravagance; but our business men show that we can be far-sighted and thrifty. We are said by some to be vicious and criminal; but our business men correct this impression by the sobriety and uprightness of their lives. When we are accused as a race of indulging too much in mere useless complaint and denunciation, we can clear ourselves by pointing to our manly, courageous and hopeful business men, who show in practice that an inch of achievement is worth a yard of complaint. Indeed, one of the greatest benefits we have received from going into business is the proof we have thus afforded that we are well able to develop those sturdy and enterprising qualities without which the highest civilization is impossible.[7]

Washington commends Negro businessmen using uplift rhetoric, suggesting that participation in American capitalism achieves the uplift ideal. Of course, the cards were stacked, and the businessman's uprightness could never wholly counter the perception of many white Americans that Black people were criminals, a threat to the social order, and unprepared for citizenship. Here as everywhere, the actual achievements of Black individuals could not compete with the imagined crimes of more numerous others. So Black film entrepreneurs engaged in a familiar kind of practice: they fought in the realm of the imaginary as they endeavored to achieve tangible economic gain and autonomy.

The men who turned to motion pictures as a tool for African American uplift did so through the lens of the Bookerite entrepreneurial philosophy. They were visible members of the Black business community, often through involvement with the NNBL. For example, in a December 1910 trip to Chicago, Washington was given a banquet by the Chicago Business League at which the celebrated photographer Peter P. Jones gave "a short well appointed talk" in which he requested to photograph Washington, who obliged the following day (figure 5.1).[8] Haynes spoke at several meetings of the NNBL.[9] William F. Watkins, an Alabama dentist and a partner in the Anderson-Watkins Film Company, served as president of the Montgomery Negro Business League. These entrepreneurs were initially involved in the NNBL because of other ventures that preceded their motion picture interests. In this period, motion picture production and exhibition gradually came to be seen as a viable Black business

FIG. 5.1 Booker T. Washington portrait by Peter P. Jones, 1910. Courtesy Prints and Photographs Division, Library of Congress, LC-DIG-ds-04383.

venture with the potential for success and autonomy, similar to other theatrical enterprises. Thus, these prominent businessmen seized the opportunity to capitalize on—while embodying and propagating—uplift ideals through filmmaking; entrepreneurial cinema would serve multiple goals.

Black filmmakers would not be the first to capture the gathering of Black businessmen on film. The 1912 NNBL convention in Chicago was filmed by the Universal Film Manufacturing Company and included in its *Animated Weekly* newsreel of September 4, along with other newsworthy items and human-interest stories: views of an automobile race, English coaches, the Women's Life Saving League, a European yachting event, shots of Governor Thomas R. Marshall (running as Woodrow Wilson's vice-presidential candidate), a cowboy wedding, and shots of Ethel Barrymore and her family at their summer home.[10] Although the film and its intertitles are not known to survive, the context of the NNBL footage suggests that the meeting was reported seriously rather than with irony or ridicule (though the possibly ironic inflection of individual accompanists could certainly have affected the tone).[11] Washington requested a copy of the segment that showed him on the steps of the Institutional Church in Chicago, which suggests that the footage was to his liking.[12] The *Moving Picture World* reported that the reel included "portraits of groups of colored people" assembled for the meeting "of which the papers have printed so much."[13] This high mainstream visibility was due in large part to Washington's popularity as a national figure and echoed the coverage of the Tuskegee moving pictures in the *Moving Picture World* and *Nickelodeon*.[14]

However, the announcement of the newsreel in the *Moving Picture World* is printed above a review for *The Haunted Bachelor* (Éclair, 1912), described as "a very farcical picture in which Sambo, a burnt cork coon, and his master, the bachelor, have the chief roles. The master thinks he has killed Sambo. The idea might be made to furnish fun; but there is little that is spontaneous or very funny in it as given here."[15] The adjacency of the coverage of the NNBL newsreel footage with a blackface comedy, where the humor pivots on the subjugation and misrepresentation of Black characters, underscores the uplift imperative. It also reveals the cultural fissures threatening to destabilize post-Reconstruction codified inequities. The prevalence of films like *The Haunted Bachelor* and the ubiquity of caricatures of African Americans in American films of this period permit us to imagine that the *Animated Weekly* newsreel would appear before such a comedy. Perhaps, then, the *Animated Weekly* would have functioned to belie the stereotypes that followed it on the screen, to render them as fictions and caricatures. The presence of photographs of actual Black men does important representational work for white audiences just as it would serve as a point of pride for Black spectators. But one of the ambiguities of uplift cinema centers on the question of adjacency: *The Haunted Bachelor* could shape the NNBL footage, uplifting the representation of Black men, but equally the racist comedy could bleed into the reception of the newsreel, ironically inflecting the respectable images.

Working in a broader culture of racialized misrepresentation, the mission of the NNBL was to combat public misconceptions about Black industriousness. Moving pictures provided an effective means of amplifying that message, and Haynes would film the 1913 NNBL meeting in Philadelphia.[16] Although Jones and Haynes were actively involved in the NNBL, there is no record that the filmmakers George W. Broome or William Foster were members. Yet the entrepreneurial emphasis of the uplift project enjoyed such a broad reach that it was a central component of the Black social and cultural zeitgeist. For example, Sherman H. Dudley, an actor and theater owner turned filmmaker, called for more "Race capitalists" to invest in moving pictures.[17] Charles H. Turpin, owner of the Booker T. Washington Theatre in St. Louis, recognized the box-office draw of uplifting moving pictures and commissioned four thousand feet of film showing "prominent colored citizens" and views of institutions "devoted to the use of the Afro-American race."[18] As the defining tenet of a widely popular belief system, the Bookerite doctrine of economic advancement was the dominant creed of African American progress across the nation in this period.

It is not surprising, then, that Broome, as discussed in chapter 2, would seek to work with Tuskegee and to promote the institute—and himself—through motion pictures, or that Louis B. Anderson and Tuskegee would find their relationship to be mutually advantageous.

In this chapter, I trace the filmmaking practices of several northern urban Black filmmaking entrepreneurs working in Chicago and New York City to show their original engagement with the medium of moving pictures. As with the filmmaking endeavors of Broome and Anderson, the work of these northern entrepreneurs represents some of the earliest instances of African American film production. But a focus on the work of Foster, Jones, and Haynes permits us to see how Black entrepreneurs engaged with moving picture technology and its possibilities in different ways than those working in the south. It also shows what happened to the cultural production of the uplift project as it intersected with broader economic concerns and the representational dynamics of image making. Creatively combining comedy and actuality filmmaking, fictional drama and scenes of everyday life, the northern entrepreneurs produced films that had complex relationships with broader strategies of Black representational politics. These different modes and their distinct appeals worked in tandem, allowing Black spectators to negotiate progress and assert uplift through moving pictures.

More broadly, I argue that entrepreneurial filmmakers offered images of African American uplift that presented its subjects as modern, civically engaged models of progress and possibility. Like the filmmakers at Tuskegee and Hampton, these entrepreneurs had an investment in the progress of the race and were imbued with uplift discourse. But their connection goes much deeper. The entrepreneurs shared strategies of representation and exhibition that we saw in the motion picture enterprises of the institutes; they engaged in actuality filmmaking and experimented with nontheatrical exhibition sites while also producing films for theatrical commercial exhibition. Black filmmaking entrepreneurs of this period employed cinema as a useful medium for promoting the uplift of the race and simultaneously endeavored to build an economically viable—and profitable—filmmaking enterprise.

Chicago Entrepreneurs and "Genuine Negro Moving Pictures"

The prominent citizens of Chicago's South Side composed a close-knit Black elite in the first decades of the twentieth century. Colonel John R. Marshall and Anderson joined forces to offer life insurance to African Americans after the two men had formed a relationship in the Eighth Regiment, where Anderson served as captain.[19] Close friends Alfred Anderson and Cary B. Lewis were prominent enough citizens to be given season passes to baseball games by Charles Comiskey, owner of the Chicago White Sox.[20] Anderson was granted the use of the White Sox's park for an annual charity baseball game to benefit Provident Hospital, where he worked.[21] Foster was a respected journalist who also owned a music publishing company, which published a set of twelve pictorial postcards of Chicago's African American churches and business places taken by Jones (who had also photographed Marshall).[22] Moving picture production was one of a number of enterprises in which these interconnected Chicagoans engaged. Filmmaking was often ancillary to their other activities or was a tool by which to exhibit the uplift of the race and extend experiences (or, rather, the images of experiences) for the rest of Chicago and beyond. In this sense, Black filmmakers were entrepreneurially engaged in contemporary enterprises that included moving pictures as one medium among many, an enterprise that worked in concert in the self-fashioning of Black modernity.

Because of these deep connections, to investigate the role of motion pictures in Chicago is to trace a series of intersecting lives and careers as well as intertwined civic involvement. Although engaged in a number of business enterprises, Black filmmakers nonetheless recognized the potential for moving pictures to challenge broader cultural misrepresentations of Black people and African American society, while also capitalizing on the public's desire for uplifting rather than degrading moving pictures. They filmed actualities, local films, fiction films, and sometimes hybrids of these modes. In so doing, they explored the potentials of the medium for the dedicated entertainment of Black audiences, while at the same time serving as an agent in the self-definition of the race.

WILLIAM FOSTER

Scholars of African American cinema have concurred, with some caution due to the paucity of surviving evidence, that William Foster was the first African American to mobilize motion picture technology for entrepreneurial purposes.[23] Considering his work alongside the films produced at Hampton and those made at Tuskegee by entrepreneurs like Broome and the Anderson-Watkins Company, Foster may more accurately be regarded as one of the earliest filmmakers working to assert a self-determined African American screen image while taking part in a range of entrepreneurial activities. Although the Black press celebrated him as a pioneer in a hostile domain, Foster was part of a larger cultural community engaged in music, theater, and journalism. He worked concurrently and in the same social milieu with other Black filmmaking entrepreneurs like Jones, Alfred Anderson, and Haynes. Before making moving pictures, Foster had been a respected journalist and had engaged in a number of successful business enterprises, mostly revolving around the entertainment industry and popular culture. He directed the tours of theatrical comedy acts such as Williams and Stevens and, as noted above, owned a music publishing company.[24] He sold popular Jack Johnson buttons to customers across the country—an aspect of his professional activity that complicates the too-facile equation of positive representation and uplift but that also shows that Johnson was a complex figure for uplift men, who admired his entrepreneurial savvy if concurrently balking at his polarizing bravado.[25] Foster also partnered with Jones to publish the photographer's images as pictorial postcards and ran the Chicago branch office of the Indianapolis *Freeman* from his music company's offices, which opened in March 1912.[26] In this way, Foster's entrepreneurial film production and exhibition ventures, along with his published film commentary in the Black press, were an urban iteration of the uplift project that promoted a visual culture aligned with the prevalent philosophy of African American progress.

Foster was popular with the Black press, which generally championed "all-colored pictures." Thus, the Indianapolis *Freeman* proclaimed: "It will be the duty of all the race to support the Foster movement."[27] Under the pen name Juli Jones Jr. (figure 5.2), Foster was a respected writer, cultural critic, sports writer, and film commentator for *Half-Century* and the *Chicago Defender*, among other outlets.[28] Given his prolific writing, he received significant press attention for his moving picture ventures. The first mention of them is in June 1913, when the *Chicago Defender* featured an announcement of his enterprise with Joe Shoecraft, a humorous monologist and theater manager who was also a band leader and ran the popular Pompeii Buffet and Café at 20–22 East 31st Street, between State Street and Wabash Avenue. The *Defender* announced: "These progressive young men have installed expensive equipments [sic] and intend to supply the public with high class films in an endeavor to offset the malicious ones produced by other companies."[29] The first motion pictures taken by the newly formed enterprise were of the dedication of the Wabash Avenue branch of the YMCA and of a baseball game featuring the star pitcher and manager Andrew "Rube" Foster and the Chicago American Giants playing at Schorling's Park.[30] These pictures celebrated milestones in Black Chicagoan life and captured key events in the social world of the South Side. The Wabash Avenue YMCA had opened in June 1913 to serve the African American community and

FIG. 5.2 Billy Evans drawing of William Foster [Juli Jones Jr., pseud.], "News of the Moving Picture," *Freeman*, December 20, 1913.

JULI JONES JR.

was funded through a donation by Julius Rosenwald and fund-raising efforts within the community. Rosenwald had insisted on a matching fund policy to ensure local buy-in for the branch, which was in keeping with Bookerite uplift principles of self-help. Through the matching fund, Rosenwald approached philanthropy as a means of providing African Americans with "an opportunity, not to be worked *for* but to be worked *with*."[31] As a result, the community paid two-thirds of the cost of the facility and the YMCA became a local hub, a symbol of pride, and a "potent uplift agency."[32] The footage of the YMCA dedication, on June 15, 1913, included popular local people such as Colonel Marshall, head of the Illinois Eighth Regiment, and others who were deemed "good subjects" by the *Defender*.[33] The parade was led by Marshall and the Eighth Regiment, and all of the city's major secret and fraternal organizations were involved. Washington, Rosenwald, William P. Sidley (president of the YMCA of Chicago), and other prominent citizens spoke.[34] The celebration of the opening of the YMCA was thus extended through moving pictures, and its significance to the community was promulgated in theaters.

Foster tested the YMCA footage on a few associates after the last show on July 2, 1913, at the Grand Theater, an upscale theater owned and operated by whites but catering exclusively to African Americans.[35] The small audience included a *Defender* reporter, who wrote on the test screening in advance of the public premiere, announcing that it was "a decided success."[36] When the motion pictures of the YMCA parade and dedication publicly premiered on July 24, they were shown to a reported four thousand people.[37] Audiences "vociferously applauded" the famous figures filmed at the parade as they were recognized on screen.[38] The YMCA footage was exhibited with two Foster narrative fictions, *The Railroad Porter* and *The Butler*, a "high-class detective or kidnapping scene" about a hero butler working in the home of a white family.[39] The *Chicago Defender* noted that the YMCA pictures were the main attraction yet expressed the opinion that "the two screams" would be *The Railroad Porter* (identified in the newspaper as the *Pullman Porter*) and *The Butler*, which starred the celebrated African American singer and performer Lizzie Hart Dorsey. The *Defender* concluded its brief article by stating that "everybody is pleased with the success of the pictures, and to know we will have the pleasure of seeing the better side of the race on canvas than always seeing some Negro making an ass of himself."[40]

Championed by the *Defender* as the "first Chicago man to make films with Afro-American in laudable pursuits," Foster produced both actualities and fiction films, including comedies and detective stories, and was deeply invested in promoting images of respectability in motion pictures designed for Black audiences.[41] Foster filmed with his own camera and wrote his own scenarios, though—according to the *Defender*—he raised the necessary capital through a loan from "a white gentleman" after "married men of the race" refused to support his endeavor, perhaps due to the infidelity plot of *The Railroad Porter*.[42] Although this may have been a statement of fact by the *Defender*, Jacqueline Stewart reads it as possibly a "joking dig" at Foster's inability to secure backers within his own community or an allusion to the "hypocritical moral standards" of Chicago's race men.[43] Whatever meaning might have been inferred by readers, Stewart cites this remark as an example of the press's investment in both the content of Black films and in the issues surrounding the financing of such endeavors.

The Railroad Porter, Foster's first fiction film, was produced and released in Chicago in 1913. Lottie Grady played the wife of the porter, who was played by Kid Brown; Cassie Burch Slaughter was the wife's friend.[44] The wife believes her husband to be on the railroad and invites a café waiter, "a fashionably dressed chap" played by Edgar Litterson, to dinner.[45] The husband returns and, as the *New York Age* reported, finds "wifey sitting at the table serving the waiter all the delicacies of the season." He chases the waiter out, guns are pulled, but "no one is hurt, despite all the shooting." The conclusion restores the couple to the status quo, and "all ends happily."[46]

The film thus largely celebrates public respectability and was popular as a positive representation of Black life, recognizable to and aspirational for its audience. Although countering the comic sensibilities of white-authored Black images, the film also raises questions, through the vehicle of humor, concerning how this public respectability is expressed. Stewart notes that the infidelity plot trumps the inclusion of images of respectability: "Despite these gestures toward racial pride and celebration, the film's comedy derives from the disruptions posed by these attractive features of modern life—travel, consumer culture, and the glamour of the stroll café scene can break up Black middle-class homes."[47] Regardless of the introduction of possible immorality into the domestic scene, as Stewart and Mark Reid have pointed out, *The Railroad Porter* champions the new professional possibilities open to African American men and the relative wealth and leisure enjoyed by Black middle-class women.[48] As part of a new wage-earning, cosmopolitan Black middle class, railway porters were emblematic of the broader social transformations taking place. The film, with its urban setting and references to travel and social encounters in the public sphere, asserts an image of Black modernity that refutes the stereotypes of African Americans as provincial and unsophisticated that permeated popular visual culture. Foster's film comedy plays off familiar tropes of Black comedic performance while setting them in real urban contexts, as Stewart notes.[49] As the film's characters are from the recognizable social milieu of respectable Black society, the comedy is an in-joke for Black audiences and provides humor that is distinct from that in productions presented to white audiences. In this sense, Foster's project should be understood as a strategy of asserting African American modernity that constituted a key iteration of uplift cinema.

The Railroad Porter was a big success and was exhibited for over five months at a number of leading Chicago theaters catering to Black audiences, including the Grand and States Theaters.[50] For example, at the States Theater, the matinees offered three times weekly were all crowded, and the *Defender* reported: "The play is a scream, and already it is known from coast to coast."[51] When the film was shown at the Majestic Theater, a downtown vaudeville theater catering to white audiences, spectators reportedly "jumped up and shouted, some laughed so loud that ushers had to silence them."[52] Stewart reads this account as one in which the white spectators "exhibited the kind of 'inappropriate' spectatorial behavior frequently attributed to Black Belt audiences."[53] Yet the film was screened as part of a program of uplift cinema, including Foster's actualities of the YMCA dedication and parade. Though Foster's films appeared on bills with a variety of entertainments, Lewis, the *Freeman*'s Chicago correspondent, noted that many spectators attended the shows principally for Foster's pictures.[54] As Foster's films toured other cities, Grady accompanied the show and sang between reels.[55] Writing in the *Freeman*, Sylvester Russell noted that "the greatest thing that happened on the Stroll recently was the first appearance of William Foster's genuine Negro moving pictures."[56]

In this period, the mere existence of a Black filmmaker was enough to receive accolades in the Black press. The *Freeman* hyperbolically lauded Foster for making "the most remarkable strides of any of the colored men in Chicago. He has snatched the moving picture from its infancy among colored people and is making it the biggest thing in Chicago."[57] The material circumstances were always highlighted, along with the importance of patronage and community encouragement for such an endeavor. The *New York Age* proclaimed that if the Foster Photoplay Company had other moving pictures like *The Railroad Porter*, "the firm would be conferring a favor on the colored playgoers of Harlem by sending them eastward."[58] In a separate article, the *New York Age* also encouraged other filmmakers to follow Foster's example: "There is only one conclusion that can be well decided upon in the vineyard of the photo plays. The aim of colored moving picture purveyors should be to give comedy stories such as those seen by the William Foster Photo Play Company."[59] The Black press knew that Foster and those like him would be unable to continue successfully without the following of a sizable Black audience. The *Chicago Defender* proclaimed: "It is always gratifying to see a member of our race embark into a new field of endeavor. Long live the Foster Film Company."[60]

In September 1913 Foster released a new film: *The Grafter and the Girl*, a drama starring Grady and Jerry Mills and featuring Richard B. Harrison; Judge Moore; Burt and Grant; Marie Burton-Hyram and her baby, Kandy Kids; and Kid Brown and Kinky Cooper.[61] Like many of Foster's actors, Grady and Mills were accomplished actors and former members of the Pekin Stock Company, the celebrated Black stock company founded by Robert T. Motts at Chicago's Pekin Theatre.[62] The *Defender* noted that Foster was making notable advances in the photography of his motion pictures, and that *The Grafter and the Girl* represented "a great improvement over previous efforts."[63] Though Sylvester Russell, critic for the "Musical and Dramatic" column of the *Defender*, cautioned that the actors "must be careful in the future to reserve complete composure in order to avoid those nervous twitches which slightly mar in pictures," he also remarked that "The railroad scene, dancing in the hay and automobile ride were ample in variety. William Foster now has the best colored photo plays that the market can supply."[64] In October 1913 Foster released *The Fall Guy*, which the *Defender* noted was "a marked improvement over some of the preceding ones and simply goes to show that practice makes perfect."[65]

As an entrepreneur seeking greater exposure for his moving pictures, in October 1913 Foster visited the western office of the *Moving Picture World*, located in Chicago, to promote his company in the trade press. We know very little about this meeting, but James S. McQuade included Foster's visit in the "Chicago Film Brevities" section of his regular "Chicago Letter" column in the magazine. There, McQuade offers insights into Foster's production practice, reporting that the filmmaker does not use a script when directing and that he shoots his films in the backyard of his studio at 3312 Wabash Avenue. McQuade also notes that Foster's films are all based on scenarios written by "colored authors." Interested in the business viability of Foster's enterprise, McQuade reports that, by Foster's count, 214 theaters in the United States were owned and operated by African Americans and that Foster's "product" plays in all of them. Calling *The Railroad Porter*, *The Fall Guy*, and *The Butler* "farce comedies of a riproarious type," McQuade concludes the brief notice by purporting to quote Foster: "'Ah don't want you to take mah word for it that these comedies are a big hit. Ah jus' want you to come an' see one of them an' laf yo head off,' said Mr. Foster in a most sincere and unaffected manner. From what I can learn, the Foster films thus far issued are laugh makers of a most infectious kind."[66]

Several things are interesting about this alleged quote. If it accurately reflects Foster's sentiment, if not his language, then it indicates that he aspired to market his films to a general audience, as evidenced by the very fact of his appearance at the *Moving Picture World*'s Chicago office. Foster might have hoped that his films could be screened in white theaters as well as for African American audiences. (Indeed, as we shall see, he ended his career working in the mainstream film industry.) Yet Foster's hopefulness is undermined by McQuade's strange quotation of Foster in an imagined racialized dialect, an attempt at humor that results in a dismissal of Foster's professional ambitions by underscoring the difference between the assumed white reader of the trade magazine and the article's African American subject. It also serves to mock Foster's efforts by infusing an otherwise straightforward report with a racialized caricature more commonly used for Black figures in front of the camera than for those behind it. The ventriloquized language undermines Foster's professionalism even as it presumes to celebrate his achievements. This rare instance of mainstream coverage of early race filmmaking provides an indication of how the trade media treated such ventures, and of the difficulties Foster and his colleagues faced in their professional endeavors. It also demonstrates one of the risks of uplift comedy. Through the adoption of a minstrel accent, the *Moving Picture World* conflates the businessman and filmmaker with the type of product he makes. In this article, Foster is presented not just as an agent of comedy but as a joke himself.

It is reasonable to assume that Foster saw the notice in the *Moving Picture World*, but it is impossible to know what he thought of it. However, a lengthy article on the business of motion pictures that he wrote in the *Freeman* a few months later contains a number of sharp criticisms of the way white people treat Black innovators: "It is a well-known fact that our brother in white handles everything Negro he touches with the roughest kind of a glove. He affects to believe that he must communicate with it by a long-distance process. After awhile, however, when profit begins to loom into sight in little more than reasonable figures, then he suddenly realizes that the black will not rub off and he nestles close to the skin of the source of the profit." Foster calls for race investment in moving pictures "if we would not finally see white men step in and grab off another rich commercial plum from what should be one of our own particular trees of desirable profit." He likewise criticizes the prevalent caricatures of Black life produced by white filmmakers: "Our brother in white is both blind and unwilling to see the finer aspects and qualities of American Negro life. His blindness and unwillingness to see, I am glad to relate, is none of our making and should be small cause of our worry. We must be up and doing for ourselves in our own best way and for our own best good." Foster sees the proliferation of misrepresentations of Black people on American screens as a motivating force for heightened race consciousness. Uplift images must be controlled and disseminated by uplift men. Invoking the appeal of the local film, Foster remarks that the relentlessness of such distorted images of the Black man "has made him hungry to see himself as he has come to be."[67] As is clear from Foster's depiction of the industry, and its challenges and possibilities for African Americans, uplift cinema may celebrate advancement, but its genesis is fueled by indignities.

The *Freeman*'s headline championed Foster as the "Biggest Man in the Business," but in the article itself Foster downplays his own achievements in keeping with uplift expectations of humility. He declares: "I dare not say too much about the part I have played in the manufacture and production of motion pictures portraying certain interesting phases of Negro life. It would sound too much like tooting a horn to do so. But I can say that my feeble efforts have been met with a more than fair share of encouragement and support. This leads me to assert that the business among Negroes is bound to become the basis of a great and profitable industry."[68] Foster envisioned a separate Black film industry offering products for Black consumers, and he closely tracked statistics on the numbers of theaters owned, operated, and catering to Black audiences.[69] Yet his appearance at the *Moving Picture World*'s Chicago office and his later work in the mainstream film industry more closely reflect the uplift project's interracial entanglements. The rhetoric of Black self-help was always in tension with the need for interracial negotiation and cooperation.

Foster spent that winter in the south, touring with his films and building an audience. After his return to Chicago in June 1914, he told the *Defender*: "The South has gone wild over moving pictures. The moving picture has been a great help to the race in the South in that an opportunity is given them to see great acts and actors that they were heretofore barred from viewing."[70] Reportedly due to European demand for African American comedies (as Micheaux would later claim there was such demand for his films), in April 1914 Foster had announced plans for the October opening of a moving picture studio in Jacksonville, Florida, on the St. Johns River, with the capital support of Jacksonville banking firm Anderson Tucker.[71] However, this apparently came to nothing, and when Foster returned to Chicago in June he was reportedly "penniless" and unable to follow through with his plans for a southern studio.[72]

Foster continued to produce actualities, filming a baseball game between the Chicago American Giants and the Brooklyn Royal Giants, including footage of Andrew "Rube" Foster receiving a bouquet from Major Robert R. Jackson and of the politicians Del Roberts and William Randolph Cowan at the game. He released the actuality in 1914 under the title *The Colored Championship Base Ball Game*. Yet not all of the figures were seen as models of uplift. Russell quipped: "Bartenders and café waiters, Foster's long suite [*sic*], were seen in abundance."[73] This remark might offer a glimpse into Foster's personal reputation, but Russell was not an unbiased reporter. When the future of the Pekin Theatre as a playhouse was under debate in 1911, following the death of Motts, Russell publicly speculated on the theater's possible future leadership but qualified his endorsement of Foster. Russell noted that despite Foster's "unquestioned experience," he would "need executive direction because of his unsteady and sudden, uncontrollable impulse."[74] Whether this was an honest reflection of Foster's character or sour grapes on the part of Russell is difficult to determine. Russell seems to have had respect for Foster but was not above the occasional dig at him, perhaps stemming from a falling out the two men had had over an advertisement Russell wrote for the Grand Theater that Foster found inadequate.[75] Thereafter Russell made frequent jabs at Foster in the *Freeman* with statements such as "Foster is a fellow who does business on the half-penny plan, but does it well for the moment."[76] Incensed by Foster's presumed responsibility for motion picture policy at the Grand Theater, Russell wrote that Foster's "movements indicated that he has a way of telling a white man how to cut down expenses and run his business, but gets nothing for it."[77] In June 1915, when the Grand was cutting down on vaudeville in favor of moving pictures, Russell wrote a verse in the *Freeman* titled "The Foster Policy": "The Foster Policy control, / Is like the 'gag' called 'watered stock'; / Robbed by tricksters, heart and soul, / The Foster policy, to be sure, / Just helps the rich, without rebate, / In aiding to cut off the poor."[78] Russell called the Grand's new policy one of "Foster's well conceived [acts of] self-preservation." Russell also accused Foster of lobbying to have *The Nigger* (Edgar Lewis, Fox Film Corporation, 1915), which had been filmed for Fox by the white director Edgar Lewis, screened at the Grand; Russell claimed that Foster had been outnumbered by "prominent men who swore the picture would ruin the prestige of the theatre."[79]

This last charge highlights a central tension in moving picture exhibition for Black audiences. Based on Edward Sheldon's 1909 play of the same name, *The Nigger* aroused strong feelings largely due to its title (some exhibitors changed it to *The Governor* or *The New Governor*) and its incendiary portrayal of rape and lynching. The *Moving Picture World* proclaimed that "nothing so nauseating" had been shown on screen.[80] Some spectators felt that *The Nigger* was more nuanced than *The Birth of a Nation*, seeing the former film as championing race reconciliation as it told the story of a gubernatorial candidate who is discovered to have a Black grandmother and who then "sacrifices his love to devote his life to the uplift of the Negro."[81] Citing the ambivalence of some contemporary Black press on the film and the accounts of some members of the NAACP, Thomas Cripps has argued that despite the "obvious patronizing references to pedigree, the film may be taken, at least in part, as a tragedy brought on by mindless racism, a testament to the influence of environment over genetic heritage, and a sermon against alcoholic excess rather than against the frailty of one race."[82] However, at the time the inclusion of objectionable scenes outweighed a potentially progressive reading of the narrative. For Russell to accuse Foster of lobbying for *The Nigger* would have been to question his allegiance to respectable theatrical entertainment and suitable representations of African Americans on screen. However compromised his motivations may have been, Russell's criticism complicates the view that Foster was an elite champion of uplift and raises the question of whether self-interest underpinned his entrepreneurial endeavors.

Although Black exhibitors were circumspect about white-produced representations of African Americans, they were just as concerned with the work of

Black filmmakers. Despite the positive response that African American motion picture production received in the Black press, there was nonetheless a measure of skepticism about moving pictures and a prevalent disbelief in their economic viability when compared to theatrical productions. In this context, Foster wrote passionately about the opportunities afforded by motion pictures for the advancement of African Americans in articles such as "Moving Pictures Offer the Greatest Opportunity to the American Negro in History of the Race from Every Point of View." Offering a primarily economic argument, Foster pointed to the international opportunities available to Black film producers as well as the necessity of self-representation: "It is the Negro business man's only international chance to make money and put his race right with the world." Foster wrote: "In a moving picture the Negro would offset so many insults to the race—could tell their side of the birth of this great nation—could show what a great man Frederic Douglas [sic] was the work of Tousant LaOverture [sic], Don Pedro and the battle of San Juan Hill, the things that will never be told only by the Negroes themselves. The world is very anxious to know more of the set-aside race, that has kept America in a political and social argument for the last two hundred and fifty years." Writing in October 1915, Foster is clearly referring to the representational damage committed by *The Birth of a Nation*. Yet he is not merely responding to the immediate crisis spurred by Griffith's slanderous blockbuster. As he notes in his article, his conclusions are the culmination of seven years of studying and working in the moving picture industry. Although he does not directly refer to his own production experience, he does point to a "personal interview with a colored picture concern that made a few pictures sometime ago that were a success, in spite of itself." Citing the number of letters sent to the unnamed company from motion picture enthusiasts and aspiring actors across the country, Foster writes: "It goes to show their heartfelt interest, that they have the nerve and courage to try as their white sisters and brothers are doing and making a success." Foster argues that motion pictures would give talented African Americans more opportunities than afforded by the theater "because the stage, with a few exceptions, never offers the Negro an opportunity to display any real talent as a playwriter." Although championing Black filmmaking as a "novelty" that would appeal to a broad public, he also recognizes the opportunity for economic advancement and representational improvement that increased Black involvement in motion pictures could catalyze.[83]

In July 1916 Foster received financing from Henry Jones, a stage comedian, and was able to produce another feature, *The Barber*, with Anna Holt, Howard Kelly, and Edgar Litterson (figure 5.3). The film is about a "society man" whose

THE BARBER

The One Reel Moving Picture Comedy Riot. By Juli Jones, Jr., Producer of the Railroad Porter

Booking Direct to All Moving Picture and Vaudeville Houses. Live Managers, Get Busy. The fastest and the clearest photographic picture ever made of Colored Actors.
ONE-SHEET HERALDS AND STILLS. WRITE OR WIRE.
FOSTER FILM COMPANY (not Inc.)
Teenan Jones, President.
GRAND THEATER BLDG., 3110 STATE ST., CHICAGO, ILL.

FIG. 5.3 Advertisement for *The Barber*, *Freeman*, November 4, 1916. Courtesy Indiana Newspaper Section, Indiana State Library.

wife loves Spanish music so much that he decides to hire a Spanish teacher for her. His plans are overheard by his barber, who in turn disguises himself and passes himself off as a Spanish music teacher by the name of Alfonso Gaston. Able to speak Spanish himself, the husband discovers the barber's ruse and chases him from the home. The film reportedly contained much action and slapstick bits.[84] With *The Barber*, Foster presents an image of Black urban sophisticates who, like the characters in *The Railroad Porter*, represent upward mobility and cultured modern subjects. The comedy, it appears, comes at the expense of the couple's aspirations toward refinement (music and a foreign language) and celebrates the barber's cunning even as he is frustrated in his plot. The film can be seen as a product of Foster's meditating on tensions within uplift aspirations and working through them via the genre of comedy.

This new influx of capital might have enabled Foster to hire Tony Langston, a columnist for the *Defender*, to serve as a booking agent for the Foster Photo Play Company. When George P. Johnson wrote the Foster Company in August 1916 with the aim of distributing the films of the newly formed Lincoln Motion Picture Company, Langston replied on Foster Company letterhead. Langston wrote that he did not purchase films, but that his office acted as an agent between producers and exhibitors in the Midwest, and that he was in close contact with "every theatre that uses colored films." Furthermore, he said that he had "the columns of The Defender allways [*sic*] opened to me for publicity."[85] Lincoln engaged Langston as an agent for the Chicago release of *The Trooper of Troop K* (Harry A. Gant, Lincoln Motion Picture Company, 1916).[86]

A year later, Foster wrote to congratulate Noble Johnson on the success of the Lincoln films and ask for advice on how to make profitable films. Foster confided: "The brother is not up to times in handling such fast business as the Moving Picture Business call [*sic*] for, only a few can be trusted." In a change from the previous year, Foster now asked Lincoln for assistance in distributing his films and promised that he could "lease a Comedy once a week for a year, easily, that has the Punches."[87] Although Foster had some success with his comedies and actualities, his ambitions were broader, and he planned to produce longer dramatic films.

Giving Foster's title as Director and Manager of the Foster Photo-Play Corporation, the company prospectus announced that he was "Producing Dramas, Comedies, Commercial, Educational Photo Plays."[88] When he advertised shares in the company, Foster listed five upcoming productions, though it is unclear if any of them were ever made. Only one film, *Mother*, was ever mentioned in the press (in 1918), and even then it was only as a coming attraction. Though his early productions had emphasized comedy, the films listed on the company's shareholder prospectus were dramas. The first film listed, *Birth Mark*, is described as a film in which the "folly of youth comes home. Comes home twenty years after one of his deadly sins." The second film, *Fool and Fire*, a "Vampire Drama," was advertised as a "story with a gasping situation that makes the world wonder can there be such a creature living. The climax will spellbind any audience." *Fool and Fire* seems to have been inspired by the contemporary popularity of "vamp" dramas such as the Theda Bara vehicle *A Fool There Was* (Frank Powell, William Fox Film Corporation, 1915), the film version of the 1909 stage play based on Rudyard Kipling's poem "The Vampire." Another "vampire" film, *A Woman's Worst Enemy*, was advertised as a "five-reel Drama starting in Oklahoma Oil Fields, ending in Chicago, when a clever vampire starts the social and business world going wrong. There's no telling what the ending will be." These narratives of wayward protagonists and women leading men astray appear to be attempts to combine entertaining elements with an uplift structure.[89]

Foster's planned six-reel drama *Brother* was described as "showing four sides of life. The bad colored man, the bad white man; the good colored man, the good white man. No race of men are [*sic*] better than their women. Every white man in the South is not a Race Hater."[90] The epic scope of this synopsis demonstrates Foster's ambition to tackle race (and gender) issues as well as to direct an interracial cast. *Mother*, a "patriotic photoplay drama" about the Eighth Regiment, was advertised in these terms: "A number of startling scenes, covering four thousand people, will be presented. The picture has many thrilling incidents woven into a beautiful story, and typifies the heroism of a mother's love in her attempt to save her boy."[91] In the prospectus, *Mother* is listed as a six-reel war drama with fifty scenes "presenting the race idea of this great World's War."[92] However, there is no evidence that the film was ever released. In the notice in the *Defender* announcing the film, Foster declares that the film has been completed but that "permission is being sought from the federal government to present the play."[93] Although the announcement concludes that the "ambition of Mr. Foster to attain great heights in the moving picture world is about to be realized," his greatest success seems to have remained his first comedy, *The Railroad Porter*.

Brother and *Mother* are the only films in Foster's prospectus whose synopses indicate a race component. From his writing, it is clear that Foster had ambitions to distribute his films in theaters with white patrons as well as those with Black audiences, so perhaps he was envisioning films with potentially broader appeal than specifically race-themed films. Furthermore, these synopses indicate Foster's interest in moving into a more ambitious, broadly popular, and—with drama—even respectable area of film production. Still, it is likely that the films were never produced. As Cripps has documented, a number of Black film companies emerged in the late 1910s, but few were able to produce and distribute a completed film. Competition was stiff in "a marketplace already beset by tiny margins, cutthroat competition, limited outlets, and empty pockets."[94] Foster's later failure was not unique, a fact that underscores the incredible achievement of the projects he did complete.

In spite of his early success in comedy and his ambitions to produce dramatic features, Foster continued to film actualities of interest to Black audiences, including local films. In 1918 he shot the Eighth Regiment and combined this actuality footage with local subjects of particular appeal to specific audiences, discussed in the local press as a "Chicago Picture."[95] He filmed the regiment departing for Texas on its way to overseas service with the intention of exhibiting the images locally, targeting families of enlisted soldiers who would want to see moving pictures of their relatives in uniform. Foster also recognized an audience in the soldiers themselves and subsequently filmed family members of the troopers to, in the words of the *Chicago Defender*, "bring comfort and cheer to our boys at the front."[96] He combined this footage of citizens (the soldiers and their families) with 250 scenes of Chicago's Black businesses and secret orders (community civic clubs) to make a 2,000-foot local subject film celebrating Black Chicago with "5,000 distinct faces."[97] With this footage, Foster recorded key institutions of life in the city at a particular moment, specifically focusing on its Black elite. This footage also reflected and projected—literally, in the case of public exhibitions—the centrality of the Eighth Regiment and other African American enlisted men to the community's sense of itself. With the American involvement in World War I, the Black soldier became an increasingly important symbol of racial uplift and national belonging.[98]

After exhibiting these moving pictures in Chicago in July, Foster sent the reels to France to show to the soldiers preparing for the trenches. No records survive to give details of the mechanics of these distant screenings, but the *Defender* reported: "It is the purpose of this film exhibition in France to give the boys an idea of home life and what the people are doing over here."[99] Foster also intended the films to be screened "in all the big film houses in London and Paris to show who is behind the trenches."[100] The *Defender* considered Foster's films to be equal to "any of the big pictures that the Pathe [*sic*] and Hearst have ever put on the screens" and said that they "will be an eye-opener to the world."[101] Then, in October 1918, Foster filmed more footage of relatives of the troops and sent the films to the military to screen to the troops over the holidays. Advertised as "smile movies," Foster published a schedule in the *Defender* to film "the Colored troops' folks."[102] A variation on the local "see yourself" films, Foster's films became travelogues, bringing images of Black Chicago to the homesick soldiers. In these foreign exhibitions of Foster's reels, the local film takes on national significance for Black soldiers fighting abroad by projecting an image of home that conflates the Black community of Chicago's South Side with the national cause. Thus, the interrelatedness of the local and national that undergirds the local film finds overt expression in Foster's filmmaking practice. Of course, tied up with these films are issues of racism in the army and ambivalence about African American investment in national causes.

In the 1910s, Foster strategically positioned his uplift filmmaking to appeal to audiences on several levels. The "Foster movement" of race film production is marked by multiple genres of moving pictures that functioned in combination to address Black spectators as participants in a broader cultural self-fashioning that was modeled on the uplift ideal.[103] If it was primarily found in Foster's own work and career, it nonetheless helped shape a wide range of other filmmaking practices. Foster's endeavors eventually took him from Chicago to Los Angeles, where he had a fascinating, if little known, second act to his filmmaking career, one that will be discussed at the end of this chapter.

PETER P. JONES

Among Foster's friends and business associates was the famed photographer Peter P. Jones (figure 5.4). One of the most celebrated and successful African American studio photographers of the early twentieth century, Jones captured the likenesses of artists and entertainers (Henry O. Tanner [figure 5.5], Bert Williams, and Aida Overton Walker), politicians and military men (Colonel Franklin A. Denison and Major John R. Lynch), educators and race leaders (Washington and W. E. B. Du Bois), religious figures (Bishop C. T. Schafer), and other prominent leaders. He also specialized in photography for theater professionals.[104] Jones portrayed his subjects with dignity, pathos, and respectability. By capturing his fellow members of the nation's Black elite, Jones might well be considered the exemplary photographer of the uplift movement.[105] His multimedia enterprise and aesthetic sensibilities were deeply invested in his community and in celebrating the advancement of the race across broad areas of cultural and political achievement. Jones was a member of the Photographers' Association of America and was reportedly represented by a number of galleries in the United States and Europe, including the Victor George Gallery, Moffett Studios, and the fashionable Matzene Studio (where for three years he worked in its development).[106]

As part of his photography business, Jones produced a large number of photo portrait postcards. Since these postcards, like Jones's films, are non-extant or unattributed, this discussion must be confined to what can be gleaned from the scant archival references to their production and circulation rather than the nuances of their visual rhetoric. However, we can gain some sense of what that rhetoric might have been like by placing Jones's postcards in the broader context of the role of postcards in African American representation.

A fad of the early twentieth century, photo postcards could be seen as emblematic of modernity: they were mechanically reproduced, circulated through the civic infrastructure of postal networks, and composed a collectable commodity. Made possible by changes to postal regulations and the development

Photography

PETER H. JONES.

To the Theatrical Profession

GREETING

I offer the latest in high class

PHOTOGRAPHY.

Correct Posing, Popular Tones, the Best Finishes for Theatrical Purposes in the Middle West.

A Trial Will Convince You.

Studio 3519 State St., Chicago.

FIG. 5.4 (*top*) Advertisement for photography, *Freeman*, January 8, 1910. Courtesy Indiana Newspaper Section, Indiana State Library.

FIG. 5.5 (*right*) Henry O. Tanner portrait by Peter P. Jones, 1909. Courtesy Henry Ossawa Tanner Papers, Archives of American Art, Smithsonian Institution.

of photographic printing processes, the photo postcard was both a private souvenir and a public marker of cosmopolitanism.[107] The relatively inexpensive production of personalized photo postcards, such as those produced by Jones, allowed Black urban consumers to procure an image that was both a private portrait and a publicly disseminated image. However, Jones's work also entered the visual sphere of other genres of real photo postcards in circulation at the time, thereby participating in a dialogue with varied iterations of the medium, ranging from larger commercial ventures (such as the promotion of motion picture actors through star postcards) to amateur and itinerant products.

The star portraits were an important intertext for Jones's postcards. As souvenir photos of stars began to circulate and be collected, photo postcards were key in publicizing actors.[108] Because of this, the photo postcard of a private person would, through its professional format and the concurrent existence of comparable examples of celebrities, take on some of that aura. The personal or family photograph might indicate upward mobility and consumerist self-reflection. It would also carry with it an inherent interactivity: although some real photo postcards were undoubtedly produced for personal collections like other studio portrait photography, the format with its verso print suggests a possible recipient or viewer apart from the subject on the front — someone who would relish receiving such a souvenir. Indeed, in the 1910s in Chicago and beyond, the Great Migration divided families across the country, making the photo postcard an especially meaningful keepsake as well as a sign to those back home of the urbaneness of the sender. Clients could fashion themselves by using the photo postcard as proof of their upward mobility, sending what the Eastman Kodak Company termed "the individuality of companionship" to relatives in the south.[109] These images offered a contrasting portrait of African Americans to that which circulated through the south on a very different kind of photo postcard: of lynchings.

As James Allen, Shawn Smith, Koritha Mitchell, Amy Wood, and others have demonstrated, photography and the circulation of images — often through the photo postcard — was integral to the dissemination of terror that was a constituent of ritual lynching.[110] Antilynching campaigns such as those of Ida B. Wells and others raised broad awareness of the horrors of lynching and its grotesque celebration through souvenir images. Often depicting the aftermath of the murder of a young Black man by a crowd of whites usually referred to by local authorities as "persons unknown," lynching postcards circulated the gruesome spectacles of white aggression in the form of a collectable commodity. As Smith notes, "postcard photographers not only capitalized on the scene of the crime but also played a crucial role in producing and reproducing the crime itself as a 'scene.' These photographers designed images not simply to document or depict but to memorialize; they created mementos and souvenirs for participants to share with family and friends."[111] Two things are important here. First, lynching photographs typically depicted the aftermath of the crime and often repositioned subjects for the camera. Second, the "profoundly unafraid" crowd that posed to record this fantasy of control, as Smith notes, asserts a social—even civic—belonging to the group with power so that the presence of murder is registered not as a threat to authority but as its assertion.[112]

Jones's postcard production worked against the sickening logic of lynching photo postcards by offering a counterimage of civic belonging. In July 1911 Jones produced a set of twelve photo postcards that Foster published through his music company. The series depicted Chicago's landmarks of African American civic life, including the vernacular architecture of local churches and businesses. In its endorsement of the postcards, the *Chicago Defender* remarked that the series consisted of "the most handsome postals ever put on the market" and reported both on their aesthetic value and the significance of the business venture in "race enterprise."[113] The series was a success, prompting Jones to go further into the photo postcard business. A year after producing the series with Foster, Jones opened the Climax Photo Studio on State Street with the goals of producing photo postcards for the public at ten cents per card and of giving "the citizens of Chicago a card that they have never seen before."[114]

Jones's naming of his photo postcard studio Climax refers to the presumed quality of his work as well as to the single moment captured through photography. Yet it also suggests the in medias res nature of his photographic subjects and, subsequently, his actuality filming. Lynching photographs for the most part depict the act as a fait accompli, a reconstruction of a murder captured outside time. In contrast, the name "Climax" for the photo studio returns the photograph to the time of a narrative's unfolding, to a moment where change is possible—to the unstaged reality of everyday life. With a present-tense defiance, Jones answers the horror of photographs depicting the aftermath of lynching.

As a name, "Climax" also temporally situates the postcard in a linear narrative, representationally akin to motion picture photography with its movement through time. In some ways the real photo postcard could be seen as the opposite of the moving picture: the spectator engages with the postcard tactilely as well as visually and individually rather than collectively, and has a relationship with the image that is one of ownership and control (where to put it, when and how to use it). Yet the experiences of both the postcard and the moving picture grew from and were constituent of American consumer culture's rise in the

Peter P. Jones.

early twentieth century, as they "relate to twentieth century traditions through their use as a mode of brief and ephemeral communication."[115] There is, then, a logical trajectory from Jones's portrait photography through his promotion of real photo postcards to his production of motion picture actualities, fictions, and hybrids.

Like his fellow entrepreneurs in Chicago's Black elite, Jones was involved in a number of professional activities (figure 5.6). In 1912 he ran unsuccessfully for alderman of the Second Ward with the backing of the *Chicago Defender*. When Jones was accused of being a stooge candidate in the pocket of white interests, Robert S. Abbott, editor of the *Defender*, came to his defense, writing: "The *Defender* would sooner, ten thousand times over, break and wear itself out assailing and exposing the legions of selfish, unprincipled whites that daily are feeding upon, growing fat and rich through the helplessness and igno-rance of the race, than put so much as a straw in the way of the humblest Negro striving to lift himself up and out of the ruts."[116] Jones lost the race to a white candidate, saying that "race prejudice" was the cause and implying that elec-tion irregularities caused the loss.[117] The *Defender* went so far as to accuse his opponents of "treachery," leading to his unfair loss.[118] Despite the controversy over his candidacy, Jones remained in the public eye and served on the committee to organize the Grand August Carnival and Negro Exposition in 1912. Davarian Baldwin has demonstrated that this carnival prefigures early Black filmmaking practices in Chicago, arguing that the event, known popularly as the State Street Fair, "consolidated various spectacles and amusements in ways that would inform later film culture. Through an amazing blend of tradition and modernity, leisure and race uplift, the State Street Fair signaled a conscious moment in the construction of the race's image." Street carnivals, Baldwin writes, "contain profound insights into the emergence of Black film culture as a visual medium of racial representation."[119] Like Jones's photographic work and postcard business, the public exposition is another emblematic spectacle of modernity with which he was professionally engaged prior to making motion pictures. As a member of the executive committee for the carnival, Jones was directly involved in coordinating its various amusements and spectacles. The mix of public forms of expression that constituted the street fair informed Jones's moving picture ventures with their hybrid forms and combination of physical comedy, expressive caricatures, and public display of civic belonging.

It is not clear that his political defeat damaged Jones's social standing or professional position, since many allies came to his defense and challenged the accusations levied against him. Nonetheless, Jones retired suddenly from studio photography in September 1912.[120] Two years later he started a moving picture venture, reportedly capitalized at $100,000 by South American businessmen with the purpose of making films depicting the progress of Black Americans.[121] Anna Everett suggests that Jones's international financing indicates the "limitations of business opportunities available to aspiring black filmmakers during America's Jim Crow era."[122] It also demonstrates the social acceptance of racial integration in South America, particularly Brazil. With the opening of the Brazilian film exhibition market in 1911, foreign films eclipsed local ones, and Brazilian film producers turned largely to newsreels and documentaries. In this context, collaboration with Jones was both an extension of the internationalism that the film industry was experiencing and a source of actuality footage for the Brazilian marketplace.[123]

Supportive of Jones's creative endeavors, the *Chicago Defender* lauded the filmmaker for engaging in "this new scientific fad" and for taking the first moving pictures of the Mystic Shriners' march in Chicago in May 1914. Jones operated the camera himself and recorded the march from in front of the storefront on State Street where his photography studio had been located. The *Defender* announced that Jones's production of moving pictures of the Shriners "marks the beginning of a series of our marching organization and other features of race life that will encourage and uplift."[124] Organizations like the Shriners were instrumental in providing civic models and places of belonging in an ever-changing environment. This combination of the social and service orientation reflects Jones's tendency to work in different forms and expressive genres. In announcing his establishment of the Peter Jones Film Company, the *Defender* stated: "While special effort will be made to develop stories with a human interest having well-laid love plots, others will be seen showing the real commercial and business thrift and prosperity of the race; the humorous side will not be overlooked."[125]

For his first narrative film, Jones worked with Alfred Anderson, a well-known songwriter with experience in show business. (With De Koven Thompson, Alfred Anderson wrote such songs as the 1911 hit "If I Forget.") The work with Jones marked Anderson's entry into moving pictures. Like many members of Chicago's Black elite, Anderson was involved in the Eighth Regiment, which would be the subject of his and Jones's first motion picture collaboration.

The Eighth Regiment of Illinois, known as the "Fighting Eighth," was a celebrated all–African American volunteer regiment. The soldiers of the Eighth Regiment were keenly aware that they were seen as representatives of the race and, as Eleanor Hannah has noted, a "test case for the honor and merit of their African American officers."[126] Military service was a way to assert national belonging and to contradict prevalent myths of Black cowardice and unruliness. The Eighth Regiment had served in Cuba during the Spanish-American War, arriving at Guantánamo Bay on August 14, 1898. Back in Chicago, they functioned as part of the Illinois National Guard. As Hannah notes, "African Americans demonstrated their belief that equality of military service would carry with it equal access to the public space in which to act out one form of responsible citizenship and disciplined manhood—the formal military parade down city streets."[127] Likewise, the summer regiment camp was a valuable space for the assertion of civic pride. Hannah writes: "African American guardsmen needed time to bond and to demonstrate via their presentation of themselves as free adult men and citizens of Illinois, that their company was an asset to their own community as both a model for manhood and as a reminder and a challenge to the larger, white audiences that lay beyond the small African American communities."[128] The value of moving pictures of the regiment was, as the *Defender* put it, to "give an opportunity to all races to see the first Afro-American regiment in camp, a call to battle, an exhibition of his [the African American soldier's] bravery and heroism."[129]

Anderson had visited the Eighth Regiment at its camp in Springfield over the course of several years as a correspondent along with the prominent journalist Cary B. Lewis. Drawing on his military experience for theatrical material, Anderson wrote *Captain Rufus*, a military musical comedy set in the Philippines, for the Pekin Stock Company in 1907; there was a revival staging of it in 1914.[130] Lawrence Chenault had appeared in the 1907 production and Leon Crosby appeared in the 1914 revival, taking over a role originally played by Charles Gilpin.[131] Like *Captain Rufus*, the new film by Anderson and Jones fictionalizes the actions of Black troops fighting in the Spanish-American War, though the musical comedy centered around a bogus captain, whereas the moving picture dramatized the actions of the popular regiment itself.

In July 1914 Anderson returned to Camp Lincoln in Springfield, Illinois, as a "war correspondent" occupying the tent of the *Chicago Defender* and its "quill drivers," in the words of Captain James S. Nelson, quartermaster of the regiment.[132] Jones accompanied Lewis and Anderson and, in late July and early August, filmed the Eighth Regiment at Camp Lincoln, working from a scenario written by Anderson. The result was a dramatic fiction-actuality hybrid film titled *For the Honor of the 8th Ill., U.S.A.* The film was set in 1898 but, rather than a fictionalized reenactment, Jones used footage of 1914 regiment maneuvers to represent the military action in the drama. The actuality footage thereby functioned as historical fiction, yet the film also included appearances of contemporary political figures, rendering the fictional time curiously anachronistic. The *Freeman* reported that the moving pictures were partially directed by Colonel Franklin A. Denison (who led the military maneuvers), who had succeeded Colonel John R. Marshall as head of the Eighth Regiment in January 1914. The paper also noted that Illinois Governor Edward Fitzsimmons Dunne, who appears in the film reviewing troops, lauded the moving pictures as the first taken of the regiment.

To weave through the actuality footage of the regiment, Anderson wrote a love story that serves as a narrative thread through the film. Few details survive about the nature of this story. It featured the colonel's daughter, Lucy, who was courted by a captain named Smith, the story's hero; a major named Duplex was the villain. While lauding the love story as "realistic," one reviewer singled out the characterization of Major Duplex: "It is a rare thing to see one of the race depicted by the race as a rascal or a scoundrel." His villainy is explained, according to the reviewer, by his hopeless love for Lucy. The reviewer does not judge Jones for the portrayal of Duplex, but his praise of the love story's depiction for its "faithfulness to the ways of men" and of the film's overall realism suggests an appreciation for the range of characters presented. It was a breadth, as the reviewer notes, not commonly seen in Black self-representation.[133]

In general, the press reports of *For the Honor of the 8th* emphasized the action sequences of the actuality film rather than the fictional story. One review praised Jones's realism here by saying: "One gets a real war glimpse with all of its possible horror."[134] Lewis reported in the *Freeman*: "The entire Eighth Regiment is shown in battle, a charge up San Juan Hill, the taking of the block house, a storming battle, the surrender, court martial, returning of the troops, review by Gov. Dunne of the state of Illinois, and the 'war correspondent' in the mix-up of battle."[135] For the fictional part of the film, Jones brought in actors from Chicago including Marie Johnson, Rosa Gordon, Lawrence Chenault, and Leon Crosby.[136] He shot them along with the Eighth Regiment exercises led by Colonel Denison and Sergeant Wilson, and Lewis appeared as the "war correspondent."[137] In advance of the premiere, the *Freeman* noted, the film "is destined to [be] the most wonderful realistic war scene ever staged."[138]

Produced for $25,000, the film opened on Saturday, September 5, 1914, at the Pekin Theatre, with tickets selling for ten cents. The *Defender* touted the film: "See the only Colored National Guard Regiment in the world at war."[139] As the film was released right after the beginning of World War I, the news of the time would have had a militarist context (though of course not yet involving the United States). Along with figuring the Black solider as actively engaged with the nation's potential military engagements, the film also coincided with the erection of a dedicated armory in Bronzeville, marking the "state commitment to their formal equality and full citizenship."[140] *For the Honor of the 8th* functioned at the nexus of the public celebration of the dedicated armory, the institution of civic engagement that the regiment represented, and the reflection to itself of the community shown in the film. As a tool of self-representation, the film connected urban monumental architecture with the visual display of military pageantry to serve as a model and celebration of African American uplift.

After the premiere, the *Defender* gave the film a glowing review (not surprising, given that Anderson was an associate editor at the newspaper). Calling it "the classiest moving picture ever witnessed on the South Side" and "the finest and most intelligent yet produced by photo players of the race," the *Defender* lauded the film for its educational aspects. The paper singled out the appearance of Governor Dunne as particularly significant: "Especial [sic] mention should be made of the magnificent appearance of Gov. Dunne while reviewing the troops on governor's day, prior to the regiment's leave [sic] for Cuba. This is the first time that a man of national character, a governor of a state, has posed for a moving picture for the Afro-American race. Gov. Dunne, immediately after reviewing the parade, set his seal of approval for the immediate erection of the new 8th Armory."[141] Dunne's presence, as well as that of Denison and other recognizable figures from 1914, is curiously anachronistic for a drama set in 1898. The apparent acceptance of this anachronism, and the celebration of Dunne's appearance in the film, gives insight into how Black spectators in Chicago consumed this narrative-actuality hybrid. Broadly speaking, although motion pictures were becoming increasingly narratively coherent and consistent, Black spectators created a different kind of coherence and narrative logic.[142] The seemingly invisible techniques of continuity editing were developing into a coherent system that would be codified by 1917, but Jones's work suggests another possibility for cinema as different spectatorial regimes of comprehension were involved. As the uplift rhetoric of the print campaigns of Hampton and Tuskegee highlighted the before-and-after trajectory of individual achievement for collective progress, Jones's fictionalized actuality conflates the past and present in a spectacle of uplift. Jones offers a mechanism by which the role of the Eighth Regiment in 1898 in Cuba can be understood as significant to the present of 1914 through the official nod of Governor Dunne. Dunne thereby serves as a punctuation but also a present marker of the significance of the historical events depicted. The anachronism becomes a mechanism for negotiating progress and asserting uplift. (It is worth comparing Jones's filmic strategy to the literary strategy of Frederick Douglass and his own investment in anachronism. For Jones, anachronism presents a way of understanding the present through the lens of the past, but it works like Douglass's pen in his cracked feet, as Robert Stepto has pointed out.[143] Anachronism, from Douglass on, is a strategy with special meaning for Black culture and is a strategy deployed by Jones to directly relate past actions of Black heroism to the present.)

For the Honor of the 8th likely served a more practical purpose for Black Chicagoans. In the first decades of the twentieth century, the Eighth Regiment encountered increasing hostility such as interruptions at parades, snubbings, threats of violence, and even physical attacks on members of the regiment by white spectators.[144] Projecting the parading regiment before a Black audience realigned the context of both spectacle and spectatorship to an all-Black space uninterrupted by reminders of white hegemony. The street, like the dominant visual culture, was a hostile site that required oppositional production practices and resistant modes of spectatorship. Such an opposition required reclaiming both the street (through acts of civic belonging and defiance of the myriad iterations of white hostility) and the screen (through the production and projection of actualities, fictions, and hybrid moving pictures that vied with the demeaning representations pervasive in mass culture). The moving pictures mitigated the contingencies that would have attended the public display of the regiment's pageantry.

Jones's hybrid strategy extended across films as well as within them. In addition to filming actualities, Jones also produced race comedies that drew on familiar vaudeville acts. These comedies were fraught with older traditions of racialized representation while concurrently working within uplift paradigms. To produce comedy films, Jones partnered with the famed comedian Matt Marshall, who served as director of productions, and J. T. Bell who served as the company's business manager.[145] Marshall had appeared in Anderson's 1907 stage production of *Captain Rufus* at the Pekin and had starred in the 1907 stage production of *Shoo-Fly Regiment*, written by J. Rosamond and James Weldon Johnson—a show that associated southern industrial education with the establishment of a Black regiment sent to the Philippines.[146] *The Shoo-Fly Regiment* combined African American soldiers in the Spanish-American War with a dramatic romantic narrative, the same combination that Jones employed in *For the Honor of the 8th*. Although Cole and Johnson avoided comedic stereotyping, departing from minstrel conventions, comedies based on stereotypes were nonetheless quite popular with Black audiences.[147] Celebrated vaudevillians Marshall and Andrew Tribble had an act called "The Troubles of Sambo and Dinah." The *Defender* noted the vast crowds gathered at the Grand Theater in April 1913 to see Marshall and Tribble perform "their clever act," in response to which the audiences were "convulsed from the moment they appear until the curtain goes down." The *Defender* noted: "if those in the audience had troubles on their minds before they entered they quickly vanished before these inimitable fun makers."[148] Basing his film *The Troubles of Sambo and Dinah* on Marshall and Tribble's popular skit, Jones's adaptation is rooted in Black vaudeville and intraracial comedy, becoming what Baldwin has termed an "uplift comedy."[149] The fact that a minstrel stage comedy could provide the source material for an uplift film demonstrates one of the inherent contradictions of the uplift project. Because cinema operated in the same sphere as vaudeville acts and minstrel comedy, uplift films drew on these other forms for source material and mechanisms of address. The adjacency of these often conflicting forms demonstrates the ways in which they engaged different but complementary aspects of the uplift project.

At the Pekin Theatre in Chicago, Jones screened twelve reels of motion pictures, including his actualities, mixed genre pictures, and *The Troubles of Sambo and Dinah*. The *Defender* called the latter a "side breaker" not to be missed, and "a killer of the 'blues.'"[150] In *Sambo and Dinah*, Marshall, the "funniest man in vaudeville," starred alongside Ethel Fletcher, Tom Lemonier, Effie Riddley, and Earl Watson. The *Defender* further announced that Marshall would direct Jones's comedies: "His ability in this direction was recognized during the palmy days of the old Pekin stock company. He surrounded himself with a galaxy of stars who can produce real legitimate fun and humor, the kind that will not cause the race to blush in shame at disgraceful actions and themes." In the wake of the controversy over the Lubin Manufacturing Company's *The Tale of a Chicken*, a comedy (discussed below) based on stereotypes from minstrelsy, the *Defender* announced: "There will be no chicken-stealing scenes or crap games to be played by this company. The pictures will be placed upon a high order and the scenes will tend to awaken the consciences of men and women to do the right thing in life and will discourage drunkenness, dishonesty and licentiousness. There will be love scenes of the purest type, ones that children, maids and patrons will relish with pleasure."[151] Here, Jones's project is explicitly aligned with the uplift of cinema, and film is presented as a model mechanism for shaping audience behavior. The *Freeman* lauded the film: "Again the unexpected happened when 'Sambo and Dinah,' a new colored life moving picture furnished by the Peter P. Jones Film Company, opened on the 14th with Matt Marshall, the popular actor in the chief character, at the States. That Marshall is the best comedy actor that has been seen in the colored pictures goes on record and what proves it is that people were turned away in the lineup at every performance. The dinner at Chateau Garden was a feature."[152] Sambo and Dinah, common names in Black minstrelsy, were appropriated by African American performers and welcomed by many spectators. The inclusion of scenes at the Chateau Garden, a popular South Side café and performance venue, set the comedy in recognizable places frequented by members of its intended audience. In this respect, even Jones's comedy contained actuality elements of "colored life" with particular appeal to Black Chicagoans.

In August and September 1915, Jones filmed the Illinois National Half Century Exposition and Lincoln Jubilee, including the Elks' parade, Baptist convention, and Governor's Day (apparently with the cooperation of Thomas Wallace Swann, the secretary of the exposition commission).[153] The result was a 5,000-foot actuality film of the events first advertised as *50 Years Freedom*, "the greatest motion picture ever produced of colored people" (figure 5.7).[154] Jones showed images of the exposition, the state exhibits, inventors and their works, and the industrial and art exhibitions. In his advertisements, Jones proclaimed, "The picture is a hummer."[155] In various configurations, Jones would exhibit this footage well into the following year, building, as Pearl Bowser puts it, a

50 Years 50 Years
FREEDOM FREEDOM

The Greatest Motion Picture Ever Produced of Colored People

The Illinois National Half Century Exposition and Lincoln Jubilee, held in Chicago from August 24 to September 16, 1915, showing the progress of the Negro. Everything we have done in 50 Years of Freedom produced in pictures, so that the entire world can see.

Ready to be Shown on the Screen

This picture shows a general view of entire exposition, each state exhibit in detail, all the inventors and their inventions, large industries and beautiful art work and artists. All of the many big days at the exposition—

Elks Day

Grand Elks' Parade. This feature alone is one of the most beautiful parades ever shown, classy to the last minute.

Baptist Day

Showing the large gathering at the Lincoln Jubilee Exhibition and their Convention at the Armory.

Governor Day

Gov. Dunne and Officials of Exposition.

Owners and Managers of Theatres: This picture is ready for bookings; write in for open time and terms. State and territory rights for sale. The picture is a hummer.

PETER P. JONES
FILMS CO.

FIG. 5.7 Advertisement for *50 Years Freedom* in *Chicago Defender*, October 2, 1915.

"complex grid of images" out of his actualities and fiction films.[156] For example, he screened two reels at the Booker T. Washington Theatre in Indianapolis on March 23, 1916, under the title *The Dawn of Truth* (*For the Honor of the 8th* was on the same program). The title comes from the name of a section of the exposition that focused on "the progress of the race" from Appomattox Court House, Virginia, to the Tuskegee Institute. The section included the domestic cotton industry and "the Genius of Liberty at home and abroad," and included life-size portraits of Ulysses S. Grant, Douglass, Washington, and Stephen A. Douglas.[157] Displaying savvy marketing skills, Jones replaced these last two portraits with images of General John A. Logan and the abolitionist Owen Lovejoy, both popular heroes in Illinois history, in a front-page advertisement in the *Freeman* featuring the "leading characters" in *The Dawn of Truth*.[158] In April Jones took the show to Ohio, where he screened the same program, along with *The Troubles of Sambo and Dinah*, for two-night engagements in Cincinnati and Cleveland. From Jones's advertisement in the *Freeman*, it is clear that the uplift potential of *The Troubles of Sambo and Dinah* was presumed (figure 5.8). The adjacency of the comedy and actualities chronicling the "progress of the Negro" and the "Re-Birth of a Nation" suggest that the older vaudeville tradition of Black caricature was not replaced by the uplift actualities but coexisted, however uneasily, with them.[159] The film and its vaudeville source were not seen as derogatory or compromised by spectators; in fact, one review pointed to Jones's comedy as "evidence of the versatility" of the filmmaker.[160]

Jones's reference to the "Re-Birth of a Nation" in his advertisement is significant. Baldwin rightly sees it as a response to Griffith, "or to what his film represented," and Bowser reads it as an affirmative gesture participating in the celebration of the fiftieth anniversary of the Emancipation Proclamation.[161] Indeed, Jones's program explicitly uses actuality footage of the "progress of the Negro" to show the "prime factors in the Re-Birth of a Nation." Jones subverts Griffith's slander by showing "the true birth of a nation as it concerns the Negro race," as one reviewer put it. After a full year of protest, pushback, and political debate, the wound made by *The Birth of a Nation* was still fresh, and Jones's audience was primed to see his exhibition as both a celebration of fifty years of freedom and an assertion of a powerful corrective to the representational injustice of Griffith's "orgy of contempt and reflection." The same reviewer lauded Jones for his promotion of the self-representation of the race, noting that although "white pictures" dominate, "there are still other lessons to be learned and they must come from pictures of ourselves by ourselves."[162]

In May 1917 Jones released *The Slacker*, a war drama "full of thrills and facts" that was likely comprised of footage reused from *For the Honor of the 8th*: "The

Red Cross nurse wins in love and the Slacker proves himself a hero."[163] A military melodrama written by Alice Jones, *The Slacker* reportedly premiered to one of the largest audiences of the year assembled at the States Theater.[164] The *Chicago Defender* reported: "From start to finish the play is full of thrills. The slacker, a Race youth, proves at last to be a hero. The encores from the audience makes one feel that he is right on the firing line, watching the slacker 're-slack,' and with his country's flag, win both glory and a wife."[165] Jones then made *The Accidental Ruler*, with Frank P. George, Marie Burton, and Sidney Perrin. Released in September 1917, the film featured two researchers exploring Africa as they encounter wild animals, are captured by natives, are judged by the native queen, and eventually become kings of the natives.[166] The film played to reportedly good audiences at the Washington Theater in Chicago.[167]

With his lens focusing on a wide range of subjects, and employing various modes of filmmaking, Jones not only entertained audiences with his motion pictures but also reflected back to them scenes of their community that would inspire a sense of pride and belonging. This was a powerful model, but it is not clear how sustainable it was. No evidence survives to suggest that Jones made films after 1917, although in the early 1920s he moved to New York and worked for David O. Selznick taking still photos, combining his expertise as a studio photographer with his moving picture experience.[168]

HUNTER C. HAYNES:
A "HUSTLING NEGRO" IN NEW YORK CITY

No more entrepreneurial a figure turned to filmmaking during this period than Haynes (figure 5.9), described as a "hustling negro" by the *Topeka Plaindealer*.[169] By 1901 Haynes had become known as the "King of Razor Traders," having established a business in shaving supplies that rapidly grew into a large enterprise, starting with secondhand razors and then moving to the manufacture of razor strops.[170] He invented, for example, a razor strop called "The New Idea," which reportedly sold well in both Europe and the United States.[171] As a prominent New York businessman with national and international ambitions, Haynes was frequently lauded in the Black press across the country. He also published a history of barbering, enthusiastically titled "Knights of the Razor!," in the Indianapolis *Freeman* in 1902.[172] Haynes's vast business expertise served as a foundation for his filmmaking ventures, and his broad travel experience informed his narrative sensibility, especially in the comedies he wrote that pivoted on clashing cultures, classes, and social mores.

The Black press lauded Haynes's entrepreneurial successes, for example

FIG. 5.9 Hunter C. Haynes portrait, *Indianapolis Recorder*, April 12, 1913. Courtesy *Indianapolis Recorder* and IUPUI University Library Digital Collections.

HUNTER C. HAYNES.

when he received the largest merchandise consignment order ever placed from London to an African American manufacturer; or when his strop was reportedly used by Francis Haby, the private barber to the German kaiser. Haynes's early career is marked by impressive professional achievements in the barbering world and other business ventures. He employed six men, four of whom were whites, to represent his company on the road. Haynes returned from a business trip to Europe in time to deliver a talk titled "The Negro as a Business Man" at the August 1904 meeting of the NNBL in Indianapolis.[173] After returning from another trip to Europe, Haynes wrote an article for the *Freeman* on "the barber's world."[174] In 1905, in true uplift fashion, Haynes opened a barber's college in Chicago for African American men and women.[175] In 1906 he left Chicago to establish the New York Razor Strop Company in New York City.[176] After forays into brokerage and loan and shipping businesses, he sold his razor strop company in 1911 and accepted a reportedly "flattering" job as foreman of the M. L. Grant Cutlery Company in New York.[177] At this point, he founded the Haynes Advertising Agency and became an active member of the National Negro Press Association. N. Barnett Dodson, writing in the *Indianapolis Record*, lauded Haynes's achievements: "Although quite young, the Haynes enterprise is proving the Afro-Americans' appreciation of present day business requirements by entering into this almost hitherto untried field among us for the purpose of bringing the advertiser and the publisher into closer relation."[178] It is unclear exactly what led Haynes to the moving pictures, but it is likely that Haynes saw that development as an extension of his work in advertising (advertising, after all, is a key to the success of useful cinema). The *Freeman* reported that the motion picture business is "the calling which engrossed him."[179]

In the summer of 1913, Haynes became the general manager of the white-owned Afro-American Film Company, based in New York City. In an article titled "Reel Colored Pictures, by Real Colored Persons," the *New York Clipper* reported that the company was capitalized at $100,000 and aimed to "specialize in the production of films intended for colored audiences. These will contain colored actors only, and will be directed by colored men." The *Clipper* noted that the company would produce comedies, dramas, and a number of educational films each month; Charles A. Pryor was listed as president, Haynes as vice president, and Clarence H. Fay as treasurer.[180] The films were directed by Frank A. Wade, a well-known producer of musical comedies on stage, who was lauded as "America's greatest Motion Picture Producer" in the Afro-American Film Company's advertisements.[181] However well known as he may have been as a theatrical producer, I have found no evidence to suggest that he had worked in moving pictures prior to his involvement with the Afro-American Film Company. This white-owned venture that catered to African American audiences prefigures such race film companies working in the 1920s through the 1940s as the Norman Film Manufacturing Company, Sack Amusement Enterprises, Million Dollar Productions, Toddy Pictures, and Reol Productions.

The Afro-American Film Company proudly produced films "with real negro characters" and aimed to show "the rapid progress of the negro in every field of human activity."[182] A shrewd businessman, Haynes diversified the motion pictures of the Afro-American Film Company, producing comedies as well as actualities, as did Foster and Jones in their moving picture ventures. Anticipating the growing interest in Black business activities, Haynes and two other operators shot footage of the NNBL's annual meeting in Philadelphia in August 1913.[183] His presence at the meeting and Washington's approval of it resulted in the mistaken report that the Afro-American Film Company was under the management of the NNBL and that Washington "is personally interested in the welfare of the new company."[184] However, given Washington's deep interest in image and self-promotion and his interest in procuring footage of himself, Tuskegee, and the NNBL, it is clear that he was a strong supporter of Haynes's endeavors.

The resulting film, *Notable Negroes and Their Achievements*, was presented as an educational film and "the first film ever produced showing millions of dollars worth of property, enterprises and noted American Negroes."[185] Like Foster, Anderson, and Jones, Haynes was interested in reaching southern audiences. When the film was exhibited at the Pekin Theatre in Savannah in April 1914, it was advertised as the greatest "scenic and Industrial production" and the first moving picture to capture Washington, J. C. Napier, Emmett J. Scott, George H. White, and Charles W. Anderson, among others. It also featured footage of the NNBL and the Knights of Pythias conclave in Baltimore.[186] In addition, *Notable Negroes* included comedic street scenes.[187] The combination of actuality footage, portraits of famous people, and comedy in *Notable Negroes* is consistent with filmmaking entrepreneurs' interest in mixing genres and modes of filmmaking to entertain audiences within a rubric of uplift.

In February 1914 the Afro-American Film Company announced the upcoming release of two comedies, *Lovey Joe's Romance* and *The Tango Queen*. The company described *Lovey Joe's Romance* as "a Masterpiece d'Art," calling it a "sensational melodramatic and classic" comedy. Featuring Stella Wiley, Bob A. Kelley, Braxton and Carter, and Anthony D. Byrd, the film was advertised as "a clean cut story taken from real life."[188] The *Freeman* reported:

> The phenomenal success of the Afro-American Film Co., has opened the eyes of managers of colored houses who have been playing legitimate attractions when they could get them. Many of the white managers as well as colored have had a revelation as to the possibilities of the productions produced by the Afro-American Film Co., as real "business gettings." Like a good business man, Mr. Haynes has carefully studied the market, and from the most unfavorable surroundings, despite his handicaps, lack of [illegible], and the almost insurmountable barriers standing between him and success, he has today outdistanced the average white manufacturer, and from a business standpoint, is far in the lead.[189]

However, from an artistic standpoint, critics viewed the Afro-American Film Company as a decided failure. No reports survive concerning *The Tango Queen*, but Herbert Meadows's report in the *Freeman* on the St. Louis screening of *Lovey Joe's Romance* eviscerated that film:

This so-called "masterpiece" proved of the most amateurish class. The play is disconnected all through. The scenery is bad; is static, even in the announcements. The camera, in most instances, was out of focus and the gun used was a toy weapon that would not shoot. "Lovie [sic] Joe" is in evidence, but the "Romance" was not discernible. The general action of the piece is absolutely absurd and it is to be regretted that the first production of the Afro-American Film Co. to come west should have shown such weakness. No one is more disappointed than Mr. Turpin, the Booker Washington Theatre owner, who is ever ready to boost race enterprise, and as in this case, confidentially invests heavily for good results.[190]

The criticism of the production values and "absurd" plot indicates the cultural discernment, at least on the part of Meadows and presumably other spectators as well, that had been underestimated by the Afro-American Film Company.

The Afro-American Film Company apparently improved its production values for its next release, *One Large Evening*, which had a successful run at the Lafayette Theatre in New York. Praising the film as "one of the best visualizations of every-day life," the *Amsterdam News* reported that "Mr. Haynes has succeeded admirably in his effort of producing a comedy production with abundance of action."[191] The film is a marital farce about a minister who woos the wife of a doctor, who in turn is wooing a grocer's wife—and the grocer is after the preacher's wife. Additionally, a deacon and a railroad porter are also wooing the doctor's wife and visit her secretly. After the doctor returns home from flirting with the grocer's wife, he discovers the deacon and the railroad porter hiding, one in the bed and the other behind the piano. As he throws them out of the house, the minister—who has been hiding in the fireplace—is able to outwit the doctor and escape. The doctor later finds the minister and chases him with a gun. In the end, the couples are all brought back together.[192] Charles Gilpin played the doctor, Marie Young the doctor's wife, and Leon Williams the minister. Also appearing were Marie Young, Sarah Greene Byrd, and Ava Johnson.[193]

Based on the plot summary, *One Large Evening* appears to be an amusing farce and comedy of manners. However, not everyone was thrilled about the film. In April 1914 the Chicago Board of Moving Picture Censors rejected it at the encouragement of Reverend Archibald J. Carey, the Black member of the board who had recently been appointed at the time of the film's rejection.[194] Films that were accepted by the National Board of Censorship of Motion Pictures were often not shown in Chicago because, as the *Defender* noted, the "cosmopolitan makeup of [the] local body protects every race from ridicule." The *Defender* alluded to Carey's rejection of *One Large Evening* as an example of the way in which he "completely revolutionized the moving pictures pertaining to the race he represents." The newspaper continued: "Before he was a member the board only concerned itself with the vicious portrayals but under the keen eyes of Rev. Carey even the ridiculous has been eliminated. A case in point is this: Recently a white firm in New York passed on to Chicago what they termed highly creditable race pictures. They had the sanction of various eastern censors but Rev. Carey saw nothing elevating in them and they were cut out."[195] A "power broker," Carey was one of the most powerful Black Chicagoans, serving as a kind of uplift gatekeeper of images promoting respectability.[196] He later played a central role in the fight against *The Birth of a Nation* in 1915, but his intervention in the exhibition of *One Large Evening* demonstrates that he was more concerned about the self-representation of Black people than he was about their misrepresentation by white filmmakers. This is also evidenced by the curious fact that Carey did not block the screening of Lubin's *The Tale of a Chicken*, although he did prevent the showing of *One Large Evening*.

Clearly, there was material in Lubin's film that Carey could have objected to. The *Moving Picture World* reported on *The Tale of a Chicken* in negative terms: "This is a burlesque on 'Sherlock Holmes' and is intended to be 'cute,' evidently. If the cruel abuse of a speckled hen can be construed into comedy then this misnomer is funny. The actors are colored individuals."[197] Although the trade journal expressed disgust over the "cruel abuse" of the chicken, the Black press was irate over the degrading buffoonery performed by Black actors. As Stewart has shown, critics and patrons would complain to the managers of Black theaters if they screened films deemed racially offensive.[198] The States Theater was chastised for showing *The Tale of a Chicken* in May 1914, as the *Defender* launched a front-page attack against it for showing Lubin's film along with Warner's Civil War drama *A Mother of Men*.[199] Calling the first film "disgusting," "raw," and "vile," the *Defender* commented, "We would think that pictures to uplift and show the good and not the bad would be the first thought of a 'Movie' proprietor."[200] William Foster told the *Defender*: "I heartily endorse the attack of *The Chicago Defender* on the theaters showing pictures that are degrading and making the race ridiculous from every viewpoint. Stealing chickens and similar pictures only appeal to the ignorant class and race-hating whites."[201] Here, Foster rehearses the uplift mission of eradicating ignorance through the promotion of images of respectability.

These tensions played out in an article written about Haynes's *One Large Evening* by the prominent arts critic Lester Walton. Writing for the *New York*

Age, Walton observed that "members of the race who have respect for their women and their ministry fail to discover one iota of humor in it." Walton praised Carey's intervention, lauding his role on the censor board as "strategic" and one that "can render the race invaluable service."[202] Walton identified the producers as Jewish and was stunned that they would produce a film ridiculing the Black clergy when "no filmmakers would have the audacity to produce a picture so seriously involving a priest or a rabbi." He continued: "When 'One Large Evening' was shown at the Lafayette Theatre there were some who were disposed to criticize Hunter C. Haynes, who had been associated with the Afro-American Film Company, for putting the picture on the market. But it is said that 'his voice did not have any sound to it' when the advisability of producing 'One Large Evening' was discussed." Walton inferred that Haynes could not have been involved because he was not included in the announcement in the newspapers that the Afro-American Film Company had been incorporated for $10,000 by Alfred W. Burg, Gertrude K. Wade, and Frank A. Wade.[203] Walton commented: "Perhaps it is the same old story—the colored man furnishing the idea, but shut out from partnership when the proposition materializes."[204] This is perhaps a bit disingenuous since the April 9 issue of the *New York Age* lauded the film as "the best mechanically that Hunter C. Haynes and his associates have yet produced." That early review notes that "there is no denying the fact that 'One Large Evening' contains much humor," and that the film would be "enjoyed by all colored Americans who do not object to the ministers and other members of the race being shown in a none too complimentary light."[205] The praise for the professional polish of *One Large Evening* makes sense given the critique of *Lovey Joe's Romance* as being amateurish.

However, Walton made a stronger, and possibly unfounded, charge: he reported that *One Large Evening* was retitled as *A Night in Coontown* for white theaters.[206] There is no surviving evidence confirming that a film called *A Night in Coontown* was ever exhibited, but Walton's report nonetheless reflects the racist tropes prevalent in Reconstruction and post-Reconstruction America. Similar derogatory cultural views were captured on the minstrel stage, as well as in popular cartoons such as the "coontown" series by Edward Winsor Kemble. Walton's accusation also makes *One Large Evening* a descendant of the celebrated Bob Cole stage production *A Trip to Coontown* (1898–1900), which was the first musical comedy written and produced by African Americans and which featured an all-Black cast.[207] Regardless of the veracity of his claim, Walton's suggestion that the film was released as *A Night in Coontown* for white audiences is revealing. The fear that filmmakers would not be able to control the use of their images suggests an underlying contingency to uplift cinema. Produced for Black audiences, uplift comedies presumed a shared perspective with the audience. White spectators would have a very different relationship to Black comedy, and the possibility of abuse puts contingency back in the equation, underscoring the danger of moving pictures. The exhibition context remained central to the definition of uplift filmmaking. Abusing the image by projecting it before a ridiculing gaze, an outsider's view, is understood as distinct from the ridiculing knowing gaze of the insider laughing from within a shared subject position. With *One Large Evening*, issues of accessibility and legibility come to the fore; the concern over the audience demonstrates that the same film *could* be released as *A Night in Coontown*, rendering the subject as one to be laughed at. If the predominant role of the Black figure in white cinema was to be laughed at, then uplift cinema constitutes a project of reclaiming the Black image for the Black audience, freed from the white gaze that had hitherto made it mean something else and had distorted it to fit the dominant expectation of what the Black figure on screen signifies.

Interestingly, it is not just the plot and circumstances of *One Large Evening* that Walton found objectionable, but the way in which the material circumstances of the characters were portrayed, which he found "exceedingly primitive" and unrealistic "compared with present day standards."[208] Here, the image of uplift is key. The fiction is asked to do what the actualities do; there is an expectation of uplift that extends across genres. In an exhibition context where actualities and fictions are presented together, the fiction's presumption of verisimilitude exceeds the limitations of the context of its production. (The issue of realism was clearly vexed. Although the anachronisms in *For the Honor of the 8th* were acceptable, viewers had a harder time accepting the poetic license of film productions in which a single set served multiple functions.) Sensitive to a portrayal that might question the success (understood as the economic status) of the characters, Walton objects to the condition in which characters are portrayed as living: "For instance, the colored doctor is represented as living with his wife in one room, which is used by the family both for the receiving of company and for indulgence in nocturnal slumber. The piano and bed are in the same room, which is poorly furnished. There is not a colored physician in Greater New York who is guilty of living with his family in practically one room. Then, despite the fact that nine out of every ten colored families reside in modern flats and apartment houses, the colored preacher's residence is portrayed as an old frame house, one of the few occupied by colored people in the Harlem district." Walton argues that if films are indeed educational, then producers should present conditions "as they are and not as they think they should be; or, as they take the liberty of assuming, what the public imagines they ought to be." The concern, implicitly, is about the white spectator: "The ignorance displayed by the average white American relative to the home life and natural development of the colored American is bad enough, and tends to make the race question more complex without motion pictures making matters worse by continually representing the race at its worst. The duty of the film manufacturer should be to emancipate the white American from his peculiar ideas and incorrect notions of the colored American, not enslave him in additional ignorance, which is hurtful to both races." Walton's use of the words *emancipate* and *enslave* in a discussion of perception and misperception is a telling reversal that points to a deep faith in the ability of motion pictures to educate whites about the truth (or the uplift version of it) in an environment where misperceptions are the foundation for actual inequities. Walton is convinced, conveniently, that Haynes had nothing to do with *One Large Evening*, as he concludes his critique by calling for more African Americans to work in motion picture production, stating that "Negro life is best known by Negroes."[209] Walton's view, of course, was not universally shared. When the film was shown in Indianapolis at the Hoosier Theater, it was described as "a real scream" in advertisements and promoted as a featured supplement to regular screenings.[210] The controversy over the film speaks to the importance that images of respectability enjoyed, demonstrating how extensively the image of uplift was understood to be a fundamental component of uplift itself.

The Afro-American Film Company followed *One Large Evening* with another comedy, *Mandy's Choice*. When the Lafayette Theatre screened *Mandy's Choice*, the *New York Age* reported that "in justice to the Afro-American Film Company it may be said that the picture contains none of the obnoxious features that made 'One Large Evening' objectionable to many."[211] *Mandy's Choice* featured the respected stage actors Charles Gilpin, Billy Harper, Anthony Byrd, and Sara Green Byrd. It was shown to large crowds at the Lincoln Theater in Chicago the week of May 11, 1914, and also at the States, where it reportedly "made people scream."[212] A comedy, the film was also a romance with the alternative title *Love Will Find a Way*, and it was advertised as "1,100 Feet Continuous Laughs."[213] Presumably a romance about a woman and her suitors, the film avoided controversy by steering clear of potentially inflammatory scenarios while also pivoting its comedy on female sexuality.

On June 15 the Afro-American Film Company released *Dandy Jim's Dream*, advertised as "a comedy eclipsing all others."[214] Again, the company drew from minstrel tropes in the cinematic portrayal of Dandy Jim. In the same month, Haynes wrote a column in the *Freeman* calling for the establishment of an exchange in New York or Chicago to furnish weekly products for theaters catering to African American audiences. His vision was interracial: "I do not believe, however, that under any condition an entire service consisting of pictures portrayed, and posed by Negro actors would prove profitable, but a service furnishing all the latest events of national interest, best white productions, with one or two Negro comedies and dramas in each week's program, would prove to be a big paying proposition, and doubtless, if conservatively managed would show at least 30 per cent [return] on the investment." He concluded with rhetorical flourish: "We're living at a mile-a-second gait in the swiftest epoch of the world's progress—in the age of incredibilities come true." Haynes extolled "the Negro who has money to invest now in the moving picture industry." He also argued for the uplift potential of the medium: "It is an agency which is right at home, it can be scorned and frowned upon and called taboo. It may, however, be welcomed and uplifted and be made a mighty agency in the general welfare of the American Negro." Announcing the end of "the old 'head hand[ker]chief' and 'candle light' ideas," Haynes lauded the new mechanisms of modernity and rehearsed the tropes of old versus new that he would take up thematically in his next film.[215]

In July 1914, after having spent nearly a year at the Afro-American Film Company, Haynes resigned and opened his own film studio in New York in a four-story residence at 159 W. 136th Street in Harlem, around the corner from the current site of the New York Public Library's Schomburg Center for Research in Black Culture. Haynes's goal was to produce two film productions per month of a higher caliber than productions currently on the market.[216] He told the *Freeman* that his goal in starting his own film studio was to "vividly" show in motion pictures "the rapid progress of the race in art, science, religious [*sic*], commerce, education, stage and every field of human endeavor."[217] Motion pictures were seen as an effective and economical way to demonstrate advances in African Americans' material circumstances and culture.

Haynes quickly released the first feature of the Haynes Photoplay Company, *Uncle Remus' Visit to New York*, shot in late July and released in early August 1914. Haynes advertised the two-reel film as "the greatest picturization of Negro life now playing to the public" and "positively the most classic melodramatic Negro production of the decade."[218] *Uncle Remus' Visit* turns the uplift narrative on its head, reimagining the before-and-after trajectory as temporally conflated. It highlights "two extremes" of African American life, as the *Freeman* noted, "from the cabin life of the Southern States to the life of the Negro in stone front flats in New York City":

The story of the play is of Rastus, a successful New York colored businessman, sending for his Uncle Remus and his wife to come and visit them [sic] from their old cabin home in the South. The comedy comes following the sending of a telegram by the inexperienced daughter of Uncle Remus to Rastus that the "Old Couple" will arrive in New York on a certain day, never mentioning what station or over what road. Of course, Rastus goes to the wrong station and the old folks arriving in New York, afraid to trust any one to tell them anything, start out in that big city to find Rastus. Rastus not finding them on the train he met starts back home. And the action from then on is fast and convulsive with laughter.[219]

Uncle Remus and his wife were played by Wesley Jones and Maude Jones, and Rastus and his wife were played by Tom Brown and Abbie Mitchell, all well-known stage performers. In announcing Brown and Mitchell as stars, Haynes noted that the leads were supported by "the highest salaried colored performers ever before assembled in any screen production."[220] He took pride in the capital investment in his actors as well as his advertising, offering lithograph posters and slides free to exhibitors.

Considered a "high class" production, *Uncle Remus' Visit* was popular in Chicago, and there was a reported rush at the Phoenix when it premiered there.[221] Sylvester Russell noted in his review that "it was the best picture by a colored film company that has yet been shown."[222] O. C. Hammond, manager of the Phoenix, reportedly stated that "the audience was carried away with enthusiasm. Endless laughter and applause greeted scene after scene."[223] Walton, who had been so critical of *One Large Evening*, lauded *Uncle Remus' Visit*, stating that it "is full of action and funny situations, it is a picture that will book itself."[224]

Reporting on a screening in Indianapolis, the *Freeman* encouraged audiences to see the film: "These pictures should be seen by every Negro because they are good pictures taken by a Negro firm acted by a Negro cast and is a Negro story."[225] Reporting on the screening in Washington, D.C., at the Howard Theater, the *Freeman* observed that "it was a highly enjoyable production and outranks anything yet gotten up with the Negro as a theme." The review stated:

The story revolves around the visit of "Uncle Remus," an unsophisticated old farmer from Awfulville, Miss., to his fashionable nephew in New York City. The mishaps and mixups which befell the old man and his wife from the time they left their delta farm to the close of their sojourn in Gotham, together with the embarrassment of the high-toned city nephew and his wife and stylish friends, form a series of situations that make for laughter, mingled with a bit of pathos. It is also a faithful portrait that contrasts the new Negro with the old and forges a chain of circumstances that vividly point out the progress the race has made in his [sic] fifty years of freedom. From the mule cart to the automobile may be a far cry, but the Negro has bridged the gap and in Hunter C. Haynes' "Uncle Remus," the modern and ante-bellum Negro are shown in sharp differentiation, imparting a lesson that cannot fail to inspire, as well as interest and amuse.[226]

In its assessment of Haynes's film, the *Freeman* pithily summarizes the goals of uplift cinema: to inspire, hold the interest of spectators, and provide appropriate amusement. The question remains, however, what "lesson" the *Freeman* imagines the film to be imparting. Certainly the progress of the race is demonstrated through a commitment to technological progress and modernity, as Rastus and his family are contrasted with his country relatives. The sending of a telegram demonstrates to the audience a means of connecting to relatives in the south and shows southerners as engaged with a modern communication technology.[227] Implicit in the fact that wireless telegraphy connects the spaces of "Awfulville" and New York City is that it enables the movement of the rural southerners to the northern metropolis. The telegram that connects the relatives and catalyzes the railway journey that brings them together, albeit circuitously, figures Remus and Rastus as modern subjects whose cinematic representation is a logical extension of the technologies that are deployed in the film's narrative (telegram, railroad, and automobile). This paradigm is taken another step because audiences participate in the progress narrative as they see it articulated as a motion picture—again, film as a technology is highlighted.

With *Uncle Remus' Visit*, Haynes models key components of urban modernity for his spectators. But the comedy pivots on the juxtaposition of the old ways and the new, southern expectations clashing with northern realities, a "mule cart" mentality up against an "automobile" environment. Thus, another aspect to the lesson of *Uncle Remus' Visit* could be derived from the embarrassment of the urbane relatives, whose snobbishness is treated with comedy just as the country folks' displacement provides amusing fodder for the narrative. As Stewart notes, the intraracial conflict serves as the catalyst for "regionalized and racialized humor."[228] This comedy would be especially accessible to Black audiences, who would recognize the types portrayed and parodied in Haynes's farce. When the *Freeman* describes the film as "a Negro story," it is this intraracial encounter that is being celebrated. In this way, comedy could serve as a means of navigating the widespread social changes taking place in Black life during this period. Haynes's uplift comedy—even in its irreverence—thus provides a useful model for its urban audience.

As with *The Troubles of Sambo and Dinah*, *Uncle Remus' Visit to New York* presents an uneasy combination of uplift themes and debasing tropes of blackness. Stewart notes that "comedy could open up opportunities for parody and critique that reflected on the changing contours of modern Black life," while at the same time it could repeat denigrating minstrel tropes prevalent in white culture.[229] The issue of the appropriation of seemingly offensive tropes raises complex questions about the nature of appropriation, assimilation, resistance, and subversion. Stewart sees the use of the name Rastus as a problem, commenting that "his respectability is compromised" by his name.[230] This critique recalls Everett's discussion of *The Troubles of Sambo and Dinah*, in which she negotiates the apparently demeaning title in the context of films such as *The Tale of a Chicken* that might mitigate the compromised appropriation of such caricature.[231] Certainly, names such as Rastus, Remus, Sambo, and Dinah have long been associated with stereotypical portrayals of Black characters stemming from blackface minstrelsy, and *Uncle Remus' Visit* must be understood as being in dialogue with these precedents. However, viewed in the context of its production and exhibition, other readings are possible. These names are derived from a blackface vaudeville tradition that had already been appropriated by Black stage figures and celebrated by Black audiences and cultural critics alike, even while being denigrated by others. With unprecedented control by Black producers, writers, directors, and performers, Black theatrical productions between 1912 and 1920 were, as Henry Sampson has demonstrated, almost exclusively presented to Black audiences.[232] In this view, Haynes arguably is appropriating material from Black subversive usage rather than from the racist origins of the stereotypical figures.

Additionally, some aspects of the narrative suggest an ironic naming of Haynes's characters. In his imagining, this Uncle Remus actually is an uncle—to the successful and urbane Rastus. Though of course there is a dialogue with Joel Chandler Harris, writer of the Uncle Remus stories, Haynes's Remus is not given an honorific that denotes his relationship to whites (as in "Uncle Tom"). His name does not depend on his relationship to whites but refers entirely to his own family.[233] In addition to upward mobility, Rastus is portrayed as having not only a wife and a daughter but also a maid and a butler; he is a completely different from the Rastus stereotype that Stewart notes is coded as a "lazy, henpecked, chicken-stealing" type.[234] The portrait of success, professionalism, and respectability is closer to the image of Haynes himself than to the stereotype suggested by his character's name.

Unlike films such as Edison's *Uncle Josh at the Moving Picture Show* (Edwin S. Porter, Edison Manufacturing Company, 1902), Haynes's film does not derive its comedy entirely at the expense of the country bumpkins—though it might seem to do so from the vantage point of the contemporary Black press. Stewart, commenting on the film's review in the *Freeman*, notes: "Relying on the idea that Black 'progress' is located in northern cities, the reviewer indicates that this particular film privileges urban Black sensibilities over the ostensibly persistently retrogressive 'Old Negro' ways of the South."[235] However, the film's reviews also suggest that the "New Negroes" in New York were not free from ridicule themselves, and that the New York and Chicago audiences would have recognized this self-satire. Indeed, the comedy is predicated on both extremes being amusing and recognizable parodies of contemporary types.

The clash of two worlds, in fact, marks the film's contemporariness, given that the first wave of the Great Migration to the north was just beginning. Haynes—originally from Selma, Alabama, and well traveled due to his razor strop business—was aptly positioned to point out the humor of both types. The simultaneity of the before-and-after tropes of Black progress reflected in *Uncle Remus' Visit* reflects Black life in the urban north at that time. Haynes's motion pictures presented comedic types that were perhaps uniquely accessible to Black audiences, and he was celebrated for filming stories they could relate to. As the *Freeman* observed, "Mr. Haynes has but scratched the surface of the wonderful possibilities that lie in stories of the Negro race, and the success of 'Uncle Remus' will doubtless encourage him to go deeper into the mass of material that simply awaits the magic touch of him and his confreres."[236]

At the same time, like his colleagues in Chicago, Haynes was invested in filming actualities. Shown together with the comedy fictions, the actualities were equally celebrated, as the *Freeman* notes: "Not less interesting and inspiring was Mr. Haynes' remarkable films that depict the scenes of the late B.M.C. [Biennial Movable Conference] convention in Boston and which follow the line of race progress through New York City, Washington and the south."[237] Like the Afro-American Film Company's feature *Notable Negroes*, Haynes's *A Review of the B.M.C. and the Colored Business World* consisted of actuality footage of highlights of Black civic life. It was produced in the fall of 1914 as a three-reel picture.[238] Haynes provided slides and lobby posters to theaters that booked the film. He advertised the footage to exhibitors as "an immense film creation" of three "stupendous, colossal reels" that contained "2,800 feet of film, consisting of 150 short, snappy subjects that will hold the intense interest of any audience anywhere."[239] The film featured the Odd Fellows dress parade at the B.M.C., held in Boston in September, "the most spectacular parade ever seen in the East in which colored men were the sole participants."[240] The footage included "moving portraits" of notable figures such as former U.S. Assistant Attorney General William H. Lewis, H. Lincoln Johnson, Charles W. Anderson, Harry S. Cummings, Edward H. Morris, Benjamin Davis, Judge and Mrs. Robert H. Terrell, Governor Pinckey B. S. Pinchback, and T. Thomas Fortune and popular figures such as Bert Williams and the boxers Sam Langford and Joe Walcott.[241] Langford was advertised as being filmed at his residence in Boston, and Walcott was advertised as "first time in any motion picture production!" (figure 5.10).[242] The film also included twenty-one businesses and enterprises operated by African Americans in New York, the field day at the Lenox Oval on 145th Street and Lenox Avenue, and a baseball game between the Lincoln Giants, an African American baseball team based in Harlem, and "a Chinese team."[243]

Haynes filmed notable sites pertaining to African American history, such as the monument to Colonel Robert Gould Shaw, the Crispus Atticus monument, Frederick Douglass's home, and the campus of Howard University. He also included footage of Washington visiting Fisk University though, as discussed in chapter 2, Tuskegee did not permit Haynes to use existing moving pictures of the institute.[244] The footage showed running races, sack races, and potato racing scenes that the *Freeman* found "very interesting."[245] The *New York Age* reported that the film "is said to be the greatest industrial Negro picture ever made."[246] The paper also commented: "It is by far the most meritorious picture of its kind ever thrown upon the screen. . . . This picture is instructive as well as entertaining and is interesting from start to finish."[247] The *Amsterdam News* reported that the "highly appreciative" audience "enthusiastically received each view with a racial pride and hearty applause that speaks volumes for our future. When a people take such keen interest in their own industries and celebrities it's the best proof of their welfare and progress."[248] Similarly, the *New York News* wrote: "We have hitherto severely condemned Mr. Haynes, because we felt that he was wasting a large amount of valuable time and money producing worthless scenarios. Writers are born, not made; and it is certain that Haynes does not belong to the author class. . . . [However,] as a film reviewer, Hunter Haynes is worthy of a place, side by side, with Bert Williams, our greatest comedian, the late Aida Walker, our greatest dancer, and Anita Patti Brown, our greatest singer."[249] The respectability of Haynes's actualities

FIG. 5.10 Advertisement for the Haynes Photoplay Company, *Freeman*, October 10, 1914. Courtesy Indiana Newspaper Section, Indiana State Library.

influenced the reception of his comedies; contemporary reviews indicate that they were not seen as distinct genres but understood as part of the same general cinematic enterprise.

A Review of the B.M.C. was screened at the Lafayette Theatre in New York for a week in October 1914 and for four nights at the Howard Theater in Washington in December.[250] At the Howard, the actualities were screened with *Uncle Remus' Visit* for reportedly large audiences, many of whom came to see the actualities in particular.[251]

In March 1915 Haynes made a distribution deal with the Universal Film Manufacturing Company to distribute fifty comedies that he would direct and produce and that would be written by Jesse Shipp and Alex Rodgers. Of the deal, the *Freeman* reported: "This is something very big in the Colored Motion Picture world, and will give the colored picture actors a chance to show just what they can do."[252] In his company, Haynes employed Charles Moore, Bobby Kemp, Julius Glen, Leon Williams, Allie Gilliam, Tom Fletcher, Abbie Mitchell, Carita Day, Jennie Sheppard, Grange LeCooke, and Madam Williams. It is not clear why, but Haynes's deal with Universal did not pan out. However, always the entrepreneur, Haynes opened a restaurant in August 1915 across the street from his studio in Harlem.[253] The Haynes Dining and Social Club aimed to promote "a healthier moral, recreational and intellectual spirit among the people of the city."[254] Haynes fell ill the following year and died in January 1918 in Saranac Lake, New York. He was buried at his birthplace in Selma, Alabama.[255]

Black Filmmaking Entrepreneurs and the Mainstream Film Industry

Uplift filmmaking entrepreneurs worked primarily within Black communities, making films for Black audiences. However, each of the filmmakers I discuss in this chapter also sought opportunities and procured work, to varying degrees, in the wider American film industry. The story of Black filmmakers who worked in various capacities in the moving picture industries of New York and Los Angeles in the 1910s and 1920s merits further exploration, in greater depth than is possible here. But the coda to the uplift cinema careers of the Black filmmaking entrepreneurs and their participation in the broader film industry indicates their investment in the professional potential of moving pictures in an interracial capacity. They may not have made uplift films in the mainstream industry, but they were still working within that conceptual grid. The endeavors of Black filmmaking entrepreneurs in the wider film industry constitutes uplift itself.

Interracial film attempts were not unheard of, but they were rare enough to be notable in the Black press. In early February 1915 a young law student at the University of Southern California named John E. McLemore (figure 5.11) sold a script to Universal based on his play *The Struggle*, the details of which do not survive. According to an article in the *Chicago Defender* lauding McLemore's success, Universal requested three rounds of rewrites before purchasing the scenario for "a fair sum."[256] Sadly, McLemore drowned while swimming in

John E. McLemore, Successful Los Angeles Scenario Writer.

Santa Monica a year after his success with Universal.[257] McLemore's success— and his untimely death—made the front pages of the *California Eagle*, an African American newspaper based in Los Angeles, and the *Defender* as the inspirational story of a promising young talent. Sarah Elaine Woods is one of the rare examples from this period of a Black woman who was an aspiring screenwriter. Very little is known about her apart from her initial success in selling a scenario to a "leading 'movie' house." A pastor's daughter, Woods was a high-school student in Milwaukee when she wrote a screenplay titled *The Sacrifice*, which the *Defender* described as "a love story with adventure and trials interwoven."[258] It is not known whether the film was ever produced, but her aspirations and the press's celebration of her success indicate a belief in the opportunities afforded to Black men and women by the moving picture business.

In the decade following the emergence of uplift cinema, Black filmmakers, writers, and technicians moved to Los Angeles and New York and sought work in the moving picture industry. William Foster was one of these, yet little is known or understood about his work in Hollywood. After filming actualities of Black troops and their families in Chicago, Foster was employed by the *Defender* as a sports writer. According to an obituary, he spent nearly a decade as a journalist before resigning to establish the Haitian Coffee Company, which he reportedly left after two years to return to filmmaking.[259] Though Foster's early filmmaking career was focused on the production of moving pictures for Black audiences, he had a second act to his career when he moved to Los Angeles in 1928. After befriending an African American doorman named Major Morris at the Pathé studios, he was given an interview with the director Paul Powell. Foster was a technical director at first and then worked as a director on *Black and Tan* (Dudley Murphy, RKO Radio Pictures, 1929), a film dealing with "the underworld, rum runners, dope fiends and murder," starring Duke Ellington and Fredi Washington, for which Dudley Murphy received full directing credit.[260] He also directed films at Pathé for Buck and Bubbles, the popular song and dance duet of Ford L. Washington and John W. Sublett. The Black press celebrated Foster's achievements in the mainstream film industry. One report lauded his perseverance, noting: "He was laughed at, scoffed at, given the run around, but he persisted." As a result of his "stick-to-itiveness," he "got a break" and became an assistant director, "much to the surprise of the Negroes whom he directs and the whites who observe him."[261] The press also noted that he had white employees working under him.[262] Foster's success was used as a lesson in "nerve, grit and persistence" in surmounting the barriers of racial prejudice.[263]

Despite his opportunities with Pathé, Foster was apparently unable to pursue the kind of filmmaking for which he had moved to Los Angeles. According to Foster, "certain conditions" made it impossible for him to "carry out his plans," so he eventually left Pathé to found the Foster Photo Play Company, where he could write his own shorts for Buck and Bubbles as well as Stepin Fetchit and Clarence Muse (it is unclear if those were ever produced).[264] Working with Norman Houston and Machlon Cooley, Foster aimed to turn his plays into short subjects and then produce "high-class pictures."[265] He also tried to bring the acts of African American stage entertainers to moving picture audiences. For example, he tried (to no avail) to locate Billy King, leader of a popular Black musical and comedy stock company in the 1910s and early 1920s, in the hope of featuring him in a film.[266] The Foster Photo Play Company also aimed to assist African American theater owners in creating theater chains. As one report on Foster's initiative in the Black press noted, "the cry from Race people is for better pictures of their race on the screen. White corporations defiantly say 'If you want better pictures of your race make them yourself,' and the reply of the Foster Photo Play company is, 'We will!'"[267] Foster lobbied for "Race-wide subscription in state quotas" to raise the capital for race films.[268] He claimed to have the support of "powerful white friends" who assured him that he would have an open market for his films as well as training for "the small army" of Black technicians (sound engineers, cinematographers, and developers) to assist in his intended bimonthly productions.[269] The Black press was excited about the opportunities that Foster's ambitions could represent for other African Americans.

In June 1929, with the organization of the new Foster Photo Play Company, Foster set out to produce sound pictures, proclaiming that "the talking picture business is the biggest uplift project the Race has ever had."[270] The motto of the company reflected the uplift ethos on which Foster had based his career: "Dedicated to the Upbuilding of Greater Opportunities for You in the Talking Picture World." In the prospectus for the company, Foster emphasized the advantages of sound film for African Americans, noting that "the low mellow voice of the Negro" was ideally suited to sound pictures. Foster proclaimed: "His songs and dances are the most copied in the world—he fits right into this new age of affairs." As an argument for his production venture, Foster bemoaned the fact that "the peculiar ability of the Negro was not given full opportunity to express itself" in sound films to date and that "pictures were not designed to play up the advancement and upbuilding thought of our people. Our psychology was not fully understood—we needed a broader chance."[271] That chance is what Foster proposed to provide in his new company, for which he was seeking shareholders.

Once critical of Foster, Russell now wrote an encouraging, if exaggerated, column on Foster's efforts in Los Angeles: "Since Mr. Foster has been in Hollywood he has been besieged by throngs of people of his own race" who were eager to support him in his effort to produce films with the "correct presentation of racial traits and character in stories that would not have to be confined entirely to the white man's idea of humiliating past conditions of servitude."[272] Foster's efforts in Hollywood were celebrated as a sign of race progress and a crucial opportunity to correct the prevalent misrepresentations of African Americans that were a mainstay of popular entertainment.

Continuing his interest in journalism into the 1930s, Foster served as a special correspondent to the *California Eagle*. During four months in 1933 he published a serialized version of *Fool and Fire* in the women's column of the paper. In the author's note that appeared over each installment, Foster proclaimed: "The story is not intended to expose youth or lower the standard of our Girls. Lottie Childress, the leading character[,] is no different from girls of all Races the world over. Her victims are no different from men since the beginning of all things. The wisest of men have been destroyed following youth since the days of Cleopatra. The wrong Road leads to destruction. Short or long."[273] The story chronicles the exploits of a vamp who manipulates men for financial gain until she is shot by a jealous husband. Published when Foster was over seventy, the serial emphasizes tensions between new fast ways and old-fashioned social decorum (represented by the main character's sister, an unfashionable prude whose greatest aspiration is to have her own school). The vamp gets her comeuppance, but the sister is portrayed as something of a bore. Although the story concludes with an uplift moral, each episode includes titillating details of the vamp's badness. From *The Railway Porter* to *Fool and Fire*, Foster's narratives explored intraracial diversity and the full range of the human experience, offering a well-rounded portrayal of Black cultural life that belied the industry's one-dimensional caricatures of Black people. In this sense, his filmmaking project was ultimately invested in the assertion of Black humanity, a core mission of the uplift project. Foster died in Los Angeles in 1940 at age seventy-eight.

Black filmmaking entrepreneurs did not just go west. Jones worked for Selznick's company in New York taking film stills and experimenting in color photography.[274] Selznick's house organ, *The Brain Exchange*, featured an article on Jones's work on color photography titled "Peter Jones Follows the Rainbow." The article's author, Myron Brinig, lauds Jones's passion: "Look in his eyes—the eyes of a man in love with his work, a man of ideals and strength of character."[275] Although noting basic biographic information about Jones and his career trajectory, Brinig does not mention or allude to Jones's race.[276] It is not clear why, but the absence is striking. Brinig concludes the short piece with near-euphoric enthusiasm for his subject: "Keep the name of Peter Jones in mind. If you are following the rainbow; if you have aspirations and ideals that you mean to come true, prepare to meet Peter Jones at the successful realization. He will be there waiting for you. He will smile and grasp your hand."[277] When Selznick's company moved its operations to Hollywood, Jones stayed behind and opened the Service Film Laboratory in Fort Lee, New Jersey, in May 1922 in the facilities formerly occupied by the Éclair Film Company.[278]

In the same year, he partnered with Trueman Bell, a Chicago businessman, to establish the Seminole Film Producing Company. Very little is known about his independent laboratory work or the Seminole company, but he provided the lab service for the company's only production, a two-reel comedy titled *How High Is Up?* (Seminole Film Producing Company, 1923), the moving picture recording of the popular vaudeville act of the comedians Arthur Moss and Edward Frye.[279]

Less is known about Haynes's work in the mainstream film industry, though the *New York News* reported that he worked for the Pathé, Hearst, and Selig newsreels.[280] When Haynes died in New York in 1918, his obituary in the *Chicago Defender* lauded him as "a conspicuous figure in the moving picture field, having at one time been connected with the Vitagraph Motion Picture company as a producer of comedies."[281] The accuracy of these claims has yet to be verified, but if he worked for or was associated with such newsreel companies, that would mark a significant instance of early interracial collaboration in the moving picture industry.

The indications that these filmmaking entrepreneurs sought work in the mainstream film industry point to the likely financial obstacles to their independent ventures as well as their belief in the possibility of viable employment in the industry. Although filmmakers like the Johnson brothers and Oscar Micheaux contended in the parallel race film industry, the interracial ambitions of these early uplift entrepreneurs suggests a hope about the future of motion pictures despite the apparent hostility of the industry concerning the Black screen image. Very little is known about the entrepreneurs' work with these companies, but the possibility of their successful employment (and potentially that of other Black workers who remain unknown to us) suggests the achievement of the central ambition of the uplift project—to bring about collective advancement through personal striving.

In these ways, moving pictures represented a new arena of professional opportunity, self-fashioning, and the collective public assertion of the possibilities for African Americans in the twentieth century. The accomplishments of these Black filmmaking entrepreneurs have not previously been understood in the aggregate, but the significance of their efforts goes beyond the fuller accounting of their work provided here. One of the key things this examination has shown is that the common conception of uplift, which is still prevalent today—that it was a uniformly calculated yet politically compromised strategy—is inadequate, as the historical material proves. Following from the contested filmmaking projects of Black educational institutions, entrepreneurial Black film production likewise reveals the instability of the concept of uplift itself. The mission of southern agricultural and industrial institutes required an image of the Black populace as both dependent on white largesse and capable of self-sufficiency within circumscribed parameters. In the films and media works that emerged from Hampton and Tuskegee, the before-and-after rhetorical strategy enabled an image of uplift that corroborated white perceptions of Black dependency while proffering the possibility of Black humanity. In contrast, the ambitions of northern Black filmmaking entrepreneurs were primarily focused on Black communities, yet these entrepreneurs also used a variety of forms of motion picture production and exhibition (without a dominant strategy like that of Hampton). The various ways these entrepreneurs had of employing moving pictures for the progress of the race, and the debates they engendered over appropriate strategies for representing African Americans in film, expose tensions in the uplift project between individual initiative and collective advancement, between so-called positive representation and alternative notions of what should constitute a public image of the race. This complexity is not a matter of chance: it reflects the world in which uplift emerged and the intraracial diversity of opinions, politics, and investments surrounding programs for the advancement of the race. Never monolithic—any more than the people it purported to affect—the uplift project functioned in myriad ways, aimed to implement a range of interventions, and had no singular political agenda. Uplift cinema demonstrates that uplift itself—as a concept and a practice—defined an era of African American striving while also reflecting the intricacies of that ambition.

EPILOGUE

The end of uplift cinema in both its northern and southern versions occurred in the late 1910s. The northern entrepreneurs who began making films for Black audiences struggled in the mainstream film industry and largely abandoned their entrepreneurial endeavors, finding work in various capacities in supporting rather than autonomous roles. In the south, the debacle caused by *The Birth of a Nation* led Hampton to be far more cautious with its filmmaking. Furthermore, the U.S. involvement in World War I resulted in the redirection of Hampton's and Tuskegee's energies toward proving African American patriotism and fitness for contributing to the war effort. These practical issues were met with a larger shift in cultural and political priorities for African Americans. With the death of Booker T. Washington, the "Representative Man," the uplift movement that had been a focal point splintered and became decentralized. The uplift philosophy, once the dominant—and dominating—strategy for the advancement of the race was increasingly criticized and was challenged by competing theories and programs. However, the strength of uplift's hold on the social psyche (both Black and white) meant that its influence continued even as its strategies and forms were picked up elsewhere.

Despite its relatively short moment of productivity, uplift cinema did not disappear. Even if no more uplift films were being made, the idea was nonetheless generative of a number of practices that would emerge more fully in the ensuing decades. Indeed, reconsidered in the light of a fuller understanding of uplift cinema, the genealogy of Black filmmaking shows that the legacy of this early moment goes beyond its immediate contexts and reverberates in significant ways across history. Uplift cinema points to the complicated landscape of moving pictures in the 1920s and afterward, including sponsored films and theatrical entertainments, local filmmaking and useful cinema, and—most importantly—hybrids of these forms. Understood in this way, uplift cinema is not just a straightforward precursor to race filmmaking and later movements. That is certainly an important aspect of its legacy, but it constitutes only one of the various forms that moving pictures have taken in their service of racial advancement. Uplift aesthetics do not simply disappear with the waning of the uplift movement in the late 1910s; they continue to permeate Black cinema in complex and enduring ways.

The traces of uplift cinema mark the trajectory of African American engagements with moving pictures in the twentieth century and beyond: social dramas in the 1950s, the Blaxploitation era of the 1970s, the independent film production of the L.A. Rebellion, and the work of Oprah Winfrey and Tyler Perry in the current media environment. But the main role of uplift cinema has been to provide a way of understanding the dynamics of the race filmmaking that emerged in the 1920s through the 1940s and the uses of moving pictures in campaigns for the material improvement of the lives of African Americans.

In the decades that followed their own filmmaking endeavors, the southern agricultural and industrial institutes were repeatedly featured in educational films sponsored by the U.S. government as well as private-sector philanthropic organizations that targeted Black communities. Hampton became the subject of films sponsored by, for example, the U.S. Department of Agriculture (USDA), such as *Helping Negroes to Be Better Farmers and Homemakers* (USDA Extension Service, 1921) and the Harmon Foundation, such as *Hampton Institute Presents Its Program of Education for Life* (Ray and Virginia Garner, Harmon Foundation, 1941).[1] Tuskegee was the subject of at least two actuality films made in the 1920s by white-owned companies, *A Tuskegee Pilgrimage* (Robert Levy, Reol Productions, 1922) and *Tuskegee Finds the Way Out* (Crusader Films, 1923).[2] Tuskegee also lent its choir to a film sponsored by the National Tuberculosis Association, *Let My People Live* (Edgar G. Ulmer, Motion Picture Service Corporation, 1938). These films are representative of a practice of educational filmmaking for rural Black communities that traces its origins to uplift cinema.

Uplift cinema's investment in self-representation—manifested in the tension between the imperative for positive images of African Americans and the demands to show the Black community as it is—was taken up by race filmmakers from George P. and Noble Johnson to the various race film enterprises of the 1920s through the 1940s. These include the Johnson brothers' Lincoln Motion Picture Company, which produced dramatic films advancing images of race pride such as *The Realization of a Negro's Ambition* (1916) and *The Trooper of Troop K* (1916).[3] It also includes Spencer Williams's acting and directing work in the 1940s, which focused on religious-themed films such as *The Blood of Jesus* (1941), which he also wrote, and *Go Down Death* (1944). Like a number of the uplift films by northern entrepreneurs, these films bend (and blend) generic conventions: *The Blood of Jesus*, for example, features extended sequences of Southern Baptist culture as well as comedy and stage spectacles that put these traditions in relief. Uplift cinema's commitment to self-representation can also be seen in the anthropological lens of Zora Neale Hurston and her desire to document southern Black cultures in the late 1920s. And the idea that moving pictures could play a role in the uplift of the race continues in the nontheatrical religious films of Eloyce and James Gist, such as *Hellbound Train* (1929–30) and *Verdict Not Guilty* (1930–33).

It is Oscar Micheaux, however, who provides the most complex instance of a negotiation with the rhetoric and politics of uplift. Micheaux is a figure who must be addressed in considerations of Black filmmaking in the first half of the twentieth century, as he possessed one of the most singular visions of the time. Even so, his work took shape against a definite background of race representation and emerged from a longer history of Black filmmaking practices. The consideration of uplift cinema and uplift aesthetics in this book should attune us to key places in Micheaux's extended oeuvre that recall the work of uplift filmmakers and that can be read in that light. The connection resonates across several levels. Micheaux's extant silent films frequently invoke uplift themes, as in the emphasis on education in *Within Our Gates* and the achievement of economic self-sufficiency and the rewarding of racial pride in *Symbol of the Unconquered*. The influence of uplift also can be seen in narrative structure, as in the way that *Body and Soul* is organized according to the familiar uplift logic of before and after. Finally, uplift aesthetics can be seen in the blending of staged drama and documentary footage that appears in Micheaux's films. In the remainder of this epilogue, I will demonstrate how a more nuanced account of Micheaux's filmmaking practice becomes possible when it is placed in the context of uplift cinema.

I began this book by showing how the place of the portrait of Washington in the mise-en-scène of Micheaux's *Body and Soul* evokes the project of social and political uplift for African Americans, establishing that context as a backdrop to Micheaux's cautionary tale of blind faith and intraracial deceit. *Body and Soul* does not shy away from depicting hypocrisy, criminality, and the unuplifted. Still, there are certainly other narrative elements such as Martha Jane's industriousness, Sylvester's ambition, and Isabelle's proper English, which indicate an uplift ethos. Micheaux rounds out the screen depiction of African Americans and complicates the prevalent emphasis on positive representation.

However, Micheaux's deepest link to uplift aesthetics involves formal strategies. Most interesting here is his use of actuality footage and the integration of nonactors into the drama. After Martha Jane has found Isabelle in Atlanta and finally believes the truth about her pastor, she returns to confront him. The scene of confrontation takes place in the church on the Sunday when, as we are told by an intertitle, Reverend Jenkins plans to preach on "Dry Bones in the Valley," noted as the ambition of every Black preacher.[4] In the lead-up to the confrontation, Micheaux carefully, and curiously, blends actuality footage of Black churchgoers in the rural south with staged dramatic actions.

The scene begins with a shot marked with a diamond masking of a rural dirt road, on which a man and three women are briskly walking diagonally toward the camera, all finely dressed (figure E.1). They notice the camera and stare at it fixedly as they continue across the frame. The second woman, carrying what appears to be a Bible, even turns as if to alert her companions to the presence of the camera. Micheaux then cuts to a shot, also masked, of a tree-lined path, thick with foliage, through which two women and four girls walk diagonally to the camera (figure E.2). Here, the second woman wears a fox stole and the girls wear white dresses with bows in their hair; they are followed by a man, also smartly dressed. We then get a reverse shot to the same family standing around a gazebo placed at the center of the frame and in front of a car (figure E.3). Micheaux cuts to the family as they enter a country church painted white (figure E.4). At this point, the scene changes to the interior of the church as Micheaux's actors file in, followed by a sequence of intercutting between the interior set and the exterior footage that suggests the arrival of the congregation (figure E.5). We are then shown Reverend Jenkins in his room, preparing for his sermon by donning aftershave and hiding a flask in his pocket. This private moment is intercut with the church exterior as more people arrive and the dirt road as more people head to church by horse-drawn cart (figure E.6) and on foot (figure E.7). As in the earlier shots, the churchgoers walk with their eyes fixed on the camera.

The recurring instances of figures staring at the camera play an important role in the scene. A key trope of the local film, the direct address to the spectator functions as a signal of self-recognition. As the figures turn toward the camera, it is as if they confront the spectator, breaking the illusory fourth wall and the relay of gazes that connect the subjects of Micheaux's film to his audience. The spectator thus becomes aware of his or her presence as a spectator as well as in relation to the figure or figures on screen. Micheaux's subjects and audience are thus connected through this two-way gaze, seeing one another through the cinematic apparatus.[5]

The preface to the climactic confrontation between Martha Jane and Reverend Jenkins ends with the return inside the church where the congregation has assembled and the deacons are taking their places. The congregation rises and Jenkins enters in pompous solemnity. He begins with the offering and, after taking the collection, launches into the sermon "Dry Bones in the Valley."[6] Micheaux uses a number of comic set pieces to parody the charismatic Black church and its duplicitous leader. Caught up in a religious fervor, Jenkins socks a deacon twice and drinks liquor from the pulpit, and a reluctant churchgoer is converted (much to his wife's approval). The congregation becomes increasingly frenzied and Jenkins closes the Bible, putting it on his shoulder as he preaches. At the crescendo of the sermon, Jenkins is interrupted by Martha Jane, who enters the church like "an angel of truth" and accuses him of killing Isabelle (figure E.8).[7] He is exposed as a fraud, and the congregation turns on him.

For this key scene, Micheaux organizes formal elements and narrative structure to complicate a straightforward reading of the story events. The intercutting between the actuality exteriors, set interior, and Jenkins's preparations suggests an interrelation between the real subjects of Micheaux's lens, the actors in the church scene, and the con man masquerading as a preacher. Although this can be read as a classic establishment of space and time, the disjunction between the actuality footage and staged interiors suggests a more complex set of identifications. Here, I am especially interested in how the actuality footage functions as a frame to this scene of exposure. J. Ronald Green is one of the few scholars who have noted the "documentary-like" shots that preface the climax, reading them as continuing "the discourse of sobriety that marks Martha Jane's investigation." Green writes: "It is an investigatory, factual, realistic style, and it arrives just in time to counter the effects of the preacher's apotheosis of escapist 'religious' spectacle and entertainment, the 'Dry Bones' sermon."[8] Green notes the similarity of these shots to the footage shot in the south by Hurston in 1927 and the footage taken by Charles Houston in South Carolina in 1934.[9] What Green couldn't have known is that another major intertext was uplift cinema, especially the iterations that combine actuality and fiction forms: Peter P. Jones's *For the Honor of the 8th*, the actualities of Boston churchgoers by George W. Broome, the Hampton and Tuskegee films, and the work of William Foster and Hunter C. Haynes. As in those works, Micheaux's employment of actuality footage is dynamic and complex. If the portrait of Washington in Martha Jane's home does more than serve as an emblem of uplift, the actuality shots of rural churchgoers do more than signal authenticity. They engage the Black audience in a personal way, gesturing to familiar tropes with a realist lens—a rare sight for feature narratives.

FIG. E.1–E.4 (*above and at right*) *Body and Soul* (Oscar Micheaux, 1925).

FIG. E.5–E.8 (*above and at right*) *Body and Soul* (Oscar Micheaux, 1925).

Of course, the footage certainly does the work of authentication, calling on the representational work of the local film to elicit a sense of recognition of the race film audience. From the dress and means of transport to the church, these scenes would be generically recognizable to the Black audience. In this sense, *Body and Soul* extends from the specificity of the representational regimes of the local film to a categorical familiarity with the types of people shown and the environment captured by the camera. For northerners, many of whom were recent migrants from the south, these shots might also elicit nostalgia in their evocation of life back home. Placed here, these shots place the staged drama within the frame of real life. As Pearl Bowser and Louise Spence note, Micheaux was invested in "claims to truth," and his gestures toward authenticity reflected the dearth of screen images of African Americans that were not ridiculing or lampooning the race.[10]

Yet what follows the shots of actual rural churchgoers could easily be described as offensive, especially in its proximity to the authenticating actuality footage. In other words, the authenticating mirror is contained in "an unflattering portrait of the community" and risks becoming a part of Micheaux's lampooning of churchgoers.[11] Are the very folks who are shown naturalistically then ridiculed? If Bowser and Spence see the "stylization or performances, makeup, and costuming" as Micheaux's method of creating "a knowing kinship with members of the audience," there is still a strong sense of mockery in the scene.[12] In the comedic set pieces and the naïve faith of the congregation, Micheaux presents a negative portrayal of a charismatic Black church spellbound by a con man, which elicited complaints from many of his contemporaries.

Here, Micheaux is more complex than he might appear. The scene moves from authentication to ridicule but then goes toward rehabilitation, as the members of the congregation discover the truth about their false preacher and drive him out. In this respect, the truth claim works both ways: the actuality footage signals a truth that will emerge, and the unmasking of the false preacher demonstrates the sophistication of the churchgoers who, in a sense, are awakened from their false frenzy when Martha Jane alerts them to Jenkins's subterfuge. The truth coming out about the false reverend lends veracity to the actuality footage, just as the footage suggests a truth about the church service.

Ironically, it is Martha Jane who is again duped by the reverend. This "angel of truth" unmasks the con man, but she remains blinded by her faith, hiding him from the bloodhounds on his trail.[13] In true Christian spirit, she forgives him — and then pays the cost. Jenkins leaves and brutally murders a young parishioner (figure E.9). The young man's last word — "Mama!" — make him a surrogate son to Martha Jane and, at least symbolically, another child lost

FIG. E.9 *Body and Soul* (Oscar Micheaux, 1925).

to her blind faith. Furthermore, the murder is shot in an exterior scene in the woods, echoing the shots of the arriving churchgoers that prefaced the climax and, as an intertext, the lynch mob of *Within Our Gates*. The allusion to both the arriving churchgoers and to the vigilante lynch mob functions to underscore Micheaux's truth telling. First, the reference to the actuality footage of arriving churchgoers signals a point of relation for the audience, thereby serving as a warning that their blind faith could have deadly consequences. Second, the way in which the setting echoes the crimes committed in *Within Our Gates* furthers the truth claim of the film concerning the result of interracial betrayal and white acrimony. After all, it is obsequious Eph that Micheaux presents as the catalyst for the lynching (and its victim), and the lynch mob contains men, women, and children—"white people as primitives"—who show the veracity of southern "justice" and, as Jane Gaines argues, "work as a kind of moral self-affirmation."[14] In contrast, the men, women, and children whom Micheaux films arriving at church in *Body and Soul* epitomize orderly community, culture, and respectability—the inverse of the lynch mob. Or, to extend Gaines's analysis of the lynch scene in *Within Our Gates* to the actuality footage in *Body and Soul*, Micheaux "chooses to show what blacks knew and northern whites would refuse to believe."[15]

The story of Isabelle's escape to Atlanta and subsequent death are framed in Martha Jane's dream, but this fact is not revealed until the end of the narrative. Bracketed in the dream, the unmasking of the fraudulent preacher nonetheless appears at the climax of the film, giving narrative weight to what is later shown to be illusion. But the fact of the dream is important in one key respect: it re-iterates the need to wake up. Charles Musser sees Martha Jane as a surrogate for the audience and argues that, "for Micheaux, it was the duty of these films to awaken their audiences and to force them to reflect on their predicament."[16] The actuality footage works in this manner. If audiences in effect saw them-selves in the faces of nonactors staring back at them, then it was those very doubles who turn on Jenkins and drive him out.

When Martha Jane wakes up as Isabelle and Sylvester enter, they announce that Sylvester's invention has been a success, and Martha Jane then permits them to marry. Significantly, Sylvester is costumed to echo the portrait of Washington, becoming, in effect, the uplift spirit made flesh. His costuming and posture also recall the after figures in Hampton's and Tuskegee's publicity photographs (figure E.10). Seen this way, the brothers are split: Jenkins be-comes the symbolic before that must be overcome for Sylvester to prevail as the after. Of course, the brothers—played by the same actor—exist concurrently rather than sequentially in the narrative (at least until the end), complicating the straightforward trajectory of uplift. Sylvester and Isabelle go off on their honeymoon and return to a new, elegantly decorated house, the after to their modest working-class home. They are finely dressed, and Isabelle marvels at her new bourgeois surroundings. Although Sylvester has become a success, the intertitles make it clear that their marriage and new home are due to Martha Jane's industriousness and thrift. The family has achieved the middle-class ideal. As Hazel Carby observes, the "uplifting portraits of leaders" are gone; the piano has replaced the portrait (figure E.11). And the real uplift man, Sylvester, replaces the ideal Washington in their home: "waking up" results in a domestic sphere of active participation rather than one of passive observation.[17]

Micheaux's oeuvre puts into relief the tentative political investments of up-lift cinema. To be clear, uplift films were not direct assaults on racism and social inequities. Rather, they were indirect, perhaps even coded, attacks on inequali-ties through the representation of Black respectability, promise, and advance-ment, along with images to counter the prevalent on-screen racism. For these reasons, uplift cinema has never entirely gone away. Although it is no longer a dominant mode of representation and politics, Black intellectuals and media makers have continued to grapple with the ideas of uplift and the public pre-sentation of images of Black respectability. From Spencer Williams to Sidney

FIG. E.10-E.11 *Body and Soul* (Oscar Micheaux, 1925).

Poitier, Melvin Van Peebles, and Lee Daniels, uplift has been incorporated, negotiated, or explicitly rejected in complex and unresolved ways. In critical debates surrounding Black media representation, the persistence of a positive-negative binary across changing social, economic, and political circumstances underscores the impact of uplift discourse in Black cinema. By producing a historically situated and theoretically grounded consideration of uplift cinema, we have seen that uplift discourse is far more nuanced and complex than a simplistic positive-negative binary allows. In this sense, a greater understanding of uplift cinema permits a more complete accounting of the critical trajectory attending Black moving pictures—and visual media more broadly—from their emergence in the early twentieth century to the present day.

NOTES

PREFACE

1. William Henry, "Correcting Oscar Misceaux," *Chicago Defender*, January 22, 1927. Henry is also quoted in Regester, "The African-American Press and Race Movies, 1909–1929," 46.

2. "Oscar Micheaux In," *Chicago Defender*, September 24, 1927.

3. Quoted in Regester, "Black Films, White Censors," 183, and Green, *With a Crooked Stick*, 78.

4. Quoted in "Going Abroad: Noted Motion Picture Producer Soon Sails for Europe," *Chicago Defender*, January 31, 1920.

5. Bowser and Spence, *Writing Himself into History*, 20.

INTRODUCTION

1. William Foster [Juli Jones Jr., pseud.], "News of the Moving Picture," *Freeman*, December 20, 1913. It is notable that a century later the Ethiopian-born independent filmmaker Haile Gerima would use the same language to describe the response by audiences to his film *Sankofa* (1993): "Why would one movie become what it became? Hunger. Not the film. Hunger" (Haile Gerima, unpublished oral history interview by Jacqueline Stewart, Allyson Nadia Field, Jan-Christopher Horak, and Zeinabu irene Davis, September 13, 2010, L.A. Rebellion Oral History Project, University of California, Los Angeles [UCLA], Film and Television Archive, Los Angeles, CA).

2. J. Gaines, *Fire and Desire*, 107.

3. Brundage, "Reconsidering Booker T. Washington and *Up From Slavery*," 9.

4. Kevin Gaines has shown that the origins of the concept of uplift preceded Washington's political activity by far and can be traced to antebellum efforts among antislavery crusaders as well as among free Black communities (*Uplifting the Race*, 31).

5. Washington, *Up from Slavery*, 99–100.

6. Du Bois, "Of Mr. Booker T. Washington and Others," 35.

7. Washington, *Up from Slavery*, 100.

8. Washington, *Up from Slavery*, 100.

9. Brundage, "Reconsidering Booker T. Washington and *Up from Slavery*," 13.

10. K. Gaines, *Uplifting the Race*, 33.

11. Tuskegee Normal and Industrial Institute, *Making Useful Citizens* (Tuskegee, AL: Normal and Industrial Institute, 1912).

12. K. Gaines, *Uplifting the Race*, 33.

13. K. Gaines, *Uplifting the Race*, 35. On the ideological conflict between Washington and Du Bois, see Bauerlein, "Booker T. Washington and W. E. B. Du Bois"; Moore, *Booker T. Washington, W. E. B. Du Bois, and the Struggle for Racial Uplift*; Harlan, "Booker T. Washington in Biographical Perspective."

14. Du Bois, "The Talented Tenth," 33.

15. K. Gaines, *Uplifting the Race*, 1.

16. K. Gaines, *Uplifting the Race*, 1.

17. K. Gaines, *Uplifting the Race*, 32.

18. K. Gaines, *Uplifting the Race*, xv.

19. Moten, "Uplift and Criminality," 330.

20. Other Black leaders shared the belief in the importance of economic independence of African Americans. In fact, as Kevern Verney points out, it was Du Bois who inspired Washington to found the NNBL (*The Art of the Possible*, 87).

21. Hampton Institute, *What Hampton Graduates Are Doing in Land-Buying*.

22. Like Frederick Douglass, Washington published three autobiographies. In Washington's case, they were first published in 1900 (*The Story of My Life and Work*), 1901 (*Up from Slavery*), and 1911 (*My Larger Education*).

23. W. Andrews, preface, viii.

24. W. Andrews, "The Representation of Slavery and the Rise of Afro-American Literary Realism," 251.

25. W. Andrews, "The Representation of Slavery and the Rise of Afro-American Literary Realism," 252.

26. Washington, *Up from Slavery*, 100.

27. Washington, *Up from Slavery*, 33.

28. Lester Walton, "Colored Motion Pictures are in Great Demand," *New York Age*, March 6, 1920.

29. Quoted in J. Gaines, *Fire and Desire*, 3.

30. Cripps, *Black Film as Genre*, 7.

31. Sampson, *Blacks in Black and White*, 3.

32. Petersen, "The 'Reol' Story"; Lupack, *Richard E. Norman and Race Filmmaking*; Bernstein and White, "'Scratching Around' in a 'Fit of Insanity'"; P. Bowser and Musser, "Richard D. Maurice and the Maurice Film Company"; Stewart, untitled forthcoming book on Spencer Williams. See also Green, *Straight Lick* and *With a Crooked Stick*; J. Gaines, *Fire and Desire*; P. Bowser, Gaines, and Musser, *Oscar Micheaux and His Circle*; P. Bowser and Spence, *Writing Himself into History*; and the documentary *Midnight Ramble: Oscar Micheaux and the Story of Race Movies* by Pearl Bowser and Pamela Thomas.

33. Regester, "The African-American Press and Race Movies"; Everett, *Returning the Gaze*.

34. P. Bowser and Spence, *Writing Himself into History*, 14.

35. P. Bowser and Spence, *Writing Himself into History*, 26.

36. See, in particular, Stewart, *Migrating to the Movies*; P. Bowser and Spence, *Writing Himself into History*; Green, *Straight Lick*; Robinson, *Forgeries of Memory and Meaning*; J. Gaines, *Fire and Desire*.

37. J. Gaines, *Fire and Desire*, 17. Gaines does not specify the period of this "heyday," though with her reference to their borrowing from "every existing Hollywood genre," I presume she refers to films made in the 1930s and 1940s. Sampson marks the peak of race film production as 1921 (*Blacks in Black and White*, 6, 15).

38. J. Gaines, *Fire and Desire*, 107.

39. Although scholarly attention to Black film culture has focused on the north, notable exceptions include Bernstein and White, "'Scratching Around' in a 'Fit of Insanity'" and "'Imitation of Life' in a Segregated Atlanta"; Streible, "The Harlem Theatre"; Waller, *Main Street Amusements*, 161–79; R. Allen and Gomery, *Film History*, 202–7.

40. J. Gaines, *Fire and Desire*, 108. See also Williams, *Playing the Race Card*.

41. Cara Caddoo's study of early Black exhibition practices in nontheatrical spaces, *Envisioning Freedom*, is an important contribution to these issues.

42. J. Gaines, *Fire and Desire*, 6.

43. J. Gaines, *Fire and Desire*, 91–126.

44. Sampson, *Blacks in Black and White*; Cripps, *Slow Fade to Black*; Klotman, *Frame by Frame*.

45. Cripps, *Slow Fade to Black*, 172. See also 70–89.

46. For discussions of white financing of Black films, see Cripps, *Black Film as Genre*, 6–7; Rhines, *Black Film, White Money*, 14–27; P. Bowser, Gaines, and Musser, *Oscar Micheaux and His Circle*, xx.

47. J. Gaines, *Fire and Desire*, 6, 17.

48. See Stewart, *Migrating to the Movies*.

49. See, for example, Sloan, *The Loud Silents*; Brownlow, *Behind the Mask of Innocence*; Stamp, "Taking Precautions, or Regulating Early Birth-Control Films" and "Lois Weber, Progressive Cinema, and the Fate of 'The Work-a-Day Girls' in *Shoes*."

50. Prelinger, *The Field Guide to Sponsored Films*, vi.

51. Acland and Wasson, "Introduction," 13, 4.

52. Acland and Wasson, "Introduction," 3.

53. Advertisement for *Adrift*, *Moving Picture World*, January 28, 1911, 166.

54. Untitled review of *The Refugee*, *Moving Picture World*, January 29, 1910, 128.

55. Advertisement for Lubin Manufacturing Company, *Moving Picture World*, August 27, 1910, 478.

56. "The Picture as a Teacher," 193; "Teachers View Historical Films," 197; and W. Stephen Bush, "Simplifying the Teaching of History," 199, all in *Moving Picture World*, October 21, 1911.

57. "Reviews of Notable Films," *Moving Picture World*, November 18, 1911, 535.

58. "Made to Persuade" was the theme of the Eighth Orphan Film Symposium held at the Museum of the Moving Image, Astoria, NY, April 11–14, 2012. Devin Orgeron, Marsha Orgeron, and Dan Streible note: "We have opted to use the term *educational*

because we believe it to be a useful umbrella under which to collect scholarship on films that were used to teach, inform, instruct, or persuade viewers in a variety of ways and contexts" (introduction, 9).

59. See, for example, Waller, "Locating Early Non-Theatrical Audiences"; Prelinger, *The Field Guide to Sponsored Films*; Slide, *Before Video*; advertisement for Kalem Company, *Moving Picture World*, October 21, 1911, 185; "Comments on the Films," *Moving Picture World*, October 28, 1911, 290.

60. See advertisement for Edison Manufacturing Company, *Moving Picture World*, August 27, 1910, 476; "Stories of the Films," *Moving Picture World*, September 3, 1910, 531; "Comments on the Films," *Moving Picture World*, September 17, 1910, 630; "Show Safety Devices for Workers," *Moving Picture World*, March 8, 1913, 1005; "Independent," *Moving Picture World*, May 3, 1913, 489; Waller, "Locating Early Non-Theatrical Audiences," 87–90; Simmon, "Program Notes."

61. "Comments on the Films," *Moving Picture World*, September 17, 1910, 630.

62. "Show Safety Devices for Workers," *Moving Picture World*, March 8, 1913, 1005; Simmon, "Program Notes," 121–25.

63. "Moving Pictures of Tuskegee," *New York Age*, January 27, 1910.

64. "The States Theater," *Chicago Defender*, August 9, 1913.

65. The Patents Company fiercely fought and drove out of business independent production companies, although the MPPC was also in decline during the years of uplift cinema's emergence. See E. Bowser, *The Transformation of Cinema*, 73–85.

66. Musser, with Nelson, *High-Class Moving Pictures*, 109.

67. Vitagraph's publicity quotes Burns's poem as "O wad the power some giftee gie us / To see ourselves as others see us." See Musser, with Nelson, *High-Class Moving Pictures*, 151.

68. Quoted in Toulmin and Loiperdinger, "Is It You?," 8.

69. M. Johnson, "The Places You'll Know," 24.

70. "Entertainments," *Southern Workman*, February 1914, 121.

71. J. Gaines, *Fire and Desire*, 12.

72. Du Bois, "Of Our Spiritual Strivings," 11.

73. J. Gaines, *Fire and Desire*, 13.

74. Davis, foreword, 6. In her discussion of the Tyler, Texas Black Film Collection, Stewart has an extended discussion of Davis's foreword ("Discovering Black Film History," 152–54).

75. J. Gaines, *Fire and Desire*, 13.

76. Joseph Clark builds on Gaines's work in his study of All-American Newsreel, noting that the newsreel's "pedagogical address could not fully escape the dilemma described by Du Bois. Even as the newsreel sought to inspire race pride and overcome the distortions of mainstream representations of African Americans, it reinscribed the self-surveillance logic of double consciousness" ("Double Vision," 276). Clark discusses a didactic segment of the newsreel that was designed to serve as a conduct lesson, after which the commentator concludes: "This has been a good chance to see ourselves as others see us. To which group do you belong? Let's make good conduct a habit, a good habit from now on" (quoted in ibid., 277).

77. David Pierce's important *The Survival of American Silent Feature Films: 1912–*

1929 focuses on surviving American feature films of the silent era. Of these, 70 percent have been completely lost, 14 percent survive in complete domestic-release versions in 35mm film, and 16 percent survive in incomplete forms or are foreign-release versions or small-gauge prints. The rate of survival for nontheatrical silent era films is far lower. Nearly all African American nontheatrical films and theatrical shorts are considered lost.

78. There has been a plethora of work dedicated to fragmentary evidence. See Bruno, *Streetwalking on a Ruined Map*; Omasta and Horwath, *Josef Von Sternberg*; O'Donoghue, "Paradise Regained"; Lunzer, "Vienna's Prater District on Film." There is also exemplary article-length scholarship concerning nonextant films. See, for example, Bergstrom, "Murnau in America"; M. Orgeron, "Multi-Purposing Early Cinema." Several volumes have been dedicated to cataloging lost films, including Tarbox, *Lost Films*, and Waldman, *Missing Reels*. In 1969 the Museum of Modern Art in New York City put on an exhibit called *The Lost Film*, which contained 130 photographs from twenty-eight films considered lost. See Weinberg, "Lost Ones." The excellent collection edited by Jon Lewis and Eric Smoodin, *Looking Past the Screen*, is exemplary for the way it demonstrates how scholarship on film can be augmented by extrafilmic evidence, but it is not concerned with the outright absence of print sources per se.

79. Stewart, "Discovering Black Film History."

80. J. Gaines, *Fire and Desire*, 93.

81. Bruno, *Streetwalking on a Ruined Map*, 147.

82. Vivian Sobchack makes a similar argument concerning the project of media archaeology. See Sobchack, "Afterword," 323.

83. Elsaesser, "General Introduction," 2.

84. See Gartenberg, "The Brighton Project"; Elsaesser, *Early Cinema*.

85. Musser, "Historiographic Method and the Study of Early Cinema," 101.

86. Staiger, "The Future of the Past," 127.

87. Elsaesser, "General Introduction," 3.

88. Robert Allen and Douglas Gomery draw on E. H. Carr's distinction between "a fact of the past" and "a historical fact": "A fact of the past becomes an historical fact when a historian decides to use that fact in constructing a historical analysis" (*Film History*, 7).

89. For a discussion of the issues pertaining to the unreliability of the film print and variability among versions, see Usai, *Silent Cinema*, 14–16.

90. The earliest surviving feature made by an African American is Oscar Micheaux's *Within Our Gates* (1920). Fragments of the Lincoln Motion Picture Company's *By Right of Birth* (1921) also survive. *Two Knights of Vaudeville* (Historical Films, 1915), distributed by Ebony Films, is likely the earliest surviving short film made by a white company and then explicitly marketed to Black audiences. For more information, see P. Bowser, Gaines, and Musser, *Oscar Micheaux and His Circle*; P. Bowser, Gaines, and Musser, "Oscar Micheaux and His Circle," *The 20th Pordenone Silent Film Festival Catalogue*, 47–74.

91. Washington, *Up from Slavery*, 99.

92. This is how Houston Baker (*Turning South Again*, 20) reads W. J. Cash.

93. Gilroy, *The Black Atlantic*, 2.

94. See, for example, Charney and Schwartz, *Cinema and the Invention of Modern Life*.

95. Scholars have begun to consider the role of cinema in issues of Black modernity. I am building on the work of, among others, Everett, *Returning the Gaze*, 12; and Stewart, *Migrating to the Movies*, xiii.

1. THE AESTHETICS OF UPLIFT

1. *4,000,000 Former Slaves Cast Adrift at End of Civil War* (Hampton, VA: Hampton Institute Press, c. 1923); Harvard College Library, Harvard University, Cambridge, MA.

2. Watkins, *The White Architects of Black Education*, 49.

3. Watkins, *The White Architects of Black Education*, 23.

4. Watkins, *The White Architects of Black Education*, 19.

5. See, for example, Blackmon, *Slavery by Another Name*.

6. Washington, *Up from Slavery*, 99.

7. Washington, *Up from Slavery*, 99.

8. Samuel Chapman Armstrong, untitled and undated brochure, Hampton Institute (Hampton, VA); Harvard College Library, Harvard University, Cambridge, MA.

9. Baker, *Modernism and the Harlem Renaissance*, 15.

10. Baker, *Modernism and the Harlem Renaissance*, 22.

11. Verney, *The Art of the Possible*, 40.

12. Washington, *Working with the Hands*, vi.

13. Barthes, *Image, Music, Text*, 25.

14. See, for example, Sampsell-Willmann, *Lewis Hine as Social Critic*; Little, "On Progressive-Era Photography."

15. Washington, *Up from Slavery*, 28, 31.

16. Baker, *Modernism and the Harlem Renaissance*, 41.

17. I. Andrews, *The Failure of Cunningham*, 5.

18. I. Andrews, *The Failure of Cunningham*, 5.

19. I. Andrews, *The Failure of Cunningham*, 5.

20. I. Andrews, *The Failure of Cunningham*, 6.

21. I. Andrews, *The Failure of Cunningham*, 6.

22. I. Andrews, *The Failure of Cunningham*, 6.

23. I. Andrews, *The Failure of Cunningham*, 7.

24. I. Andrews, *The Failure of Cunningham*, 9.

25. I. Andrews, *The Failure of Cunningham*, 9.

26. I. Andrews, *The Failure of Cunningham*, 10.

27. I. Andrews, *The Failure of Cunningham*, 3.

28. I. Andrews, *The Failure of Cunningham*, 12.

29. I. Andrews, *The Failure of Cunningham*, 7.

30. Washington takes a different view of this when he critiques the image of a young man trying pathetically to continue his formal education while neglecting his home:

"In fact, one of the saddest things I saw during the month of travel which I have described was a young man, who had attended some high school, sitting down in a one-room cabin, with grease on his clothing, filth all around him, and weeds in the yard and garden, engaged in studying a French grammar" (*Up from Slavery*, 58).

31. I. Andrews, *The Failure of Cunningham*, 10.

32. See, for example, the case of Frances Benjamin Johnston discussed later in this chapter.

33. I. Andrews, *The Failure of Cunningham*, 12.

34. *The Failure of Cunningham* originally appeared without images. Five editions were published by the Hampton Institute Press between 1898 and 1916.

35. I. Andrews, *The Failure of Cunningham*, 9.

36. H. Frissell, "Address of Dr. Frissell," 20–21.

37. Verney, *The Art of the Possible*, 135.

38. Jones, "Harvard Square."

39. Sollors, Titcomb, and Underwood, *Blacks at Harvard*, 153–54.

40. "Columbia Faculty Club Served by Colored Votary of the Muse," *New York Times*, February 16, 1913. The *Times* published one of Jones's poems, "Contentment," as a letter to the editor, August 4, 1913, 6.

41. There were Black students enrolled at Harvard in 1910, but only a few. See Sollors, Titcomb, and Underwood, *Blacks at Harvard*, 153–54.

42. Washington, *Working with the Hands*, 230.

43. Washington, *Working with the Hands*, 242.

44. Washington, *Working with the Hands*, 244.

45. Washington, *Working with the Hands*, 245–46.

46. Hampton Institute, *What Hampton Graduates Are Doing*, 10.

47. Hampton Institute, *What Hampton Graduates Are Doing*, 10.

48. Hampton Institute, *What Hampton Graduates Are Doing*, 98.

49. H. Frissell, "Address of Dr. Frissell," 19.

50. Washington, *Up from Slavery*, 99.

51. In the *Southern Workman*, there is a fuller version of the photograph, which shows three figures working on the window and is captioned "Indoor construction work" (May 1913, 279).

52. Hampton Institute, untitled brochure, c. 1910, n.p.

53. *Southern Workman*, June 1915, 356–57.

54. The 1900 exposition inaugurated Hampton's consistent presence at fairs and expositions. The *Southern Workman* mentions that the photos were taken for the Paris exposition, "but many others [were] designed for the stereopticon and for other illustration[s]" (January 1900, 49).

55. Lincoln Kirstein found the images in a leatherbound album in a Washington bookstore during World War II and brought them to the Museum of Modern Art in New York City in the 1960s. See Johnston, *The Hampton Album*. There are 159 platinum prints in *The Hampton Album*, although the *Southern Workman* mentions only 140. In 1966, MOMA published a collection of forty-four prints under the title *The Hampton Album* with an introduction by Kirstein.

56. *Southern Workman*, January 1900, 49.

57. H. Frissell, "Thirty-Second Annual Report of the Principal," *Southern Workman*, May 1900, 289.

58. *Southern Workman*, January 1900, 8.

59. "Hampton School Record: Every Day Affairs," *Southern Workman*, January 1900, 49–50.

60. *Southern Workman*, January 1900, 8.

61. Wexler, *Tender Violence*, 129, 148.

62. Wexler, *Tender Violence*, 130.

63. Wexler, *Tender Violence*, 136–37.

64. Ellison, *Invisible Man*, 39.

65. Wexler, *Tender Violence*, 142.

66. Wexler, *Tender Violence*, 152, 144.

67. Washington, *Working with the Hands*, 4–5, 9, 29, 30, 63.

68. For a discussion of this incident, see Wexler, *Tender Violence*, 291–98.

69. Wexler, *Tender Violence*, 293.

70. Wexler, *Tender Violence*, 295.

71. Hampton Institute, *The Need for Hampton*, n.p.

72. S. Frissell, *Hampton's Message*, 8–10.

73. Washington, *Working with the Hands*, 235.

74. Du Bois, *Some Notes on Negro Crime*.

75. Baker, *Turning South Again*, 58.

76. Baker, *Turning South Again*, 58.

77. Baker, *Turning South Again*, 60.

78. Moten, "Uplift and Criminality," 332.

79. Wallace, "Framing the Black Soldier," 251.

80. Wallace, "Framing the Black Soldier," 257–58.

81. *Making Useful Citizens* (Tuskegee, AL: Normal and Industrial Institute, 1912).

82. "Moving Pictures of Tuskegee," *New York Age*, January 27, 1910.

83. H. Frissell, "Address of Dr. Frissell," 22.

84. Hampton Institute, *Everyday Life at Hampton Institute*, 5.

85. For a thorough study of Native Americans at Hampton, see Lindsey, *Indians at Hampton Institute*.

86. Sapirstein, "Out from behind the Mask," 186.

87. For a discussion of seriality as a key strategy for reading photographs, see Campt, *Image Matters*.

88. Miner graduated from the Academy of Design in New York and worked at the Pennsylvania Museum in Philadelphia before taking a position as a drawing teacher at Hampton in 1898. For more on Miner's career, see Dabbs, *Face of an Island*; Sapirstein, "Out from behind the Mask: The Illustrated Poetry of Paul Laurence Dunbar and Photography at Hampton Institute."

89. Hampton Institute, *Everyday Life at Hampton Institute*, 28.

90. W. E. B. Du Bois, "Booker T. Washington," *Crisis*, December 1915, 82.

91. Wexler, *Tender Violence*, 151.

92. Although the photographs were credited to the Hampton Institute Camera

Club, Miner was the lead photographer of the group and went on to photograph the images for thee Dunbar volumes by himself. For more on the club and its members' Dunbar illustrations, see Sapirstein, "Out from behind the Mask."

93. Wexler, *Tender Violence*, 147.

94. Wexler, *Tender Violence*, 291.

95. Wexler, *Tender Violence*, 148.

96. Anderson, "Education for Servitude," 168.

97. Dunbar, *The Paul Laurence Dunbar Reader*, 261.

98. Gates, *The Signifying Monkey*, 176.

99. Gates, *The Signifying Monkey*, 176.

100. Balestrini, "National Memory and the Arts in Paul Laurence Dunbar's War Poetry," 30, note 33.

101. See S. Smith, *Photography on the Color Line*.

102. Du Bois, "Of Mr. Booker T. Washington and Others," 40.

103. S. Smith, *Photography on the Color Line*, 147.

104. Washington, *Up from Slavery*, 100.

105. Miller, "Radicals and Conservatives," 188.

2. "TO SHOW THE INDUSTRIAL PROGRESS OF THE NEGRO ALONG INDUSTRIAL LINES"
—————

1. Washington, "General Introduction," 6.

2. Broome later wrote Washington that he would be leaving Boston for Tuskegee "to take Moving Pictures of the Institute that you gave me the privilege of doing sometime ago" (George W. Broome letter to Washington, November 1, 1909, frame 323, microfilm reel 300, Booker T. Washington Papers, 1853–1946, Manuscript Division, Library of Congress, Washington, DC [hereafter Washington Papers]).

3. Brooks, *Lost Sounds*, 464.

4. "Moving Pictures of Tuskegee," *New York Age*, January 20, 1910.

5. Broome to Washington, November 1, 1909, Washington Papers.

6. George W. Broome letter to Washington, February 12, 1910, frame 528, microfilm reel 312; Broome invoice to Emmett J. Scott, no date (paid February 4, 1910), frame 503, reel 312, both Washington Papers.

7. George W. Broome letter to Washington, June 8, 1910, frame 15, microfilm reel 313, Washington Papers.

8. Broome to Washington, November 1, 1909, Washington Papers. The photographer is unnamed.

9. Broome to Washington, November 1, 1909, Washington Papers.

10. *Southern Workman*, March 1909, 137–38.

11. Quoted in "Moving Pictures of Tuskegee," *New York Age*, January 20, 1910.

12. Samuel E. Courtney letter to Emmett J. Scott, January 8, 1910, frame 542, microfilm reel 313, Washington Papers.

13. George P. Phenix letter to Washington, January 11, 1910, frame 30, microfilm reel 320, Washington Papers.

14. [Name redacted] letter to George P. Phenix, January 7, 1910, frame 31, microfilm reel 320, Washington Papers.

15. [Name redacted] to Phenix, January 7, 1910, Washington Papers.

16. [Name redacted] to Phenix, January 7, 1910, Washington Papers.

17. Washington letter to Emmett J. Scott, January 15, 1910, frame 29, microfilm reel 320, Washington Papers.

18. Advertisement in *New York Age*, February 3, 1910. This advertisement does not mention Broome by name, but the subject of the moving pictures, the timing, and the location of the exhibition indicate that this was indeed a Broome program.

19. "Tuskegee's Moving Pictures," *Freeman*, March 12, 1910.

20. "Tuskogee [sic] in Moving Pictures Business," *Chicago Defender*, December 31, 1910.

21. "Tuskogee [sic] in Moving Pictures Business," *Chicago Defender*, December 31, 1910.

22. Musser, with Nelson, *High-Class Moving Pictures*, 109.

23. See Musser, with Nelson, *High-Class Moving Pictures*.

24. Broome Exhibition Company letterhead, 1910, frame 755, reel 312, Washington Papers.

25. Quoted in P. Bowser and Spence, *Writing Himself into History*, 109.

26. Stewart, *Migrating to the Movies*, 103.

27. Higginbotham, *Righteous Discontent*, 185.

28. Higginbotham, *Righteous Discontent*, 187.

29. Washington to H. J. Streyckmans, *The Show World*, March 4, 1910, frame 397, microfilm reel 321, Washington Papers.

30. "Moving Pictures of Tuskegee," *New York Age*, January 20, 1910.

31. "Moving Pictures of Tuskegee," *New York Age*, January 20, 1910. The article concluded that Hampton, Fisk, and Shaw would all be "given consideration in the future." Although there is no surviving evidence that the Broome Company filmed Fisk or Shaw (both Black colleges) at this time, Hampton embraced the new industrial medium. However, after Hampton vice principal George Phenix's strong disapproval of Broome's Tremont Temple exhibition, Hampton officials were concerned about working with outside filmmakers and produced their campaign films themselves.

32. Emmett Jay Scott letter to Washington, January 12, 1910, in Washington, *Booker T. Washington Papers*, 10:261.

33. Scott to Washington, January 12, 1910, Washington, *Booker T. Washington Papers*, 10:262.

34. Robert E. Park, "Bring School Here. That Is, by Means of Moving Pictures," *New York Tribune*, January 16, 1910.

35. Robert E. Park, "Bring School Here. That Is, by Means of Moving Pictures," *New York Tribune*, January 16, 1910.

36. "Moving Pictures of Tuskegee Institute," *Nickelodeon*, May 15, 1910, 262. The *New York Age* published Park's article as "Moving Pictures of Tuskegee" on January 20, 1910, without attribution but nearly verbatim, changing "negroes" to "colored people," for example.

37. Carnegie Hall was a popular venue for lectures that included moving pictures in

the 1910s, such as frequent travelogue and other nonfiction events by showmen like Burton Holmes and Dwight L. Elmendorf. Rob Hudson, the associate archivist at Carnegie Hall, informed me that the first moving picture screened at Carnegie Hall, on December 14, 1898, was of Pope Leo XIII, which accompanied a lecture by Thomas H. Malone.

38. Following Washington's death in 1915, Riley published *The Life and Times of Booker T. Washington*.

39. Quoted in "Moving Pictures of Tuskegee," *New York Age*, January 27, 1910.

40. Quoted in "Moving Pictures of Tuskegee," *New York Age*, January 27, 1910.

41. Quoted in "Moving Pictures of Tuskegee," *New York Age*, January 27, 1910.

42. Quoted in "Moving Pictures of Tuskegee," *New York Age*, January 27, 1910.

43. "Moving Pictures of Tuskegee," *New York Age*, January 27, 1910.

44. "Moving Pictures of Tuskegee," *New York Age*, January 27, 1910. The day after the event, the *New York Times* ran an article titled "Low Joins in Appeal to Help Tuskegee" (January 25, 1910) in which there is a reference to stereopticon views, not motion pictures. The speeches were reported using the same text that had appeared in the *Age*, suggesting that the *Times* reporter might not have attended the event and was reporting from transcripts of the speeches. The *Times* did mention the philanthropists in attendance, focusing on the "prominent women in boxes" at the event. It is also possible that the misreport of stereopticon views was due to a press release from Tuskegee prior to the event since Scott made the decision not to include the slides only after the January 12 private screening.

45. Washington letter to Robert T. Motts, January 31, 1910, frame 690, microfilm reel 318, Washington Papers.

46. J. O. Spencer letter to Emmett J. Scott, February 16, 1910, frame 361, microfilm reel 321, Washington Papers.

47. William A. Creditt letter to Washington, January 29, 1910, frame 362, microfilm reel 312, Washington Papers.

48. George W. Broome letter to Washington, February 17, 1910, frame 543, microfilm reel 312, Washington Papers.

49. Broome to Washington, February 17, 1910, Washington Papers.

50. George W. Broome letter to Emmett J. Scott, April 11, 1910, frame 704, microfilm reel 312, Washington Papers.

51. Emmett J. Scott letter to George W. Broome, April 14, 1910, frame 712, microfilm reel 312, Washington Papers.

52. The *Trenton Evening Times* reported: "Moving pictures of Booker T. Washington's great industrial school, Tuskegee Institute showing the students at their work and other phases of the enterprise conducted by this famous negro leader will be shown tomorrow evening at Mt Zion A M E Church, Perry Street, this city under the auspices of the United Societies of the congregation. The pastor the Rev H. P. Anderson will be in charge of the affair" ("To Show Motion Pictures of Tuskegee Institute," March 1, 1910).

53. George W. Broome letter to Washington. June 8, 1910, frame 15, microfilm reel 313, Washington Papers.

54. Washington letter to George W. Broome, June 15, 1910, frame 31, microfilm reel 313, Washington Papers.

55. George W. Broome letter to Washington, July 18, 1910, frame 85, microfilm reel 313, Washington Papers.

56. Washington letter to George W. Broome, July 21, 1910, frame 90, microfilm reel 313, Washington Papers.

57. George W. Broome letter to Washington, November 2, 1910, frame 297, microfilm reel 313, Washington Papers.

58. *Clayton's Weekly*, October 18, 1919, 3.

59. Tim Brooks, *Lost Sounds*, 464–72.

60. Tim Brooks, *Lost Sounds*, 469.

61. Stewart, *Migrating to the Movies*, 101.

62. Stewart, *Migrating to the Movies*, 276, note 19.

63. I have not been able to find any information about Broome's other films except for a few references to their existence.

64. Cary B. Lewis, "The 8th Illinois Regiment Hold Their Fifteenth Anniversary amid Pomp, Dignity and Military Glory," *Freeman*, November 12, 1910. Anderson was legal adviser of the Chicago Leland Giants and president of the Appomattox Club, and he was involved in various fraternal and social organizations in Chicago.

65. Washington, *A New Negro for a New Century*, 339.

66. See "Fires from His Pocket," *Salt Lake Telegram*, March 1, 1905; "Shot One of the Thugs," *Aberdeen Daily News*, March 2, 1905.

67. "The First Negro Colonel: John R. Marshall of Chicago to Enjoy that Distinction," *New York Times*, June 22, 1898.

68. "John Arthur Johnson, Champion Heavy Weight Prize Fighter of the World," *Broad Ax*, October 26, 1912.

69. Louis B. Anderson, Dr. George C. Hall, E. H. Wright, Julius F. Taylor, George W. Ellis, B. F. Moseley, ex-officio, "Statement by Conference of Representative Chicago Colored Citizens, October 23, 1912," *Broad Ax*, October 26, 1912.

70. See Gatewood, "Booker T. Washington and the Ulrich Affair"; Harlan, *Booker T. Washington*, 379–404.

71. "John Arthur Johnson, Champion Heavy Weight Prize Fighter of the World," *Broad Ax*, October 26, 1912.

72. United Press Association to Booker T. Washington, October 22, 1912, Washington, *Booker T. Washington Papers*, 12:43.

73. "A Statement on Jack Johnson for the United Press Association," October 23, 1912, Washington, *Booker T. Washington Papers*, 12:43. The statement was prepared by Emmett J. Scott and Robert E. Park, in consultation with Washington while he was away from Tuskegee.

74. Anderson wrote to Emmett J. Scott on February 25, 1913: "I am breaking my silence with the announcement that the moving picture films of 'A Day at Tuskegee,' have been developed and an initial private exhibition of them has been given" (Washington, *Booker T. Washington Papers*, 12:121).

75. "Col. John B. Marshall, and His Trip through the South," *Broad Ax*, January 15, 1913.

76. "Negroes of State Holding Meeting: Alabama State Negro Business League

Opens Three-Day Session with Addresses of Welcome and Responses," *Montgomery Advertiser*, April 22, 1914; "Negroes Desirous of Organizing for Active Borer Duty," *Montgomery Advertiser*, June 23, 1916.

77. Quoted in "Birds Eye View of Camp Lincoln at Springfield, Ill.," *Broad Ax*, September 2, 1911.

78. See Emmett J. Scott letter to Louis B. Anderson, January 20, 1913, frame 820, microfilm reel 347, Washington Papers; *Tuskegee Student*, January 25, 1913.

79. *Tuskegee Student*, January 25, 1913.

80. "Tuskegee in Motion Pictures," *Broad Ax*, March 15, 1913.

81. Emmett J. Scott letter to Louis B. Anderson, January 20, 1913, frame 820, microfilm reel 347, Washington Papers.

82. See Scott to Anderson, January 20, 1913, Washington Papers; "Col. John R. Marshall, and His Trip through the South," *Broad Ax*, January 25, 1913; *Freeman*, February 1, 1913.

83. Louis B. Anderson letter to Emmett Jay Scott, February 25, 1913, Washington, *Booker T. Washington Papers*, 12:121.

84. "A Day at Tuskegee," *Chicago Defender*, March 29, 1913.

85. Anderson to Scott, February 25, 1913, Washington, *Booker T. Washington Papers*, 12:121–22.

86. "Hear the Man Who Founded Tuskegee Institute," *Broad Ax*, March 29, 1913.

87. The advertisement appeared in *Moving Picture World* on March 15, 22, and 29, 1913.

88. Anderson to Scott, February 25, 1913, Washington, *Booker T. Washington Papers*, 12:122.

89. For example, see, Louis B. Anderson letter to Emmett J. Scott, March 3, 1913, frame 5, microfilm reel 348, Washington Papers.

90. Anderson to Scott, February 25, 1913, Washington, *Booker T. Washington Papers*, 12:123.

91. Emmett J. Scott letter to Louis B. Anderson, March 1, 1913, frame 3, microfilm reel 348, Washington Papers.

92. Emmett J. Scott letter to Louis B. Anderson, February 28, 1913, frame 817, microfilm reel 347, Washington Papers.

93. Scott to Anderson, February 28, 1913, Washington Papers.

94. "A Day at Tuskegee," *Chicago Defender*, March 29, 1913.

95. Louis B. Anderson letter to Emmett J. Scott, March 3, 1913, frame 5, microfilm reel 348, Washington Papers.

96. "A Day at Tuskegee," *Chicago Defender*, March 29, 1913.

97. Carey B. Lewis letter templates to principals of public schools, prominent citizens, club presidents, and prominent ministers, no date, frames 32–50, microfilm reel 348, Washington Papers.

98. Louis B. Anderson letter to Emmett J. Scott, March 25, 1913, frame 48, microfilm reel 348, Washington Papers. The clubs invited included Appomattox, University, Criterion, Tuskegee, Fisk, Swastika, Peerless, Pandora, Bethel Literary, Standard, Fellowship League, Navarre, Men's Civic, Midlothian, Phalanx, Umbrian Glee, Federal Glee,

Young Peoples' Progressive, Chicago Girls' Civic, Wendell Phillips Settlement Club, 20th Century, West Side Women's, and Federation of Women's Clubs of Chicago. Advertisement in *Broad Ax*, March 29, 1913.

99. Letter templates, no date, frame 50, microfilm reel 348, Washington Papers.

100. Cary B. Lewis, "Film Co. Incorporated," *Freeman*, March 8, 1913.

101. Cary B. Lewis, "J. P. Faulkner Speaks," *Freeman*, March 15, 1913.

102. "Movies," *Chicago Defender*, March 8, 1913.

103. Emmett J. Scott letter to Washington, March 18, 1913, frame 39, microfilm reel 348, Washington Papers.

104. Louis B. Anderson letter to Emmett J. Scott, April 28, 1913, frame 122, microfilm reel 348, Washington Papers.

105. Advertisement in *Broad Ax*, March 22, 1913.

106. Letter template, March 20, 1913, frame 49, microfilm reel 348, Washington Papers.

107. Louis B. Anderson letter to Emmett J. Scott, March 6, 1913, frame 15, microfilm reel 348, Washington Papers.

108. Text for the "amusement column" of Chicago's Sunday newspapers, March 30, 1913, frame 49, microfilm reel 348, Washington Papers.

109. "Tuskegee in Moving Pictures," *Broad Ax*, March 15, 1913.

110. Louis B. Anderson letter to Emmett J. Scott, March 8, 1913, frame 20, microfilm reel 348; Scott letter to Anderson, March 11, 1913, frame 24, microfilm reel 348, both Washington Papers.

111. "Tuskegee in Moving Pictures," *Broad Ax*, March 15, 1913; "An Evening at Tuskegee Institute," *Broad Ax*, April 5, 1913; Abbott and Seroff, *To Do This, You Must Know How*, 224.

112. "A Day at Tuskegee," frame 818, microfilm reel 347, Washington Papers.

113. Emmett J. Scott letter to Louis B. Anderson, March 12, 1913, frame 25, microfilm reel 348, Washington Papers.

114. Louis B. Anderson letter to Emmett J. Scott, March 14, 1913, frame 26, microfilm reel 348, Washington Papers.

115. Emmett J. Scott letter to Louis B. Anderson, March 19, 1913, frame 41, microfilm reel 348, Washington Papers.

116. Cary B. Lewis, "Moving Pictures of Tuskegee," *Tuskegee Student*, April 5, 1913. At sixteen feet per second, 4,000 feet of film would run for approximately one hour.

117. Jas. S. McQuade, "Chicago Letter," *Moving Picture World*, March 29, 1913, 1322.

118. "The Moving Picture Educator," *Moving Picture World*, May 3, 1913, 491.

119. "Facts and Comments," *Moving Picture World*, June 21, 1913, 1227. The trade journal also mentions "pictures of the students of the Agricultural and Mechanical College down in Texas and scores of similar undertakings."

120. See, for example, Gaycken, "The Cinema of the Future."

121. "In the Educational Field," *Moving Picture World*, January 21, 1911, 128–29. See also D. Orgeron, Orgeron, and Streible, "A History of Learning with the Lights Off," 16; Gaycken, "The Cinema of the Future," 85–86.

122. "In the Educational Field," *Moving Picture World*, January 21, 1911, 128.

123. "A Day at Tuskegee," *Chicago Defender*, March 29, 1913; Harlan, *Booker T. Washington*, 434.

124. Louis B. Anderson letter to Emmett J. Scott. April 7, 1913, frame 77, micofilm reel 348, Washington Papers.

125. "An Evening at Tuskegee Institute," *Broad Ax*, April 5, 1913.

126. Advertisements in *Moving Picture World*, March 15, 1913, 1167; March 22, 1913, 1277; and March 29, 1913, 1385; and in *Freeman*, November 22, 1913.

127. Louis B. Anderson letter to Emmett J. Scott, March 14, 1913, frame 26, microfilm reel 348, Washington Papers.

128. In Larry Richards's filmography, *A Day at Tuskegee* is the only film credited to the Anderson-Watkins Film Company (*African American Films through 1959*, 246).

129. Louis B. Anderson letter to Emmett J. Scott, April 7, 1913, frame 77, microfilm reel 348, Washington Papers.

130. Anderson to Scott, April 7, 1913, frame 79, Washington Papers.

131. "An Evening at Tuskegee Institute," *Broad Ax*, April 5, 1913.

132. "An Evening at Tuskegee Institute," *Broad Ax*, April 5, 1913.

133. George W. Broome letter to Louis B. Anderson, March 26, 1913, frame 67, microfilm reel 348, Washington Papers.

134. Anderson to Scott, April 7, 1913, frame 79, Washington Papers.

135. Anderson to Scott, April 7, 1913, frame 79, Washington Papers.

136. Louis B. Anderson letter to Emmett J. Scott, April 22, 1913, frame 114, microfilm reel 348; Anderson letter to Scott, April 28, 1913, frame 122, microfilm reel 348, both Washington Papers.

137. Louis B. Anderson letter to Emmett J. Scott, April 29, 1913, frame 123, microfilm reel 348, Washington Papers.

138. Anderson to Scott, April 7, 1913, frame 77, Washington Papers.

139. Louis B. Anderson letter to Emmett J. Scott, April 28, 1913, frame 122, microfilm reel 348, Washington Papers.

140. *Tuskegee Student*, May 17, 1913.

141. Scott to Anderson, May 9, 1913, frame 131, Washington Papers.

142. Emmett J. Scott letter to Louis B. Anderson, May 9, 1913, frame 131, microfilm reel 348, Washington Papers.

143. The *Moving Picture World* described the footage included in Pathé News, No. 94, November 24, 1915: "The body of Booker T. Washington is carried to its last resting place by favorite pupils of the great negro leader" ("Stories of the Films: Pathe Exchange, Inc.," December 4, 1915, 1906).

144. "A Day at Tuskegee," *Montgomery Advertiser*, May 6, 1913.

145. William F. Watkins letter to Emmett J. Scott, May 18, 1913, frame 156, microfilm reel 348, Washington Papers.

146. "A Day at Tuskegee," *Savannah Tribune*, May 17, 1913.

147. Watkins to Scott, May 18, 1913, Washington Papers.

148. No records survive indicating the nature of the photograph. Washington letter to Louis B. Anderson, May 23, 1913, frame 165, microfilm reel 348, Washington Papers.

149. The screening was advertised in the *St. Paul Appeal* on June 28 and July 5, 1913.

150. Cary B. Lewis, "Jerry Mills and Lizzie Wallace at the Grand," *Freeman*, August 9, 1913.

151. Waller, *Main Street Amusements*, 311, note 65.

152. Hunter C. Haynes letter to Emmett J. Scott, November 25, 1913, frame 518, microfilm reel 348, Washington Papers.

153. Emmett J. Scott letter to Hunter C. Haynes, November 29, 1913, frame 526, microfilm reel 348, Washington Papers.

3. "PICTORIAL SERMONS"

1. Hampton Institute faculty meeting minutes, January 6, 1912, Hampton University Archives, Hampton University Museum, Hampton, Virginia (hereafter Hampton Archives).

2. Folsom was also the primary coordinator of Hampton's Native American work and handled the correspondence with Native American graduates. See Washington, *Booker T. Washington Papers*, 2:84, note 3.

3. Fritz J. Malval, introduction to Cora M. Folsom, unpublished essay, Hampton Archives. Malval served as Hampton's curator of archives from 1970 until 1995. This unpublished essay is a more comprehensive version of the abbreviated biographical note to the listed letters of Cora Mae Folsom archived at Hampton that was published in Malval, *A Guide to the Archives of Hampton University*, 100.

4. "Hampton's Winter Campaigns," *Southern Workman*, February 1915, 72.

5. Although it has become legendary, the attribution of the statement that *The Birth of a Nation* is like "history written in lightning" to Woodrow Wilson has been shown to be very likely false. For a discussion of the available evidence concerning this statement, see McEwan, "Lawyers, Bibliographies, and the Klan," 63.

6. Hampton's director of applied art, Leigh Richmond Miner, began work on a new film in 1921, and his third film, *Cephas Returns*, was used through 1919 (Hampton Institute summary of faculty meeting minutes, Hampton Archives).

7. Hampton Institute summary of faculty meeting minutes, December 15, 1909, Hampton Archives.

8. Hampton Institute faculty meeting minutes, January 27, 1910, Hampton Archives.

9. Hampton Institute faculty meeting minutes, December 12, 1911, Hampton Archives.

10. Hampton Institute faculty meeting minutes, December 20, 1911, Hampton Archives.

11. Hampton Institute faculty meeting minutes, January 27, 1910, Hampton Archives.

12. [Name redacted] letter to George P. Phenix, January 7, 1910, frame 31, microfilm reel 320, Booker T. Washington Papers, 1853–1946, Manuscript Division, Library of Congress, Washington, DC.

13. The premiere date is given in "'John Henry's' Four Years at Hampton," *Southern Workman*, August 1913, 459. *John Henry* is identified as the first film made at Hampton by "Entertainments," *Southern Workman*, March 1915, 184.

14. Library of Congress U.S. Copyright Office, *Catalogue of Copyright Entries*, 128.

15. "'John Henry's' Four Years at Hampton," *Southern Workman*, August 1913, 459.

16. *John Henry* was screened on December 29, 1914, during the holiday break, followed by another film. The *Southern Workman* mentions a screening of *The Old Curiosity Shop* (Essanay Film Mfg. Co., 1909) on December 26 ("The Holidays," February 1915, 118–19). Other films were brought to Hampton to be screened for students. At the 1916 summer school, "three evenings were devoted to moving pictures": *John Barleycorn* (Bosworth, 1914), *Tess of the D'Urbervilles* (Famous Players Film Co., 1913), and *The Wonderful Wizard of Oz* (Selig Polyscope Co., 1910) ("Entertainments," *Southern Workman*, August 1916, 480). In 1915 "on the evening of Labor Day, September 6, and again on Monday, September 13, students and workers were entertained by amusing moving pictures" ("Entertainments," *Southern Workman*, October 1915, 570). And in 1916, on September 6, "the story of Aladdin and the wonderful lamp was shown in moving pictures" ("Entertainments," *Southern Workman*, October 1916, 577).

17. "Hampton Students to Organize," *Chicago Defender*, July 12, 1913; "Hampton Graduates Organize in Chicago," *Chicago Defender*, July 19, 1913.

18. "Moving Picture Story: Achievements of a Hampton Student Portrayed in Didactic Manner," *Broad Ax*, July 26, 1913; "Moving Picture Story: Achievements of a Hampton Student Portrayed in Didactic Manner," *Cleveland Gazette*, August 2, 1913.

19. "'John Henry's' Four Years at Hampton," *Southern Workman*, August 1913, 459–60. The Whittier School was founded in 1889 as a day school serving primary students and was used for training for Hampton students studying to become teachers.

20. "Entertainments," *Southern Workman*, February 1914, 121.

21. It is also possible that the films were shown concurrently for some events.

22. The advertisement for William Foster's *The Barber* (1916), discussed in chapter 5, is likely a publicity still given the staging (see figure 5.3).

23. Undated and untitled program (circa 1914), Hampton Archives.

24. Undated and untitled program (circa 1914), Hampton Archives.

25. "Tableaux for Hampton," *New York Times*, March 11, 1913.

26. "Hampton Institute's Northern Campaign," *Afro-American*, March 8, 1913.

27. "Tableaux for Hampton," *New York Times*, March 11, 1913.

28. "Hampton Institute's Northern Campaign," *Afro-American*, March 8, 1913.

29. R. Nathaniel Dett, "The Emancipation of Negro Music," *Southern Workman*, April 1918, 175.

30. R. Nathaniel Dett, "The Emancipation of Negro Music," *Southern Workman*, April 1918, 175.

31. R. Nathaniel Dett, "The Emancipation of Negro Music," *Southern Workman*, April 1918, 175.

32. R. Nathaniel Dett, "The Emancipation of Negro Music," *Southern Workman*, April 1918, 175.

33. Quoted in R. Nathaniel Dett, "The Emancipation of Negro Music," *Southern Workman*, April 1918, 172.

34. R. Nathaniel Dett, "The Emancipation of Negro Music," *Southern Workman*, April 1918, 176.

35. Undated and untitled program (circa 1914), Hampton Archives.

36. Peabody, *Education for Life*, 132. Lincoln Kirstein echoes Peabody in noting the role of students in building their own institution: "While students fired their own bricks in their own kiln, the signers 'sang up' new buildings" ("Foreword," 8).

37. Nelson, *Steel Drivin' Man*, 52, 59, 77, 86–91, 93.

38. J. Smith, *Managing White Supremacy*, 30–31.

39. Dorson, "The Career of 'John Henry,'" 163.

40. Nelson, *Steel Drivin' Man*, 114.

41. Washington, *Up from Slavery*, 99.

42. Trachtenberg, foreword, xv.

43. Hampton Institute faculty meeting minutes, January 10, 14, and 19, 1914, Hampton Archives.

44. "Entertainments," *Southern Workman*, February 1914, 121.

45. "Northern Campaign of the Hampton Institute," *Afro-American*, January 24, 1914; "Hear of Hampton's Work," *New York Times*, January 28, 1914.

46. Quoted in "Hampton Institute North," *Afro-American*, February 7, 1914.

47. Quoted in "Hampton Institute North," *Afro-American*, February 7, 1914.

48. "Hampton Institute North," *Afro-American*, February 7, 1914.

49. "Lecture in Aid of Hampton Institute," *Boston Journal*, February 4, 1914.

50. "Hampton Institute Entertainers in the High School," *Wilkes-Barre Times-Leader*, February 13, 1914; *Wilkes-Barre Times-Leader*, February 16, 1914.

51. Henry, "Correspondence: New England," *Moving Picture World*, February 21, 1914, 979; "Moving Picture Educator," *Moving Picture World*, March 7, 1914, 1220.

52. Henry, "Correspondence: New England," *Moving Picture World*, February 21, 1914, 979.

53. Henry, "Correspondence: New England," *Moving Picture World*, February 21, 1914, 979.

54. "Moving Picture Educator," *Moving Picture World*, March 7, 1914, 1220.

55. William Scoville letter to Rev. George T. Scott, Presbyterian Missions, New York City, October 16, 1914, Hampton Archives. The African Union Company was incorporated in New York on March 20, 1914, as an African trading company. According to the *Southern Workman*, "the company controls the mahogany trees on 4900 square miles of Gold Coast territory, the value of which is several millions of dollars, and has a contract with one mahogany firm to take all the logs shipped for five years. . . . Among the officers are Dr. W. R. Pettiford, of Birmingham, Ala., and Mr. E. J. Scott, of Tuskegee" ("A New Negro Corporation," June 1914, 376).

56. Hampton Institute faculty meeting minutes, October 24, 1914, Hampton Archives.

57. Hampton Institute faculty meeting minutes, December 2, 1914, Hampton Archives.

58. Hampton Institute faculty meeting minutes, February 25 and March 4, 1914, Hampton Archives; Library of Congress U.S. Copyright Office, *Catalogue of Copyright Entries*, 7385.

59. Hampton Institute faculty meeting minutes, October 8, 1913, Hampton Archives.

60. Hampton Institute faculty meeting minutes, October 17, 1914, Hampton Archives.

61. Hampton Institute faculty meeting minutes, October 24, 1914, Hampton Archives.

62. Hampton Institute faculty meeting minutes, October 24, 1914, Hampton Archives.

63. Summary, faculty meeting minutes, December 2, 1914, Hampton Archives.

64. The *Southern Workman* identifies him as Leo Bock from Long Island ("Visitors," December 1914, 708). The February 1915 *Southern Workman* refers to him as "Mr. Bok." ("Addresses," *Southern Workman*, February 1915, 120.) Faculty meeting minutes also refer to him as Mr. Bok. Hampton Institute faculty meeting minutes, December 2, 1914, Hampton Archives.

65. "Addresses," *Southern Workman*, February 1915, 120.

66. "Entertainments," *Southern Workman*, March 1915, 184–85.

67. "Entertainments," *Southern Workman*, March 1915, 184–85.

68. "Making Negro Lives Count," *Outlook*, May 12, 1915, 56.

69. G. D. Crain Jr., "Making Negro Lives Count," *Moving Picture World*, March 27, 1915, 1952. The summary in the *Outlook* is echoed verbatim in "Giving the Negro a Chance," *Evangelical Herald*, May 20, 1915, 1.

70. "Entertainments," *Southern Workman*, March 1915, 184–85.

71. I am grateful to Ray Sapirstein for identifying Peyton.

72. Du Bois, *The Souls of Black Folk*, 154.

73. Program of "Hampton Meeting," Carnegie Hall, February 8, 1915, Hampton Archives.

74. "News of the Nation's Metropolis," *Freeman*, February 20, 1915; program of "Hampton Meeting," Carnegie Hall, February 8, 1915, Hampton Archives.

75. Quoted in "News of the Nation's Metropolis," *Freeman*, February 20, 1915.

76. "The Western Campaign," *Southern Workman*, April 1915, 250. Hampton had several quartets traveling and performing simultaneously, though this was the principal one. Bailey replaced Freeman W. Crawley for the western campaign. According to Natalie Curtis-Burlin, the 1915 quarter consisted of Tynes ("Lead"), Crawley (tenor), Phillips (baritone), and Wainwright (bass) (*Negro Folk-Songs*, 32). Curtis-Burlin writes: "The above group of singers is the oldest quartet at Hampton, some of the members having graduated from the school over thirty years ago. Though none of them have had technical musical training, all are musicians by the grace of God and have sung together for so long that the blending interplay of their voices has attained rare artistic perfection. At the Panama-Pacific International Exposition, where they sang all summer at the Educational Exhibit, they were awarded a medal" (ibid., 32–33). The Hampton Quartet for the 1915 campaign is identified, with some misspellings, as C. H. Tynes, tenor; J. H. Wainwright, bass; J. A. Beasley, second tenor; and S. E. Phillips, second bass, in P. F. Hale, "Twin Cities in Review," *Chicago Defender*, May 1, 1915. The names are also misreported as C.H. Taynes, John Phillips, James H. Wainwright, James A. Bailey in "Hampton Quartet Visits Chicago," *Chicago Defender*, May 8, 1915.

77. Program of "Hampton Meeting," Carnegie Hall, February 8, 1915, Hampton Archives; "Meeting Held in Aid of Hampton," *Afro-American*, February 20, 1915.

78. Program of "Hampton Meeting," Carnegie Hall, February 8, 1915, Hampton Archives.

79. "Hampton's Work a Needed Factor," *New York Age*, February 11, 1915.

80. William S. Dodd, brother-in-law of Hollis B. Frissell, replaced Sydney Frissell and Moton during portions of the campaign. Dodd had become a teacher at Hampton in 1908 and was head of the newly formed business department.

81. "Hampton Singers in Plantation Songs," *Cedar Rapids Republican*, April 11, 1915.

82. "Hampton Quartet Visits Chicago," *Chicago Defender*, May 8, 1915.

83. "The Western Campaign," *Southern Workman*, April 1915, 250; "Hampton Campaigns," *Southern Workman*, September 1915, 509.

84. "Making Negro Lives Count," *Moving Picture World*, March 27, 1915, 1952.

85. Sydney Dodd Frissell, "Hampton in Thirty States," *Southern Workman*, October 1915, 526.

86. "The Hampton Spirit Was Here," *Freeman*, March 27, 1915.

87. "Hampton Institute Aim to Be Explained," *Indianapolis Star*, March 21, 1915; "Scenes and Persons Portraying Life at the Hampton Institute in Virginia," *Indianapolis Star*, March 22, 1915; "Hampton Institute Funds Are Boosted," *Indianapolis Star*, March 25, 1915; "The Hampton Spirit Was Here," *Freeman*, March 27, 1915.

88. "Hampton Institute Funds Are Boosted," *Indianapolis Star*, March 25, 1915; "The Hampton Spirit Was Here," *Freeman*, March 27, 1915.

89. "Madam C. J. Walker Entertains in Honor of Major R. R. Moton of Hampton," *Freeman*, April 3, 1915.

90. "Indiana Brief Notes," *Moving Picture World*, April 10, 1915, 263.

91. "Hampton Singers Here," *Lawrence Journal-World*, March 31, 1915.

92. In Eau Claire, Wisconsin, the *Eau Claire Leader* printed the program that Hampton provided ("Would you know the souls of black folk") verbatim ("Hampton Boys to Sing Tonight," April 16, 1915). Likewise, the *Anaconda Standard* incorporated language from the program in its announcement of the upcoming Montana appearance ("Famed Hampton Singers Are Coming to This City," June 6, 1915).

93. "Hampton Singers in Plantation Songs," *Cedar Rapids Republican*, April 11, 1915.

94. Quoted in Sydney Dodd Frissell, "Hampton in Thirty States," *Southern Workman*, October 1915, 524.

95. Quoted in Sydney Dodd Frissell, "Hampton in Thirty States," *Southern Workman*, October 1915, 525.

96. "Negro Melodies and Motion Pictures," *Eau Claire Leader*, April 17, 1915.

97. "St. Paul: Week's Record of Happenings in Minnesota's Capitol," *St. Paul Appeal*, April 3, 1915.

98. "The Five Byrons Entertained by Mr. and Mrs. Williams," *Chicago Defender*, April 24, 1915; *Duluth News-Tribune*, April 16, 1915; *Duluth News-Tribune*, April 21, 1915.

99. P. F. Hale, "Twin Cities in Review," *Chicago Defender*, May 1, 1915.

100. "Famed Hampton Singers Are Coming to This City," *Anaconda Standard*, June 6, 1915.

101. Sydney Dodd Frissell, "Hampton in Thirty States," *Southern Workman*, October 1915, 524.

102. "Hampton at the Exposition," *Southern Workman*, April 1915, 249.

103. "Government Features Educational," *Moving Picture World*, September 4, 1915, 1684.

104. *Salt Lake Tribune*, September 5, 1915.

105. G. D. Crain Jr., "Making Negro Lives Count," *Moving Picture World*, March 27, 1915, 1952.

106. W. H. Scoville letter to H. H. Mack, May 1, 1915, Hampton Archives.

107. Hampton Institute faculty meeting minutes, May 1, 1915, Hampton Archives.

108. G. D. Crain Jr., "Pictures That Disturb," *Moving Picture World*, March 27, 1915, 1952; Bernstein, *Screening a Lynching*, 19.

109. G. D. Crain Jr., "Pictures That Disturb," *Moving Picture World*, March 27, 1915, 1952.

4. "A VICIOUS AND HURTFUL PLAY"

1. Washington, *Up from Slavery*, 39–40.

2. Thomas F. Dixon Jr., author of a trilogy of Reconstruction-era novels celebrating the Ku Klux Klan—*The Leopard's Spots* (1902), *The Clansman* (1905, which became the source of *The Birth of a Nation*), and *The Traitor* (1907)—had once praised Washington, thinking that industrial education trained Black people for subordination (Harlan, *Booker T. Washington*, 431). Dixon then changed his mind and wanted to debate Washington, promising "not to refer to my play," referring to the stage adaptation of *The Clansman*, but Washington refused (ibid., 432).

3. On October 22, 1914, Emmett J. Scott wrote to J. S. Johnson thanking him for sending the "Story of Paramount" and asking for the name of the employee of the Jesse L. Lasky Feature Play Show who would be able to advise him "as to the picturizing" of *Up from Slavery*. Scott wrote: "From an entertainment point of view, I feel quite sure that 'Up From Slavery,' if properly filmed, will prove a satisfactory entertainment for presentation by the Paramount Pictures Corporation" (Washington, *Booker T. Washington Papers*, 13:147–48). Louis Harlan notes: "In 1914 Washington and Scott tried to interest two of the major white motion picture companies, Edison and Paramount, in a movie version of *Up from Slavery* but without success" (Harlan, *Booker T. Washington: The Wizard of Tuskegee*, 434).

4. Emmett J. Scott letter to Edwin L. Barker, October 18, 1915, in Washington, *Booker T. Washington Papers*, 13:401–2.

5. Booker T. Washington was widely considered the "representative man" of African Americans in his era. See, for example: "Small Talk," *Independent*, October 26, 1901, 2547.

6. For discussions of the African American response to *Birth of a Nation*, see Cripps, "The Reaction of the Negro to the Motion Picture *Birth of a Nation*" and *Slow Fade to Black*; Everett, *Returning the Gaze*; Stokes, *D. W. Griffith's "The Birth of a Nation."*

7. Cripps, "The Reaction of the Negro to the Motion Picture *Birth of a Nation*," 345.

8. For a thorough discussion of *Lincoln's Dream* and other attempts at counter-

ing *The Birth of a Nation* with film, see Stokes, *D. W. Griffith's "The Birth of a Nation,"* 162–68.

9. This outcry was certainly related to the response to Dixon's play, *The Clansman*, whose stage appearance sparked much controversy in 1905.

10. See Fleener, "Answering Film with Film." This article is the most comprehensive discussion of the Hampton epilogue to date and represents the consideration of significant archival sources. However, Fleener does not appear to be aware of the extent of Hampton's filmmaking project or the provenance of *The New Era*.

11. See, in particular, Stokes, *D. W. Griffith's "The Birth of a Nation,"* chapter 6.

12. Stokes, *D. W. Griffith's "The Birth of a Nation,"* 142–44.

13. Advertisement in the *Boston Globe*, April 9, 1915.

14. Philip J. Allston letter to Washington, April 12, 1915, in Washington, *Booker T. Washington Papers*, 13:261–62.

15. Samuel Edward Courtney letter to Washington, April 12, 1915, in Washington, *Booker T. Washington Papers*, 13:274.

16. "Big Negro Mass Meeting Denounces Photo-Play," *Boston Journal*, April 19, 1915.

17. Washington letter to Samuel Edward Courtney, April 23, 1915, Washington, *Booker T. Washington Papers*, 13:277–78.

18. Washington letter to Samuel Edward Courtney, April 23, 1915, *Booker T. Washington Papers*, 13:277.

19. "Confers on Cuts in Photo Play Films," *Boston Daily Globe*, April 13, 1915.

20. "Confers on Cuts in Photo Play Films," *Boston Daily Globe*, April 13, 1915.

21. "Progress of Negro Race," *Boston Daily Globe*, April 15, 1915; "Will Improve Big Picture," *Boston Evening Record*, April 15, 1915, microfilm reel 2, D. W. Griffith Papers, 1897–1954, Frederick, MD: University Publications of America, 1982 (hereafter Griffith Papers); "Will Add New Film to 'The Birth of a Nation,'" *Boston Herald*, April 15, 1915, Griffith Papers; "'Birth of a Nation' to Have New Film," *Traveler and Evening Herald*, April 15, 1915, Griffith Papers.

22. "Court to Rule Today on 'Birth of a Nation,'" *Boston Journal*, April 21, 1915; "New Film Shows Negro's Progress," *Boston Journal*, April 17, 1915; "New Film Added," *Boston Daily Globe*, April 17, 1915. The *Crisis* reported: "A new feature is added to the film in Boston 'portraying the advance of Negro life.' A prominent New York lawyer informs us that this was done at the suggestion of Mr. Booker T. Washington" ("Fighting Race Calumny," June 1915, 86).

23. The press referred to the inserts as "title material," suggesting intertitles and perhaps still images. See "Court to Rule Today on 'Birth of a Nation,'" *Boston Journal*, April 21, 1915.

24. "New Film Added," *Boston Daily Globe*, April 17, 1915.

25. "New Film Added," *Boston Daily Globe*, April 17, 1915. The language of this article echoes very close wording in a similar article in the *Christian Science Monitor* from the same day, suggesting that Epoch Producing Corporation had issued a press release announcing the additions. See "Theater Notes," *Christian Science Monitor*, April 17, 1915.

26. "New Film Shows Negro's Progress," *Boston Journal*, April 17, 1915.

27. "'Birth of a Nation' Approved by Mayor," *Boston Daily Globe*, April 11, 1915. Curley requested edits to the Gus chase scene, scenes with Austin Stoneman and his mulatto housekeeper, Silas Lynch's attempted "forced marriage" of Elsie Stoneman, and the South Carolina House of Representatives scene. Curley added these cuts in addition to the changes made in the original film in New York. All evidence suggests that the cuts in New York were no more than "minor, cosmetic changes to the film," with the offensive scenes left intact although the Gus chase scene was shortened (Stokes, *D. W. Griffith's "The Birth of a Nation,"* 139). The *Dramatic News* reported that "the cuts were all trivial and will not hurt the engagement [in Boston] which looks good at present" (April 17, 1915, microfilm reel 2, Griffith Papers).

28. W. Stephen Bush, "The Birth of a Nation," *Moving Picture World*, March 13, 1915, 1586. In surviving prints, you can see the woman fanning herself as the child returns to the front of the congregation. The woman is played by Jennie Lee, who also plays Mammy later in the film (Cuniberti, *The Birth of a Nation*, 38).

29. Stokes notes that the mayor of New York insisted on the removal of the smell incident (*D. W. Griffith's "The Birth of a Nation,"* 104). However, the review by W. Stephen Bush in the *Moving Picture World* includes it ("The Birth of a Nation," March 13, 1915, 1586). Bush states he saw the film at a private screening in New York. There is no indication the shot was removed from the New York print apart from John Cuniberti's reference to the record of the hearing on April 1 in New York (*The Birth of a Nation*, 38). Offended both by the portrayal of abolitionism in the film as well as its overarching racism, the Wendell Phillips Memorial Association, dedicated to the history of abolitionism, held a meeting in protest of *The Birth of a Nation* at Faneuil Hall on April 18, 1915 ("To Protest Film Play," *Boston Daily Globe*, April 17, 1915).

30. After a private screening in the White House, President Woodrow Wilson reportedly said of *The Birth of a Nation*, "It is like writing history with lightning. My only regret is that it is all so terribly true." However, this is unsubstantiated legend. See Stokes, *D. W. Griffith's "The Birth of a Nation,"* 111; McEwan, "Lawyers, Bibliographies, and the Klan," 363.

31. Although today's surviving prints are derived from the 1921 reissue of the film, there is no reason to assume that the opening sequence of the original film differed significantly from the surviving versions, beyond the edits discussed here. See Kaufman, "Non-Archival Sources."

32. See Du Bois, "Of Our Spiritual Strivings," 9; Washington, *The Negro Problem*.

33. For discussions of the use of intertitles in *The Birth of a Nation* as a means to claim historical accuracy for a fictional film, see White, "'The Birth of a Nation'"; Stokes, "The Use of Intertitles in D.W. Griffith's 'The Birth of a Nation.'"

34. "'Birth of Nation' Causes Near-Riot," *Boston Daily Globe*, April 18, 1915.

35. J. Gaines, *Fire and Desire*, 222.

36. "Say Box Office Discriminated," *Boston Daily Globe*, May 1, 1915.

37. Quoted in "'Birth of Nation' Causes Near-Riot," *Boston Daily Globe*, April 18, 1915.

38. "The Birth of a Nation," *Fitchburg Daily Sentinel*, May 4, 1915.

39. "The Birth of a Nation," *Fitchburg Daily Sentinel*, May 4, 1915.

40. Fox, *The Guardian of Boston*, 192–93; Stokes, *D. W. Griffith's "The Birth of a Nation,"* 145–46; "Gov Walsh and O'Meara Will Appeal to Courts on 'Nation' Film," *Boston Evening Globe*, April 19, 1915.

41. Stokes, *D. W. Griffith's "The Birth of a Nation,"* 146.

42. "'The Birth of a Nation' Pictures at the Tremont," *Boston Daily Globe*, April 18, 1915.

43. Quoted in "Blames Governor for Photo-Play Agitation," *Boston Journal*, April 28, 1915. See also "Legislators to See Photo-Play," *Boston Daily Globe*, April 28, 1915.

44. Quoted in "One Scene Must Be Cut Out," *Boston Globe*, April 21, 1915.

45. Quoted in "Confers on Cuts in Photo Play Films," *Boston Daily Globe*, April 13, 1915.

46. Quoted in "Blames Governor for Photo-Play Agitation," *Boston Journal*, April 28, 1915. For more on Fleischer's position, see "500 in Room Meant for 200," *Boston Evening Globe*, April 26, 1915.

47. "Court to Rule Today on 'Birth of a Nation,'" *Boston Journal*, April 21, 1915.

48. Hampton Institute Faculty Meeting Minutes, April 10, 1915, Hampton University Archives, Hampton University Museum, Hampton, Virginia (hereafter Hampton Archives).

49. William G. Willcox letter to Julius Rosenwald, May 12, 1915, Tuskegee University Archives, Tuskegee, AL (hereafter Tuskegee Archives); Hollis B. Frissell letter to Francis J. Grimké, November 6, 1915, in Grimké, *The Works of Francis J. Grimké*, 4:153.

50. Hampton Institute Faculty Meeting Minutes, April 10, 1915, Hampton Archives.

51. Stamp, "Moral Coercion," 41.

52. Grieveson, *Policing Cinema*, 98.

53. Stamp, "Moral Coercion," 42.

54. This was true for a film like *The Inside of the White Slave Traffic* (Frank Beal, Moral Feature Film Company, 1913). See Stamp, "Moral Coercion," 50–57.

55. Grieveson, *Policing Cinema*, 100. In 1916 the board changed its name to the National Board of Review to more accurately reflect its mandate.

56. Grieveson notes that "the board focused in the main less on content and more on the organization of content" (*Policing Cinema*, 101).

57. Grieveson, *Policing Cinema*, 101. Grieveson cites the board's statement of intent and standards published in "National Board of Censorship of Motion Pictures," *Moving Picture World*, October 16, 1909, 524: "The National Board of Censorship has been organized for the improvement of motion pictures and for their further extension in this country as social and educational forces" (ibid.).

58. Quoted in Grieveson, *Policing Cinema*, 103.

59. Hollis B. Frissell to Francis J. Grimké, November 6, 1915, in Grimké, *The Works of Francis J. Grimké*, 4:153.

60. Hollis B. Frissell, "Forty-Seventh Annual Report of the Principal," *Hampton Bulletin*, May 1915, 36.

61. Hampton Institute Faculty Meeting Minutes, April 14, 1915, Hampton Archives.

62. Hampton Institute Faculty Meeting Minutes, April 20, 1915, Hampton Archives.

63. W. D. McGuire Jr. to George Foster Peabody, April 21, 1915, Hampton Archives.

The George Foster Peabody Awards recognizing public service–related media productions were established after Peabody's death and named in his honor.

64. W. D. McGuire Jr. to George Foster Peabody, April 21, 1915, Hampton Archives. See also Francis Hackett, "Brotherly Love," *New Republic*, March 20, 1915, 185; Cuniberti, *The Birth of a Nation*, 166–67.

65. The reuse of footage is a common practice in industrial filmmaking, where films are adapted to best suit various exhibition contexts, becoming what Yvonne Zimmermann has called "provisional assemblages of working material to be (re)used in new combinations" depending on the desired functions of the footage ("'What Hollywood Is to America, the Corporate Film Is to Switzerland,'" 111.

66. "Entertainments," *Southern Workman*, March 1915, 185.

67. Cuniberti, *The Birth of a Nation*, 166–67; Hackett, "Brotherly Love," 86; *Motography*, March 20, 1915, 432. It is unclear if the deportation was conveyed through the intertitle alone or included a scene as well, though there are spectators' accounts of such scenes (Cuniberti, *The Birth of a Nation*, 167).

68. In spite of the letter from McGuire to Peabody, no evidence suggests that *The New Era* replaced this scene at all venues. W. D. McGuire Jr. to George Foster Peabody, April 21, 1915, Hampton Archives. However, Joseph J. McCarthy referred to the Hampton material fitting "over against the imaginative scene of the great Liberia once dreamed of by Lincoln" in a letter to the *Boston Journal* ("Journal Mail Bag," *Boston Journal*, May 5, 1915).

69. C. F. Lothrop, "Journal Mail Bag," *Boston Journal*, April 20, 1915.

70. Eugene V. Debs's account of the film also indicates that the "screen record" was moved to the end ("Debs Flays Bad Motion Picture," *California Eagle*, March 18, 1916).

71. Joseph J. McCarthy, "Journal Mail Bag," *Boston Journal*, May 5, 1915.

72. Booker T. Washington, "Time to Fight Bad Movies Is before They Are Shown," *Chicago Defender*, May 22, 1915.

73. Jesse H. Harris letter to Washington, May 3, 1915, in Washington, *Booker T. Washington Papers*, 13:285 (emphasis in original).

74. Jesse H. Harris letter to Washington, May 3, 1915, in Washington, *Booker T. Washington Papers*, 13:285.

75. Florence E. Sewell Bond letter to Washington, June 27, 1915, Washington, *Booker T. Washington Papers*, 13:335, note 1.

76. Washington to Florence E. Sewell Bond, June 30, 1915, Washington, *Booker T. Washington Papers*, 13:335.

77. "'Birth of a Nation' at the Tremont," *Boston Daily Globe*, June 8, 1915.

78. "'The Birth of a Nation' Spectacle at the Tremont," *Boston Daily Globe*, June 27, 1915.

79. "Summer-Time Amusements," *Boston Daily Globe*, July 4, 1915.

80. Washington to Charles Ellis Mason, May 28, 1915, Washington, *Booker T. Washington Papers*, 13:296.

81. "The Screen," *New York Times*, December 5, 1922. The *Times* editorialized: "It doesn't strike one as history but rather as an inflammatory document born of preju-

dice and an appreciation of its paying possibilities. And the social value of its revival at the present time is open to question—to say the least. As if to remove from the picture the taint of racial prejudice, however, scenes of the work done at the negro school at Hampton, with complimentary references to the Hampton and Tuskegee institutes, were shown following the exhibition of the Griffith film."

82. "'The Birth of a Nation' a Great Spectacle," *Baltimore Sun*, February 27, 1916.

83. "'Birth of Nation' Shows to 3,200," *Harrisburg Patriot*, February 15, 1916.

84. Quoted in "Amusements," *Fitchburg Daily Sentinel*, September 3, 1915.

85. *Boston Daily Globe*, June 16, 1915.

86. Quoted in "Questions Motive of City in Fight on Birth of Nation," *Chicago Daily Tribune*, June 8, 1915.

87. Microfilm reel 2, Griffith Papers.

88. "Censorship Loses Again," *Motography*, June 19, 1915, 1007.

89. Quoted in "Ohio's Censors Ban Photo Play," *New York Age*, October 7, 1915.

90. Quoted in "Debs Flays Bad Motion Picture," *California Eagle*, March 18, 1916.

91. Quoted in "Atlantic City Men Denounce Photo Play," *New York Age*, August 12, 1915. See also "Colored People to Storm State House," *Boston Daily Globe*, April 19, 1915.

92. May Childs Nerney letter to R. Granville Curry, September 21, 1915, frame 54, microfilm reel 33, NAACP Records, 1842–1999, Manuscript Division, Library of Congress, Washington, DC (hereafter NAACP Records).

93. John P. Turner, "Does Not Approve Birth of a Nation," *Philadelphia Tribune*, July 31, 1915. See also "Dr. Turner Writes," *New York Age*, August 5, 1915.

94. It is not clear to what extent Mrs. Washington was involved in the letter-writing campaign, but it is striking given Tuskegee's encouragement of the addition.

95. Ida Anderson letter to Hollis B. Frissell, January 14, 1916, Hampton Archives.

96. "Out of Town Correspondence," *New York Age*, February 3, 1916.

97. Leslie Pinckney Hill letter to Mr. Emlen, Pennsylvania Armstrong Association, September 23, 1915, Hampton Archives.

98. James W. Johnson, "A Trap," *New York Age*, May 6, 1915.

99. "Birth of a Nation Case Dismissed," *New York Age*, May 27, 1915.

100. Hampton Institute Faculty Meeting Minutes, May 19, 1915, Hampton Archives.

101. Hampton Institute Faculty Meeting Minutes, May 1, 1915, Hampton Archives.

102. Stokes, *D. W. Griffith's "The Birth of a Nation,"* 137; Grieveson, *Policing Cinema*, 194; Kenneth Miller, *From Progressive to New Dealer*, 192.

103. William G. Willcox letter to Julius Rosenwald, May 12, 1915, Tuskegee Archives.

104. May Childs Nerney letter to Desha Breckenridge, September 20, 1915, NAACP Records. Nerney cites an unnamed teacher at Hampton, a white woman, whom she believed to be "absolutely reliable." William Howard Taft, the former president of the United States and future chief justice of the Supreme Court, was president of the Board of Trustees at the time.

105. Hampton Faculty Meeting Minutes, November 3, 1915, Hampton Archives.

106. Grimké, *The Birth of a Nation*, 2–3.

107. Hollis B. Frissell letter to Francis J. Grimké, November 6, 1915, in Grimké, *The Works of Francis J. Grimké*, 4:153.

108. Francis J. Grimké letter to Hollis B. Frissell, November 8, 1915, in Grimké, *The Works of Francis J. Grimké*, 4:154.

109. Work, *Negro Year Book*, 46.

110. Hollis B. Frissell letter to Lillian R. Williams, president, Women's Friendly Club, Pawtucket, Rhode Island, January 5, 1916, Hampton Archives. A marginal note corrected one trustee to two.

111. Faculty Meeting Minutes, November 3, 1915, Hampton Archives.

112. Faculty Meeting Minutes, November 3, 1915, Hampton Archives. According to Edith Dabbs in *Face of an Island*, Miner visited St. Helena only in 1907 and 1923. However, the Hampton Faculty Meeting Minutes indicate that he filmed *Cephas Returns* at the Penn School in November 1915.

113. Faculty Meeting Minutes, November 3, 1915, Hampton Archives.

114. "The National Hampton Association," *Southern Workman*, February 1916, 136.

115. "Declares South Best for Negro Industrially," *Boston Journal*, January 13, 1916; "Solving the Race Problem," *Boston Daily Globe*, January 13, 1916.

116. Sydney Dodd Frissell, "The National Hampton Association," *Southern Workman*, February 1916, 136.

117. Sydney Dodd Frissell, "The National Hampton Association," *Southern Workman*, February 1916, 136.

118. Thompson, "The Formulation of the Classical Style, 1909–28," 182.

5. TO "ENCOURAGE AND UPLIFT"

1. The assertion that national identity is predicated on the defining representation of African Americans has been well argued by various authors. See, for example, Fiedler, *The Inadvertent Epic*; Morrison, *Playing in the Dark*; Rogin, *Blackface, White Noise*; Taylor, "The Rebirth of the Aesthetic in Cinema"; Williams, *Playing the Race Card*.

2. See, for example, Howard, *Blaxploitation Cinema*, 10.

3. See, for example, Leab, *From Sambo to Superspade*, 233–63; Guerrero, *Framing Blackness*; Cook, *Lost Illusions*, 259–66; Lawrence, *Blaxploitation Films of the 1970s*, 24–25, 94–98.

4. See, for example, Regester, "From the Buzzard's Roost"; Sampson, *Blacks in Black and White*; Stewart, *Migrating to the Movies*; J. Gaines, *Fire and Desire*; P. Bowser, Gaines, and Musser, *Oscar Micheaux and His Circle*; Green, *Straight Lick* and *With a Crooked Stick*; Cripps, *Slow Fade to Black* and *Black Film as Genre*; Robinson, *Forgeries of Memory and Meaning*.

5. Kelley, foreword, ix.

6. Washington, *The Negro in Business*, 269–70.

7. Washington, *The Negro in Business*, 18–19.

8. "Booker T. Washington Takes Chicago by Storm," *Chicago Defender*, December 10, 1910.

9. "Hunter C. Haynes, Chicago's Famous Negro Manufacturer, Who Will Sail for Europe 22nd," *Freeman*, June 18, 1904; "Official Program N.N.B.L. Meeting," *Chicago Defender*, August 17, 1912.

10. "Comments on the Films: Independent," *Moving Picture World*, September 12, 1912, 1177.

11. Mary Carbine shows how musical accompaniment could undercut the meaning of screen action in silent-era Black theaters in Chicago ("'The Finest outside the Loop'"). For examples of how musical accompaniment could affect the tone of moving pictures in another context, see, Tsivian, *Early Cinema in Russia and Its Cultural Reception*.

12. Booker T. Washington letter to Hal Reid, March 24, 1913, frame 44, microfilm reel 348, Booker T. Washington Papers, 1853–1946, Manuscript Division, Library of Congress, Washington, DC (hereafter Washington Papers). Hal Reid, a manager of *Animated Weekly*, had sent Washington a copy of the film taken of him on the steps of the Institutional Church in Chicago in August 1913. Washington wrote to Reid in March stating he had misplaced the film and requesting another copy.

13. "Comments on the Films: Independent," *Moving Picture World*, September 12, 1912, 1177.

14. Jas. S. McQuade, "Chicago Letter," *Moving Picture World*, March 29, 1913, 1322; "The Moving Picture Educator," *Moving Picture World*, May 3, 1913, 491; "Facts and Comments," *Moving Picture World*, June 21, 1913, 1227; "Moving Pictures of Tuskegee Institute," *Nickelodeon*, May 15, 1910, 262.

15. "Comments on the Films: Independent," *Moving Picture World*, September 12, 1912, 1177.

16. "News of Greater New York," *New York Age*, August 21, 1913. Haynes attended the 1912 convention as a businessman and spoke about his entrepreneurial ventures.

17. Sherman H. Dudley, "Open Letter," *Chicago Defender*, December 15, 1917. More research is needed on Dudley's filmmaking enterprise. See, for example, Jas. S. McQuade, "Chicago Letter," *Moving Picture World*, June 21, 1913, 1257; "Correspondence: Louisville," *Moving Picture World*, June 21, 1913, 1262.

18. Giebler, "Exhibitors News: St. Louis," *Moving Picture World*, June 27, 1914, 1850.

19. "The Proposed Formation of the Progressive National Life Insurance Co.," *Broad Ax*, May 17, 1913.

20. "Chips," *Broad Ax*, April 20, 1912.

21. "The Convention City!," *Freeman*, June 8, 1912.

22. "Enterprising Mr. Wm. Foster," *Chicago Defender*, July 29, 1911; *Chicago Defender*, May 28, 1910.

23. Pearl Bowser, Jane Gaines, and Charles Musser assert that Foster was "the first African-American producer to make films specifically for black audiences" (*Oscar Micheaux and His Circle*, xix). Others who have made similar assertions include Stewart, *Migrating to the Movies*, 174; Reid, *Redefining Black Film*, 7; Sampson, *Blacks in Black and White*, 68; Cripps, *Slow Fade to Black*, 79–80; Waller, *Main Street Amusements*, 162.

24. Advertisement for the William Foster Music Company, *Freeman*, January 1, 1910.

25. Cary B. Lewis, "W. L. Houston in Chicago," *Freeman*, April 30, 1910.

26. "Enterprising Mr. Wm. Foster," *Chicago Defender*, July 29, 1911; *Freeman*, March 16, 1912.

27. "Foster's Colored Photo Plays," *Freeman*, August 30, 1913.

28. See, for example, Everett, *Returning the Gaze*, 136–41, 319, note 9. For a profile of Foster that documents his multimedia activities, see also Sampson, *Blacks in Black and White*, 172–76.

29. "Foster and Shoecraft Make 'Movies,'" *Chicago Defender*, June 21, 1913.

30. "Foster and Shoecraft Make 'Movies,'" *Chicago Defender*, June 21, 1913; "Foster's Moving Pictures," *Freeman*, August 9, 1913.

31. Quoted in Mjagkij, "A Peculiar Alliance," 592.

32. "Potent Uplift Agency," *Afro-American*, June 7, 1913.

33. "Foster's Moving Pictures a Success," *Chicago Defender*, July 5, 1913.

34. "Y.M.C.A. Bldg. Completed," *Chicago Defender*, June 14, 1913; "New Y.M.C.A. Building Dedicated," *Afro-American*, June 21, 1913.

35. For a thorough discussion of the Grand Theater, see Stewart, *Migrating to the Movies*, 168–71.

36. "Foster's Moving Pictures a Success," *Chicago Defender*, July 5, 1913.

37. "Foster's Movies Make Big Hit," *Chicago Defender*, July 26, 1913.

38. Sylvester Russell, "Special Stage Review," *Freeman*, August 16, 1913.

39. "The States Theater," *Chicago Defender*, August 9, 1913.

40. "Foster's Movies Make Big Hit," *Chicago Defender*, July 26, 1913.

41. "Foster, the Moving Picture Man, Returns," *Chicago Defender*, June 20, 1914.

42. No records survive to indicate what kind of camera Foster owned. "Foster's Moving Pictures," *Freeman*, August 9, 1913; "The States Theater," *Chicago Defender*, August 9, 1913.

43. Stewart, *Migrating to the Movies*, 195.

44. There is significant evidence to suggest that the release of the film occurred in July 1913 in Chicago. See "Foster's Movies Make Big Hit," *Chicago Defender*, July 26, 1913; "The States Theater," *Chicago Defender*, August 9, 1913.

45. The full cast is listed in "The States Theater," *Chicago Defender*, August 9, 1913.

46. The *New York Age* reports the film's title as *The Pullman Porter* ("Colored Pictures a Hit," September 25, 1913). See also Reid, *Redefining Black Film*, 8.

47. Stewart, *Migrating to the Movies*, 195.

48. Stewart, *Migrating to the Movies*, 195; Reid, *Redefining Black Film*, 8.

49. Stewart, *Migrating to the Movies*, 196.

50. "Foster's R.R. Porter Biggest Success of the Year at the Majestic," *Chicago Defender*, November 22, 1913.

51. "The States Theater," *Chicago Defender*, August 9, 1913.

52. "Foster's R.R. Porter Biggest Success of the Year at the Majestic," *Chicago Defender*, November 22, 1913.

53. Stewart, *Migrating to the Movies*, 298, note 21.

54. Cary B. Lewis, "Star Quartette Makes a Hit at the Grand," *Freeman*, September 6, 1913.

55. "Lottie Grady a Star," *Chicago Defender*, January 3, 1914.

56. Sylvester Russell, "Special Stage Review," *Freeman*, August 16, 1913.

57. "Foster's Moving Pictures," *Freeman*, August 9, 1913.

58. "Colored Pictures a Hit," *New York Age*, September 25, 1913.

59. "The Vineyard of the Photo Plays," *New York Age*, December 20, 1913.

60. *Chicago Defender*, August 30, 1913.

61. A Broadway actor, Richard Harrison also appeared in *How High Is Up?* (Seminole Film Company, 1923) and *Easy Street* (Oscar Micheaux, 1930). Harrison created the role of "De Lawd" in the stage production of *The Green Pastures* but died in 1935, before production commenced on the Warner Bros. film adaptation. For more on Harrison, see Daniel, *De Lawd*; and Sampson, *Blacks in Black and White*.

62. "Uncle Eph Says," *Chicago Defender*, April 12, 1919. For more on Lottie Grady, see Sampson, *The Ghost Walks*. Jerry Mills went on to direct or codirect Oscar Micheaux's *The Homesteader* (1919). For his collaboration with Micheaux, Mills drew on his experience working with Foster, who was also reportedly involved in Micheaux's production and served as an advance agent for the film.

63. "States Theater," *Chicago Defender*, September 27, 1913.

64. Sylvester Russell, "Chicago Weekly Review," *Freeman*, October 4, 1913. For a lengthy discussion of Russell, see Everett, *Returning the Gaze*, 36–49.

65. "The States," *Chicago Defender*, October 18, 1913.

66. James S. McQuade, "Chicago Letter," *Moving Picture World*, October 25, 1913, 363.

67. William Foster [Juli Jones Jr., pseud.], "News of the Moving Picture World: What the 'Biggest Man in the Business' has to say of the Early History and the Future Outlook," *Freeman*, December 20, 1913.

68. William Foster [Juli Jones Jr., pseud.], "News of the Moving Picture World: What the 'Biggest Man in the Business' has to say of the Early History and the Future Outlook," *Freeman*, December 20, 1913.

69. William Foster [Juli Jones Jr., pseud.], "News of the Moving Picture, World: What the 'Biggest Man in the Business' has to say of the Early History and the Future Outlook," *Freeman*, December 20, 1913; William Foster, "Negro Theaters," *Freeman*, March 9, 1907; William Foster, "A Partial List of the Colored Theaters in the United States," *Freeman*, December 20, 1913; William Foster [Juli Jones Jr., pseud.], "Moving Pictures Offer the Greatest Opportunity to the American Negro in History of the Race from Every Point of View," *Chicago Defender*, October 9, 1915.

70. Quoted in "Foster, the Moving Picture Man, Returns," *Chicago Defender*, June 20, 1914.

71. "Foster, the Moving Picture Man, Returns," *Chicago Defender*, June 20, 1914; "Going Abroad," *Chicago Defender*, January 31, 1920; J. Gaines, *Fire and Desire*, 276–77, note 21; "Foster Photoplay Co. Licensed in Florida," *Chicago Defender*, April 11, 1914.

72. Sylvester Russell, "Chicago Weekly Review," *Freeman*, June 12, 1915.

73. Sylvester Russell, "Chicago Weekly Review," *Freeman*, September 12, 1914.

74. Sylvester Russell, "Future of the Pekin Theater," *Chicago Defender*, July 29, 1911.

75. Sylvester Russell, "Chicago Weekly Review," *Freeman*, June 12, 1915.

76. Sylvester Russell, "Chicago Weekly Review," *Freeman*, September 12, 1914.

77. Sylvester Russell, "Chicago Weekly Review," *Freeman*, June 12, 1915.

78. Sylvester Russell, "Chicago Weekly Review," *Freeman*, June 12, 1915.

79. Sylvester Russell, "Chicago Weekly Review," *Freeman*, July 3, 1915.

80. "A Picture to Be Suppressed," *Moving Picture World*, March 27, 1915, 1914.

81. "Fox Film Corp.," *Moving Picture World*, July 24, 1915, 734.

82. Cripps, *Slow Fade to Black*, 65.

83. William Foster [Juli Jones Jr., pseud.], "Moving Pictures Offer the Greatest Opportunity to the American Negro in History of the Race from Every Point of View," *Chicago Defender*, October 9, 1915.

84. "Foster Film Co.," *Chicago Defender*, July 29, 1916; William Foster [Juli Jones, pseud.], "The Barber," *Chicago Defender*, August 5, 1916. The synopsis in the *Defender* differs in some plot points from that in Sampson, *Blacks in Black and White* (240–41). Sampson does not indicate the source of his synopsis.

85. Tony Langston letter to George P. Johnson, August 10, 1916, George P. Johnson Negro Film Collection, Department of Special Collections, University of California, Los Angeles, Los Angeles, CA (hereafter Johnson Collection).

86. "The Trooper of Co. [*sic*] K," *Chicago Defender*, October 14, 1916.

87. William Foster letter to Noble Johnson, June 1, 1917, Johnson Collection.

88. Foster Photo-Play Company Incorporation announcement, Johnson Collection.

89. Foster Photo-Play Company Incorporation announcement, Johnson Collection. The popularity of Theda Bara might explain Foster's interest in vampires. Bara's films played at South Side Chicago theaters. For example, *Her Double Life* (J. Gordon Edwards, Fox Film Corporation, 1916) showed at the Star the same week as *The Railroad Porter* in July 1917, and Bara was advertised as "the great vampire." See "The Star," *Chicago Defender*, July 7, 1917.

90. Foster Photo-Play Company Incorporation announcement, Johnson Collection.

91. "Foster Photoplay Co. Stages Drama," *Chicago Defender*, August 17, 1918.

92. Foster Photo-Play Company Incorporation announcement, Johnson Collection.

93. Quoted in "Foster Photoplay Co. Stages Drama," *Chicago Defender*, August 17, 1918.

94. Cripps, *Slow Fade to Black*, 85.

95. "Foster Photo Play Co. Completes Chicago Picture," *Chicago Defender*, June 29, 1918.

96. "Something New in Movies," *Chicago Defender*, April 27, 1918.

97. "Foster Photo Play Co. Completes Chicago Picture," *Chicago Defender*, June 29, 1918.

98. For a detailed discussion of the significance of World War I for Black film activities, see Stewart, *Migrating to the Movies*, 210–18.

99. "Foster Photo Play Co. Completes Chicago Picture," *Chicago Defender*, June 29, 1918.

100. "Moving Picture of Chicago's Activities and Scenes," *Chicago Defender*, July 20, 1918.

101. "Moving Picture of Chicago's Activities and Scenes," *Chicago Defender*, July 20, 1918.

102. "Infantry Relatives to Be Taken in 'Smile' Movie Sunday," *Chicago Defender*, October 26, 1918.

103. "Foster's Colored Photo Plays," *Freeman*, August 30, 1913.

104. Advertisement for Peter P. Jones Studio, *Freeman*, January 1, 1910; advertisement for Peter P. Jones Studio, *Freeman*, January 8, 1910.

105. Jones's photography has yet to be discussed in a sustained manner. On the history of Black photographers, see the work of Deborah Willis, in particular *Posing Beauty*, *Reflections in Black*, and *Let Your Motto Be Resistance*.

106. "Featuring Negro Progress in Moving Pictures," *Freeman*, April 1, 1916. See also P. Bowser, "Pioneers of Black Documentary Film," 13.

107. Geary and Webb, "Introduction," 2–3.

108. See Bowers, "Souvenir Postcards and the Development of the Star System."

109. Quoted in Snow, "Correspondence Here," 44.

110. See Allen, Als, Lewis, and Litwak, *Without Sanctuary*; S. Smith, *Photography on the Color Line*, chapter 4; Mitchell, *Living with Lynching*; Wood, *Lynching and Spectacle*; Goldsby, *A Spectacular Secret*; Apel and Smith, *Lynching Photographs*.

111. S. Smith, *Photography on the Color Line*, 121.

112. S. Smith, *Photography on the Color Line*, 125.

113. "Enterprising Mr. Wm. Foster," *Chicago Defender*, July 29, 1911.

114. Jones hired G. W. Neighbours to operate the camera and produce the postcards. In an announcement of the opening of the studio, Neighbours is described as a "post card expert" who was a "student of the man that invented card photography" ("The Climax Photo Studio," *Chicago Defender*, June 8, 1912). Sampson places the opening of the studio in April 1913, but the report in the *Defender* indicates it was the previous year (*Blacks in Black and White*, 183).

115. Snow, "Correspondence Here," 43.

116. Robert S. Abbott, "Vicious Publications Repudiated," *Chicago Defender*, March 23, 1912.

117. "Peter P. Jones Thanks Voters for 1,200 Votes," *Chicago Defender*, April 6, 1912.

118. "Peter P. Jones," *Chicago Defender*, April 6, 1912.

119. Baldwin, *Chicago's New Negroes*, 111–12.

120. "Peter P. Jones, the Photographer Retires," *Chicago Defender*, August 31, 1912.

121. "Peter P. Jones Takes Moving Pictures of Shriners," *Chicago Defender*, May 23, 1914.

122. Everett, *Returning the Gaze*, 113.

123. See R. Johnson and Stam, *Brazilian Cinema*.

124. "Peter P. Jones Takes Moving Pictures of Shriners," *Chicago Defender*, May 23, 1914.

125. "Peter P. Jones Heads Moving Picture Company," *Chicago Defender*, June 13, 1914.

126. Hannah, "A Place in the Parade," 98.

127. Hannah, "A Place in the Parade," 87.

128. Hannah, "A Place in the Parade," 92.

129. "'For the Honor of the 8th' Playing Big Houses," *Chicago Defender*, September 12, 1914.

130. "Chicago Weekly Review," *Freeman*, June 20, 1914.

131. Sampson, *Blacks in Blackface*, 174–75.

132. Quoted in "Colonel Denison Leads Gallant Eighth Regiment to Camp," *Chicago Defender*, July 25, 1914.

133. "Featuring Negro Progress in Moving Pictures," *Freeman*, April 1, 1916. Al-

though Jones's representation of a negative character is noted rather than directly critiqued by the reviewer, later press reception of Oscar Micheaux's work, for example, took Micheaux to task for seemingly unuplifting portrayals.

134. "Featuring Negro Progress in Moving Pictures," *Freeman*, April 1, 1916.

135. Cary B. Lewis, "Photo Play of Eighth Regiment!," *Freeman*, August 15, 1914.

136. Cary B. Lewis, "7,000 People See 8th Regiment on Dress Parade," *Chicago Defender*, August 1, 1914.

137. "8th Regiment to be Thrown upon Canvas," *Chicago Defender*, August 8, 1914; Cary B. Lewis, "Photo Play of Eighth Regiment!," *Freeman*, August 15, 1914.

138. "Eighth Regiment Has Ground Broken for New Armory," *Freeman*, August 8, 1914. Peter P. Jones is misidentified in the article as Peter P. Imes.

139. "Great War Drama and Battle Scenes," *Chicago Defender*, September 5, 1914.

140. Hannah, "A Place in the Parade," 100.

141. "'For the Honor of the 8th' Playing Big Houses," *Chicago Defender*, September 12, 1914.

142. This is a strategy of oppositional reading that is a thread through Black culture. See, for example, the editing in *Bush Mama* (Haile Gerima, 1975) that follows a logic of Black experience rather than classical Hollywood's notion of spatial and temporal coherence.

143. In his 1845 *Narrative of the Life of Frederick Douglass, an American Slave*, Frederick Douglass famously remarks: "My feet have been so cracked with the frost, that the pen with which I am writing might be laid in the gashes." Stepto points to this passage in noting Douglass's "ability to conjoin past and present" to illustrate different moments in his story that "in their fusion, speak of his evolution from slavery to freedom" (Stepto, *From Behind the Veil*, 20).

144. Hannah, "A Place in the Parade."

145. "Peter P. Jones Heads Moving Picture Company," *Chicago Defender*, June 13, 1914.

146. See Sampson, *Blacks in Blackface*, 304.

147. Library of Congress, "The Development of an African-American Musical Theatre 1865–1910," accessed September 5, 2012, http://memory.loc.gov/ammem /collections/sheetmusic/brown/aasmsprs6.html.

148. "The Grand," *Chicago Defender*, April 19, 1913.

149. Baldwin, *Chicago's New Negroes*, 117.

150. "Eight [*sic*] Regiment in Movies at Pekin Saturday and Sunday," *Chicago Defender*, September 12, 1914.

151. "Peter P. Jones Heads Moving Picture Company," *Chicago Defender*, June 13, 1914.

152. Sylvester Russell, "Chicago Weekly Review," *Freeman*, June 20, 1914.

153. *Freeman*, March 18, 1916.

154. Advertisement for *50 Years Freedom* in *Chicago Defender*, October 2, 1915.

155. Advertisement for the Peter P. Jones Film Company in *Chicago Defender*, October 9, 1915; *Chicago Defender*, November 13, 1915; *Chicago Defender*, November 20, 1915.

156. P. Bowser, "Pioneers of Black Documentary Film," 12.

157. N. Barnett Dodson, "Pushing Plans for Exposition," *Cleveland Gazette*, August 15, 1915.

158. Advertisement for *The Dawn of Truth* in *Freeman*, March 25, 1916.

159. "In the Movies!" advertisement, *Freeman*, April 8, 1916.

160. "Featuring Negro Progress in Moving Pictures," *Freeman*, April 1, 1916.

161. Baldwin, *Chicago's New Negroes*, 126. See also P. Bowser, "Pioneers of Black Documentary Film," 13–14.

162. "In the Movies!" advertisement, *Freeman*, April 8, 1916; "Featuring Negro Progress in Moving Pictures," *Freeman*, April 1, 1916.

163. Advertisement for *The Slacker, Chicago Defender*, June 23, 1917.

164. "The Slacker," *Chicago Defender*, June 2, 1917.

165. "The Slacker," *Chicago Defender*, June 2, 1917.

166. Advertisement for *The Accidental Ruler* in *Chicago Defender*, September 1, 1917.

167. "Among the Movies," *Chicago Defender*, September 22, 1917.

168. Everett, *Returning the Gaze*, 168–70.

169. "Handles a Razor," *Topeka Plaindealer*, May 17, 1901.

170. "Handles a Razor," *Topeka Plaindealer*, May 17, 1901.

171. *Freeman*, November 7, 1903.

172. Hunter C. Haynes, "Knights of the Razor!," *Freeman*, November 22, 1902.

173. "Hunter C. Haynes, Chicago's Famous Negro Manufacturer, Who Will Sail for Europe 22d," *Freeman*, June 18, 1904.

174. Hunter C. Haynes, "General Review of the Barber's World of America and Europe," *Freeman*, January 21, 1905.

175. Hunter C. Haynes, "H. C. Haynes of Razor Strop Fame Soon to Appear in New Role—Will Open 'Barber's College,'" *Freeman*, October 21, 1905.

176. Henry F. Manns, "The Right Man in the Right Place," *Freeman*, February 28, 1914.

177. Henry F. Manns, "The Right Man in the Right Place," *Freeman*, February 28, 1914; "Doings of the Race," *Cleveland Gazette*, October 21, 1911.

178. N. Barnett Dodson, "New Movement for Business," *Indianapolis Record*, April 12, 1913.

179. Henry F. Manns, "The Right Man in the Right Place," *Freeman*, February 28, 1914.

180. "Reel Colored Pictures, by Real Colored Persons," *New York Clipper*, August 30, 1913.

181. See advertisement for the Afro-American Film Co., *Freeman*, February 7, 1914.

182. Afro-American Film Co. letterhead, November 1913, frame 518, microfilm reel 348, Washington Papers.

183. "News of Greater New York," *New York Age*, August 21, 1913.

184. "Reel Colored Pictures, by Real Colored Persons," *New York Clipper*, August 30, 1913.

185. Advertisement for the Afro-American Film Company in *Freeman*, February 28, 1914.

186. "Hunter Haynes in Town," *Baltimore Afro-American*, August 30, 1913.

187. Advertisement for the Pekin Theatre in *Savannah Tribune*, April 11, 1914.

188. Advertisement for the Afro-American Film Company in *Freeman*, February 7, 1914.

189. Henry F. Manns, "The Right Man in the Right Place," *Freeman*, February 28, 1914.

190. Herbert T. Meadows, "St. Louis Theatrical News," *Freeman*, March 28, 1914. See also Sampson, *Blacks in Black and White*, 259.

191. "The Afro-American Film Co.," *Freeman*, April 18, 1914.

192. The plot is outlined by Lester A. Walton, "Chicago Censor Board Rejects 'One Large Evening,'" *New York Age*, April 23, 1914.

193. According to the *Amsterdam News*, quoted in "The Afro-American Film Co.," *Freeman*, April 18, 1914.

194. Carey was appointed to the board on March 13, 1914, by Mayor Carter Harrison Jr. to serve under the second deputy superintendent of police, Major M. L. C. Funkhouser, who was head of the board.

195. "Funkhouser to Preach at Institutional Church," *Chicago Defender*, April 18, 1914.

196. Dickerson, *African American Preachers and Politics*, 42.

197. "Licensed," *Moving Picture World*, May 16, 1914, 968. Here, the title is listed as *A Tale of a Chicken*.

198. Stewart, *Migrating to the Movies*, 175.

199. *A Mother of Men* featured a scene in which a slave is whipped for attacking the son of the plantation owner. The film also employed four African American actors who were reportedly born in slavery. See "Notes of the Trade," *Moving Picture World*, May 2, 1914, 684; George Blaisdell, Review of "A Mother of Men," *Moving Picture World*, May 30, 1914, 1238; George Blaisdell, "At the Sign of the Flaming Arcs," *Moving Picture World*, May 30, 1914, 1245.

200. "States Theatre Displays Vile Race Pictures," *Chicago Defender*, May 30, 1914.

201. Quoted in "Foster, the Moving Picture Man, Returns," *Chicago Defender*, June 20, 1914.

202. Lester A. Walton, "Chicago Censor Board Rejects 'One Large Evening,'" *New York Age*, April 23, 1914.

203. "New Picture Companies," *New York Dramatic Mirror*, April 15, 1914.

204. Lester A. Walton, "Chicago Censor Board Rejects 'One Large Evening,'" *New York Age*, April 23, 1914. The amount of capitalization differs by a factor of ten from the account in the *New York Clipper*.

205. "One Large Evening," *New York Age*, April 9, 1914.

206. Lester A. Walton, "Chicago Censor Board Rejects 'One Large Evening,'" *New York Age*, April 23, 1914.

207. Sampson, *Blacks in Blackface*, 9.

208. Lester A. Walton, "Ridiculing the Race," *New York Age*, April 23, 1914.

209. Lester A. Walton, "Ridiculing the Race," *New York Age*, April 23, 1914.

210. Advertisements for the Hoosier Theater in *Indianapolis Recorder*, May 16, 1914; *Indianapolis Recorder*, May 23, 1914.

211. "The Lafayette Theatre," *New York Age*, May 21, 1914.

212. Tony Langston, "Review of the Theaters," *Chicago Defender*, May 16, 1914;

Sylvester Russell, "Chicago Weekly Review," *Freeman*, May 16, 1914. No evidence survives to indicate the plot of *Mandy's Choice*.

213. The film was advertised as "*Mandy's Choice* Or *Love Will Find a Way*" in the *Freeman* on May 30 and June 13, 1914.

214. Advertisement for the Afro-American Film Company in *Freeman*, June 13, 1914.

215. Hunter C. Haynes, "Amazing Figures on 'Movies,'" *Freeman*, June 13, 1914.

216. "Hunter C. Haynes Opens Motion Picture Studio in New York," *Freeman*, August 1, 1914.

217. Quoted in "Hunter Haynes in Boston," *Freeman*, September 12, 1914.

218. Advertisement for the Haynes Photoplay Company, *Freeman*, August 8, 1914.

219. "'Uncle Remus's Visit to New York,'" *Freeman*, December 12, 1914.

220. Advertisement for the Haynes Photoplay Company in *Freeman*, August 8, 1914.

221. See "Afro-American Play House Circuit to Be Formed," *Chicago Defender*, August 22, 1914; Sylvester Russell, "Chicago Weekly Review," *Freeman*, August 22, 1914; "Biggest Motion Picture Deal," *Freeman*, March 13, 1915.

222. Sylvester Russell, "Chicago Weekly Review," *Freeman*, August 22, 1914.

223. Quoted in "Haynes Latest Release a Big Hit," *Freeman*, September 12, 1914.

224. Lester A. Walton quoted in "Haynes Latest Release a Big Hit," *Freeman*, September 12, 1914.

225. "'Uncle Remus's Visit to New York,'" *Freeman*, December 12, 1914.

226. AR-W-TEE, "The Passing Show in Washington," *Freeman*, December 26, 1914.

227. See Gunning, "Heard over the Phone." See also Gunning, "Systematizing the Electric Message: Narrative Form, Gender, and Modernity in *The Lonedale Operator*" on phone calls and communication shaping narrative form.

228. Stewart, *Migrating to the Movies*, 193.

229. Stewart, *Migrating to the Movies*, 193.

230. Stewart, *Migrating to the Movies*, 193.

231. Everett, *Returning the Gaze*, 115.

232. Sampson, *Blacks in Blackface*, 19–20.

233. The *Chicago Defender* quoted an unidentified source claiming Haynes's *Uncle Remus* to be "a most pretentious and beautiful screen version" of Harris's stories. However, it is likely that this source was unfamiliar with either the film or Harris's stories, as Haynes's film bears no similarities to the stories. See "John E. M'Lemore Shows Talent; Writes Scenario," *Chicago Defender*, February 6, 1915.

234. Stewart, *Migrating to the Movies*, 193. See also "'Uncle Remus's Visit to New York,'" *Freeman*, December 12, 1914.

235. Stewart, Migrating to the Movies, 194.

236. AR-W-TEE, "The Passing Show in Washington," *Freeman*, December 26, 1914.

237. AR-W-TEE, "The Passing Show in Washington," *Freeman*, December 26, 1914.

238. Advertisement for the Haynes Photoplay Company in *Freeman*, October 10, 1914. Though the advertising for the film does not identify a title but rather a subject ("The B.M.C. and the Odd Fellows on Dress Parade in Boston"), the *Freeman* refers to the film in quotation marks (as "A Review of the B.M.C. and the Colored Business

World" in "Hunter C. Haynes' New Releases in the Photo Play World," *Freeman*, October 24, 1914).

239. Advertisement for the Haynes Photoplay Company in *Freeman*, October 10, 1914.

240. "To Produce Picture," *New York Age*, October 8, 1914.

241. "Hunter C. Haynes' New Releases in the Photo Play World," *Freeman*, October 24, 1914; AR-W-TEE, "The Passing Show in Washington," *Freeman*, December 26, 1914.

242. Advertisement for the Haynes Photoplay Company in *Freeman*, October 10, 1914.

243. "To Produce Picture," *New York Age*, October 8, 1914; see also "Hunter C. Haynes' New Releases in the Photo Play World," *Freeman*, October 24, 1914.

244. AR-W-TEE, "The Passing Show in Washington," *Freeman*, December 26, 1914.

245. "Hunter C. Haynes' New Releases in the Photo Play World," *Freeman*, October 24, 1914.

246. "To Produce Picture," *New York Age*, October 8, 1914.

247. "Lafayette Theatre," *New York Age*, October 15, 1914.

248. Quoted in "Hunter C. Haynes' New Releases in the Photo Play World," *Freeman*, October 24, 1914.

249. Quoted in "Hunter C. Haynes' New Releases in the Photo Play World," *Freeman*, October 24, 1914.

250. "Lafayette Theatre," *New York Age*, October 15, 1914; AR-W-TEE, "The Passing Show in Washington," *Freeman*, December 26, 1914.

251. AR-W-TEE, "The Passing Show in Washington," *Freeman*, December 26, 1914.

252. "Biggest Motion Picture Deal," *Freeman*, March 13, 1915.

253. "At the Nation's Metropolis," *Freeman*, August 7, 1915.

254. "At the Nation's Metropolis," *Freeman*, March 18, 1916.

255. "Hunter Haynes Dies at Saranac Lake," *New York Age*, January 12, 1918.

256. Eloise Bibb Thompson, "John E. M'Lemore Shows Talent; Writes Scenario," *Chicago Defender*, February 6, 1915. While in law school, McLemore worked as an advertising manager at the *California Eagle* and organized a theatrical troupe, the Juvenile Stock Company, to put on his original plays.

257. "John McLemore Drowned," *California Eagle*, March 25, 1916; "Young Man Drowned," *Chicago Defender*, April 1, 1916.

258. Genevie Reubin, "Miss Sarah E. Woods Movie Picture Writer," *Chicago Defender*, May 22, 1915.

259. "William Foster, Veteran Newspaper Man, Dies in California at 78," unsigned obituary of Foster, who died April 9, 1940, in unknown newspaper, Johnson Collection.

260. "Bill Foster Gets Chance to Enter Movies," *Chicago Defender*, June 1, 1929.

261. "Perseverance," *Pittsburgh Courier*, July 6, 1929.

262. "Bill Foster Gets Chance to Enter Movies," *Chicago Defender*, June 1, 1929.

263. "Perseverance," *Pittsburgh Courier*, July 6, 1929.

264. Foster Photo-Play Company Incorporation announcement, Johnson Collec-

tion. See also "William Foster, Veteran Newspaper Man, Dies in California at 78," unsigned obituary of Foster, who died April 9, 1940, in unknown newspaper, Johnson Collection.

265. "Race Movie Company," unsigned and undated clipping from unknown newspaper, Johnson Collection.

266. "King Sought for Movies," *Pittsburgh Courier*, February 8, 1930.

267. "Race Movie Co. Given Charter to Make Films," *Chicago Defender*, November 23, 1929.

268. Salem Tutt Whitney, "Promoter Says Race Gets Little Return from Rush West to Movie Gold Coast," *Chicago Defender*, September 21, 1929.

269. "Plans Million Dollar Studio," *Pittsburgh Courier*, June 22, 1929.

270. Quoted in "Bill Foster Organized Talkie Movie Company," *Chicago Defender*, November 2, 1929.

271. Foster Photo-Play Company Incorporation announcement, Johnson Collection.

272. Sylvester Russell, "William Foster Forming Million-Dollar Movie Syndicate at Hollywood," *Pittsburgh Courier*, July 27, 1929.

273. William Foster, "Fool and Fire," *California Eagle*, June 23 and September 5–22, 1933.

274. See Everett, *Returning the Gaze*, 169–70.

275. Myron Brinig, "Peter Jones Follows the Rainbow," *Brain Exchange*, March 6, 1922, 6.

276. Brinig notes that Jones worked in Chicago for the Matzene and Moffett studios, having entered the motion picture business through Rothacker but makes no mention of Jones's independent film productions. No records survive of Jones's involvement in these other concerns.

277. Myron Brinig, "Peter Jones Follows the Rainbow," *Brain Exchange*, March 6, 1922, 6.

278. Everett, *Returning the Gaze*, 170; *New York Age*, June 17, 1922.

279. "Now a Superfilm," *Billboard*, October 21, 1922, 48; "Richard B. Harrison and Corrine Smith Starring in New Movie Production," *Pittsburgh Courier*, September 29, 1923; Sampson, *Blacks in Black and White*, 185. The Seminole Company planned to film a feature titled *Shadows and Sunshine*, but the production fell through when its star, the famous Black aviatrix Bessie Coleman, withdrew.

280. Cited in "Hunter C. Haynes' New Releases in the Photo Play World," *Freeman*, October 24, 1914.

281. "Hunter Haynes, Dead," *Chicago Defender*, January 19, 1918.

EPILOGUE

1. For more on *Helping Negroes*, see Jennifer Zwarich, "Federal Films," 231–63.

2. P. Bowser, "Pioneers of Black Documentary Film," 32, note 20; Sampson, *Blacks in Black and White*, 623.

3. For a discussion of the productions of the Lincoln Motion Picture Company, see Stewart, *Migrating to the Movies*, 202–18.

4. For a discussion of the Valley of Dry Bones as a metaphor and of the African American spirituals tradition, see Powery, *Dem Dry Bones*.

5. J. Ronald Green discusses another instance of direct address in *Body and Soul*, that of Martha Jane following her unmasking of Jenkins (*With a Crooked Stick*, 88–92).

6. The collection segment is punctuated with an intertitle indicating "an hour later," suggesting that the collection is not just foregrounded but a significant part of this false service, as Jenkins is lining his own pockets with the church donations.

7. P. Bowser and Spence, *Writing Himself into History*, 199.

8. Green, *With a Crooked Stick*, 83.

9. Green, *With a Crooked Stick*, 83.

10. P. Bowser and Spence, *Writing Himself into History*, 185.

11. P. Bowser and Spence, *Writing Himself into History*, 183.

12. P. Bowser and Spence, *Writing Himself into History*, 195.

13. P. Bowser and Spence, *Writing Himself into History*, 199.

14. J. Gaines, *Fire and Desire*, 169.

15. J. Gaines, *Fire and Desire*, 168.

16. Musser, "To Redream the Dreams of White Playwrights," 128.

17. Carby, *Race Men*, 71.

BIBLIOGRAPHY

Items in newspapers and magazines are cited in the notes. They are not included in the bibliography.

ARCHIVES AND SPECIAL COLLECTIONS

Booker T. Washington Papers, 1853–1946, Manuscript Division, Library of Congress, Washington, DC.

D. W. Griffith Papers, 1897–1954. Frederick, MD: University Publications of America, 1982.

George P. Johnson Negro Film Collection, Department of Special Collections, University of California, Los Angeles, Los Angeles, CA.

Hampton University Archives, Hampton University Museum, Hampton, VA.

L.A. Rebellion Oral History Project, University of California, Los Angeles, Film and Television Archive, Los Angeles, CA.

NAACP Records, 1842–1999, Manuscript Division, Library of Congress, Washington, DC.

Tuskegee University Archives, Tuskegee, AL.

Harvard College Library, Harvard University, Cambridge, MA.

SECONDARY SOURCES

Abbott, Lynn, and Doug Seroff. *To Do This, You Must Know How: Music Pedagogy in the Black Gospel Quartet Tradition.* Jackson: University Press of Mississippi, 2013.

Acland, Charles R., and Haidee Wasson. "Introduction: Utility and Cinema." In *Useful Cinema,* edited by Charles R. Acland and Haidee Wasson, 1–14. Durham, NC: Duke University Press, 2011.

Allen, James, Hilton Als, Congressman John Lewis, and Leon F. Litwack. *Without Sanctuary: Lynching Photography in America.* Santa Fe, NM: Twin Palms, 2000.

Allen, Robert C., and Douglas Gomery. *Film History: Theory and Practice*. New York: Knopf, 1985.

Anderson, James D. "Education for Servitude: The Social Purposes of Schooling in the Black South, 1870–1930." PhD diss., University of Illinois, Urbana-Champaign, 1973.

Andrews, Isabella M. *The Failure of Cunningham*. 1892. Hampton, VA: Hampton Institute Press, 1898.

Andrews, William L. Preface to Booker T. Washington, *Up from Slavery*, edited by William L. Andrews, vii–xi. New York: W. W. Norton, 1996.

———. "The Representation of Slavery and the Rise of Afro-American Literary Realism, 1865–1920." In Booker T. Washington, *Up from Slavery*, edited by William L. Andrews, 249–58. New York: W. W. Norton, 1996.

Apel, Dora, and Shawn Michelle Smith. *Lynching Photographs*. Berkeley: University of California Press, 2007.

Baker, Houston A., Jr. *Modernism and the Harlem Renaissance*. Chicago: University of Chicago Press, 1987.

———. *Turning South Again: Re-Thinking Modernism/Re-Reading Booker T*. Durham, NC: Duke University Press, 2001.

Baldwin, Davarian L. *Chicago's New Negroes: Modernity, the Great Migration, and Black Urban Life*. Chapel Hill: University of North Carolina Press, 2007.

Balestrini, Nassim W. "National Memory and the Arts in Paul Laurence Dunbar's War Poetry." In *We Wear the Mask: Paul Laurence Dunbar and the Politics of Representative Reality*, edited by Willie J. Harrell Jr., 17–31. Kent, OH: Kent State University Press, 2010.

Barthes, Roland. *Image, Music, Text*. Translated by Stephen Heath. New York: Hill and Wang, 1977.

Bauerlein, Mark. "Booker T. Washington and W. E. B. Du Bois: The Origins of a Bitter Intellectual Battle." *Journal of Blacks in Higher Education*, no. 46 (2004–5): 106–14.

Bean, Jennifer M., and Diane Negra, eds. *A Feminist Reader in Early Cinema*. Durham, NC: Duke University Press, 2002.

Bergstrom, Janet. "Murnau in America: Chronicle of Lost Films (*4 Devils, City Girl*)." In *Looking Past the Screen: Case Studies in American Film History and Method*, edited by Jon Lewis and Eric Smoodin, 303–52. Durham, NC: Duke University Press, 2007.

Bernstein, Matthew H. *Screening a Lynching: The Leo Frank Case on Film and Television*. Athens: University of Georgia Press, 2009.

Bernstein, Matthew H., and Dana F. White. "'Imitation of Life' in a Segregated Atlanta: Its Promotion, Distribution and Reception." *Film History* 19, no. 2 (2007): 152–78.

———. "'Scratching Around' in a 'Fit of Insanity': The Norman Manufacturing Company and the Race Film Business in the 1920's." *Griffithiana* 62–63 (May 1998): 80–127.

Blackmon, Douglas A. *Slavery by Another Name: The Re-Enslavement of Black Americans from the Civil War to World War II*. New York: Anchor, 2008.

Bowers, Q. David. "Souvenir Postcards and the Development of the Star System, 1912–1914." *Film History* 3, no. 1 (1989): 39–45.

Bowser, Eileen. *The Transformation of Cinema, 1907-1915.* Berkeley: University of California Press, 1994.

Bowser, Pearl. "Pioneers of Black Documentary Film." In *Struggles for Representation: African American Documentary Film and Video,* edited by Phyllis R. Klotman and Janet K. Cutler, 1–33. Bloomington: Indiana University Press, 1999.

Bowser, Pearl, Jane Gaines, and Charles Musser. *Oscar Micheaux and His Circle: African-American Filmmaking and Race Cinema of the Silent Era.* Bloomington: Indiana University Press, 2001.

———. "Oscar Micheaux and His Circle." *The 20th Pordenone Silent Film Festival Catalogue,* Sacile/Udine, Italy, October 13–20, 2001: 47–74.

Bowser, Pearl, and Charles Musser. "Richard D. Maurice and the Maurice Film Company." In *Oscar Micheaux and His Circle: African-American Filmmaking and Race Cinema of the Silent Era,* edited by Pearl Bowser, Jane Gaines, and Charles Musser, 190–94. Bloomington: Indiana University Press, 2001.

Bowser, Pearl, and Louise Spence. *Writing Himself into History: Oscar Micheaux, His Silent Films, and His Audiences.* New Brunswick, NJ: Rutgers University Press, 2000.

Bowser, Pearl, and Pamela Thomas. *Midnight Ramble: Oscar Micheaux and the Story of Race Movies.* Alexandria, VA: Northern Light Productions, 1994.

Brooks, Tim. *Lost Sounds: Blacks and the Birth of the Recording Industry, 1890–1919.* Urbana: University of Illinois Press, 2004.

Brownlow, Kevin. *Behind the Mask of Innocence: Sex, Violence, Prejudice, Crime: Films of Social Conscience in the Silent Era.* New York: Alfred A. Knopf, 1990.

Brundage, W. Fitzhugh. "Reconsidering Booker T. Washington and *Up From Slavery.*" In *Booker T. Washington and Black Progress: "Up From Slavery" 100 Years Later,* edited by W. Fitzhugh Brundage, 1–18. Gainesville: University Press of Florida, 2003.

Bruno, Giuliana. *Streetwalking on a Ruined Map: Cultural Theory and the City Films of Elvira Notari.* Princeton, NJ: Princeton University Press, 1993.

Caddoo, Cara. *Envisioning Freedom: Cinema and the Building of Modern Black Life.* Cambridge, MA: Harvard University Press, 2014.

Campt, Tina M. *Image Matters: Archive, Photography, and the African Diaspora in Europe.* Durham, NC: Duke University Press, 2012.

Carbine, Mary. "'The Finest outside the Loop': Motion Picture Exhibition in Chicago's Black Metropolis, 1905–1928." *Camera Obscura* 23 (May 1990): 9–41.

Carby, Hazel. *Race Men.* Cambridge, MA: Harvard University Press, 1998.

Charney, Leo, and Vanessa R. Schwartz, eds. *Cinema and the Invention of Modern Life.* Berkeley: University of California Press, 1995.

Clark, Joseph. "Double Vision: World War II, Racial Uplift, and the All-American Newsreel's Pedagogical Address." In *Useful Cinema,* edited by Charles R. Acland and Haidee Wasson, 263–88. Durham, NC: Duke University Press, 2011.

Cook, David A. *Lost Illusions: American Cinema in the Shadow of Watergate and Vietnam, 1970–1979.* Berkeley: University of California Press, 2002.

Cripps, Thomas R. *Black Film as Genre.* Bloomington: Indiana University Press, 1978.

———. "The Reaction of the Negro to the Motion Picture *Birth of a Nation.*" *Historian* 25, no. 3 (1963): 344–62.

———. *Slow Fade to Black: The Negro in American Film, 1900–1942*. New York: Oxford University Press, 1977.

Cuniberti, John. *The Birth of a Nation: A Formal Shot-by-Shot Analysis Together with Microfiche*. Woodbridge, CT: Research, 1979.

Curtis-Burlin, Natalie. *Negro Folk-Songs*. Hampton Series, Book 4, *Work and Play Songs*. New York: G. Schirmer, 1919.

Dabbs, Edith M. *Face of an Island: Leigh Richmond Miner's Photographs of Saint Helena Island*. Charleston, SC: Wyrick, 2004.

Daniel, Walter C. *"De Lawd": Richard B. Harrison and the Green Pastures*. Westport, CT: Greenwood Press, 1986.

Davis, Ossie. Foreword to G. William Jones, *Black Cinema Treasures: Lost and Found*, 1–12. Denton: University of North Texas Press, 1991.

Dickerson, Dennis C. *African American Preachers and Politics: The Careys of Chicago*. Jackson: University Press of Mississippi, 2010.

Dorson, Richard M. "The Career of 'John Henry.'" *Western Folklore* 24, no. 3 (1965): 155–63.

Douglass, Frederick. *Narrative of the Life of Frederick Douglass, an American Slave*. Boston: Anti-Slavery Office, 1845.

Du Bois, W. E. B. "Booker T. Washington." *Crisis*, December 1915, 82.

———. "Of Mr. Booker T. Washington and Others." In *The Souls of Black Folk*, edited by Henry Louis Gates Jr. and Terri Hume Oliver, 34–45. New York: W. W. Norton, 1999.

———. "Of Our Spiritual Strivings." In *The Souls of Black Folk*, edited by Henry Louis Gates Jr. and Terri Hume Oliver, 9–16. New York: W. W. Norton, 1999.

———, ed. *Some Notes on Negro Crime, Particularly in Georgia: Report of a Social Study Made under the Direction of Atlanta University; Together with the Proceedings of the Ninth Conference for the Study of the Negro Problems, Held at Atlanta University, May 24, 1904*. Atlanta, GA: Atlanta University Press, 1904.

———. *The Souls of Black Folk*. Edited by Henry Louis Gates Jr. and Terri Hume Oliver. New York: W. W. Norton, 1999.

———. "The Talented Tenth." In *The Negro Problem: A Series of Articles by Representative Negroes of To-Day*, edited by Booker T. Washington, 31–76. New York: James Pott, 1903.

———, comp. *Types of American Negroes, Georgia, U.S.A.* 1900. Daniel Murray Collection, Prints and Photographs Division, Library of Congress.

Dunbar, Paul Laurence. *Candle-Lightin' Time*. New York: Dodd, Mead, 1901.

———. *The Paul Laurence Dunbar Reader: A Selection of the Best of Paul Laurence Dunbar's Poetry and Prose, Including Writings Never before Available in Book Form*. Edited by Jay Martin and Gossie H. Hudson. New York: Dodd, Mead, 1975.

Ellison, Ralph. *Invisible Man*. 2nd ed. New York: Vintage International, 1995.

Elsaesser, Thomas, ed. *Early Cinema: Space, Frame, Narrative*. London: British Film Institute, 1990.

———. "General Introduction—Early Cinema: From Linear History to Mass Media Archaeology." In *Early Cinema: Space, Frame Narrative*, edited by Thomas Elsaesser, 1–8. London: British Film Institute, 1990.

Everett, Anna. *Returning the Gaze: A Genealogy of Black Film Criticism, 1909–1949.* Durham, NC: Duke University Press, 2001.

Fiedler, Leslie A. *The Inadvertent Epic: From "Uncle Tom's Cabin" to "Roots."* Toronto: Canadian Broadcasting Corporation, 1979.

Fleener, Nickie. "Answering Film with Film: The Hampton Epilogue, A Positive Alternative to the Negative Black Stereotypes Presented in *The Birth of a Nation.*" *Journal of Popular Film and Television* 7, no. 4 (1980): 400–425.

Fox, Stephen R. *The Guardian of Boston: William Monroe Trotter.* New York: Atheneum, 1970.

Frissell, Hollis B. "Address of Dr. Frissell." In *The Work and Influence of Hampton: Proceedings of a Meeting Held in New York City February 12, 1904, under the Direction of the Armstrong Association*, 16–26. New York: Lehmaier, 1904.

Frissell, Sydney Dodd. *Hampton's Message.* Hampton, VA: Press of the Hampton Normal and Agricultural Institute, 1914.

Gaines, Jane M. *Fire and Desire: Mixed-Race Movies in the Silent Era.* Chicago: University of Chicago Press, 2001.

Gaines, Kevin K. *Uplifting the Race: Black Leadership, Politics, and Culture in the Twentieth Century.* Chapel Hill: University of North Carolina Press, 1996.

Gartenberg, Jon. "The Brighton Project: Archives and Historians." *Iris* 2, no. 1 (1984): 5–16.

Gates, Henry Louis, Jr. *The Signifying Monkey: A Theory of African-American Literary Criticism.* New York: Oxford University Press, 1988.

Gatewood, Willard B. "Booker T. Washington and the Ulrich Affair." *Phylon* 55, no. 1 (1970): 29–44.

Gaycken, Oliver. "The Cinema of the Future: Visions of the Medium as Modern Educator, 1895–1910." In *Learning with the Lights Off: Educational Film in the United States*, edited by Devin Orgeron, Marsha Orgeron, and Dan Streible, 67–89. New York: Oxford University Press, 2012.

Geary, Christraud M., and Virginia-Lee Webb. "Introduction: Views on Postcards." In *Delivering Views: Distant Cultures in Early Postcards*, edited by Christraud M. Geary and Virginia-Lee Webb, 1–12. Washington: Smithsonian Institution Press, 1998.

Gilroy, Paul. *The Black Atlantic: Modernity and Double Consciousness.* Cambridge, MA: Harvard University Press, 1993.

Goldsby, Jacqueline. *A Spectacular Secret: Lynching in American Life and Literature.* Chicago: University of Chicago Press, 2006.

Green, J. Ronald. *Straight Lick: The Cinema of Oscar Micheaux.* Bloomington: Indiana University Press, 2000.

———. *With a Crooked Stick: The Films of Oscar Micheaux.* Bloomington: Indiana University Press, 2004.

Grieveson, Lee. *Policing Cinema: Movies and Censorship in Early-Twentieth-Century America.* Berkeley: University of California Press, 2004.

Griffiths, Alison. *Wondrous Difference: Cinema, Anthropology, and Turn-of-the-Century Visual Culture.* New York: Columbia University Press, 2002.

Grimké, Francis J. *The Birth of a Nation.* Washington, DC, October 30, 1915.

————. *The Works of Francis J. Grimké*. Edited by Carter G. Woodson. Vol. 4: *Letters*. Washington: Associated, 1942.

Guerrero, Ed. *Framing Blackness: The African American Image in Film*. Philadelphia, PA: Temple University Press, 1993.

Gunning, Tom. "Heard over the Phone: *The Lonely Villa* and the de Lorde Tradition of the Terrors of Technology." *Screen* 32, no. 2 (1991): 184–96.

————. "Systematizing the Electric Message: Narrative Form, Gender, and Modernity in *The Lonedale Operator*." In *American Cinema's Transitional Era: Audiences, Institutions, Practices*, edited by Charlie Keil and Shelley Stamp, 15–50. Berkeley: University of California Press, 2004.

Hackett, Francis. "Brotherly Love." In *Focus on The Birth of a Nation*. Edited by Fred Silva, 84–86. Englewood Cliffs, NJ: Prentice Hall, 1971.

Hampton Institute. *Everyday Life at Hampton Institute*. Hampton, VA: Hampton Institute Press, 1907.

————. *The Need for Hampton*. Hampton, VA: Hampton Institute Press, 1915.

————. *What Hampton Graduates Are Doing in Land-Buying, in Home-Making, in Business, in Teaching, in Agriculture, in Establishing Schools, in the Trades, in Church and Missionary Work, in the Professions, 1868-1904*. Hampton, VA: Hampton Institute Press, 1904.

Hannah, Eleanor L. "A Place in the Parade: Citizenship, Manhood, and African American Men in the Illinois National Guard, 1870–1917." In *Brothers to the Buffalo Soldiers: Perspectives on the African American Militia and Volunteers, 1865-1917*, edited by Bruce A. Glasrud, 86–111. Columbia: University of Missouri Press, 2011.

Harlan, Louis R. "Booker T. Washington in Biographical Perspective." *American Historical Review* 75, no. 6 (1970): 1581–99.

————. *Booker T. Washington: The Wizard of Tuskegee, 1901-1915*. New York: Oxford University Press, 1983.

Higginbotham, Evelyn Brooks. *Righteous Discontent: The Women's Movement in the Black Baptist Church, 1880-1920*. Cambridge, MA: Harvard University Press, 1993.

Howard, Josiah. *Blaxploitation Cinema: The Essential Reference Guide*. Surrey, UK: Fab Press, 2008.

Johnson, Martin L. "The Places You'll Know: From Self-Recognition to Place Recognition in the Local Film." *Moving Image* 10, no. 1 (2010): 24–50.

Johnson, Randal, and Robert Stam, eds. *Brazilian Cinema*. Exp. ed. New York: Columbia University Press, 1995.

Johnston, Frances Benjamin. *The Hampton Album: 44 Photographs from an Album of Hampton Institute*. Edited by Lincoln Kirstein. New York: Museum of Modern Art, 1966.

Jones, Edward Smyth. "Harvard Square." In Edward Smyth Jones, *The Sylvan Cabin; A Centenary Ode on the Birth of Lincoln, and Other Verses*, 86–95. Boston: Sherman, French, 1911.

Kaufman, J. B. "Non-Archival Sources." In *The Griffith Project*, edited by Paolo Cherchi Usai, 8:107–12. London: British Film Institute, 2004.

Kelley, Robin D. G. Foreword to Deborah Willis, *Reflections in Black: A History of Black Photographers, 1840 to the Present*, ix–xi. New York: W. W. Norton, 2000.

Kirstein, Lincoln. "Foreword." *The Hampton Album: 44 Photographs by Frances B. Johnston from an album of Hampton Institute*. Edited by Lincoln Kirstein, 5–11. New York: Museum of Modern Art, 1966.

Klotman, Phyllis Rauch. *Frame by Frame: A Black Filmography*. Bloomington: Indiana University Press, 1979.

Lawrence, Novotny. *Blaxploitation Films of the 1970s: Blackness and Genre*. New York: Routledge, 2008.

Leab, Daniel J. *From Sambo to Superspade: The Black Experience in Motion Pictures*. Boston: Houghton Mifflin, 1975.

Lewis, Jon, and Eric Smoodin, eds. *Looking Past the Screen: Case Studies in American Film History and Method*. Durham, NC: Duke University Press, 2007.

Library of Congress, "The Development of an African-American Musical Theatre 1865–1910," accessed September 5, 2012, http://memory.loc.gov/ammem/collections/sheetmusic/brown/aasmsprs6.html.

Library of Congress U.S. Copyright Office. *Catalogue of Copyright Entries*. Part 4, vol. 9, no 1. Washington: Government Printing Office, 1914.

Lindsey, Donal F. *Indians at Hampton Institute, 1877–1923*. Urbana: University of Illinois Press, 1995.

Little, Kimberly. "On Progressive-Era Photography." *Environmental History* 14, no. 1 (2009): 146–50.

Lunzer, Martina. "Vienna's Prater District on Film, or: Looking at the World Again." *Senses of Cinema* 50 (April 2009).

Lupack, Barbara Tepa. *Richard E. Norman and Race Filmmaking*. Bloomington: Indiana University Press, 2014.

Malval, Fritz J. *A Guide to the Archives of Hampton Institute*. Westport, CT: Greenwood, 1985.

McEwan, Paul. "Lawyers, Bibliographies, and the Klan: Griffith's Resources in the Censorship Battle over *The Birth of a Nation* in Ohio." *Film History* 20, no. 3 (2008): 357–66.

Miller, Kelly. "Radicals and Conservatives." In Booker T. Washington, *Up from Slavery*, edited by William L. Andrews, 185–192. New York: W. W. Norton, 1996.

Miller, Kenneth E. *From Progressive to New Dealer: Frederic C. Howe and American Liberalism*. University Park: Pennsylvania State University Press, 2010.

Mitchell, Koritha. *Living with Lynching: African American Lynching Plays, Performance, and Citizenship, 1890–1930*. Urbana: University of Illinois Press, 2011.

Mjagkij, Nina. "A Peculiar Alliance: Julius Rosenwald, the YMCA, and African-Americans, 1910–1933." *American Jewish Archives* 44, no. 2 (1992): 585–605.

Moore, Jacqueline M. *Booker T. Washington, W. E. B. Du Bois, and the Struggle for Racial Uplift*. Wilmington, DE: Scholarly Resources, 2003.

Morrison, Toni. *Playing in the Dark: Whiteness and the Literary Imagination*. 1st Vintage Books ed. New York: Vintage, 1993.

Moten, Fred. "Uplift and Criminality." In *Next to the Color Line: Gender, Sexuality, and W. E. B. Du Bois*, edited by Susan Gillman and Alys Eve Weinbaum, 317–49. Minneapolis: University of Minnesota Press, 2007.

Musser, Charles. "Historiographic Method and the Study of Early Cinema." *Cinema Journal* 44, no. 1 (2004): 101–7.

———, with Carol Nelson. *High-Class Moving Pictures: Lyman H. Howe and the Forgotten Era of Traveling Exhibition, 1880–1920*. Princeton, NJ: Princeton University Press, 1991.

———. "To Redream the Dreams of White Playwrights." In *Oscar Micheaux and His Circle: African-American Filmmaking and Race Cinema of the Silent Era*, edited by Pearl Bowser, Jane Gaines, and Charles Musser, 97–131. Bloomington: Indiana University Press, 2001.

Nelson, Scott Reynolds. *Steel Drivin' Man: John Henry, the Untold Story of an American Legend*. New York: Oxford University Press, 2006.

O'Donoghue, Darragh. "Paradise Regained: *Queen Kelly* and the Lure of the 'Lost' Film." *Senses of Cinema* 27 (July 2003).

Omasta, Michael, and Alexander Horwath, eds. *Josef Von Sternberg: The Case of Lena Smith*. Vienna: Austrian Filmmuseum, 2008.

Orgeron, Devin, Marsha Orgeron, and Dan Streible. "A History of Learning with the Lights Off." In *Learning with the Lights Off: Educational Film in the United States*, edited by Devin Orgeron, Marsha Orgeron, and Dan Streible, 15–66. New York: Oxford University Press, 2012.

———. Introduction to *Learning with the Lights Off: Educational Film in the United States*, edited by Devin Orgeron, Marsha Orgeron, and Dan Streible, 3–14. New York: Oxford University Press, 2012.

Orgeron, Marsha. "Multi-Purposing Early Cinema: A Psychological Experiment Involving *Van Bibber's Experiment* (Edison 1911)." In *Beyond the Screen: Institutions, Networks and Publics of Early Cinema*, edited by Marta Braun et al., 153–60. New Barnet, UK: John Libbey, 2012.

Peabody, Francis Greenwood. *Education for Life: The Story of Hampton Institute*. New York: Doubleday, Page, 1920.

Petersen, Christina, "The 'Reol' Story: Race Authorship and Consciousness in Robert Levy's Reol Productions, 1921–1926." *Film History* 20, no. 3 (2008): 308–24.

Pierce, David. *The Survival of American Silent Feature Films: 1912–1929*. Washington: Council on Library and Information Resources and the Library of Congress, 2013.

Powery, Luke A. *Dem Dry Bones: Preaching, Death, and Hope*. Minneapolis, MN: Fortress, 2012.

Prelinger, Rick. *The Field Guide to Sponsored Films*. San Francisco: National Film Preservation Foundation, 2006.

Regester, Charlene. "The African-American Press and Race Movies, 1909–1929." In *Oscar Micheaux and His Circle: African-American Filmmaking and Race Cinema of the Silent Era*, edited by Pearl Bowser, Jane Gaines, and Charles Musser, 34–49. Bloomington: Indiana University Press, 2001.

———. "Black Films, White Censors: Oscar Micheaux Confronts Censorship in New York, Virginia, and Chicago." In *Movie Censorship and American Culture*, edited by Francis G. Couvares, 159–86. 2nd ed. Amherst: University of Massachusetts Press, 2006.

————. "From the Buzzard's Roost: Black Movie-Going in Durham and Other North Carolina Cities during the Early Period of American Cinema." *Film History* 17, no. 1 (2005): 113–24.

Reid, Mark A. *Redefining Black Film*. Berkeley: University of California Press, 1993.

Rhines, Jesse Algeron. *Black Film, White Money*. New Brunswick, NJ: Rutgers University Press, 1996.

Richards, Larry. *African American Films through 1959: A Comprehensive, Illustrated Filmography*. Jefferson, NC: McFarland, 1998.

Riley, Benjamin Franklin. *The Life and Times of Booker T. Washington*. New York: Fleming H. Revell, 1916.

————. *The White Man's Burden: A Discussion of the Interracial Question with Special Reference to the Responsibility of the White Race to the Negro Problem*. Birmingham, AL: B. F. Riley, 1910.

Robinson, Cedric J. *Forgeries of Memory and Meaning: Blacks and the Regimes of Race in American Theater and Film Before World War II*. Chapel Hill: University of North Carolina Press, 2007.

Rogin, Michael Paul. *Blackface, White Noise: Jewish Immigrants in the Hollywood Melting Pot*. Berkeley: University of California Press, 1996.

Sampsell-Willmann, Kate. *Lewis Hine as Social Critic*. Jackson: University Press of Mississippi, 2009.

Sampson, Henry T. *Blacks in Black and White: A Source Book on Black Films*. 2nd ed. Metuchen, NJ: Scarecrow, 1995.

————. *Blacks in Blackface: A Source Book on Early Black Musical Shows*. Metuchen, NJ: Scarecrow, 1980.

————. *The Ghost Walks: A Chronological History of Blacks in Show Business, 1865–1910*. Metuchen, NJ: Scarecrow, 1988.

Sapirstein, Ray. "Out from behind the Mask: Paul Laurence Dunbar, the Hampton Institute Camera Club, and Photographic Performance of Identity." In *Pictures and Progress: Early Photography and the Making of African American Identity*, edited by Maurice O. Wallace and Shawn Michelle Smith, 167–203. Durham, NC: Duke University Press, 2012.

————. "Out from behind the Mask: The Illustrated Poetry of Paul Laurence Dunbar and Photography at Hampton Institute." PhD diss., University of Texas, Austin, 2005.

Simmon, Scott. "Program Notes." In *Treasures III: Social Issues in American Film, 1900–1934*. DVD. San Francisco: National Film Preservation Foundation, 2004.

Slide, Anthony. *Before Video: A History of the Non-Theatrical Film*. New York: Greenwood, 1992.

Sloan, Kay. *The Loud Silents: Origins of the Social Problem Film*. Urbana: University of Illinois Press, 1988.

Smith, J. Douglas. *Managing White Supremacy: Race, Politics, and Citizenship in Jim Crow Virginia*. Chapel Hill: University of North Carolina Press, 2002.

Smith, Shawn Michelle. *Photography on the Color Line: W. E. B. Du Bois, Race, and Visual Culture*. Durham, NC: Duke University Press, 2004.

Snow, Rachel. "Correspondence Here: Real Photo Postcards and the Snapshot Aesthetic." In *Postcards: Ephemeral Histories of Modernity*, edited by David Prochaska and Jordana Mendelson, 42–53. University Park: Pennsylvania State University Press, 2010.

Sobchack, Vivian. "Afterword: Media Archaeology and Re-presencing the Past." In *Media Archaeology: Approaches, Applications, and Implications*, edited by Erkki Huhtamo and Jussi Parikka, 323–33. Berkeley: University of California Press, 2011.

Sollors, Werner, Caldwell Titcomb, and Thomas A. Underwood, eds. *Blacks at Harvard: A Documentary History of African-American Experience at Harvard and Radcliffe*. New York: New York University Press, 1993.

Staiger, Janet. "The Future of the Past." *Cinema Journal* 44, no. 1 (2004): 126–29.

Stamp, Shelley. "Lois Weber, Progressive Cinema, and the Fate of 'The Work-a-Day Girls' in *Shoes*." *Camera Obscura* 19, no. 2 (2004): 140–69.

———. "Moral Coercion, or the National Board of Censorship Ponders the Vice Films." In *Controlling Hollywood: Censorship and Regulation in the Studio Era*, edited by Matthew Bernstein, 41–59. New Brunswick, NJ: Rutgers University Press, 1999.

———. "Taking Precautions, or Regulating Early Birth-Control Films." In *A Feminist Reader in Early Cinema*, edited by Jennifer M. Bean and Diane Negra, 270–97. Durham, NC: Duke University Press, 2002.

Stepto, Robert B. *From Behind the Veil: A Study of Afro-American Narrative*. 2nd ed. Urbana: University of Illinois Press, 1991.

Stewart, Jacqueline Najuma. "Discovering Black Film History: Tracing the Tyler, Texas Black Film Collection." *Film History* 23, no. 2 (2011): 147–73.

———. *Migrating to the Movies: Cinema and Black Urban Modernity*. Berkeley: University of California Press, 2005.

Stokes, Melvyn. *D. W. Griffith's "The Birth of a Nation": A History of "The Most Controversial Motion Picture of All Time."* New York: Oxford University Press, 2007.

———. "The Use of Intertitles in D. W. Griffith's 'The Birth of a Nation.'" In *Le cinéma en toutes lettres: jeux d'écritures à l'écran*, edited by Nicole Cloarec, 15–26. Paris: Michel Houdiard, 2007.

Streible, Dan. "The Harlem Theatre: Black Film Exhibition in Austin, Texas: 1920–1973." In *Black American Cinema*, edited by Manthia Diawara, 221–36. New York: Routledge, 1993.

Tarbox, Charles H. *Lost Films: 1895–1917*. Los Angeles: Film Classic Exchange, 1983.

Taylor, Clyde R. "The Rebirth of the Aesthetic in Cinema." In Clyde R. Taylor, *The Mask of Art: Breaking the Aesthetic Contract — Film and Literature*, 103–23. Bloomington: Indiana University Press, 1998.

Thompson, Kristin. "The Formulation of the Classical Style, 1909–28." In *The Classical Hollywood Cinema: Film Style and Mode of Production to 1960*, edited by David Bordwell, Janet Staiger, and Kristin Thompson, 155–240. New York: Columbia University Press, 1985.

Toulmin, Vanessa, and Martin Loiperdinger. "Is It You? Recognition, Representation and Response in Relation to the Local Film." *Film History* 17, no. 1 (2005): 7–18.

Trachtenberg, Alan. Foreword to Wolfgang Schivelbusch, *The Railway Journey: The Industrialization of Time and Space in the 19th Century*, xiii–xvi. Berkeley: University of California Press, 1986.

Tsivian, Yuri. *Early Cinema in Russia and Its Cultural Reception*. Translated by Alan Bodger. Edited by Richard Taylor. New York: Routledge, 1994.

Tuskegee Normal and Industrial Institute. *Making Useful Citizens*. Tuskegee, AL: Normal and Industrial Institute, c. 1912.

Usai, Paolo Cherchi. *Silent Cinema: An Introduction*. London: British Film Institute, 2000.

Verney, Kevern. *The Art of the Possible: Booker T. Washington and Black Leadership in the United States, 1881–1925*. New York: Routledge, 2001.

Waldman, Harry. *Missing Reels: Lost Films of American and European Cinema*. Jefferson, NC: McFarland, 2000.

Wallace, Maurice O. "Framing the Black Soldier: Image, Uplift, and the Duplicity of Pictures." In *Pictures and Progress: Early Photography and the Making of African American Identity*, edited by Maurice O. Wallace and Shawn Michelle Smith, 244–73. Durham, NC: Duke University Press, 2012.

Waller, Gregory A. "Locating Early Non-Theatrical Audiences." In *Audiences: Defining and Researching Screen Entertainment Reception*, edited by Ian Christie, 81–95. Amsterdam: Amsterdam University Press, 2012.

———. *Main Street Amusements: Movies and Commercial Entertainment in a Southern City, 1896–1930*. Washington: Smithsonian Institution, 1995.

Washington, Booker T. *Booker T. Washington Papers*, edited by Louis R. Harlan and Raymond W. Smock. 14 vols. Urbana: University of Illinois Press, 1972–89.

———. "General Introduction." In *Tuskegee and Its People: Their Ideals and Achievements*, edited by Booker T. Washington, 1–15. New York: D. Appleton, 1905.

———. *The Negro in Business*. Boston: Hertel, Jenkins, 1907.

———, ed. *The Negro Problem: A Series of Articles by Representative American Negroes of To-Day*. New York: James Pott and Company, 1903.

———. *A New Negro for a New Century: An Accurate and Up-to-Date Record of the Upward Struggles of the Negro Race*. Chicago: American, 1900.

———. *Up from Slavery*. Edited by William L. Andrews. New York: W. W. Norton, 1996.

———. *Working with the Hands; Being a Sequel to "Up from Slavery," Covering the Author's Experiences in Industrial Training at Tuskegee*. New York: Doubleday, Page, 1904.

Watkins, William H. *The White Architects of Black Education: Ideology and Power in America, 1865–1954*. New York: Teachers College Press, 2001.

Weinberg, Herman G. "Lost Ones." *Film Comment* 5, no. 3 (1969): 6–11.

Wexler, Laura. *Tender Violence: Domestic Visions in an Age of U.S. Imperialism*. Chapel Hill: University of North Carolina Press, 2000.

White, Mimi. "'The Birth of a Nation': History as Pretext." In *"The Birth of a Nation": D. W. Griffith, Director*, edited by Robert Lang, 214–24. New Brunswick, NJ: Rutgers University Press, 1994.

Williams, Linda. *Playing the Race Card: Melodramas of Black and White from Uncle Tom to O. J. Simpson*. Princeton, NJ: Princeton University Press, 2001.

Willis, Deborah, ed. *Let Your Motto Be Resistance: African American Portraits*. Washington: National Museum of African American History and Culture, Smithsonian Institute, 2007.

———. *Posing Beauty: African American Images from the 1890s to the Present*. New York: W. W. Norton, 2009.

———. *Reflections in Black: A History of Black Photographers 1840 to the Present*. New York: W. W. Norton, 2000.

Wood, Amy Louise. *Lynching and Spectacle: Witnessing Racial Violence in America, 1890–1940*. Chapel Hill: University of North Carolina Press, 2009.

Work, Monroe N. *Negro Year Book: An Annual Encyclopedia of the Negro 1916–1917*. Tuskegee, AL: Negro Year Book, Tuskegee Institute, 1916.

Zimmermann, Yvonne. "'What Hollywood Is to America, the Corporate Film Is to Switzerland.'" In *Films That Work: Industrial Film and the Productivity of Media*, edited by Vinzenz Hediger and Patrick Vonderau, 101–17. Amsterdam: Amsterdam University Press, 2009.

Zwarich, Jennifer. "Federal Films: Bureaucratic Activism and the U.S. Government Motion Picture Initiative, 1901–1941." PhD diss., New York University, 2014.

INDEX

NOTE: Page numbers followed by *f* indicate a figure.